Food as a Medicine for the Heart

Tissa Kappagoda, M.D.,
Debbie Lucus, R.D., Jill Burns, R.D.,
and
Linda Paumer, M.A.

This book is dedicated to the patients who entrusted
their care to us over an extended period.

CONTENTS

Preface		IV
Part One:	**Background Information Introduction**	1
Chapter 1	How Much Food Do I Need?	5
Chapter 2	How Much Should I Weigh?	9
Chapter 3	How Much Food Am I Eating Now	13
Chapter 4	How Do I Know How Much Fat Is In My Food?	20
Chapter 5	Cholesterol and Fat in Food	25
Chapter 6	Be Serious! Can You Actually Eat Fiber?	32
Chapter 7	Add Salt to Taste	35
Chapter 8	What about Alcohol?	38
Chapter 9	The Recommendations	42
Chapter 10	The Big Picture (As We See It)	47
Part Two:	**Meal Planning**	50
Chapter 11	Menu Plans From the Grocery to the plate…	50
Part Three:	**Recipes**	60
Breakfast		60
Lunch		92
Salads		93
Sandwiches		127
Soups		134
Dinner		163
Beans		164
Breads		176
Egg/Meat substitutes		187
Mexican Food		205
Pasta		222
Potatoes		239
Rice & Grains		252
Vegetables		271
Appetizers		298
Desserts		318
Sauces/Miscellaneous		366
Favorite Marinades		374
Index		387

PREFACE

Food is an integral part of any program of health care. The nature of the diet consumed is especially important in the maintenance of cardiovascular health. It is particularly relevant to those recovering from a major cardiac event such as a heart attack or coronary artery bypass surgery and also to those who are at risk of developing diseases such as atherosclerosis. While recognizing the benefits that accrue from procedures such as the placement of stents in the coronary arteries and the use of medications for the treatment of high blood pressure and elevated levels of cholesterol, we believe that these effects could be enhanced by instituting changes in lifestyle such as cessation of tobacco abuse, participation in a regular exercise program and the consumption of a diet that is low in saturated fat and cholesterol. For a period of more than 20 years, the authors of this book have promoted a low-fat, plant-based diet for patients who have evidence of coronary atherosclerosis. This book is a collection of recipes that we recommended to patients who came under our care. The individual items were contributed by patients who adapted their favorite recipes so that they fell within the low fat vegetarian guidelines we provided for them. Wherever possible we have acknowledged the source of these recipes.

Two individuals merit special acknowledgement for this collection of recipes. Ginny Goodrow, a spouse from group 25, was a great cook and actively promoted the potlucks for patients. She was very helpful in the production of early versions of this recipe collection. Jane Hue, a spouse from group 28, was also a great cook and continued to help with potlucks for their entire existence (long after she and her husband had completed two years of participation). She was also a great organizer who kept immaculate records of recipes. These two women illustrate the profound effect good support has on successful dietary management of health.

Finally the authors would like to thank Meah Wilson who assisted in the development of this project from its earliest stages and Mary Kappagoda for many suggestions that improved the overall quality of the material presented in this book. It is abundantly clear to us that the production of this book could not have been brought to a successful conclusion without their help.

The book is divided into three parts:

Part One: Background information designed to guide readers through the basic concepts of nutrition. Included are some summaries of clinical studies to document our program experience.

Part Two: Meal plans based on the low fat vegetarian concept.

Part Three: Recipes

C. Tissa Kappagoda
Linda C. Paumer
Debbie Lucus
Jill Burns

PART ONE: BACKGROUND INFORMATION

INTRODUCTION

"It's the Holidays..."

I had heard the same kind of story many times before. It was early January and the patient sitting in front of me was waiting for me to comment on the results of her follow up tests. She had been referred three months earlier, after recovering from a heart attack, because she had experienced difficulties with managing her weight. In many ways, it was a losing battle as she had no intention of making any changes to her lifestyle. What was required was nothing short of a cosmic intervention.

'How am I doing, doctor?" she asked.

I looked up from the computer screen and said, "The numbers look good but that was not why you came here in the first place."

"What do you mean?" she asked, somewhat puzzled.

"Well, for a start you have gained 8 pounds since the last time I saw you, making that a total of 21 pounds over the last year. Your own doctor sent you because you needed to lose weight!"

"Listen! This is what happened! I was doing very well until the holidays. First there was Thanksgiving and then there was my birthday. Then it was the other holidays. Y'know, Christmas and the New Year and all these goodies in the shops. Pretty soon, I was eating a lot of things that, I knew, were really bad for me. That's the problem!! But you wait and see! Things will get better now that the holidays are over."

"But, your arteries don't know that it is Christmas or the New Year or any other holiday!!! There is no free pass that way!" I was beginning to sound like a broken record and I let her go.

Four days went by and I received a telephone call from her. She could barely contain her excitement.

"I told you it will work! I have lost a pound and a half!"

"What did you do?"

"I", she paused for effect and continued, 'I have joined a gym!"

Two weeks later, she came by my office wanting to speak to me. The smile was gone. I knew that the proverbial glitch had been hit.

"What's up now?" I asked.

"I have hit a plateau and I am stuck at this weight. I have been exercising regularly. My trainer says I am putting on musclc. Is that possible?"

I had nothing against the trainer and he had to earn a living as well! I stayed clear of the question and said, "Why don't you just eat less?"

"What do you mean? I hardly eat anything as it is! Anyway that's what you always say," was the immediate rejoinder.

The time was almost noon and it was nearly time for her lunch. I asked her, "Are you going for lunch now?"

"In a few minutes," she replied.

"So, what will you have?"

She thought for a moment and said, "A bowl of chili and a plate of salad."

"Who will serve you the chili?"

"I'll serve myself, it is a self service place." she said with a slight frown.

"OK! This is what you are going to do. Get the usual bowl and fill it till it is half full. Then have the salad using a smaller plate."

She looked at me for a full fifteen seconds and then her frown cleared.

"Oh! Is that what you mean when you ask me to eat less?"

****

Over the past twenty odd years, we have had the privilege of caring for patients who have developed coronary artery disease. Our strategy for managing them has been to focus on seven major areas which have been shown to enhance long-term survival and prevent subsequent heart attacks (Figure 1.1). This relationship between caregivers and patients was a partnership designed not only to increase life expectancy but also to enhance the overall quality of life.

Although weight management is an overriding concern for the majority of these patients, the type of food a person eats impacts all aspects of care shown in Figure 1 and for this reason it is a major focus of interest for people with coronary artery disease. Following the pioneering studies of Dr. Dean Ornish and his associates, we have promoted the use of a low fat vegetarian diet, particularly for those who have recovered from a heart attack, undergone coronary artery bypass surgery or placement of a stent in a coronary artery.

- **Figure 1.1 The 7 Areas of Interest for Patients with Coronary Artery Disease.**

1) "Know your risk" refers to the risk (chance) of having a heart attack in the next 10 years. For those who have recovered from one it refers to the risk of a second heart attack.
2) Maintain or achieve a weight that is appropriate for your height.
3) Maintain blood pressure as close to 120/80 mmHg as possible.
4) Maintain an appropriate level of serum cholesterol, in particular LDL cholesterol (see later chapters). This value should be less than 80 mg / 100 ml. in those with confirmed arterial disease.
5) Quit smoking.
6) Commence an exercise program that would gradually increase to 45 minutes per day.
7) Manage your stress level. Stress is an important risk factor which interferes with a person's ability to take steps to safeguard his/her health and to follow prescribed treatments.

Several of the areas shown in Figure1.1 are interdependent. For instance, the lack of physical exercise influences other factors such as body weight, blood pressure and blood cholesterol. Similarly, when people quit smoking they tend to eat more food resulting in weight gain.

This book contains a selection of recipes which have been shared by patients who have attended our programs at the University of California, Davis Medical Center (UCDMC). They have been preserved for posterity by our colleagues, principally the dietitians, to be used by others who may need them. Wherever possible we have acknowledged the source of the recipe. It is emphasized that these recipes have not been endorsed by the UCDMC. Opinions expressed are entirely those of the authors unless a specific source has been identified.

The nutrient contents of each recipe have been analyzed using a commercially available computer program (http://www.esha.com/product/food-processor).

The book is arranged in three sections:

Part One: Background information designed to guide readers through the basic concepts of nutrition. Included are some summaries of clinical studies to document our program experience.
Part Two: Meal plans based on the low-fat vegetarian concept.
Part Three: Recipes.

Suggested Further Reading

1. Ornish D, Brown SE, Billings JH *et al.* Can lifestyle changes reverse coronary heart disease?: The Lifestyle Heart Trial. *The Lancet* 1990, 336(8708):129-133.
2. Ornish D, Scherwitz LW, Billings JH *et al*: Intensive Lifestyle Changes for Reversal of Coronary Heart Disease. *The Journal of the American Medical Association* 1998, 280:2001-2007.
3. Rutledge JC, Hyson DA, Garduno D, Cort DA, Paumer L, Kappagoda CT: Lifestyle Modification Program in Management of Patients With Coronary Artery Disease:

The Clinical Experience in a Tertiary Care Hospital. *Journal of Cardiopulmonary Rehabilitation and Prevention* 1999, 19:226-234.
4. Kappagoda C, Ma A, Cort D, Paumer L, Lucus D, Burns J, Amsterdam E: Cardiac event rate in a lifestyle modification program for patients with chronic coronary artery disease. *Clin Cardiol* 2006, 29:317-321.
5. Balady GJ, Williams MA, Ades PA et al. Core components of cardiac rehabilitation and secondary prevention programs 2007 update. *Journal of Cardiopulmonary Rehabilitation and Prevention* 2007, 27:121-129.
6. Smith SC, Benjamin EJ, Bonow RO *et al*. AHA/ACCF Secondary Prevention and Risk Reduction Therapy for Patients with Coronary and Other Atherosclerotic Vascular Disease: 2011 Update. *Circulation*, 124 :2458-2473.

CHAPTER 1

HOW MUCH FOOD DO I NEED?

After five minutes it was apparent that the discussion was about to turn into another exercise in frustration for the patient. She had just been told once again that she had to lose weight to avoid transitioning into Type 2 diabetes. Her distress was evident on her face. The physician sitting across the desk asked, "Have I said something you don't understand?"

"It is not that I don't understand......My problem is that I don't know how to do it!"
"What is so difficult about it?"
"I have this fear. If I eat less, how would I know I will not be harming myself?"
The doctor was nonplussed. Here was a person who was at least fifty pounds over her ideal weight and she was experiencing fears about malnutrition. As he was thinking about a response, he heard the woman say, "I mean how much food do I really need?"

****

This is the first problem that needs to be settled! The primary purpose of food is to provide energy for the body. Energy, in the context of one's body, is a word that most people associate with how much "pep" or "get up and go" they feel. In terms of daily living, it is associated with oil, gas or electricity. To complicate matters further, energy, unlike the body weight or height cannot be easily measured and for that reason it is hard to relate it to food.

In fact, energy is related to the capacity to do work. The scientific way to think of it is in terms of "calories". The popular website Wikipedia defines Energy this way:

*"In physics, **energy** (from the Greek ἐνέργεια - energeia, "activity, operation", from ἐνεργός - energos, "active, working") is a scalar physical quantity that describes the amount of work that can be performed by a force, an attribute of objects and systems that is subject to a conservation law. Different forms of energy include kinetic, potential, thermal, gravitational, sound, light, elastic, and electromagnetic energy. The forms of energy are often named after a related force."*
http://en.wikipedia.org/wiki/Energy

Huh?
Yes, it is accurate! However, it does not help when one is out shopping for food at a supermarket or waiting in line at a self-service buffet.

A Canadian government website has a working definition which serves us better. It goes like this:

"When a car drives by, it is being powered by gasoline, a type of stored energy. The food we eat contains energy. We use that energy to work and play." We should also add "and to stay alive". (http://www.energyquest.ca.gov/story/chapter01.html)

If the gasoline simply remains in the tank it does nothing to move the car. It has to be altered and burned to produce energy which will move the car. The engine is responsible for that change. Similarly, if food is eaten, it has to be altered by the body to generate energy for it to function in much the same way as the engine alters the gasoline. Moment to moment normal bodily functions such as the heart beat, the act of breathing, even thinking, require energy. To that extent, food equals energy. *Unlike a car with a limited size of fuel tank that spills over when too much gasoline is added, the human body has an almost unlimited capacity to store the energy from food in the form of body fat.*

Gram and Kilogram Calories

To make formal estimates of energy needed, we use a unit, just like gallons or liters for gasoline. That unit is called the calorie and in this context, it represents energy derived from any food item. That is where we run into the second problem. What is a calorie? There are two definitions: a) the "small calorie" (calorie or cal), more commonly used in sciences such as physics and chemistry and b) the large "Calorie" (kilocalorie or kcal). This becomes confusing because the kilocalories in food are more often referred to as "calories", which is technically not correct but much more commonly accepted. ***In the context of food energy the word calorie generally refers to the kilocalorie.*** In this book the word calorie will be used in reference to a kilocalorie derived from food.

A kilocalorie is the amount of energy (i.e. heat) required to raise the temperature of one kilogram of water by one degree Celsius (which is a unit of temperature, like the degree centigrade). This unit, the kilogram calorie is the same as a large calorie, food calorie, Calorie (capital *C*) or just calorie (lowercase *c*).

The main point about the definition is that if the kilogram of water cools by 1 °C, it will give off that heat to the atmosphere. The body handles the excess energy in a different way to heated water. It keeps the energy over and above that needed for survival to be used for activities such as exercise. In the absence of such activity, the energy is deposited in a "fat bank". So, if a person eats more than he or she needs, the (fat) bank balance will grow and the weighing machine (often a scale) will record it.

How many calories?

The calories required for survival ***(basal calorie requirement)*** depends on age, weight and height. There are different requirements for men and women. It is estimated that as a person gets older, for each decade, assuming the level of activity remained the same, *the energy expenditure* would decrease by approximately 70 calories/day. However, with aging, most people tend to undertake fewer activities and their calorie requirements are likely to diminish even further. Thus as one gets older, weight gain is inevitable unless there is a reduction in the amount of food consumed or an increase in physical activity. ***Since the majority of people who develop heart attacks do so in their fifties and sixties, they also have a tendency to be overweight.***

As we discussed earlier, the daily requirement of calories is the sum of the basal requirement (to remain alive) and that needed for activity. The Food and Nutrition Board in the U.S. refers to the latter as the Personal Activity Level (PAL). The basal energy requirement is multiplied by a factor depending upon a person's PAL to yield the total energy requirement as shown on Page 7.

> **Estimated Energy Requirement (EER) in calories for Men (19 years and older)**
>
> EER = 662 − 9.53 x Age [years] + PA x (15.91 x Weight [kilograms] + 539.6 x Height [metres])
>
> PA refers to Physical Activity in this calculation. There are 4 values for PA depending on the Physical Activity Level (PAL) of each person.
>
> >   PA = 1.0   if PAL is estimated to be between 1.0 and 1.4 (Sedentary)
> >   PA = 1.11 if PAL is estimated to be between 1.4 and 1.6 (Low Active)
> >   PA = 1.25 if PAL is estimated to be between 1.6 and 1.9 (Active)
> >   PA = 1.48 if PAL is estimated to be between 1.9 and 2.5 (Very Active)
>
> **Estimated Energy Requirement (EER) in calories for Women (19 years and older)**
>
> EER = 354 − 6.91 x Age [years] + PA x (9.36 x Weight [kilogram] + 726 x Height [metres])
>
> >   PA = 1.0   if (PAL) is estimated to be between 1.0 and 1.4 (Sedentary)
> >   PA = 1.12 if (PAL) is estimated to be between 1.4 and 1.6 (Low Active)
> >   PA = 1.27 if (PAL) is estimated to be between 1.6 and 1.9 (Active)
> >   PA = 1.45 if (PAL) is estimated to be between 1.9 and 2.5 (Very Active)
>
> **Note on the Physical Activity Level (PAL)**
>
> PAL is in the **Sedentary** category if the individual's activities do not include any of those listed on page 16.
> PAL is in the **Low Active** category if the individual undertakes *30 minutes/day* of moderate activity (e.g. walking 2 miles in 30 min)

The most important items of information contained in the Table above are two equations (formulas) that describe the Estimated Energy Requirements (EER) in men and women.

Men	EER = 662 − 9.53 x Age [years] + PA x (15.91 x **Weight [kilogram]** + 539.6 x Height [meters])
Women	EER = 354 − 6.91 x Age [years] + PA x (9.36 x **Weight [kilogram]** + 726 x Height [meters])

Apart from the fact that the calculations are different they illustrate another important aspect. Let us think of two people (of either gender) of identical heights, age and Personal Activity Levels; it becomes apparent that the estimated energy requirement will depend on their weight. *Thus the heavier person will have to consume more calories than the lighter one in order to maintain his/her current weight.*

However, when it comes to *losing weight,* a person has two options: consume fewer calories and increase activity level to spend more calories (More in the next Chapter).

For those not mathematically inclined, the following Table provides a good approximation of this calculation of the energy requirement (in calories) for a 30 year old person of ideal body weight (Body weight: 64 kg (140 lbs); Height: 66 inches (168 cm) after adjustment for the Personal Activity Level.

Gender	Age (yr)	Energy Requirement (calories) Based on Personal Activity Level		
		Sedentary	Low Active	Active
Male	30	2296	2504	2772
	40	2200	2409	2667
	50	2103	2313	2582
	60	2009	2218	2487
	70	1912	2123	2391
	80	1817	2028	2296
Female	30	1959	2159	2413
	40	1890	2090	2344
	50	1821	2021	2274
	60	1752	1952	2205
	70	1683	1882	2136
	80	1614	1813	2067

It should be noted once again that, with each passing decade, both men and women tend to require fewer calories/day (~75 for women and ~100 for men) to maintain their weight, provided their activity level remains unchanged.

Suggested Further Reading

1. Dietary Reference Intakes for Energy, Carbohydrate, Fiber, Fat, Fatty Acids, Cholesterol, Protein, and Amino Acids Food and Nutrition Board (Released: September 5, 2002)
   http://www.iom.edu/Reports/2002/Dietary-Reference-Intakes-for-Energy-Carbohydrate-Fiber-Fat-Fatty-Acids-Cholesterol-Protein-and-Amino-Acids.aspx

CHAPTER 2

HOW MUCH SHOULD I WEIGH?

The dietitian had said, "Let's start by checking your height and weight. That way we will have some information about what we have to do." Hank had been referred to her because he was concerned about his weight. His brother had just been diagnosed with diabetes. After his height was measured, Hank stepped up to a small machine on the floor in his bare feet. A few minutes later a second machine nearby began to spew out a report. The dietitian tore off the sheet and took it across to her table. Hank followed and sat in a chair nearby.

"All right! Tell me the bad news!"

"The machine says that you weigh 198 pounds. For your height that is about 30 pounds too many. And your body fat is estimated to be 23% which is also somewhat high. Those are the facts."

"So where do we go from here? I mean, what should I weigh? According to some chart my wife looked up I should probably weigh something like 160 lbs and I have not weighed that since I left college. That was …….never mind! Nobody my age weighs that little! Who stipulates these things anyway?"

"Nobody! There are a bunch of diseases which are associated with being overweight. The number of people with these conditions increases when the weight goes beyond a certain point. What that means is that if you are a certain height, you should weigh within a certain range."

"You mean it is like a ratio of some sort?"

"Exactly! It is called the Body Mass Index and it is defined as……….."

"Oh boy! I was never very good at math. I majored in history…….!

****

BODY MASS INDEX

The Body Mass Index (BMI) is a common means of estimating overweight and obesity in humans. It is a calculated number, based on height and weight, used to compare and analyze the health effects in people of all heights. BMI is calculated the same way for both adults and children. It was developed by the Belgian polymath, Adolphe Quetelet, in the course of working out his system of "social physics" between 1830 and 1850 (and is therefore also known as the Quetelet Index). It is equal to the weight, divided by the square of the height: The calculation is based on the following formulae:

Kilograms and meters (or centimeters)	**Formula: weight (kg) / [height (m)]^2** With the metric system, the formula for BMI is weight in kilograms divided by height in meters squared. Since height is commonly measured in centimeters, divide height in centimeters by 100 to obtain height in meters. **Example:** Weight = 68 kg, Height = 165 cm (1.65m) **Calculation:** 68 ÷ (1.65)^2 = 24.98

Pounds and inches	Formula: weight (lb) / [height (in)]^2 x 703 Calculate BMI by dividing weight in pounds (lbs) by height in inches (in) squared and multiplying by a conversion factor of 703. **Example:** Weight = 150 lbs, Height = 5'5" (65") **Calculation:** [150 ÷ (65)^2] x 703 = 24.96

A simpler approach would be to refer to the Table shown below which permits one to estimate the BMI from the height (inches) and weight (pounds).

Determining Your Body Mass Index (BMI)

To use the table, find the appropriate height (feet and inches) in the left-hand column. Move across the row to the given weight (pounds). The number in each box is the BMI for that height and weight. The numbers have already been adjusted to fit the formula given above.

http://www.cdc.gov/healthyweight/assessing/bmi/adult_BMI/index.html

ARE YOU AT A HEALTHY WEIGHT? WHAT IS YOUR BODY MASS INDEX?

Weight in Pounds

Height	120	130	140	150	160	170	180	190	200	210	220	230	240	250
4'6	29	31	34	36	39	41	43	46	48	51	53	56	58	60
4'8	27	29	31	34	36	38	40	43	45	47	49	52	54	56
4'10	25	27	29	31	34	36	38	40	42	44	46	48	50	52
5'0	23	25	27	29	31	33	35	37	39	41	43	45	47	49
5'2	22	24	26	27	29	31	33	35	37	38	40	42	44	46
5'4	21	22	24	26	28	29	31	33	34	36	38	40	41	43
5'6	19	21	23	24	26	27	29	31	32	34	36	37	39	40
5'8	18	20	21	23	24	26	27	29	30	32	34	35	37	38
5'10	17	19	20	22	23	24	26	27	29	30	32	33	35	36
6'0	16	18	19	20	22	23	24	26	27	28	30	31	33	34
6'2	15	17	18	19	21	22	23	24	26	27	28	30	31	32
6'4	15	16	18	18	20	21	22	23	24	26	27	28	29	30
6'6	14	15	16	17	19	20	21	22	23	24	25	27	28	29
6'8	13	14	15	17	18	19	20	21	22	23	24	25	26	28

Healthy Weight   Overweight   Obese

Interpretation of BMI for adults

For adults 20 years old and older, BMI is interpreted using standard weight status categories that are the same for all ages and for both men and women. The categories associated with BMI ranges for adults are shown in the following table. Typically, the unit kg/m² is not included.

BMI	Weight Status
Below 18.5	Underweight
18.5 – 24.9	Normal
25.0 – 29.9	Overweight
30.0 and Above	Obese

For example, here are the weight ranges, the corresponding BMI ranges, and the weight status categories for a sample height (5 feet 9 inches).

Height	Weight Range	BMI	Weight Status
5' 9"	124 lbs or less	Below 18.5	Underweight
	125 lbs to 168 lbs	18.5 to 24.9	Normal
	169 lbs to 202 lbs	25.0 to 29.9	Overweight
	203 lbs or more	30 or higher	Obese

The BMI number and body fat are fairly closely related but there is some variation associated with gender, race and age. For instance, at the same BMI:
- women tend to have more body fat than men.
- older people, on average, tend to have more body fat than younger adults.
- highly trained athletes may have a high BMI because of increased muscularity rather than increased body fat.

It is also important to remember that BMI is only one factor related to risk for disease. For assessing someone's likelihood of developing overweight- and obesity-related diseases, the National Heart, Lung, and Blood Institute guidelines recommend looking at two other predictors:
- the individual's waist circumference (because abdominal fat is a predictor of risk for obesity-related diseases),
- other risk factors the individual has for diseases and conditions associated with obesity (for example, high blood pressure or physical inactivity).

Ethnicity or race is also a factor. The World Health Organization has recommended that the normal/overweight threshold for South East Asian body types be lowered to a BMI of 23. The new cut-off BMI index for obesity in Asians is 27.5 compared with the traditional WHO figure of 30. An Asian adult with a BMI of 23 or greater is now considered overweight and the ideal normal range is 18.5-22.9.

Research has shown that as weight increases to reach the levels referred to as "overweight" and "obesity," the risks for the following conditions also increase.
- Coronary heart disease
- Type 2 diabetes
- Cancers (endometrial, breast, and colon)
- Hypertension (high blood pressure)
- Dyslipidemia (for example, high total cholesterol or high levels of triglycerides in the blood)
- Stroke
- Liver and Gallbladder disease
- Sleep apnea and respiratory problems
- Osteoarthritis (a degeneration of cartilage and its underlying bone within a joint)
- Gynecological problems (abnormal menstrual cycle, infertility)

The number of people with each of these diseases tends to increase sharply when the BMI increases beyond 25 kg/m^2.

There are discussions in the scientific literature that other measurements such as the waist-hip ratio may be better predictors of various diseases such as coronary artery disease. However for most practical purposes the BMI is sufficient.

An even simpler measure is to determine how much one is above the expected weight. For instance a BMI chart such as that shown above provides an estimate of the expected weight based on age and height. Obesity is defined as being 30 pounds more than the expected weight. This is an essential step in embarking upon on a weight management program for patients with heart disease.

Suggested Further Reading

1. Overweight and Obesity Division of Nutrition, Physical Activity and Obesity, National Center for Chronic Disease Prevention and Health Promotion. http://www.cdc.gov/obesity/adult/causes/index.html (Page last updated: April 27, 2012).
2. National Institutes of Health, NHLBI Obesity Education Initiative. Clinical Guidelines on the Identification, Evaluation, and Treatment of Overweight and Obesity in Adults. Available online: http://www.nhlbi.nih.gov/guidelines/obesity/ob_gdlns.pdf.

CHAPTER 3

HOW MUCH FOOD AM I EATING NOW AND HOW MUCH DO I HAVE TO CHANGE?

The Tables in the previous chapter provided a few ideas about the amount of food (i.e. the number of calories) a person needs to live, function normally and maintain one's current weight. If one is interested in either gaining or losing weight it is equally important to establish how much food is consumed and what changes need to be made.

At any period in time, a person's weight depends on food (calories) consumed and energy (calories) spent. If the person's weight is steady, then the calories provided by the food consumed must match the energy needed for survival and activities (Fig. 3.1). Thus, in order to lose weight, one has to either increase the amount of energy spent on activities or reduce the amount consumed as food. It is estimated that a daily negative balance of 500 calories (i.e. energy expenditure exceeding intake by 500 calories) would result in a weight loss of 1 pound per week. In order to accomplish this task it is necessary to have a reliable estimate of the amount of food consumed

The usual method employed in most clinics is to first obtain an accurate estimate of food consumed in household measures such as cups and tablespoons. This is called a food diary. Once that is accomplished the items recorded in the diary are analyzed using a computer program which provides a great deal of useful additional information such as the average consumption of calories, amounts of fats, carbohydrates and proteins as well as micronutrients.

Figure 3.1. The relationship between food eaten, energy spent and fat stores in the body.

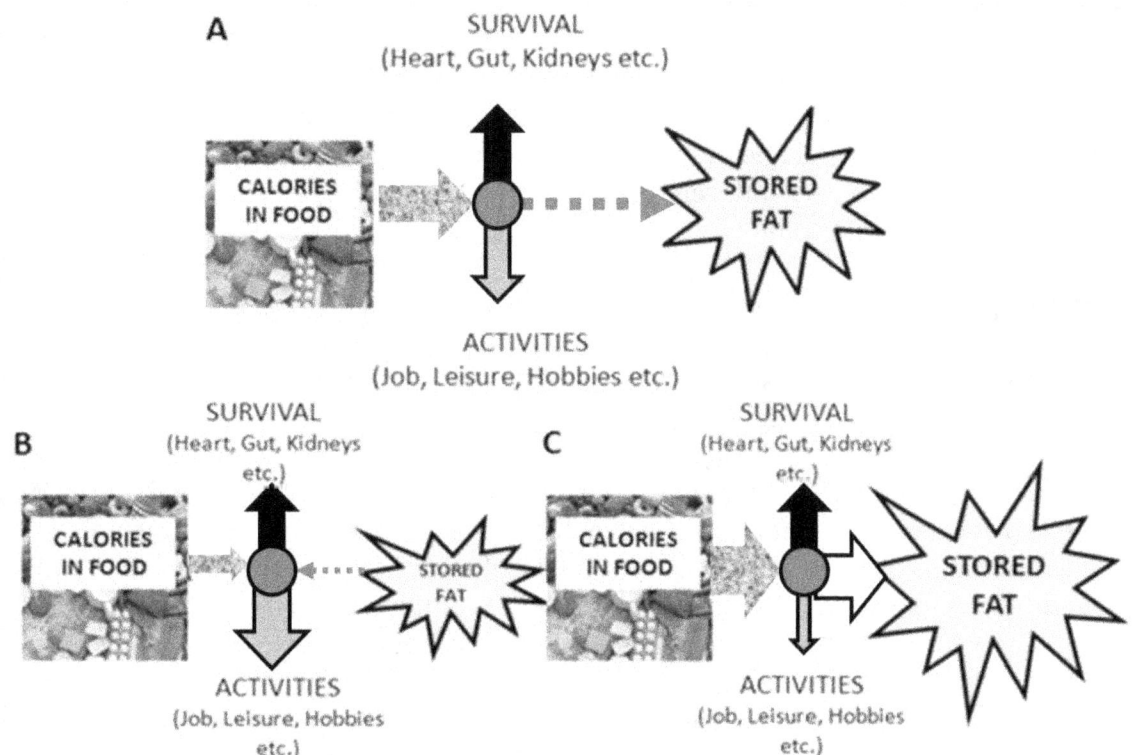

A) Baseline condition: Energy consumed as food is shown by the stippled arrow. A fixed portion of this is used for survival (black arrow). Another portion is used for activities and this would vary with the level of activity (grey arrow). Any excess is stored as fat (dashed arrow to right).

B) Weight loss: The amount of calories consumed is decreased (stippled arrow). The amount of energy used for activities is increased (grey arrow pointing down) while the amount used for survival remains the same as in A (black arrow pointing up). The difference is made up by mobilizing energy from stored fat.

C) Weight gain: The amount of calories consumed is increased (stippled arrow). The amount of energy used for activities is decreased (grey arrow pointing down) while the amount used for survival remains the same as in A) (black arrow pointing up). The excess energy is stored as fat (white arrow).

For patients who have various forms of coronary artery disease, besides the issue of the total calories consumed, we also recommend that they reduce the total fat intake to 12% of the daily consumption of calories with a quarter of it derived from saturated fats. The protein intake should be no more than 25% of the daily consumption of calories. The remaining calories will be derived from carbohydrates.

Although a food diary is a simple instrument to identify what a person eats, it has both advantages and disadvantages.

Advantages
1) It provides an overall pattern of food consumption including the frequency of eating at restaurants and the type of restaurant patronized.
2) Unexpected sources of calories such as alcohol ("I thought red wine was good you.") are identified. One could even consume too much fruit!
3) If the estimated calorie (food) intake is unrealistically low, the need for specialized counseling could be identified.
4) Unanticipated calories derived from the method of preparation could be identified. A simple example of this would be the dressing on a salad. A green salad with a simple vinaigrette dressing is a very different proposition to one with dressing purchased from a supermarket or at a restaurant.

Disadvantages
1) Inaccuracy

Inaccuracies occur for several reasons. The obvious one is that people often forget to write things down as they go along. They rely on their memory and complete the diary at night before going to bed. Things are simply forgotten. Another common mistake is that drinks are omitted because they are not considered food items and hence not a source of calories. The other important issue is the inability to estimate quantities. It is not practical to weigh the things one eats even for a week. It is necessary to compare things to a standard size. A four ounce serving of meat is often compared to a deck of cards which is something most people are familiar with in Western societies.

2) Inconvenience

It is difficult to be inconspicuous while maintaining a food diary. Invariably there are irritating questions from friends and many do not wish to draw attention to the fact that they may be grappling with a weight problem.

Instructions for completing a Food Diary

The information you record in your food diary will help you and your Registered Dietitian to develop an eating plan based on the recipes in this book. Providing information relating to 5 to 7 days would be ideal for this purpose.

How much:
In this space indicate the amount of the particular food item you ate. Estimate the size (2" x 1" x 1"), the volume (1/2 cup), the weight (2 ounces) and/or the number of items (1,2,3,) of that type of food.

What kind:
In this column, write down the type of food you ate. Be as specific as you can. Include sauces and gravies. Include items such as soda, salad dressing (brand if known), mayonnaise (brand if known), butter, sour cream, sugar and ketchup.

Time:
Write the time of day you ate the food.

Where:
Write what room or part of the house you were in when you ate. If you ate in a restaurant, fast-food chain or your car, write that location down.

Alone or with someone:
If you ate by yourself, write "alone." If you were with friends or family members, list them.

Activity:
In this column, list any activities you were doing while you were eating (for example, working, watching TV or ironing).

Mood:
How were you feeling while you were eating (for example, sad, happy or depressed)?

Helpful Hints:
- Do not change your eating habits while you are keeping your food diary, unless your family doctor has given you specific instructions to do so.
- It is important to be as accurate as possible. Your RD can help only if you record what you really eat.
- Record what you eat on all days your RD recommends.
- **Be sure to bring the completed forms back with you to your next doctor's appointment.**

Sample Food Diary

Food or Drink						
How much	What kind	Time	Where	Alone or with whom	Associated Activity	Mood
3	pancakes	3:00 p.m.	office	alone	working on computer	bored
1	cheeseburger	6.00 p.m.	Drive through	alone	Driving home	Anxious to get back home
1	regular French fries					
1	coffee					
1 cup	buttered popcorn	10:00 p.m.	kitchen	alone	watching TV	Feeling sleepy

Dietitians are aware of the issues associated with food diaries and make allowances for possible errors. Such errors tend to be under-estimations because it is common for people who are trying to lose weight to record a lower food intake. The reverse is often the case in people with "eating disorders". In people who are overweight, it is recognized that the underestimation may be as much as 300-400 calories/day. Such discrepancies can be readily detected if the calculated energy intake based on the food diary does not match the expected (calculated) food intake based on the formula described in the earlier chapter. Once a person's energy requirement and energy consumption are known, it is possible to develop an eating plan which will help the individual achieve a calorie balance specific to his/her needs.

If a person is overweight or obese, the plan should include a regimen for weight reduction which would place the individual in a negative calorie balance of approximately 500 calories/day. Patients, who find themselves in this situation, should seek the services of Registered Dietitian who is familiar with these procedures. Very often such a deficit can be accomplished by a combination of small reductions ("sacrifices") in the food eaten and physical activity. The 2 charts provided here contain information about how small changes in food and exercise could be used in combination to create the 500 calories/day deficit. Please note that these values are approximate and may vary with specific individuals.

Calories Associated With Various Activities

Activity (1-hour duration)	Weight of person and calories burned		
	160 pounds (73 kilograms)	200 pounds (91 kilograms)	240 pounds (109 kilograms)
Aerobics, high impact	533	664	796
Aerobics, low impact	365	455	545
Aerobics, water	402	501	600
Backpacking	511	637	763
Basketball game	584	728	872
Bicycling, < 10 mph, leisure	292	364	436
Bowling	219	273	327
Canoeing	256	319	382
Dancing, ballroom	219	273	327
Football, touch or flag	584	728	872
Golfing, carrying clubs	314	391	469
Hiking	438	546	654
Ice skating	511	637	763

Racquetball	511	637	763
Resistance (weight) training	365	455	545
Rollerblading	548	683	818
Rope jumping	861	1,074	1,286
Rowing, stationary	438	546	654
Running, 5 mph	606	755	905
Running, 8 mph	861	1,074	1,286
Skiing, cross-country	496	619	741
Skiing, downhill	314	391	469
Skiing, water	438	546	654
Softball or baseball	365	455	545
Stair treadmill	657	819	981
Swimming, laps	423	528	632
Tae kwon do	752	937	1,123
Tai chi	219	273	327
Tennis, singles	584	728	872
Volleyball	292	364	436
Walking, 2 mph	204	255	305
Walking, 3.5 mph	314	391	469

Examples of "Small Sacrifices"
100 Calories Portions

MEATS
2 ounces of skinless roasted chicken breast
2 ounces of grilled pork tenderloin
5 thin slices of lean ham or turkey
3 thin slices of roast beef
FISH AND SEAFOOD
2.5 ounces of salmon fillet or tuna
3 ounces of cod, halibut or other white fish
3 ounces of boiled lobster or crab meat
20 blanched large shrimp
DAIRY PRODUCTS AND SUBSTITUTES
1 cup of skimmed milk
One cup of sweetened almond milk
One cup of unsweetened soy milk
One 1 slice of regular, 2 slices of reduced fat or 3 slices of fat-free cheese
6 ounces of low-fat or 8 ounces of fat-free yogurt
1 jumbo size egg
½ cup of egg substitutes
GRAINS AND BREAD
1 slice of whole grain bread
2 slices of light bread
1 light English muffin.
½ of a regular bagel or 1 petite 100-calorie bagel
½ cup of steamed brown rice or 1 cup of steamed white rice.
5 tablespoons of dried oatmeal
3 ounce of wheat pasta
1 slice of whole grain bread
NUTS AND SEEDS
2 tablespoons of sunflower seeds
2 tablespoons of cashews bits or halves
8 walnut halves
12 raw or dry roasted almonds
16 raw or dry roasted peanuts
28 kernels of pistachios
2 tablespoons of sunflower seeds
FRUITS
1 medium apple or large pear
1 medium orange or grapefruit
1 small size banana
1 cup of grapes

Suggested Further Reading

1. Ainsworth BE, Haskell WL, Herrmann SD et al. 2011 compendium of physical activities: A second update of codes and MET values. Medicine & Science in Sports & Exercise. 2011;43:1575.
2. Mike's Calorie And Fat Gram Chart For 1000 Foods
http://www.ntwrks.com/~mikev/chart1.html]

CHAPTER 4

HOW DO I KNOW HOW MUCH FAT IS IN MY FOOD?

The dietician had spent 30 minutes explaining the intricacies involved in reading food labels. It was becoming increasingly clear that she was losing her audience despite the fact that the material presented was factually correct. Finally an elderly lady sitting at the back of the room raised her hand and asked, "So how does all this information help with my shopping at the grocery store. I get the idea about calories but now I am beginning to form the impression that there are different kinds of calories in foods. I don't get it!"

Another sitting in the front row added, "A teaspoon of sugar is different from a teaspoon of butter! So a teaspoon is not always what it seems, is it?"

The dietician said, "You are both correct and that is what makes things difficult when you go shopping. The labels help but only up to a point. Let me try to explain this again…"

****

All foods are made up of four nutrients, three of which contribute calories. These three are fats, carbohydrates and proteins. The fourth is fiber which plays a significant role in the absorption of food in the gut (digestive tract) but contributes no calories. Also, the calories contributed by fats, carbohydrates and proteins are not equal. An appropriate comparison would be the energy emitted by different light bulbs. Just as they emit different amounts of light and heat, the different types of food also yield different quantities of energy (Figure 4.1).

Figure 4.1. Calories in different types of food

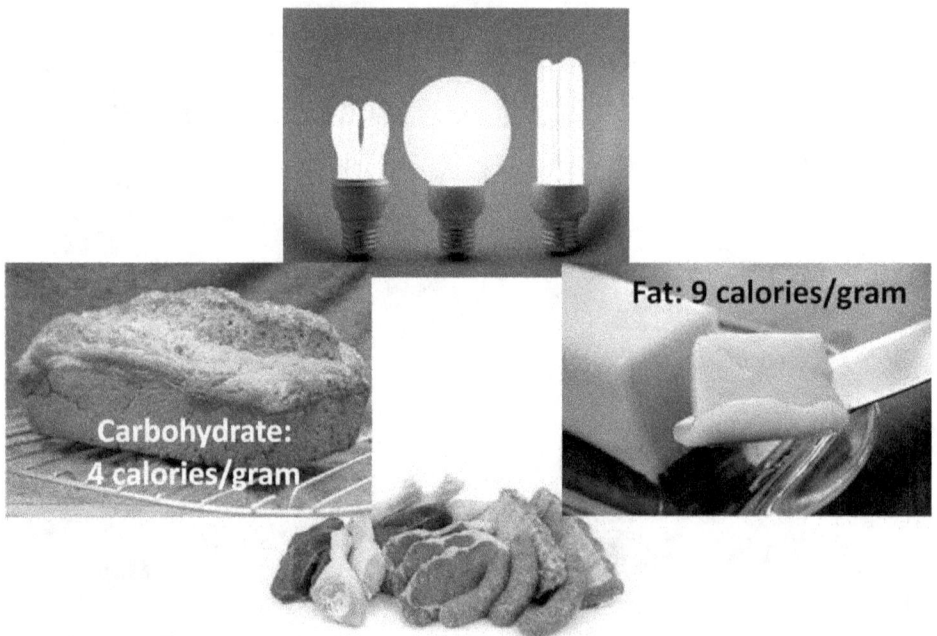

One gram of carbohydrate and protein yields 4 calories each while one gram of fat produces 9 calories. Armed with that knowledge let us consider someone who eats a meal consisting of fish (6 ounces or 180 grams of salmon), potatoes (4 ounces or 120 grams) and peas (half a cup) and sliced boiled carrots (half a cup or 1/6 of a pound or 80 grams) sautéed in butter (1 tablespoon) for lunch and followed it up with a cup of black coffee. The items in the meal in the raw state have the capacity to generate a certain number of calories that can be calculated fairly easily if one knows how much protein, fat and carbohydrates are present in the meal.

In the following table, the 2 columns in the middle show the quantities of protein, fat and carbohydrate present in 100 grams of the **raw ingredients** that formed the meal and the calories derived from them. The last column shows the same items in the portions that were eaten. This information was obtained from the USDA nutrient database and the numbers have been rounded off to the nearest whole number to make the calculations easier. (Note: The remaining component besides protein, fat and carbohydrates in these foods is water).

SALMON			
	100 grams of salmon contains	Calories contributed by 100 gram of salmon	Calories contributed to meal by 180 grams of salmon
Protein	20	80	144
Total fat	6	54	97
Carbohydrate	0	0	0
Energy (kcal)		134	241
POTATO			
	100 grams of potato contains	Calories contributed by 100 gram of potato	Calories contributed to meal by 120 grams of potato
Protein	3	11	13
Total fat	0	0	0
Carbohydrate	12	47	56
Energy (kcal)		58	69
CARROTS			
	100 grams of carrots contains	Calories contributed by 100 gram of carrots	Calories contributed to meal by 80 grams of carrots
Protein	1	4	3
Total fat	0	0	0
Carbohydrate	10	40	32
Energy (kcal)		44	35

PEAS			
	100 grams of peas contains	Calories contributed by 100 gram of peas	Calories contributed to meal by 57 grams of peas
Protein	5	20	11
Total fat	0	0	0
Carbohydrate	15	60	34
Energy (kcal)		**80**	**45**

An additional factor that needs to be considered is the manner in which these items were cooked. The fish was grilled in a tablespoon of butter (14 grams). A pat (5 grams) of butter was added to both the peas and carrots making a total of 24 grams. This quantity of butter is almost exclusively made up of fat and yields 216 calories.

The total number of calories in the meal can be easily calculated by adding the highlighted numbers in the fourth column.

The total number of calories in the meal was 390 which is the sum of 241 + 69 + 35 + 45. To this one must add the 216 calories derived from butter, thus making a total of 606. The black coffee did not provide any calories.

By adding the various nutrient components in the last column it is possible to derive a table which provides the sources of calories in the meal. This is shown below.

The composition of the meal (1 portion) Total calories 606 (including butter used for cooking) Table shows the percentage of calories derived from protein, carbohydrates and fat		
Protein	171	% calories from Protein = (171/606) x 100 = 28 %
Carbohydrates	122	% calories from Carbohydrate = (122/606) x 100 = 20 %
Fat	313	% calories from Fat incl. butter = (313/606) x 100 = 52 %

All the recipes included in this book have been adjusted so as to contain 10-12 % fat, 25-30% protein and 60% carbohydrate. If the amount of calories in a portion is known, then it is possible to consume three meals and two snacks and remain within the overall calories goal for the day and the recommended percentage of fat. A collection of meal plans is provided in subsequent chapters of this book. *It is also important to remember that if one exceeds the recommended amounts during one meal, it is possible to make appropriate adjustments during other meals in the same or next week to get back on track.*

However, the average household or person does not usually plan meals in this manner. It is not practical to weigh or measure ingredients this way to stay within specified dietary guidelines. This is an especially onerous task for those recovering from a heart attack. What we suggest instead is to adopt a series of recipes and an overall meal plan which falls within recommended guidelines and have confidence that one would remain within them.

MAKING SENSE OF FOOD LABELS
Calories, Grams and Percentages

The majority of items that are sold in packets in supermarkets carry a food label like the one shown below on the left. The same label is shown below on the right with sections defined by boxes (A,B,C,D).

Box A indicates that the packet contained 4 servings, each weighing 113 grams or 4 ounces.

Box B states that **each serving** contains 280 calories of which 130 calories are derived from fat. Based on the calculations shown previously one could conclude that 46% of the calories in the serving are derived from fat (i.e. [130/280] x 100).

Box C contains information on individual nutrients (fat, carbohydrate and protein). Most people have problems understanding this information. Take the fat content as an example, which at first sight appears to be 22%. The amount of fat is given as 14 grams per serving. One would expect the percentage value to refer to the amount of fat in a serving, which is 14 grams out of a serving of 113 grams, i.e. 12%. Alternatively, one could expect the percentage value to reflect calories. A serving provided 280 calories and 130 of that were derived from fat yielding the value of 46% stated above. What then does the 22% refer to?

The answer lies in Box D. An individual whose daily requirement is 2000 calories should consume 65 grams of fat daily while trying to maintain a daily fat intake of 30%. This amount of fat (65 x 9) yields 585 calories. The 130 calories derived from fat in the serving is 22% out of these 585 calories (i.e [130/585] x 100).

Thus, the value of 22% stated in the label is really applicable only to a person whose calorie and fat requirement are 2000 calories and 65 grams respectively.

Is there a way out of this food labeling maze for such a person? Fortunately there is. One practical solution would be to determine the percentage of calories derived from fat in the serving. This calculation is easily done as follows:

[(Fat Calories/Total calories) x 100].

In the food label on page 23, the fat calories per serving is 46% when calculated in this manner, which is much greater than the requirement for a "heart healthy" diet (see page22). <u>This value (46%) is not stated anywhere in the label.</u> The only way in which this item could be retained in the diet is by eating other things which have less fat in order to compensate for the excess fat.

Another important number in the food label is the amount of cholesterol in the serving. More on that in the next chapter.

In summary, many of the figures in food labels have <u>little or no relevance</u> to an individual attempting to lose weight as a part of a regimen of care after recovering from a heart attack, or to one wanting to have a diet designed to promote reversal of coronary artery disease.

CHAPTER 5

CHOLESTEROL AND FAT IN FOOD

What about cholesterol?

The discussion had gone along familiar lines........" Cholesterol is a waxy, fat-like substance found in all cells of the body. The human body requires cholesterol to make hormones (in both men and women), vitamin D, and substances that help you digest foods. Your body makes all the cholesterol it needs. However, cholesterol is also found in some of the foods you eat........" Eventually, the inevitable questions came from a somewhat perplexed audience. Is there such a thing as cholesterol deficiency? What is the connection between fat and cholesterol and why are they lumped together? If it causes arterial disease, why are we so concerned about the cholesterol found in the blood stream, especially if it is made in the liver......."

****

Different types of fat

All fats (lipids) are hydrophobic, i.e. they do not dissolve in water. They include oils, waxes, phospholipids, steroids (like cholesterol), and some other related compounds. **In food science, a fat** is solid or semi-solid at room temperature while an **oil** is liquid. This classification is based mainly on the fatty acid composition of the product, i.e. whether the fatty acid is saturated or unsaturated. In chemistry, a **fatty acid** is a carboxylic acid with a long aliphatic tail (chain), which is either **"saturated" or " unsaturated".** Most naturally occurring fatty acids have a chain of an even number of carbon atoms, from 4 to 28. When they are not attached to other molecules, they are known as "free" fatty acids.

Fats and **oils** are made from two kinds of molecules: i) **glycerol** (a type of alcohol with a hydroxyl group on each of its three carbons) and ii) **fatty acids** joined to the glycerol by a process called dehydration synthesis. Fats that have three fatty acids molecules attached to each molecule of glycerol are known as **triglycerides.** (See Figure on left). Fats that have one or two molecules of fatty acids attached to a glycerol molecule are called mono- and di-glycerides respectively. Bread and pastries from a commercial bread factory often contain mono- and di-glycerides as "dough conditioners."

The nature of fatty acids

Fatty acids themselves are made up of smaller units that contain a single carbon atom. The carbon atoms are linked to each other to yield different types of fatty acids based upon the number of carbon units they contain. Each carbon atom has 4 possible linkages. Usually, 2 of these 4 are linked to adjacent carbon atoms while the other 2 are each attached to a hydrogen atom (see above).

Saturated fatty acids are made up of a series of units containing a single carbon atom. Each carbon atom (C) is linked to an adjacent carbon atom and to two hydrogen atoms (H). Thus all the carbons are also bonded to the maximum number of hydrogen atoms possible. These fats are found in animal sources.

Unsaturated fatty acid has one or more double bonds in the fatty acid chain (indicated by star in diagram on left). A fat molecule is monounsaturated if it contains one double bond, and polyunsaturated if it contains more than one double bond. Where double bonds are formed, hydrogen atoms are eliminated. **Thus, a saturated fat is "saturated" with hydrogen atoms.**

Hydrogenated vegetable oil (as in shortening and commercial peanut butters) has had all the double bonds artificially broken and hydrogen units artificially added to turn it into saturated fat that bears no resemblance to the original oil making it solid at room temperature.

Trans fatty acids are another artificially induced variation on naturally occurring unsaturated fatty acids. They are made by adding hydrogen to vegetable oil through a process called hydrogenation, which makes the oil less likely to spoil. Using trans fats in the manufacturing helps foods stay fresh longer, have a longer shelf life and a less greasy feel.

In unsaturated fatty acids, there are two ways the pieces of the hydrocarbon tail can be arranged around a C=C double bond. In <u>cis bonds</u>, the two pieces of the carbon chain on either side of the double bond are either both "up" or both "down," such that both are on the same side of the molecule. In <u>trans bonds</u>, the two pieces of the molecule are on opposite sides of the double bond, that is, one "up" and one "down" across from each other.

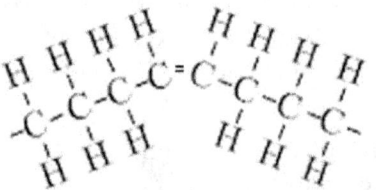

Cis configuration – bent molecule

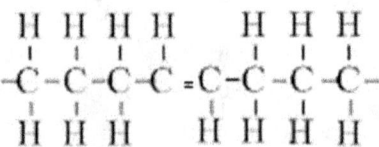

Trans configuration – straight molecule

Naturally occurring unsaturated vegetable oils have almost all cis bonds. Prolonged heating of unsaturated oils (such as repeatedly using the same oil in a fryer to make French fries) causes some of the cis bonds to convert to trans bonds. The levels of trans fatty acids in highly processed lipid-containing products tends to be quite high which has resulted in requiring manufacturers of certain types of food to list the amount of trans fats on the label. **It should be noted that quantities less than 0.5% can be designated as zero on labels and consumption of multiple portions of such manufactured foods could result in excessive consumption of trans fats. The overall effect of trans fats is to increase the serum LDL and decrease HDL.**

Essential fatty acids are a special category of fatty acids because humans and other animals cannot synthesize them. The term "essential fatty acid" refers to the fact these fatty acids are required for biological processes unlike others which provide a source of energy. There are two such fatty acids: alpha-linolenic acid (an omega-3 fatty acid) and linoleic acid (an omega-6 fatty acid). The terms omega-3 and omega-6 refer to the location of the double bond in the fatty acid molecule as measured from the last carbon atom in the molecule. During the past decade there has been an increasing body of evidence that omega-3 fatty acid supplementation has a beneficial effect on the secondary prevention of coronary artery disease. Some of the food sources of omega-3 and omega-6 fatty acids are fish, shellfish, flaxseed, hemp oil, soya oil, canola oil, chia seeds, pumpkin seeds, sunflower seeds, leafy vegetables, and walnuts.

In addition to the LDL produced naturally by the body, saturated fat, *trans*-fatty acids and dietary cholesterol can also raise blood cholesterol. Monounsaturated fats and polyunsaturated fats appear to not raise LDL cholesterol; some studies suggest they might even help lower LDL cholesterol slightly when eaten as part of a diet that is low in saturated and *trans*-fat.

Cholesterol Metabolism (Probably More Chemistry Than You Want To Know!)

Cholesterol is synthesized by the liver starting with small chemical units called acetyl-CoA. Acetyl-CoA is a molecule that has a role in many different biochemical reactions and its main function is to serve as a source of carbon atoms, which can then be used by the body for many different processes. **Acetyl-CoA is created from the metabolism of carbohydrates, fats and proteins.** For cholesterol synthesis, acetyl-CoA is made from the breakdown of fatty acids (lipids, essentially) or pyruvate (a sugar). Once three molecules of acetyl-CoA have been created, they can be converted to another compound, known as Hydroxy Methyl Glutaraldehyde – CoA (HMG-CoA). HMG-CoA is made up of six carbon atoms (four oxygen and nine hydrogen atoms attached to co-enzyme A). The next step is the conversion of HMG-CoA into another intermediate called, called mevalonate by an enzyme called HMG-CoA reductase. This compound undergoes a series of chemical reactions which eventually results in the formation of cholesterol. The step that results in the formation of mevalonic acid is important because it is the slowest part of cholesterol synthesis (which makes it known as the "rate-limiting step").

Cholesterol, while commonly associated with diseases that affect the heart and circulation, is an important molecule which plays a central role in regulating functions of the human body. Approximately half of the cholesterol required for normal function is obtained from the foods we eat. Only animals and animal products (including eggs, milk, and cheese) contain cholesterol. The other half is generated by cells all over the body as described above. Regardless of how the body acquires cholesterol, it has to be transported to cells for a variety of important functions such as the production of certain hormones.

Cholesterol travels in the bloodstream in small packages called lipoproteins which are made of fat on the inside and proteins on the outside. Two kinds of lipoproteins carry the bulk of the cholesterol throughout the body: low-density lipoproteins (LDL) and high-density lipoproteins (HDL). When the LDL cholesterol (sometimes called "bad" cholesterol) concentration in blood is high, there is a buildup of cholesterol in most arteries of the body including the coronary arteries. HDL cholesterol is sometimes also called "good" cholesterol because it carries cholesterol from other parts of the body back to the liver for removal.

Cholesterol eaten as a part of the diet is transported from the small intestine to the liver within small particles made of proteins called chylomicrons. The process of linking to proteins is a method by which cholesterol, which is insoluble in water, can be transported in blood plasma which is mainly made up of water.

Cholesterol synthesized by the liver, as well as any excess dietary cholesterol is transported in the serum within LDLs. The first step in this process is the manufacture of another particle called Very Low Density Lipoproteins (VLDLs). These are later converted to LDLs when they come in contact with the cells that line the inside of arteries (endothelial cells). This process is achieved through the action of an enzyme called endothelial cell-associated lipoprotein lipase. LDLs carry cholesterol to various cells throughout the body. These cells possess receptors for LDL, that capture the particles as they pass and transport them into the cell. Once inside the cell, the machinery of the cell begins to use cholesterol for various metabolic functions.

In contrast, cholesterol found in the inner lining of arteries can be extracted and esterified by the HDL-associated enzyme, Lecithin-Cholesterol-Acyltransferase (LCAT). The cholesterol acquired from peripheral tissues by HDLs can then be transferred to VLDLs and LDLs via the action of cholesteryl ester transfer protein (CETP) (also known as apolipoprotein -D) which is associated with HDLs. This reverse cholesterol transport allows cholesterol in the peripheral circulation to be returned to the liver in LDLs. Ultimately, cholesterol is excreted in the bile as free cholesterol or as bile salts following conversion to bile acids in the liver.

Thus when a laboratory reports the results of a "cholesterol test" it includes at least the following items: a) Total cholesterol, b) LDL cholesterol, c)HDL cholesterol and d) Triglycerides.

Those interested in reading further about cholesterol formation are referred to article Number 6 listed at the end of this chapter.

The importance of "High" Blood Cholesterol

High blood cholesterol is a condition in which there is too much cholesterol in the blood. By itself, the condition usually has no signs or symptoms. However, people who have high blood cholesterol have a greater chance of developing a form of heart disease called atherosclerosis that affects the arteries that supply blood to the heart. The higher the level of LDL cholesterol in the blood, the GREATER the chance of acquiring the disease. Conversely. the higher the level of HDL cholesterol in blood, the LOWER the chance.

Coronary atherosclerosis is a condition in which blockages build up inside the coronary arteries. These blockages (also known as plaques) are made up of cholesterol, fat, calcium, and other substances found in the blood.

The Nutrition Committee of the American Heart Association (AHA) strongly advises the following dietary guidelines for daily fat intake for healthy Americans over age 20 years:

- Limit **total fat** intake to less than 25–35% of total calories
- Limit **saturated fat** intake to less than 7%
- Limit *trans* **fat** intake to less than 1%
- Limit **cholesterol intake** to less than 300 mg per day. People diagnosed with coronary artery disease or those who have an LDL concentration greater than 100 mg/dL should consume less than 200 mg of cholesterol/day.
- The **remaining fat** should be derived from sources of monounsaturated and polyunsaturated fats such as nuts, seeds, fish and vegetable oils.

It should be noted that eating according to the recipes contained in this book will result in the consumption of much less cholesterol than the amounts recommended by the AHA even for people with coronary artery disease. However, there is no deficiency that would result from cholesterol deprivation as the liver has the capacity to manufacture the daily requirements of cholesterol.

Fat consumption and blood cholesterol
Eggs

Eggs are a major source of dietary cholesterol. Yet, there is no consensus on the effect of egg consumption on cholesterol levels in blood. The important fact to remember is that one large egg (50 gram) contains 187 mg of cholesterol (almost exclusively in the yolk). This amount of cholesterol accounts for almost the entire daily recommended allowance for patients with coronary artery disease (American Heart Association). Regardless of the arguments relating to the effect of eggs on serum cholesterol, whole eggs are not recommended for patients who have coronary artery disease and are experiencing problems controlling their blood cholesterol levels.

Saturated fats

The effects of saturated fatty acids on serum lipids depends on the type consumed.

Saturated Fat	Source	Effect on serum lipids
Stearic acid (C 18)	Animal products	No effect (Converted to oleic acid in liver).
Palmitic acid (C 16)	Palm oil, palm kernel oil, coconut oil, meat and dairy products	Raises blood cholesterol levels and cause a low HDL/ LDL ratio
Myristic acid (C 14)	Palm oil, coconut oil, dairy products and whale oil	Raises blood cholesterol levels
Lauric acid (C 12)	Coconut oil and palm kernel oil	Effect on cholesterol levels is unresolved - slightly raises blood cholesterol levels but lowers triglyceride levels.

Other sources of fat and cholesterol

Product (Raw)	Portion	Cholesterol (mg)	Total Fat (g)	Saturated Fat (mg)
Milk (non-fat)	1 cup	5	0.6	0.4
Milk (low-fat) (1%)	1 cup	10	2.4	1.5
Milk (whole)	1 cup	24	8	4.6
Yogurt (non-fat)	1 cup	5	0.4	0.3
Yogurt (whole)	1 cup	32	8	5.1
Cheddar Cheese	1 oz	29	9.6	5.5
Cottage Cheese (low-fat -1%)	1 cup	9	2.3	1.5
Butter	1 tsp	11	4.1	2.6
Margarine	1 tsp	0	3.8	0.7
Vegetable Oils (canola)	1 tsp	0	4.5	0.3
Egg	1	187	4.8	1.6
Halibut	3 ½ oz	49	1.3	0.3
Salmon	3 ½ oz	53	6.3	1.0
Oysters	3 ½ oz	50	2.3	0.5
Crab	3 ½ oz	59	1	0.1
Lobster	3 ½ oz	126	0.74	0.2
Tuna (in water)	3 ½ oz	42	3.0	0.8
Shrimp	3 ½ oz	160	0.5	0.1
Beef (ground, lean - 90%)	3 ½ oz	64	10	3.9
Beef (sirloin)	3 ½ oz	77	14	5.7
Beef Liver	3 ½ oz	273	3.6	1.2
Veal (top round)	3 ½ oz	77	3	1.2
Lamb (fore shank)	3 ½ oz	262	15.2	5.1
Pork (tenderloin)	3 ½ oz	64	3.5	1.2
Pork (chop center loin)	3 ½ oz	69	8.9	1.9
Chicken (no skin)	3 ½ oz	79	13.5	4.7

From USDA database: http://ndb.nal.usda.gov/ndb/

Food labels and fat
When reading labels for fat content, focus on the following:
a) Calories/portion.
b) Fat: both total and saturated.
c) Cholesterol content.
d) Check on trans-fat content.

As discussed previously, in the label shown below, the percentage of fat calories/portion is 46. **The value of 22% is <u>only</u> applicable to individuals who require 2000 calories/day to maintain a healthy weight.**

Nutrition Facts	
Serving Size 4 oz. (113g)	
Servings Per Container 4	
Amount Per Serving	
Calories 280	Calories from Fat 130
	% Daily Value*
Total Fat 14g	22%
Saturated Fat 3.5g	18%
Trans Fat 2.5g	
Cholesterol 120mg	40%
Sodium 640mg	27%
Total Carbohydrate 13g	4%
Dietary Fiber 1g	4%
Sugars 0g	
Protein 24g	
Vitamin A 2% • Vitamin C 2%	
Calcium 2% • Iron 6%	

*Percent Daily Values are based on a 2,000 calorie diet. Your daily values may be higher or lower depending on your calorie needs:

	Calories	2,000	2,500
Total Fat	Less Than	65g	80g
Saturated Fat	Less Than	20g	25g
Cholesterol	Less Than	300mg	300 mg
Sodium	Less Than	2,400mg	2,400mg
Total Carbohydrate		300g	375g
Dietary Fiber		25g	30g

Calories per gram:
Fat 9 • Carbohydrate 4 • Protein 4

Suggested Further Reading

1. Smith SC, Benjamin EJ, Bonow RO *et al*: AHA/ACCF Secondary Prevention and Risk Reduction Therapy for Patients With Coronary and Other Atherosclerotic Vascular Disease: 2011 Update. *Circulation*, 124:2458-2473.
2. Reiner Z, Catapano AL, De Backer G *et al*: ESC/EAS Guidelines for the management of dyslipidaemias. *European Heart Journal*, 32:1769-1818.
3. Lichtenstein AH, Appel LJ, Brands M *et al*: Diet and Lifestyle Recommendations Revision 2006. *Circulation* 2006, 114:82-96.
4. Sun Q, Ma J, Campos H, Hankinson SE et al. A Prospective Study of Trans Fatty Acids in Erythrocytes and Risk of Coronary Heart Disease. *Circulation* 2007, 115(14):1858-1865.
5. Terry A J: Secondary Prevention of Coronary Artery Disease with Omega-3 Fatty Acids. The American Journal of Cardiology 2006, 98(4, Supplement 1):61-70.
6. Mason W. Freeman, M.D. Junge C. CHAPTER 1: Understanding Cholesterol: The Good, the Bad, and the Necessary. The Harvard Medical School Guide to Lowering Your Cholesterol McGraw-Hill Companies.

CHAPTER 6

BE SERIOUS! CAN YOU ACTUALLY EAT FIBER?

In an attempt to save on gasoline, two neighbors, Jane and Janet, decided to do their weekly grocery shopping as a joint expedition. They parted company at the store entrance and each followed their usual pattern of shopping until they met at the shelves that contained rice and cereals. They loaded their respective selections into the two carts and proceeded to the checkout. Jane noticed that their selections were similar except for their choices of cereals and rice. Janet had purchased items that carried labels proclaiming they were "High Fiber Items". Jane had purchased items that did not mention anything about fiber. She also did not know what the difference implied. On the way home she decided to ask her friend about fiber in food.

"It's good for you!"
"How so?"
"I've no idea but my sister who is a nurse said so. She knows about that sort of thing."
"Really?"
"Yes! You've got to have a lot of fiber in the diet. If you don't all kinds of bad stuff happens."
"What sort of bad stuff" the other persisted.
"I don't know and it is a lot easier to follow what she says. She also asked me to start with cereals and rice. It is a good place to start. Less grief all around to do as she says!"

****

The term dietary fiber is used to identify certain materials derived from the edible portions of plants. (They form the cell walls of plant cells). Dietary fiber is not digested and therefore not absorbed. It is not a source of energy (i.e. calories). However, dietary fiber is important because of its influence on the way in which the gut handles food. Also, food items that have a lot of fiber contain other useful chemicals such as anti-oxidants which promote health.

There are two types of fiber, soluble and insoluble. A soluble fiber dissolves in water while an insoluble one does not. A balanced diet should contain an abundance of insoluble fiber (approximately 75% of the fiber content). As the Table below shows, the two types of fiber have different effects.

Type of fiber	Some Common Sources	*Short Term* Benefits
Soluble (pectins, gums, mucilages, some hemicelluloses)	Beans, corn, oats, barley, lentils, carrots, cabbage, apples, bananas, citrus fruits	Reduces the absorption of fat Slows down the absorption of sugars
Insoluble (Cellulose, lignins, and hemicelluloses)	Bran (the outer covering of corn, oats, rice and wheat), cereals, whole grains, edible portion of skins of fruits and vegetables, and celery	Bulks up the stool and prevents constipation

Fiber Content of Foods (Grams/ Servings)

	Serving Size	Fiber		
		Total	Soluble	Insoluble
Vegetables, cooked				
Asparagus	½ cup	2.8	1.7	1.1
Beets, flesh only	½ cup	1.8	0.8	1.0
Broccoli	½ cup	2.4	1.2	1.2
Brussels sprouts	½ cup	3.8	2.0	1.8
Corn, whole kernel, canned	½ cup	1.6	0.2	1.4
Carrots, sliced	½ cup	2.0	1.1	0.9
Cauliflower	½ cup	1.0	0.4	0.6
Green beans, canned	½ cup	2.0	0.5	1.5
Kale	½ cup	2.5	0.7	1.8
Peas, green, frozen	½ cup	4.3	1.3	3.0
Potato, sweet, flesh only	½ cup	4.0	1.8	2.2
Spinach	½ cup	1.6	0.5	1.1
Turnip	½ cup	4.8	1.7	3.1
Vegetables, raw				
Cabbage, red	1 cup	1.5	0.6	0.9
Carrots, fresh	1, 7 ½ in. long	2.3	1.1	1.2
Celery, fresh	1 cup chopped	1.7	0.7	1.0
Onion, fresh	½ cup chopped	1.7	0.9	0.8
Pepper, green, fresh	1 cup chopped	1.7	0.7	1.0
Tomato, fresh	1 medium	1.0	0.1	0.9
Fruits				
Apple, red, fresh w/skin	1 small	2.8	1.0	1.8
Apricots, fresh w/skin	4	3.5	1.8	1.7
Banana, fresh	½ small	1.1	0.3	0.8
Blueberries, fresh	¾ cup	1.4	0.3	1.1
Cherries, black, fresh	12 large	1.3	0.6	0.7
Figs, dried	1 ½	3.0	1.4	1.6
Grapefruit, fresh	½ medium	1.6	1.1	0.5
Grapes, fresh w/skin	15 small	0.5	0.2	0.3
Kiwifruit, fresh, flesh only	1 large	1.7	0.7	1.0
Mango, fresh, flesh only	½ small	2.9	1.7	1.2
Melon, cantaloupe	1 cup cubed	1.1	0.3	0.8
Orange, fresh, flesh only	1 small	2.9	1.8	1.1
Peach, fresh, w/skin	1 medium	2.0	1.0	1.0
Pear, fresh, w/skin	½ large	2.9	1.1	1.8
Plum, red, fresh	2 medium	2.4	1.1	1.3
Prunes, dried	3 medium	1.7	1.0	0.7
Raisins, dried	2 tbsp	0.4	0.2	0.2
Raspberries, fresh	1 cup	3.3	0.9	2.4
Strawberries, fresh	1 ¼ cup	2.8	1.1	1.7
Watermelon	1 ¼ cup cubed	0.6	0.4	0.2

Adapted from Anderson JW. *Plant Fiber in Foods*. 2nd ed. HCF Nutrition Research Foundation Inc, PO Box 22124, Lexington, KY 40522, 1990.

In the ***long term*** dietary fiber protects against the development of cancers of the colon and rectum, stomach and some regions of the mouth. A recent meta-analysis of 25 trials has suggested that it may be the type of dietary fiber which has a beneficial effect on preventing cancers. The results were a vindication of many of the current dietary recommendations relating to dietary fiber. In a U.S. study, a high intake of dietary fiber was associated with a lower incidence of colorectal adenomas which is a pre-cancerous condition. In a European study a high dietary fiber intake was associated with a reduced incidence of colorectal cancer. The greatest level of protection was obtained by consuming approximately 25-30 grams of fiber daily. The European study also indicated that this amount should be slightly higher in men. One other point of interest in the U.S. study was that fiber derived from grain, cereal and fruit appeared to confer a greater benefit than fiber from other sources.

Most national organizations in the U.S. such as the American Heart Association, The National Cholesterol Education Panel and the American Diabetes Association recommend a daily intake of about 25 grams. The Institute of Medicine and the National Academy of Science in its most recent report recommended a daily intake of 25 grams for women and 38 grams for men. The slightly higher recommendation for men is borne out by recent studies. In order to achieve this level of fiber intake there has to be a deliberate emphasis on cereals, whole grains and fruit. In fact, many food labels carry this information (see food label on Page 31).

Suggested Further Reading

1. Gonzalez CA, Riboli E: Diet and cancer prevention: Contributions from the European Prospective Investigation into Cancer and Nutrition (EPIC) study. *European Journal of Cancer*, 46:2555-2562.
2. Aune D, Chan D, Lau R et al. Dietary fibre, whole grains, and risk of colorectal cancer: systematic review and dose-response meta-analysis of prospective studies. *BMJ* 2011, 343. doi: 10.1136/bmj.d6617

CHAPTER 7

ADD SALT TO TASTE ......

Joe called his friend Fred to set up their monthly breakfast meeting for the first Tuesday of the month. They met at their usual place and each ordered their meals. Joe had been diagnosed with high blood pressure a few years previously and had managed to control his pressure by a combination of medications and a salt restricted diet. He ordered a bowl of cereal, a muffin and a cup of decaffeinated coffee. Fred who was much younger ordered a helping of scrambled eggs, toast and regular coffee. After a few minutes their orders arrived and they interrupted their discussion to start on their meals. Joe watched his young friend sprinkle his meal with a liberal helping of salt.

Even though this was a ritual going back many months, on this morning Joe was moved to observe, "How come you add so much salt even before tasting the food?"
"I don't know.....It's what I do, I guess."
"Have you any idea what too much salt could do to you?"
"What could it do? If have too much I'd probably pass it in the urine. Isn't that right? In any case we have to die of something!"
Joe shrugged and began to eat his own breakfast.

****

Reducing salt (sodium chloride) intake is one of several ways that people can lower their blood pressure. Reducing blood pressure, ideally to the normal range, reduces the chance of developing a stroke, heart disease, heart failure, and kidney disease. The relationship between salt intake and blood pressure is direct and progressive without an apparent threshold. On average, the higher a person's salt intake, the higher is his or her blood pressure. Thus, reducing salt intake as much as possible is one way to lower blood pressure. Another dietary measure to lower blood pressure is to consume a diet rich in potassium. A potassium-rich diet also blunts the effects of salt on blood pressure, may reduce the risk of developing kidney stones, and possibly decreases bone loss with age.

The first issue that needs to be resolved is the difference between sodium and salt in the shaker. The latter is a compound called sodium chloride and the recommendation refers to the chemical element sodium. Due to the different molecular weights of sodium and chloride, salt contains approximately 39% of sodium. This is a calculation that is of little practical value to the person making meals at home. The following may prove to be a little more helpful.

¼ teaspoon salt (sodium chloride) ~ 600 mg sodium
½ teaspoon salt (sodium chloride) ~ 1,200 mg sodium
¾ teaspoon salt (sodium chloride) ~ 1,800 mg sodium
1 teaspoon salt (sodium chloride) ~ 2,300 mg sodium

Current dietary guidelines for Americans recommend that adults in general should consume no more than 2,300 mg of **sodium** and 4,700 mg of potassium per day. This goal for sodium is expressed in terms of sodium rather than salt because the Nutrition Facts Labels on food products list sodium content.

The following population groups should consume no more than 1,500 mg of sodium per day:
- 51 years of age or older
- African American
- have high blood pressure
- have diabetes
- have chronic kidney disease

The 1,500 mg recommendation applies to about half of the U.S. population overall and the majority of adults. Nearly everyone benefits from reduced sodium consumption. Eating less sodium can help prevent, or control, high blood pressure.

Alternative Seasonings to Salt

- **Allspice:** Lean ground meats, stews, tomatoes, peaches, applesauce, cranberry sauce, gravies, lean meat
- **Almond extract:** Puddings, fruits
- **Basil:** Fish, lamb, lean ground meats, stews, salads, soups, sauces, fish cocktails
- **Bay leaves:** Lean meats, stews, poultry, soups, tomatoes
- **Caraway seeds:** Lean meats, stews, soups, salads, breads, cabbage, asparagus, noodles
- **Chives:** Salads, sauces, soups, lean meat dishes, vegetables
- **Cider vinegar:** Salads, vegetables, sauces
- **Cinnamon:** Fruits (especially apples), breads, pie crusts
- **Curry powder:** Lean meats (especially lamb), veal, chicken, fish, tomatoes, tomato soup, mayonnaise
- **Dill:** Fish sauces, soups, tomatoes, cabbages, carrots, cauliflower, green beans, cucumbers, potatoes, salads, macaroni, lean beef, lamb, chicken, fish
- **Garlic** (not garlic salt): Lean meats, fish, soups, salads, vegetables, tomatoes, potatoes
- **Ginger:** Chicken, fruits
- **Lemon juice:** Lean meats, fish, poultry, salads, vegetables
- **Mace:** Hot breads, apples, fruit salads, carrots, cauliflower, squash, potatoes, veal, lamb
- **Mustard (dry):** Lean ground meats, lean meats, chicken, fish, salads, asparagus, broccoli, Brussels sprouts, cabbage, mayonnaise, sauces
- **Nutmeg:** Fruits, pie crust, lemonade, potatoes, chicken, fish, lean meat loaf, toast, veal, pudding
- **Onion powder** (not onion salt): Lean meats, stews, vegetables, salads, soups
- **Paprika:** Lean meats, fish, soups, salads, sauces, vegetables
- **Parsley:** Lean meats, fish, soups, salads, sauces, vegetables
- **Peppermint extract:** Puddings, fruits
- **Pimiento:** Salads, vegetables, casserole dishes
- **Rosemary:** Chicken, veal, lean meat loaf, lean beef, lean pork, sauces, stuffings, potatoes, peas, lima beans
- **Sage:** Lean meats, stews, biscuits, tomatoes, green beans, fish, lima beans, onions, lean pork
- **Savory:** Salads, lean pork, lean ground meats, soups, green beans, squash, tomatoes, lima beans, peas
- **Thyme:** Lean meats (especially veal and lean pork), sauces, soups, onions, peas, tomatoes, salads
- **Turmeric:** Lean meats, fish, sauces, rice

The current view of both the Institute of Medicine and the American Heart Association is to work towards the goal of reducing the sodium intake to 1500 mg/day by 2020. It has been argued that this 2-step process should provide manufacturers with time to reformulate products and identify acceptable salt substitutes. Many of these recommendations stem from a study undertaken under the sponsorship of the National Institutes of Health on the effect of reducing sodium intake upon management of hypertension (see suggested reading below)

It is of interest that the Centers for Disease Control and Prevention have recently reported that the American population consumes more salt than amounts recommended and that bread is the No. 1 source of sodium. In fact, they have concluded that people get twice as much from bread and rolls as they do from snacks such as potato chips and pretzels.

Suggested Further Reading

1. Your guide to Lowering Your Blood Pressure With DASH
   [http://www.nhlbi.nih.gov/health/public/heart/hbp/dash/new_dash.pdf]
2. Sacks FM, Moore TJ, Appel LJ et al: A dietary approach to prevent hypertension: A review of the dietary approaches to stop hypertension (DASH) study. Clinical Cardiology 1999, 22(S3):6-10.
3. Cogswell ME, Zhang Z, Carriquiry AL, et al. Sodium and potassium intakes among US adults: NHANES 2003-2008. The American Journal of Clinical Nutrition;96:647-57.
4. Centers for Disease Control. Nine in 10 U.S. adults get too much sodium every day. http://www.cdc.gov/media/releases/2012/p0207_sodium_food.html February 7, 2012.
5) Centers for Disease Control and Prevention. Where's the sodium? There's too much in many common foods. http://www.cdc.gov/vitalsigns/Sodium/index.html February 7, 2012.

CHAPTER 8

WHAT ABOUT ALCOHOL?

The patient had read something about a phenomenon called the French Paradox and was attempting to convince his physician of the health promoting properties of red wine. The French Paradox refers to the idea that red wine protects people against developing coronary artery disease. This idea originated in France and the rest, as the saying goes, is history. However, this patient's problem was not coronary artery disease but the fact that he had a Body Mass Index of 32 which meant that he was seriously overweight.

As discussed in previous chapters, the essential nutrients that the body needs are carbohydrates, protein, fat, vitamins, minerals, and water. The term "essential" means that if you remove one of these nutrients from your diet there will be a deficiency that causes health problems. Alcohol (chemically called ethyl alcohol) is not an essential nutrient because there is no health problem that is the result of not consuming it. However, some argue that there are added health benefits from consuming alcohol and that it should be added to our diets for that reason. This view brings to mind a phrase popularized by Bert Lance who was the Director of the Office of Management and Budget in Jimmy Carter's 1977 administration, "If it ain't broke, don't fix it!"

As discussed previously, carbohydrates, protein and fat provide calories (energy) for our bodies to function. Besides these nutrients, alcohol is also capable of providing calories. Each gram yields the following number of calories (Figure 8.1)

Figure 8.1. Calories in Nutrients

Since, different drinks contain varying amounts of ethyl alcohol, a standard has been set for the quantity of ethyl alcohol in various drinks. In general, a 12 ounce bottle of beer containing 4% alcohol by volume (some craft beer can range up to 9% in alcohol by volume), a 4 ounce glass of wine and a 1.5 ounce shot of 80 proof spirits all contain the same amount of ethyl alcohol (one half ounce). Each of these is considered a "drink equivalent."

Alcohol proof is a measure of how much alcohol (ethyl alcohol) is contained in an alcoholic beverage. The term was originally used in the United Kingdom and was defined as 7/4 times the alcohol by volume (ABV). In the United States, alcoholic proof is defined as twice the percentage of ABV. So a drink with 12% alcohol per volume is 24 proof. A 12 ounce glass of beer, a 5 ounce glass of wine and a 1.5 ounce shot of liquor all contain a ½ ounce of pure alcohol and are considered one drink.

For the present discussion, it would be useful to remember the calories derived from one's favorite beverage or drink.

Calories in common alcoholic beverages. Generally, a 12 ounce glass of beer, a 5 ounce glass of wine and a 1.5 ounce shot of liquor all contain a ½ ounce of pure alcohol and are considered one drink.

Alcoholic Drink	Size	Calories
Note: 100 ml = 3.4 ounces. The average wine glass contains 3-5 ounces		
Beer	half Liter	184
Lager	half Liter	180
Cider	half Liter	200
Whisky	100ml	220
Gin	100ml	220
Brandy	100ml	220
Rum	100ml	220
Wine red	100ml	70
Wine white dry	100ml	65
Wine white medium	100ml	70
Wine white sweet	100ml	90
Wine white sparkling	100ml	74
Rose	100ml	62
Champagne	100ml	126
Pernod	100ml	140
Tia Maria	100ml	155
Southern Comfort	100ml	184
Drambuie	100ml	184
Sherry dry	100ml	110
Sherry medium	100ml	112
Sherry sweet	100ml	130
Port	100ml	160
Martini	100ml	175
Malibu	100ml	204
Baileys Cream	1 glass	120
Bacardi	1 glass	118

A little about the chemistry of alcohol

How is alcohol made?

Alcohol, also known as ethyl alcohol or ethanol, is made using a process called fermentation which is started using yeast. Yeast breaks down sugar into ethanol and carbon dioxide. When this process is completed, the carbon dioxide gas bubbles out into the air, leaving ethanol and water behind. A second process called distillation removes the water leaving spirits, such as vodka, rum, gin, and whisky. Sugar used for making alcoholic drinks is derived from several sources depending on the beverage manufactured. The sugar from crushed grapes is used to make wine; malted barley is used to make beer; sugar cane or molasses makes rum. Vodka is made from sugar obtained from grain, potatoes, beets and molasses.

Cardiovascular risks associated with drinking alcohol

Drinking too much alcohol can raise the levels of some fats in the blood such as triglycerides. It can also lead to high blood pressure, heart failure and a higher calorie intake resulting in weight gain and a higher risk of developing diabetes. Excessive drinking and binge drinking can lead to stroke. Other serious problems include fetal alcohol syndrome, cardiomyopathy, cardiac arrhythmia and sudden cardiac death.

Potential benefits of drinking wine or other alcoholic beverages

The best known effect of alcohol is a small increase in HDL ("good") cholesterol. However, regular physical activity is another effective way to raise HDL cholesterol "naturally". How alcohol or wine affects cardiovascular risk is the subject of current research, but for the present, the American Heart Association does not recommend drinking alcohol for potential benefits.

Red wine and heart disease

Over the past several decades, many scientific studies have addressed moderate alcohol consumption and its association with reduced deaths from heart disease in certain populations. Some researchers have suggested that the benefits may be derived from compounds present in red wine such as flavonoids and related antioxidants. However, these compounds may also be found in foods such as grapes or red grape juice. No direct prospective comparison trials have been done to determine the specific effect of wine or other alcoholic drinks on the risk of developing heart disease or stroke.

However, other studies have demonstrated no significant difference between different kinds of alcoholic drinks. A large group of people (56,926 men and 72,008 women) in the Northern California Kaiser Health System was followed from 1978 through 1998. As expected, heavy drinkers (*more than* 6 drinks daily) had a higher mortality. People who drank moderate quantities of wine (1–2 drinks daily) had a lower coronary mortality compared to abstainers. Similar differences were observed in moderate beer drinkers and spirit consumers. However, when the various types of wine were examined, there was no difference in risk reduction between white, red, and other wines.

It is not recommended that people who have some form of coronary artery disease (heart attack, coronary bypass surgery, placement of stents), should increase their alcohol intake in the expectation that they would experience some of these

apparent benefits. The main reason for not doing so is that alcohol is a source of calories. Two 4 ounce drinks of wine would provide approximately 160 calories.

Suggested Further Reading

1. Pearson TA. Alcohol and Heart Disease. *Circulation* 1996, 94(11):3023-3025.
2. Lindberg ML, Amsterdam EA. Alcohol, Wine, and Cardiovascular Health. *Clinical Cardiology* 2008, 31(8):347-351.
3. O'Keefe JH, Bybee KA, Lavie CJ. Alcohol and Cardiovascular Health: The Razor-Sharp Double-Edged Sword. *Journal of the American College of Cardiology* 2007, 50:1009-1014.
4. Klatsky AL, Friedman GD, Siegelaub AB. Alcohol and mortality. A ten-year Kaiser-Permanente experience. *Ann Intern Med* 1981, 95:139-145.
5. Movva R, Figueredo V.M. ,Alcohol and the heart: To abstain or not to abstain? International Journal of Cardiology (2012) http://dx.doi.org/10.1016/j.ijcard.2012.01.030
6. Britton KA, Gaziano JM, Sesso HD, Djoussé L. Relation of alcohol consumption and coronary heart disease in hypertensive male physicians (from the Physicians' Health Study). Am J Cardiol. 2009;104: 932-5.

CHAPTER 9

THE RECOMMENDATIONS

The group had nearly completed the dietary sessions and a few issues remained to be resolved. Several people gathered around the dietitian and asked for clarification on two specific matters. The first said, "My husband just recovered from a heart attack and is doing well but I have a son who is just turning forty. Is there anything he could be doing to avoid going down the same road as his Dad?" Several in the group nodded their head in agreement thinking of the younger people in their own families.

The second who had been silent during most of the sessions had a more critical question. " I have listened to everything you have said and even understood quite a bit of it, except the bits about how cholesterol is formed and some other matters that seemed technical. But I feel I don't need to know all that stuff to improve my husband's prognosis. There is quite a lot I could be doing with the knowledge I do have. My question is this. " How do I make this work on a day-to-day basis?" The recommendations are fine but what do I do when I go shopping for groceries?"

Both questions were on the money. There are two categories of recommendation. The first consist of guidelines which form a part of public health measures. The second consist of the more specific suggestions that apply to individuals. In this Chapter we will move from the first category to the second.

****

Overall, several national and international bodies have made specific dietary recommendations to lower the risk of heart disease. The most recent joint report of the Food and Nutrition Board and the Institute of Medicine has provided a comprehensive series of recommendations for diet and physical activity to reduce the risk of coronary artery disease. These are itemized below.

- Adults should get 45 percent to 65 percent of their calories from carbohydrates, 20 percent to 35 percent from fat, and 10 to 35 percent from protein. Acceptable ranges for children are similar to those for adults, except that infants and younger children need a slightly higher proportion of fat (25 -40 percent).
- To maintain cardiovascular health, regardless of weight, adults and children should achieve *a total of at least one hour of moderately intense physical activity each day.*
- Added sugars should comprise no more than 25 percent of total calories consumed. *Added sugars are those incorporated into foods and beverages during production which usually provide insignificant amounts of vitamins, minerals, or other essential nutrients. Major sources include soft drinks, fruit drinks, pastries, candy, and other sweets.*
- The recommended intake for total fiber for adults 50 years and younger is set at 38 grams for men and 25 grams for women, while for men and women over 50 it is 30 and 21 grams per day, respectively, due to decreased food consumption.
- The report reaffirms previously established recommended levels of protein intake, which is 0.8 grams per kilogram of body weight for adults; however recommended levels for pregnancy are higher.

- The report does not set levels for saturated fat, cholesterol, or trans fatty acids, as increased risk exists at levels above zero. However the recommendation is to eat as little of these items as possible while consuming a diet adequate in other important essential nutrients.
- Recommendations are made for linoleic acid (an omega-6 fatty acid) and for alpha-linolenic acid (an omega- 3 fatty acid).

The American Heart Association's Nutrition Committee strongly advises these guidelines for fat consumption for healthy Americans over age 20 years.

- Limit total fat intake to less than 25–35 percent of your total calories each day.
- Limit saturated fat intake to less than 7 percent of total daily calories.
- Limit *trans* fat intake to less than 1 percent of total daily calories..
- The remaining fat should come from sources of monounsaturated and polyunsaturated fats such as nuts, seeds, fish and vegetable oils.
- Limit cholesterol intake to less than 300 mg per day, for most people. If you have coronary heart disease or your LDL cholesterol level is 100 mg/dL or greater, limit your cholesterol intake to less than 200 milligrams a day.

These recommendations are broadly similar to those provided by the Food and Nutrition Board except for the added emphasis on limiting the cholesterol intake.

Recommendations from the Heart Disease Reversal Program.

The recipes contained in this book are directed at those who have recovered from an event related to coronary artery disease or those who are candidates for such an event. This diet is designed to promote regression of atherosclerosis in coronary arteries and is based on the findings of coronary angiography and long term survival data (see Part 3). The main elements of the diet are given below:

1) Mainly a plant based diet which includes non-fat dairy and egg whites.
2) Total calories consumed directed at achieving an appropriate body weight.
3) Total fat in the diet to be lower than AHA recommendations, with saturated fats extremely limited.
4) Focus on high dietary fiber (as per Food and Nutrition Board recommendations).
5) Omega-3 and 6-fatty acids should be included as part of the daily fat allowance.
6) Low sodium content highly recommended.

For *reversing heart disease*, we recommend that carbohydrates, proteins and fat be consumed in the following proportions (Note: these proportions are somewhat different from those recommended by the American Heart Association and the Institutes of Medicine in the Unites States.

Proportions of calories derived from carbohydrates, proteins and fat per day	
CARBOHYDRATES	50 - 70 %
PROTEIN	15-25%
FAT	Less than 12 %
Saturated fat	3%
Cholesterol	15 mg/day
Other diet features	Diet is ovo-lacto (non-fat dairy allowed) <1500 mg sodium 25 grams fiber for women 38 grams fiber for men

DIET RECOMMENDATIONS

WHERE DO I START?

The diet plan that is recommended for patients who are interested in reversing coronary artery disease is a vegetarian one with a very low intake of saturated fat and cholesterol. The final aim is to consume approximately 12% of the daily calorie intake as fat and 20% as protein. The remaining calories would be consumed as carbohydrates. As described in previous sections of this book, one should approach changing eating habits in stages.

Stage 1: Estimate the *current* daily (energy) calorie intake   (see chapter 1)

Stage 2: Estimate daily (energy) calorie target

If a person is at his/her ideal body weight the estimated calories intake could be used as the target value. If the weight is not appropriate, (either too low or too high) it would be necessary to set a new target. This value is based on the Body Mass Index (BMI). (See chapter 2)

Back to the diet……….

Let us take an example of a person who weighs 200 pounds and is 5 feet 8 inches tall. This individual's BMI is 31, placing him/her in the obese category. This means that the person should lose approximately 50 pounds to reach the healthy range of BMI.

A realistic goal for such an individual would be to try to lose 1 pound per week. Such a weight loss could then be achieved after approximately one year. In order to lose 1 pound in weight/week the person has to achieve a calories deficit of 3500 calories each week or 500 calories/day. This deficit could be achieved exclusively through diet or exercise or a combination of both. Since we are dealing with people with coronary artery disease, exercising to lose weight may not be an option at least initially. So, it may be necessary to reduce calorie intake as the initial goal.

How many calories does this person need to lose weight at this rate?

Based upon the formulae described earlier, if this individual is a 69 year old man who is sedentary, the calculated energy requirement to maintain his current weight is 2465 calories. This means that in order to lose 1 pound of weight/week he would need to drop his calories intake to under 2000/day (assuming his activity level remains the same).

At this point it is necessary to consult a Registered Dietitian and evaluate the food diary critically and establish which items could be eliminated or reduced in amount to achieve weight loss.

Stage 3: Planning meals

Most people tend to eat three meals and 1 mid-morning and 1 afternoon snack per day. How does one separate a daily requirement of 2,000 calories into these meals and snacks? One way to do so would be to consider the daily requirement as a pie with each slice representing a meal with an approximate calorie value. The energy derived from each meal could be assigned values depending on a person's habits and eating pattern. If each meal is prepared so that all the major food groups are included in the proportions in the pie chart below, wouldn't that solve the problem? Not quite.......

Calories in each meal

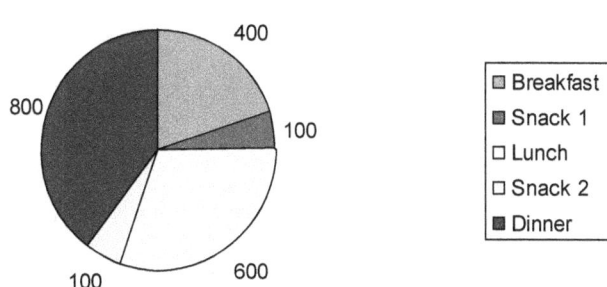

Suggested daily proportion of calories in each meal for a 2000 calories/day diet

There are several problems with this way of thinking about meals. The first is that the calorie values have to be translated into something that appears on a person's plate at meal time. The second is that the food has to contain the recommended proportions of carbohydrates and fats. This way of doing things makes it necessary to plan meals in advance and do one's grocery shopping to suit the plan.

All that sounds easy but let us stop a minute and have a brief reality check here! Does this mean that one cannot fall off the wagon, as it were, occasionally? The operative word is "occasionally". An occasional indiscretion is not a life-threatening catastrophe as long as adjustments are made to other meals on that day or the next. **The main reason why matters get out of control is because no adjustments are made at other meals**.

It is also clear that this method of eating would not come easily to most people who have been brought up on a standard "Western Diet". It is something that has to be embraced as a way of life for an extended period. This means that meal planning becomes an integral part of this process.

Suggested Further Reading

1. Dietary Reference Intakes for Energy, Carbohydrate, Fiber, Fat, Fatty Acids, Cholesterol, Protein, and Amino Acids Food and Nutrition Board (Released: September 5, 2002) http://www.iom.edu/Reports/2002/Dietary-Reference-Intakes-for-Energy-Carbohydrate-Fiber-Fat-Fatty-Acids-Cholesterol-Protein-and-Amino-Acids.aspx
2. Balady GJ, Williams MA, Ades PA et al. Core components of cardiac rehabilitation and secondary prevention programs 2007 update. *Journal of Cardiopulmonary Rehabilitation and Prevention* 2007, 27:121-129.
3. Poslusna K, Ruprich J, de Vries JHM, Jakubikova M, and van't Veer P. (). Misreporting of energy and micronutrient intake estimated by food records and 24 hour recalls, control and adjustment methods in practice. Br J Nutr. 2009;101 Suppl 2:S73-85.

CHAPTER 10

THE BIG PICTURE (AS WE SEE IT)

Several controlled trials have established that procedures such as insertion of stents and bypass surgery, medicines that reduce blood cholesterol concentration, blood pressure and the formation of blood clots in vessels, reduce the death rate in patients who have recovered from a heart attack. To these treatments one could also add the benefits that result from participating in cardiac rehabilitation programs after leaving the hospital. One of the aims of these programs is to persuade patients to focus on lifestyle issues which interfere with effective self care. They emphasize the value of a comprehensive approach combining conventional outpatient cardiac care with several other forms of treatment, such as exercise training, dietary advice and stress management. All these activities take place against a background of educating patients regarding the nature of their illnesses and their treatment so that they "buy into" the process of care. Very often, that process includes convincing patients of the need to comply with their medications as prescribed. A recent study has shown that a significant proportion of patients fail to take a daily medication to lower blood cholesterol even when it is provided free.

****

For a period of nearly 20 years, we provided such a program of comprehensive care which included a vegetarian diet. This diet was adapted from the pioneering work in this field initiated by Dr. Dean Ornish which showed that a low-fat vegetarian diet was capable of promoting the reversal of atherosclerosis in the coronary arteries.

All the patients admitted to the program had either atherosclerosis of the coronary arteries or had recovered from a recent heart attack. A significant number also had undergone coronary artery bypass surgery. The overall goal of the program was to minimize the effects of risk factors, associated with coronary artery disease, according to the recommendations of the National Cholesterol Education Program Adult Treatment Panel (NCEP II and III). The program also focused on educating patients about this type of heart disease, weight management, exercise training and stress management. Smokers were accepted only after they had successfully completed a smoking cessation program. The patients were enrolled in small groups of 6 – 8 and were managed by a team composed of cardiologists, nurses, registered dietitians, an exercise physiologist and a clinical psychologist. A spouse or a support person was encouraged to participate in the program.

The program was implemented in 4 stages: 1) a preliminary screening to determine eligibility (based upon the presence of angiographically documented coronary artery disease and a history of a recent myocardial infarction (heart attack), 2) comprehensive medical, dietary and psychological screening, 3) a 2-day non-residential workshop of lectures, interactive sessions and activities to improve bonding between members within each group, 4) a 24-month program of outpatient care. After completion of the program, the patients were not only encouraged to remain in contact with the program and attend educational sessions but also to continue with a hospital based exercise program.

These patients were tracked for a period of 10 years during which we evaluated their main heart related events. Two categories of events were identified: 1) "hard" events which consisted of cardiovascular deaths, fatal and non-fatal strokes and heart attacks,

2) admission to hospital for revascularization procedures (placement of a stent in a coronary artery or for coronary artery bypass surgery).

A total of 137 patients (105 men, 32 women; average age 61 years) enrolled in the program during the period from May 1992 to May 2002. 77 patients completed the two years and 60 dropped out at various times during the two-year period (average participation: 8.1 months). Three patients in the latter group were lost to follow-up. Thus, complete follow up data was available on 77 patients who completed the program and on 57 patients who dropped out. The average follow up in the two groups of patients was 86 months and 81 months respectively. Patients who followed a vegetarian diet and attended 60% of all the sessions relating to other aspects of the program were deemed to have completed the program. The reasons for discontinuing participation in the program fell into three equal categories: a) logistic reasons such as moving away from the area, b) program was too time-consuming and c) dissatisfaction with a specific aspect of the program.

Among those who completed the program, several changes were viewed as related to the diet. The estimated energy consumption increased from 1620 ± 43 to 1724 ± 51 kilocalories/day over the two years. Despite this increase in food intake there was a decrease in weight from 80.3 ± 1.8 to 76.8 ± 1.9 kg and daily intakes of total and saturated fat and cholesterol declined. Over 24-months, the serum cholesterol and LDL cholesterol concentrations were reduced significantly. Serum HDL cholesterol and triglyceride concentrations were unchanged. Of these patients 41% required medications for lowering serum lipids. The majority of them were already on lipid lowering therapy at the time of entry to the program.

Treadmill exercise times, oxygen consumption, peak ventilation and the highest heart rate attained during the exercise test increased significantly. Three patients reported angina during the initial exercise test and none after completion of the two years.

It should be noted that fat and cholesterol intakes in this diet are significantly lower than that recommended by the American Heart Association. The dietary changes resulting from participating in the program are summarized in the Table below.

	Start	End of 2 years
Total calorie intake/day	1627 ± 43	1725 ± 51
Fat intake (g /day)	34.2 ± 2.5	15.7 ± 0.7
Saturated Fat intake (g/day)	10.2 ± 1.2	3.8 ± 0.3
% Fat Calorie intake/day	18.3 ± 1.0	8.0 ± 0.3
Cholesterol intake (mg/day)	120 ± 14	16 ± 2.0

Eight hard cardiac events (myocardial infarctions, cardiovascular deaths) were identified in the 134 subjects over a 120-month period as follows:

a) In the group of 77 patients who completed the two-year program there was one hard event (1 fatal myocardial infarction).
b) In the group of 57 patients who dropped out of the program there were seven hard events (3 cardiac deaths, 1 non-fatal myocardial infarction, 1 fatal stroke, 2 non-fatal strokes).).

This low event rate in patients who participated in a comprehensive lifestyle modification has been shown to be associated with both a reduction in the progression and actual regression of arterial disease. It is generally recognized that in patients with advanced disease the arteries tend to become calcified. Recent studies have shown that even this form of the disease (i.e. calcified arteries) could be reversed by a comprehensive program of care as discussed above.

This study highlighted two unique aspects of the care received by these patients. The first was the extended period of follow up. It appears that participation in the program for two years had a lasting effect on long term outcomes possibly due to consolidation of lifestyle changes. The second was the frequency of use and dosage of statins. Less than half the patients required lipid-lowering drugs to achieve target LDL levels and in those who did, the average dose was considerably lower than that advocated in recent clinical trials.

Suggested further reading

1. Ornish D, Brown S, Scherwitz LW et al. Can lifestyle changes reverse coronary heart disease? The Lifestyle Heart Trial. Lancet. 1990;336:129-33.
2. Ornish D, Scherwitz LW, Billings JH et al. Intensive lifestyle changes for reversal of coronary heart disease. JAMA. 1998;280:2001-7.
3. Rutledge JC, Hyson DA, Garduno D, Cort DA, Paumer L, Kappagoda,CT. Lifestyle modification program in management of patients with coronary artery disease: the clinical experience in a tertiary care hospital. J Cardiopulm Rehabil. 1999;19:226-34.
4. Kappagoda C, Ma A, Cort D, et al. Cardiac event rate in a lifestyle modification program for patients with chronic coronary artery disease. Clin Cardiol 2006;29:317-21.
5. Schaefer S, Hussein H, Gershony GR, Rutledge JC, Kappagoda CT. Regression of severe atherosclerotic plaque in patients with mild elevation of LDL cholesterol. J Investig Med. 1997; 45(9):536-41.
6. Goh V K, Lau Chu-Pak, Mohlenkamp S, Rumberger J A, Achenbach S, Budoff, Matthew J. Cardiovascular Ultrasound 2010 8:5

PART TWO: MEAL PLANNING

CHAPTER 11

MENU PLANS - FROM THE GROCERY STORE TO THE PLATE AND ONWARD........

The basic components of the heart disease reversal diet are summarized below:

CARBOHYDRATES	50 - 70 % of daily calories	
PROTEIN	15 - 25% of daily calories	
FAT	Less than 12 % of daily calories	
	Saturated fat	3% of daily calories
	Cholesterol	20 mg/day
FIBER	Men: 38 gram/day Women: 25 gram/day	
SODIUM (See p. 35)	1500 mg/day	

The recipes in this book will provide quick, nutritious meals for you and your family. You can make a large batch for recipes that take a little longer to prepare, for 'planned-leftovers'. For instance, if you need quick breakfasts, then whip up a batch of muffins or one of the hot cereal recipes and freeze the extra portions as individual servings to be used on days when you don't have much time. Just add a fruit to round out the meal. The soups and stews also freeze quite well, so when you make those, you will have future lunches or dinners.

The suggested meal plans contain one of the recipes from this book per meal. The meal can then be completed by including a vegetable and/or a fruit. You can use the plans as a template - entree, vegetable, fruit – with individual meals being completed using the recipes and seasonal produce of your choice. Remember, that ideally your diet will consist of whole foods in their most natural form in order to increase fiber and nutrient content. Even though there are only 2 weeks of recipes presented here, it can easily extend to 3-4 weeks utilizing your planned-leftovers.

To make your life a little easier, you can also cook up a pot of a grain and a pot of beans weekly to combine into many of the recipes. For example, on Sunday, cook a pot of bulgur and a pot of black beans and then use them during the week. The bulgur can be served on the side (such as a pilaf), it can be turned into a cold salad, it can be stirred into a quick soup or stew, or it can be heated up in the morning for a hot breakfast cereal. The beans can be used in a burrito or taco, used as a protein source on a salad, served as a side dish or added to soups and stews. Most grains and beans are interchangeable in this way. Try a variety of grains: brown rice, quinoa, millet, barley, cracked wheat and amaranth, just to name a few.

GETTING STARTED
a)   The Vegetarian Pantry

To get started, you will want to stock your pantry with the appropriate foods. You can make a week's menu, write out a grocery list and then head to the store. If you do not have the right foods at home, it is a challenge to make dietary changes. You will want to develop some 'go-to' meals that you can whip up quickly. If you always have the makings for these meals in the pantry/refrigerator/freezer, it will ensure your success. In order to be successful in making the change to a plant-based diet, it is important to stock your kitchen and pantry with staples that will help you to put together quick meals. No doubt you will develop your own list of staples, but these will get you started.

Refrigerated items
Non-fat milk, yogurt, cottage cheese
Tofu
Fat- free sour cream
"I Can't Believe It's Not Butter" Spray
Fat free or soy cheeses (i.e. Veggie Shreds)
Egg substitutes
Fat-free salad dressings, barbecue sauce, salsa
Condiments
Meat substitutes
Hummus (garbanzo bean spread)
Pantry
Canned beans, all varieties, whole and refried
Pastas, noodles
Tortillas, corn and wheat
Whole wheat bread, pitas, bagels
Vegetable broth or No-Chicken broth
Canned tomatoes -various shapes & flavors
Brown instant rice, basmati or jasmine rice
Whole grain breakfast cereals -hot & cold
Spaghetti sauce
Spices and seasonings (i.e. taco, chili, beef stew)
Low-sodium canned soups, chili
Non-stick cooking spray
Natural peanut butter
Freezer items
Vegetables: corn, peas, soybeans, mixed vegetables, greens, pepper strips
Garden/Boca burgers, meat substitutes
Frozen whole grain waffles
Fat free frozen yogurt
Trader Joe's rice mixes
Leftovers !
Boxed mixes
Annie Chun's
Fat free instant soup mixes (Nile Spice)
Krusteaz mixes for muffins, brownies, pancakes
Couscous -various flavors & plain
Zatarain's
Fresh
Lots of fruits & vegetables

b) Meat Substitutes

While meat substitutes are not a necessity when following a plant-based diet, many patients feel that it helps them to give up animal protein and increases their protein intake. If it has been a while since you tried meat substitutes, you will be amazed at the variety and quality of the products. There is a wide range of likes and dislikes, so if you try one and dislike it, don't give up, try another. Most of the meat substitutes are made from soy, but there are some made from gluten (the protein in wheat flour) or mushroom mycoproteins (Quorn). These are available at most major grocery stores. Some stores have an extensive selection in their natural foods sections. At other grocery stores, refrigerated items are found in the produce section where you might also find tofu. The following listing is just a sampling of the types of substitutes on the market.

Ground "beef"

These items are found in either the freezer or refrigerated sections. They may be packaged like a pound of ground beef, or as loose soy crumbles, while others are already shaped into burgers. These work well in any recipe that calls for ground beef, such as tacos, chili, sloppy joes, spaghetti sauce or lasagna. You can shape these into meatballs, meatloaf or burgers. Beware of varieties that add cheese or are high in fat.

> *Name brands*: Boca Ground Burger, Yves Veggie Ground Round, Lightlife Smart Ground, Quorn Grounds, Boca Burgers, Gardenburgers (many varieties add cheese)

"Chick'n"

Found in freezer or refrigerated sections, these are available in nuggets, chunks, breasts or roasts. Use them just like chicken in your favorite recipes.

> *Name brands*: Lightlife Smart Menu Chick'n Strips, Veat Bites, Nuggets or Breast, Quorn Naked Breast, Nuggets or Roast

"Sausage"

These meat substitutes have the flavor of sausage because of the seasonings. They are available in patties, links, or bulk (you have to crumble). Some can be high in fat, so check your labels.

> *Name brands:* Gimme Lean Sausage Style, Boca Breakfast Patties, Morningstar Farms Veggie Breakfast Sausage Patties, Boca Italian Sausages or Brats.

Textured Vegetable Protein (TVP)

TVP is soy flour made into various shapes and dehydrated. You can purchase dehydrated shapes (looks like dried cereal) and then rehydrate it to utilize it in recipes calling for meat. This is the least expensive of the meat substitutes and is available in crumbles (like ground beef), chunks, strips and flavors. You can purchase these in bulk in the natural food sections of markets. A more extensive variety is available on-line at www.healthy-eating.com.

c) What to do with Tofu?

You can:

BLEND it (make smoothies by combining a block of tofu with fruit & juice).

CUBE it (try adding cubes of tofu, some vegetables and vegetable broth to the Annie Chun's noodle mix and you've got a great soup).

MARINATE it (in barbeque sauce or soy sauce or fat-free dressing, then grill, bake or stir-fry).

SUBSTITUTE with it (use in cream soups instead of the real thing, use instead of ricotta cheese in lasagna or stuffed shells).

FREEZE it (to give it a "meatier" texture, CRUMBLE it for chili or SCRAMBLE it for "eggs").

QUICK MEAL COMBOS
a)   What's for Breakfast?
　　Cold or hot cereal, milk/yogurt, fruit, Egg Beaters, whole grain toast, whole grain freezer waffles, soy sausage links or patties can all be used for a quick breakfast in any preferred combination bearing in mind the calorie content of the meal. Fruit could be consumed in its natural state or a smoothie. Hardboiled egg whites can pair with almost anything to complete the meal.

"Grab & go" breakfasts
- Non-fat yogurt and a piece of fruit
- Bite sized cereals (like Shredded Wheat) - take to work and eat with a yogurt or milk and a piece of fruit when you get there
- Frozen waffles (Van's are whole grain)
- Whole wheat bagels, toast, English muffins, etc. topped with jam, small amount peanut butter or fat-free cream cheese
- Graham Cracker Sandwich (Graham Crackers with peanut butter or flavored cream cheese, topped with a few raisins-make ahead and grab out of the fridge on your way out the door). Add a non-fat Milk Chug (individual milk servings)
- Non-fat, whole grain cereal bars and fruit and non-fat milk or yogurt
- Smoothies (blend juice, yogurt or tofu and frozen fruit)

If you've got time to sit down before you head out the door
- Cottage cheese and fruit
- Pizza, English muffin or bagel
- Leftovers from last night (Breakfast does not have to be 'breakfast food')
- Egg Beaters scrambled and put into a pita pocket, top with fat-free cheese, some veggies and salsa
- Cereal and milk (hot or cold whole grain cereals)
- French Toast made with whole grain bread and eggbeaters

b)   What's for Lunch?
　　Of course, bringing your lunch or eating at home will ensure that you have a healthy choice. Leftovers are a great lunch, so when cooking dinner, plan to have a little leftover for lunch the next day. Sandwiches can be made with any of the delicious spreads described in this book. Together with veggies and fruit, leftover soup or stews and whole grain crackers they round off a great lunch. Most raw vegetables can be added to any meal.

Sandwich ideas
　　If you are wondering what you can put on a sandwich when you are a vegetarian, here are some ideas for sandwich combos borrowed from "Cookin' Healthy With One Foot Out The Door" by Pitchford & Quigley:
BREAD: pita, tortilla, hoagie, French, Kaiser roll, English muffin, sliced, sour dough, cracker bread
SPREAD: Hummus, tofu burger, Boca or garden burger, tempeh burger, bean spread, tofu, soy cheese, nut butter or avocado (but just a little to spread)
VEGETABLES: Red onion, avocado, tomato, cucumber, lettuce, sprouts, peppers, pickle

CONDIMENTS: fat-free mayonnaise, mustard, ketchup, fat-free salad dressing, lime juice, lemon juice, jam, apple butter, honey

Other quick lunches:
Canned soups or chili
Veggie Burgers
Subway veggie sandwich
Salads
Bean burritos , Quesadillas
Pasta with spaghetti sauce

c)   What's for Dinner?

See the recipes in this book for dinner ideas. Remember to cook a little extra to have on hand for lunches or dinners later in the week. Some particularly quick meals are described below.

Rice and Beans

Cook up some instant brown rice (or use the extra you prepared from a previous dinner) and top with canned kidney, pinto or black beans (or S &W flavored beans) then top with chopped tomatoes or salsa and a little fat free cheese. Serve with tortillas and some steamed broccoli.

Breakfast for dinner!

Eggbeaters come in plain or flavors such as Southwestern and Garden Vegetable. Make them into scrambled eggs or an omelet, serve with whole grain toast, fruit and a glass of milk.

Annie Chun's Noodle Mixes

These are ready in 10 minutes. The package contains noodles for boiling, and you just mix the packet of sauce with the noodles. They are a bit high in sodium (690 mg/serving), but if you are careful about the portion, these can still fit easily into a 1500 mg sodium diet. Throw frozen vegetables or soybeans in with the noodles while they boil to get your vegetables.

5-Ingredient meal "Chick'n" Rice Casserole
1 package meat substitute or 1 cup rehydrated TVP
1 cup uncooked white or brown rice
2 cups vegetable broth
1 cup frozen mixed vegetables
1 tsp Italian seasoning (or more to taste)
Place all ingredients in a 2-quart microwave container. Cover and cook on medium power until rice is done, about 20-25 minutes. Stir occasionally. Serves 4. While it is cooking, throw together a tossed salad or fruit salad and slice some French bread.

How long does it take to make chili? As long as it takes to open some cans.

Combine a 16 oz can of kidney beans,16 oz can diced tomatoes, 16 oz can tomato sauce, 1 cup frozen corn, 1 cup frozen chopped onion, 1 envelope chili seasoning (like Lawry's or McCormick) and ¼ cup cornmeal. Mix, heat and eat. You can also use the Veggie Ground Round or TVP (sauté with the onions before adding other ingredients).

d)   Quick meals
Breakfast burritos

Cook some Egg Beaters in the microwave, mix together with beans and salsa and wrap in a tortilla. Add a piece of fruit and/or a glass of milk and you are set!

Rice and Veggies
Grab a bag of shredded cabbage (usually for coleslaw), a bag of shredded or chopped carrots, a container of sliced mushrooms and some broccoli florets (usually available in the produce section already chopped). While instant brown rice is cooking, sauté your collection of veggies with a little garlic and canola oil or vegetable oil spray. This should take about 3-5 minutes. You can even add tofu chunks, TVP or other meat alternative. Top cooked rice with stir-fried veggies, some ginger & light soy sauce. Have some fruit and fat-free frozen yogurt for dessert.

Quick-cooking grains
Cook 1 cup bulgur with 2 cups water for about 10 minutes. Add a box of frozen corn, a can of beans, a small bag of frozen chopped greens (collard, spinach, etc.), 1 tsp. of cumin and 2 Tbsp. lemon juice and heat through (about 10 more minutes). Serve with fruit salad and pita bread.

Boxed Beans and Rice
Give a box of Zatarain's a try -- Red Beans and Rice is a great one. You add water and cook in the microwave for 20-25 minutes or on the stovetop. It doesn't need the margarine they suggest adding with the water. You can add Boca Sausages, Veggie Ground Round, Gimme Lean or TVP to increase the protein content. While it is cooking, you can throw together a salad and steam some veggies. Make a yogurt parfait for dessert by layering strawberries, non-fat yogurt and almost fat- free granola or Grape Nuts cereal.

Quick Pizza
Use premade crusts or use other breads for the crust (English muffins, bagels, pita bread, French bread). Spread with pre-made pizza sauce or your favorite spaghetti sauce, top with diced veggies and sprinkle with fat free mozzarella or veggie shreds (soy cheese). Bake at 450°F for about 10-12 minutes. Serve with salad and a glass of milk.

Quick Veggie Fajitas
Sauté a bag of frozen mixed peppers with a sliced onion. Add a package of Fajita Seasoning Mix (i.e. McCormick's). Add water per seasoning directions. That's it! You could also add soy protein, TVP, tofu, etc. Serve in tortillas and top with fat-free cheese and fat-free sour cream. Heat a can of fat-free refried beans to serve on the side. You've got a meal in 10 minutes. You can mix the leftover veggies in with Egg Beaters for breakfast.

Pasta Bake
Mix 8 oz cooked pasta with a package of Veggie Ground Round (or break up some Garden/Boca burgers), add a jar of your favorite spaghetti sauce (28 oz) and ¾ cup of Parmesan Veggie Shreds. Spoon into a 9 x13 inch pan (sprayed with vegetable oil cooking spray). Top with 8 oz fat free mozzarella (or Veggie Shreds mozzarella) and bake at 375°F for 25-30 minutes. Serves 8. You can also add a package of chopped frozen spinach, thawed and drained to boost your vegetable intake. Serve with a salad and French bread.

Quick stew
Mix a package of Garden Burger Crumbles (or the equivalent in Veggie Ground Round, TVP, etc.) with a package of your favorite frozen vegetable medley, a can of diced tomatoes, some garlic, a bay leaf and ¼ cup red wine (optional). Heat until hot enough to serve. Serve with chunky bread, a salad and some fruit for dessert.

Refried Roll-ups
Mix together a can of fat-free refried beans, ½ cup of corn and ⅓ cup salsa. You can heat the mixture or leave cold. Spread on a corn or whole wheat tortilla, top with a lettuce leaf, roll it up and enjoy. Serve with some baked chips and salsa and some steamed broccoli or a salad. Ole!

Garden Burger meal
You cannot get much quicker than throwing one of these in the microwave, serving it on a whole grain bun or in a pita pocket, top with a Veggie Slice (soy cheese) and some lettuce and tomato. If the grill is fired up, they are great on the grill, too. Serve with tomato and basil.

Couscous
Cook a box of couscous according to package directions (this usually means pouring boiling water over some couscous and waiting 5 minutes). Toss it with a couple of chopped tomatoes, ½ cup fresh basil, a clove or two of garlic and about ½ cup fat-free feta cheese crumbled. Serve with the veggie burgers and some steamed or grilled asparagus.

Frozen Rice Combos
Look for the Biryani Curried Rice at Trader Joe's. This is a flavored rice with some veggies mixed in. You can reheat in the microwave or on the stovetop. Add a can of garbanzo beans or a bag of the frozen, shelled soybeans (edamame). It is ready in minutes. You can serve it with some pita bread, or quick quesadillas and a salad and/or cooked veggie.

SAMPLE MENUS

WEEK ONE						
Monday	**Tuesday**	**Wednesday**	**Thursday**	**Friday**	**Saturday**	**Sunday**
Breakfast						
Oatmeal Blueberries	Tofu Scramble Smoothie	Breakfast Parfait	French toast Raspberries	Cold cereal Skim Milk Melon	Crepes Pears	Frittata Sautéed Tomato Soy sausage
Lunch						
Falafel sandwich Chilled asparagus Leek soup	Baked tofu Apple sweet potato medley	Taco soup Zucchini curry	Oriental cabbage salad	Vegetarian chili Oven-baked potato	Okra curry Brown rice Green beans	Black bean soup, Water crisped tortilla chips Salsa, Mango
Dinner						
Leftover from lunch OR Tofu stir fry Vinaigrette Dried seaweed	Leftover from lunch OR Tamale pie Cool green fruit salad	Leftover from lunch OR Spiced couscous Snow pea salad Pomegranate, Mandarin and Kiwi salad	Leftover from lunch OR Lentil salad Sliced red bell pepper Peach	Leftover from lunch OR Veggie pizza Spinach salad with pears	Leftover from lunch OR Stuffed bell peppers, Grilled asparagus, Oven baked sweet potato	Leftover from lunch OR Eggplant Parmesan, Caesar salad
Snacks						
Cottage cheese and pineapple	Hummus with veggies	Chocolate banana muffin	Celery and peanut butter	Mint chocolate icebox cake	Carrots and dip	Yogurt and fruit

WEEK TWO						
Monday	**Tuesday**	**Wednesday**	**Thursday**	**Friday**	**Saturday**	**Sunday**
Breakfast						
Cranberry orange breakfast barley 1 banana	Vegetable omelet 1 whole wheat thin sandwich with jam	Smoothie (Frozen strawberry, mango), Fat-free vanilla yogurt, Apple carrot muffin with flaxseed	Cold cereal, Skim milk, Blueberries	Breakfast sandwich (English muffin, Egg beaters, Slice of fat-free cheese, Tomato,	French toast, 1 cup of strawberry or blueberry yogurt	Flaxseed pancake, Fruit salad
Lunch						
Barley bean salad 2 cups mixed greens, 1 cup cantaloupe	Falafel sandwich, carrot and celery sticks 1 peach	Grilled cheese with tomato and basil sandwich, Broccoli salad	Lentil sweet potato stew, 1 apple	1Tbsp Hummus with garlic, Carrots, Cherry tomato, Jicama, Pita bread 1 cup corn chowder, 1 nectarine	Hot vegetarian hero, Mushroom, celery and sliced bell pepper with dip. 1 diced mango	Pita pizza, Tossed salad. 1 pear.
Dinner						
Dave's Hearty burrito, Sautéed sliced bell pepper and Summer squash.	Stuffed Portobello mushrooms, Green beans	Vegetable lasagna, Mixed greens	Meatless jambalaya and cooked broccoli	Quinoa stuffed peppers, Honey wheat rolls and Greek salad	Shepherd's pie Spinach salad	Sloppy Joe's Roasted broccoli and cauliflower, Melon
Snacks						
Kale chips	Garbanzo nuts	Crunchy munchies	Bean dip with baked tortilla chips	Apple carrot muffins	Sliced apple with peanut butter	Hummus with Veggies.

MODIFYING YOUR RECIPES WITH HEALTHY SUBSTITUTIONS

Some quick and helpful tips to reduce the fat and cholesterol in your favorite recipes, as well as increase the fiber are listed below.
- Use non-fat ingredients in place of high fat ingredients.
- Use egg whites or egg substitutes in place of whole eggs.
- Use applesauce in place of butter or oil.
- Use whole wheat flour in place of all-purpose flour.
- Use oats in place of all-purpose flour.
- Use low-fat nonstick cooking spray in place of butter or oil.
- Add fresh fruits and vegetables whenever possible.

Specific Substitutions

First, it is a good idea to review your recipe and identify which ingredients are high in fat. Next, you should think about what that ingredient is needed for in the recipe. For example, it might be used as a thickener, to add texture, or to add flavor to the recipe. Once you have determined these pieces of information, you can then decide what might work in its place as a healthier substitution. Below is a list of specific ingredients and their possible healthier substitutions.

Healthy Substitutions for Common Ingredients

Common Ingredient	Healthier Ingredient
Grains, breads, cereals, etc,	
White bread	Whole wheat bread
White rice or pasta	Brown rice or whole wheat pasta
All-purpose flour	Whole wheat flour Oats Oat bran or wheat germ
Fruits and Vegetables	
Canned fruits or vegetables	Fresh fruits or vegetables Add water if recipe calls for "liquid from can" No-sugar added canned fruits Canned fruits "in their own juice" Low sodium or no-salt added canned vegetables
Fruit juice	No-sugar added fruit juice or water
Vegetable juice	Low sodium vegetable juice or water
Dairy	
Whole milk	Non-fat or skim milk Evaporated non-fat milk Non-fat soy milk or rice milk
Heavy cream, Evaporated milk, or Half & Half	Evaporated non-fat milk
Whole egg	2 egg whites ¼ cup egg substitute 1 oz mashed tofu 2 Tbsp cornstarch + 2 Tbsp water
Cream cheese	Non-fat cream cheese or non-fat ricotta cheese
Cheese	Non-fat cheese or soy cheese
Cottage cheese	Non-fat cottage cheese
Meats	
Chicken, beef, pork, etc	Meat substitutes Light tofu Cooked dried beans (black, pinto, lentils, etc.)
Bacon	Meat substitute with smoke flavoring
Sausage	Meat substitute
Chicken or beef broth	Low sodium vegetable broth (see recipe)

Fats and oils	
Butter, margarine, oil	Applesauce Non-fat plain yogurt Non-fat mayonnaise Mashed banana Pureed prune Pumpkin Pureed tofu Marshmallow cream
Oil to sauté or fry	Wine Non-fat broth Water Juice Low-fat nonstick vegetable spray ½ applesauce + ½ buttermilk mixture
Mayonnaise	Non-fat mayonnaise
Sour cream	Non-fat sour cream or Non-fat plain yogurt
Salad dressing or marinade	Non-fat or fat-free salad dressing Sugar free dressing Make your own using fruit juice or non-fat broth as the liquid
Chocolate (1 oz unsweetened chocolate)	3 Tbsp cocoa powder + 1 Tbsp applesauce
Sugar	Substitute flour for omitted sugar Splenda, Sweet n Low, Equal Cinnamon, nutmeg, vanilla, for sweeter flavor when reducing sugar Natural fruit juice (if only for flavor) Add fresh, whole fruits

PART THREE: THE RECIPES

BREAKFAST

APPLE CARROT MUFFINS WITH FLAXSEED

Grind flaxseeds into a meal with a coffee bean grinder, blender, or food processor. Flaxseed meal can also be found in 1 lb packages (Bob's Red Mill), sold at larger grocery stores. Store flaxseed in refrigerator or freezer.

Makes 12 muffins

Ingredients:

1½	cups	whole wheat flour
¾	cup	flaxseed flour
¾	cup	oat bran, raw
1	cup	brown sugar
2	tsp	baking soda
1	tsp	baking powder
½	tsp	salt
1½	cups	grated carrots
1	cup	sliced apple
½	cup	seedless raisins
¾	cup	skim milk
4		egg whites
1	tsp	vanilla extract
1	Tbsp	olive oil

Nutrition Facts
Serving Size 1 muffin (106g)
Servings Per Container 12

Amount Per Serving

Calories 220   Calories from Fat 25

% Daily Value*

Total Fat 3g — 5%
Saturated Fat 0g — 0%
Trans Fat 0g
Cholesterol 0mg — 0%
Sodium 390mg — 16%
Total Carbohydrate 46g — 15%
Dietary Fiber 7g — 28%
Sugars 24g
Protein 7g

Vitamin A 45% • Vitamin C 2%
Calcium 6% • Iron 8%

*Percent Daily Values are based on a 2,000 calorie diet. Your daily values may be higher or lower depending on your calorie needs:

		2,000	2,500
Total Fat	Less than	65g	80g
Saturated Fat	Less than	20g	25g
Cholesterol	Less than	300mg	300mg
Sodium	Less than	2,400mg	2,400mg
Total Carbohydrate		300g	375g
Dietary Fiber		25g	30g

Calories per gram:
Fat 9 • Carbohydrate 4 • Protein 4

Preparation:

- Preheat oven to 350°F. Coat muffin cups with cooking spray or line with paper muffin cups.
- In a large bowl, mix together flours, oat bran, brown sugar, baking soda, baking powder, salt and cinnamon.
- Stir in carrots, apples and raisins. In a separate bowl, combine milk, egg whites, vanilla and oil.
- Pour liquid ingredients into dry ingredients.
- Stir until just moistened.
- Fill muffin cups ¾ full.
- Bake for about 15-25 minutes, or until done.

Thanks to: Jill Burns

Category: Breads

Apricot Bread

A good brunch offering.

Makes 2 loaves, ~15 slices each

Ingredients:

1	cup	boiling water
1 ½	cup	dried apricots
½	tsp	baking soda
½	cup	granulated sugar
½	cup	egg substitute
2 ¾	cups	all-purpose flour
3	tsp	baking powder
1	cup	chopped nuts

Preparation:

- Pour boiling water over the apricots and let stand until just tender; do not over soak them.
- Drain off the water, measure, adding water to make 1 cup.
- Chop the apricots roughly.
- Pour apricot water into a large mixing bowl. Add soda, sugar and egg substitute and mix with a wooden spoon.
- Add flour, baking powder, chopped nuts and apricots and mix well again.
- Lightly oil two small loaf pans. Divide the batter between the prepared pans.
- Bake at 350°F for about 45 minutes, or until the breads have risen, are dark in color, and a toothpick or knife comes out clean when inserted in the center.
- Cool on racks and serve.

Thanks to: Walt and Phyllis Quinn, Group 25

Category: Breads

Nutrition Facts

Serving Size 1/30 recipe (38g)
Servings Per Container 2 loaves, 15 slices each

Amount Per Serving

Calories 100   Calories from Fat 25

% Daily Value*

Total Fat 2.5g	4%
Saturated Fat 0g	0%
Trans Fat 0g	
Cholesterol 0mg	0%
Sodium 80mg	3%
Total Carbohydrate 17g	6%
Dietary Fiber 1g	4%
Sugars 7g	
Protein 3g	

Vitamin A 2%	•	Vitamin C 0%
Calcium 2%	•	Iron 4%

*Percent Daily Values are based on a 2,000 calorie diet. Your daily values may be higher or lower depending on your calorie needs:

	Calories:	2,000	2,500
Total Fat	Less than	65g	80g
Saturated Fat	Less than	20g	25g
Cholesterol	Less than	300mg	300mg
Sodium	Less than	2,400mg	2,400mg
Total Carbohydrate		300g	375g
Dietary Fiber		25g	30g

Calories per gram:
Fat 9 • Carbohydrate 4 • Protein 4

Breakfast Frittata

Most frittatas (Italian omelets) are too high in cholesterol to be served as a main course. In this recipe, egg substitute is used to replace eggs.

Serves 4

Ingredients:

1½	lbs	potatoes (3 medium-large), peeled and finely diced
1	tsp	canola oil
1½	cups	fresh or frozen broccoli
6		scallions or green onions, cut diagonally into ½ inch slices
1½	cups	egg substitute
½	cup	grated non-fat cheddar cheese
½	cup	non-fat cottage cheese
2	Tbsp	minced fresh parsley or 2 tsp dried parsley flakes
½	tsp	salt, if desired
½	tsp	freshly ground black pepper

Nutrition Facts

Serving Size 1/4 recipe (382g)
Servings Per Container 4

Amount Per Serving

Calories 240 Calories from Fat 10

% Daily Value*

- Total Fat 1.5g — 2%
-   Saturated Fat 0g — 0%
-   Trans Fat 0g
- Cholesterol 5mg — 2%
- Sodium 700mg — 29%
- Total Carbohydrate 39g — 13%
-   Dietary Fiber 5g — 20%
-   Sugars 8g
- Protein 23g

Vitamin A 25% • Vitamin C 120%
Calcium 25% • Iron 20%

*Percent Daily Values are based on a 2,000 calorie diet. Your daily values may be higher or lower depending on your calorie needs:

		Calories:	2,000	2,500
Total Fat	Less than		65g	80g
Saturated Fat	Less than		20g	25g
Cholesterol	Less than		300mg	300mg
Sodium	Less than		2,400mg	2,400mg
Total Carbohydrate			300g	375g
Dietary Fiber			25g	30g

Calories per gram:
  Fat 9 • Carbohydrate 4 • Protein 4

Preparation:

- In a large, covered oven-proof nonstick skillet, cook the potatoes in the oil over medium heat, stirring them once or twice, for about 10 minutes or until they are tender and lightly browned.
- Add the broccoli and scallions, cover the skillet, cook the mixture for another 5 minutes (the broccoli should be tender-crisp).
- Preheat oven to 350°F.
- Meanwhile in a medium bowl beat the egg substitute with the cheese, parsley, salt and pepper.
- Pour this over the vegetable mixture and cook the frittata for about 5 minutes, pushing the ingredients occasionally with a spatula to allow any uncooked egg to make contact with the skillet.
- Place the skillet in the preheated oven for 5 minutes or until set on top.

Thanks to: *Jane Brody*

Category: Egg/MeatSubstitute

Breakfast Parfait

A little non-fat dairy and some vitamin rich fruit and you've just started your day right, nutritionally speaking!

Ingredients:

¾	cup	fat-free cottage cheese
1	cup	pineapple chunks, papaya chunks or cling peaches
2	tsp	toasted wheat germ

Preparation:

- Place cottage cheese in a small bowl.
- Top with fruit and sprinkle with wheat germ.

Nutrition Facts
Serving Size (436g)
Servings Per Container 1

Amount Per Serving
Calories 220   Calories from Fat 5

% Daily Value*
- Total Fat 0.5g — 1%
- Saturated Fat 0g — 0%
- Trans Fat 0g
- Cholesterol 10mg — 3%
- Sodium 650mg — 27%
- Total Carbohydrate 33g — 11%
- Dietary Fiber 3g — 12%
- Sugars 27g
- Protein 22g

Vitamin A 8% • Vitamin C 30%
Calcium 15% • Iron 8%

*Percent Daily Values are based on a 2,000 calorie diet. Your daily values may be higher or lower depending on your calorie needs:

	Calories:	2,000	2,500
Total Fat	Less than	65g	80g
Saturated Fat	Less than	20g	25g
Cholesterol	Less than	300mg	300mg
Sodium	Less than	2,400mg	2,400mg
Total Carbohydrate		300g	375g
Dietary Fiber		25g	30g

Calories per gram:
Fat 9 • Carbohydrate 4 • Protein 4

Breakfast Parfait with Yogurt

A small variation on the Breakfast Parfait

Ingredients:

¾	cup	non-fat plain yogurt
1	cup	pineapple chunks, papaya chunks or cling peaches
2	tsp	toasted wheat germ

Preparation:

- Place yogurt in a small bowl.
- Top with fruit and sprinkle with wheat germ.

Nutrition Facts
Serving Size (320g)
Servings Per Container

Amount Per Serving
Calories 160   Calories from Fat 10

% Daily Value*
- Total Fat 1g — 2%
- Saturated Fat 0g — 0%
- Trans Fat 0g
- Cholesterol 5mg — 2%
- Sodium 115mg — 5%
- Total Carbohydrate 32g — 11%
- Dietary Fiber 3g — 12%
- Sugars 22g
- Protein 10g

Vitamin A 45% • Vitamin C 160%
Calcium 25% • Iron 4%

*Percent Daily Values are based on a 2,000 calorie diet. Your daily values may be higher or lower depending on your calorie needs:

	Calories:	2,000	2,500
Total Fat	Less than	65g	80g
Saturated Fat	Less than	20g	25g
Cholesterol	Less than	300mg	300mg
Sodium	Less than	2,400mg	2,400mg
Total Carbohydrate		300g	375g
Dietary Fiber		25g	30g

Calories per gram:
Fat 9 • Carbohydrate 4 • Protein 4

Breakfast Rolls

16 servings

Ingredients:

2½	tsp	active dry yeast
1⅓	cups	water
2	Tbsp	honey
1	Tbsp	canola oil
3	cups	all-purpose flour
¾	cup	whole wheat flour
1	tsp	salt

Preparation:

- The evening before, mix ingredients and knead briefly.
- Place in oiled bowl, cover with plastic wrap and towel, let rest in refrigerator overnight (8-12 hours).
- The next morning, preheat oven to 400°F.
- Remove dough from refrigerator, and divide dough into 16 parts, using two spoons or a dough knife.
- Roll each piece into desired shape and place 2 inches apart on oiled baking sheet, cover, and let rest for 10 minutes.
- Bake for 15-20 minutes, or until golden brown.

Nutrition Facts

Serving Size 1 roll (53g)
Servings Per Container 16

Amount Per Serving

Calories 120　　Calories from Fat 10

% Daily Value*

Total Fat 1.5g	2%
Saturated Fat 0g	0%
Trans Fat 0g	
Cholesterol 0mg	0%
Sodium 150mg	6%
Total Carbohydrate 24g	8%
Dietary Fiber 1g	4%
Sugars 2g	
Protein 3g	

Vitamin A 0%　•　Vitamin C 0%
Calcium 0%　•　Iron 8%

*Percent Daily Values are based on a 2,000 calorie diet. Your daily values may be higher or lower depending on your calorie needs:

		Calories:	2,000	2,500
Total Fat		Less than	65g	80g
Saturated Fat		Less than	20g	25g
Cholesterol		Less than	300mg	300mg
Sodium		Less than	2,400mg	2,400mg
Total Carbohydrate			300g	375g
Dietary Fiber			25g	30g

Calories per gram:
　Fat 9　•　Carbohydrate 4　•　Protein 4

Thanks to: Dave Hansen, Group 40

Chocolate Banana Muffins

Who doesn't love a fat-free chocolate muffin? To further reduce carbohydrates, leave off the glaze.

makes 18 muffins

Ingredients:

2	cups	all-purpose flour
¾	cup	sugar, divided
¼	cup	unsweetened cocoa powder
¾	tsp	baking soda
½	tsp	baking powder
¼	tsp	salt
1½	cups	plain non-fat yogurt
½	cup	mashed ripe banana
¼	cup	skim milk
2	tsp	vanilla extract
3		egg whites

White Glaze:

½	cup	powdered sugar
3-4	tsp	warm water

Nutrition Facts
Serving Size 1 muffin (63g)
Servings Per Container 18

Amount Per Serving
Calories 120   Calories from Fat 5

% Daily Value*
- Total Fat 0g — 0%
- Saturated Fat 0g — 0%
- Trans Fat 0g
- Cholesterol 0mg — 0%
- Sodium 125mg — 5%
- Total Carbohydrate 26g — 9%
- Dietary Fiber 1g — 4%
- Sugars 14g
- Protein 3g

Vitamin A 2% • Vitamin C 2%
Calcium 4% • Iron 4%

*Percent Daily Values are based on a 2,000 calorie diet. Your daily values may be higher or lower depending on your calorie needs:

	Calories:	2,000	2,500
Total Fat	Less than	65g	80g
Saturated Fat	Less than	20g	25g
Cholesterol	Less than	300mg	300mg
Sodium	Less than	2,400mg	2,400mg
Total Carbohydrate		300g	375g
Dietary Fiber		25g	30g

Calories per gram:
Fat 9 • Carbohydrate 4 • Protein 4

Preparation:

- Preheat oven to 350°F. Line 2 ½ inch muffin pan cups with paper liners.
- Stir together flour, ¼ cup sugar, cocoa, baking soda, baking powder and salt in a large bowl. Set aside.
- Stir together yogurt, banana, milk, and vanilla in medium-sized bowl. Set aside. In small bowl with electric mixer at high speed, beat egg whites until soft peaks form. Gradually beat in remaining ½ cup sugar until stiff peaks form.
- Stir yogurt mixture into flour mixture until moistened. With rubber spatula or wire whisk, fold in one-third egg white mixture. Gently fold in remaining egg white mixture until blended.
- Fill muffin cups ¾ full with batter.
- Bake 20 to 25 minutes, or until wooden toothpick inserted in center comes out clean.
- Cool completely in pan on wire rack.
- Meanwhile, prepare White Glaze by stirring powdered sugar together with warm water, beating until smooth and of desired consistency. Drizzle on cooled cupcakes.

Thanks to: Wendy Mueller. R.D.

Corn Frittata

A good choice for a brunch or supper entree.

Prep time: about 25 minutes   Cooking time: 20-25 minutes

4 servings

Nutrition Facts
Serving Size 1/4 recipe (442g)
Servings Per Container 4

Amount Per Serving	
Calories 270	Calories from Fat 10

	% Daily Value*
Total Fat 1g	2%
Saturated Fat 0g	0%
Trans Fat 0g	
Cholesterol 5mg	2%
Sodium 420mg	18%
Total Carbohydrate 46g	15%
Dietary Fiber 5g	20%
Sugars 8g	
Protein 21g	

Vitamin A 30%	•	Vitamin C 45%
Calcium 30%	•	Iron 10%

*Percent Daily Values are based on a 2,000 calorie diet. Your daily values may be higher or lower depending on your calorie needs:

	Calories:	2,000	2,500
Total Fat	Less than	65g	80g
Saturated Fat	Less than	20g	25g
Cholesterol	Less than	300mg	300mg
Sodium	Less than	2,400mg	2,400mg
Total Carbohydrate		300g	375g
Dietary Fiber		25g	30g

Calories per gram:
Fat 9 • Carbohydrate 4 • Protein 4

Ingredients:

¾	cup	egg substitute
¼	cup	egg whites (2 large)
2	Tbsp	fat-free milk
1	Tbsp	cornstarch
2	tsp	fresh basil, chopped OR ½ tsp dried basil
⅛	tsp	salt
⅛	tsp	pepper
1	lb	russet potatoes, peeled and finely chopped
½	cup	water
3	med	ears corn, kernels only*
OR		
2½	cup	frozen corn
¼	cup	green onions, thinly sliced
2	large	tomatoes (about 1 lb total), each cut into 6 wedges
1	cup	fat-free cheddar cheese (4 oz) (Veggie Shreds melt well)

Preparation:

- Prepare Eggs: Beat egg substitute and egg whites with milk, cornstarch, basil and salt and pepper in a medium bowl, until well blended. Set aside.
- Prepare Potatoes: Spray vegetable oil spray in a wide ovenproof frying pan. Add potatoes and water over medium heat.
- Cover and cook, stirring occasionally, until potatoes are tender to bite (12 - 15 minutes). If pan appears dry, add more water, 1 Tbsp at a time.
- Uncover and cook until all liquid has evaporated.
- Assemble: Combine corn kernels and green onions in medium bowl. Whisk egg mixture and pour over corn. Stir quickly to blend well.
- Pour corn mixture over potatoes. Increase heat to medium-high and cook, lifting edges with a spatula to let uncooked eggs flow underneath, until frittata is set around edges (2 - 3 minutes).
- Broil about 4 inches below heat until puffed and golden (about 2 minutes).
- Decoratively arrange tomatoes over frittata. Sprinkle with cheese and broil until cheese is melted.
- Garnish with basil sprigs.

*Preparing fresh cut corn kernels: In a large, shallow bowl, hold one ear of corn upright and, with a sharp knife, cut kernels from cob. Then, using blunt edge of knife, scrape juice from cob into bowl. Discard cobs.

CRANBERRY ORANGE BREAKFAST BARLEY

Add this to your list of favorite breakfasts. Barley is a great alternative to oatmeal and has the same cholesterol lowering properties.

Makes 4 servings, ~1 cup each

Prep time: 5 minutes. Cook time: 45 minutes

Ingredients:

3	cups	water
1	cup	barley, rinsed and drained
1½	cups	orange juice
½	cup	dried cranberries
3	Tbsp	honey (or artificial sweetener)
¼	tsp	cinnamon

Preparation:

- Place water and barley in a medium saucepan and bring to a boil.
- Reduce heat and simmer, covered, for 30 minutes, stirring occasionally.
- Stir in remaining ingredients and continue cooking over low heat, uncovered, for 15 – 30 minutes or until most of the liquid has been absorbed and the barley is thick and creamy.

Nutrition Facts
Serving Size (352g)
Servings Per Container 4

Amount Per Serving

Calories 320 Calories from Fat 5

% Daily Value*

Total Fat 0.5g	1%
Saturated Fat 0g	0%
Trans Fat 0g	
Cholesterol 0mg	0%
Sodium 15mg	1%
Total Carbohydrate 75g	25%
Dietary Fiber 9g	36%
Sugars 33g	
Protein 6g	

Vitamin A 2% • Vitamin C 50%
Calcium 4% • Iron 8%

*Percent Daily Values are based on a 2,000 calorie diet. Your daily values may be higher or lower depending on your calorie needs:

		2,000	2,500
Total Fat	Less than	65g	80g
Saturated Fat	Less than	20g	25g
Cholesterol	Less than	300mg	300mg
Sodium	Less than	2,400mg	2,400mg
Total Carbohydrate		300g	375g
Dietary Fiber		25g	30g

Calories per gram:
Fat 9 • Carbohydrate 4 • Protein 4

Adapted from Raley's Something Extra Magazine. I usually make the whole recipe, put it in individual containers and reheat all week in the microwave. It is carbohydrate heavy, but that could be reduced by using Light orange juice (or just water and some orange peel for flavor instead), Splenda instead of honey and ½ the amount of dried cranberries.

Thanks to: Debbie Lucus, R.D.

Category: Cereal

CREPES

Fill these luscious crepes with sautéed veggies and cream sauce for a savory meal, or pureed fruit for a sweeter version.

Makes 20 crepes, 6 inches each

Ingredients:

1	cup	cold water
1	cup	cold skim milk
6		egg whites
½	tsp	salt or less
2	cups	sifted flour
1	tsp	olive oil

Preparation:

- Combine liquids, egg whites and salt into blender jar; add flour, then oil.
- Blend at top speed, scraping any flour adhering to sides of the jar.
- Cover and refrigerate 2 hours. This is an important step. It allows the flour particles to expand in the liquid and ensures a tender, thin crepe. The batter should be a very light creamy texture (just thick enough to coat a wooden spoon).
- For each crepe, heat a 6 inch nonstick fry pan over moderately high heat.
- When hot, pour a scant ¼ cup of the batter in the skillet; immediately rotate pan until batter covers bottom.
- Cook until light brown. Turn and brown on other side. Slide onto warm plate and proceed in same manner with the rest of the batter.
- Put waxed paper between crepes.
- Keep covered as they cool to prevent them from drying out. The crepes are now ready to be filled.

Serving, Storing, Freezing Crepes:
These versatile crepes can be:
a) Filled, folded or rolled and served immediately.
b) Prepared ahead of time, with layers of waxed paper between each one.
c) Wrapped in foil, refrigerated and reheated when ready to be filled and served.
d) Prepared in advance, frozen and reheated at the last minute.
e) Wrapped in heavy foil to freeze. They will keep for weeks.

Source: Adapted from New American Diet

Nutrition Facts
Serving Size 1 crepe (47g)
Servings Per Container 20

Amount Per Serving

Calories 60 — Calories from Fat 5

% Daily Value*

Total Fat 0g	0%
Saturated Fat 0g	0%
Trans Fat 0g	
Cholesterol 0mg	0%
Sodium 80mg	3%
Total Carbohydrate 10g	3%
Dietary Fiber 0g	0%
Sugars 1g	
Protein 3g	

Vitamin A 0% • Vitamin C 0%
Calcium 2% • Iron 4%

*Percent Daily Values are based on a 2,000 calorie diet. Your daily values may be higher or lower depending on your calorie needs:

	Calories:	2,000	2,500
Total Fat	Less than	65g	80g
Saturated Fat	Less than	20g	25g
Cholesterol	Less than	300mg	300mg
Sodium	Less than	2,400mg	2,400mg
Total Carbohydrate		300g	375g
Dietary Fiber		25g	30g

Calories per gram:
Fat 9 • Carbohydrate 4 • Protein 4

Date Bread

Gift Suggestion: Pour batter into recycled 15 oz cans that have been cleaned, labels removed, and coated with cooking spray. Fill ¾ full. Wrap cooked "loaf" in foil for holiday gifts.

Makes 1 loaf. ~ 15 slices

Nutrition Facts
Serving Size 1 slice (51g)
Servings Per Container about 15

Amount Per Serving	
Calories 120	Calories from Fat 25

	% Daily Value*
Total Fat 2.5g	4%
Saturated Fat 0g	0%
Trans Fat 0g	
Cholesterol 0mg	0%
Sodium 210mg	9%
Total Carbohydrate 22g	7%
Dietary Fiber 1g	4%
Sugars 11g	
Protein 2g	

Vitamin A 0%	•	Vitamin C 0%
Calcium 2%	•	Iron 4%

*Percent Daily Values are based on a 2,000 calorie diet. Your daily values may be higher or lower depending on your calorie needs:

	Calories:	2,000	2,500
Total Fat	Less than	65g	80g
Saturated Fat	Less than	20g	25g
Cholesterol	Less than	300mg	300mg
Sodium	Less than	2,400mg	2,400mg
Total Carbohydrate		300g	375g
Dietary Fiber		25g	30g

Calories per gram:
Fat 9 • Carbohydrate 4 • Protein 4

Ingredients

1	cup	hot water
1	cup	dates, pitted and chopped
¼	cup	egg substitute, beaten
¼	cup	white or brown sugar
1½	cups	flour
1	tsp	baking powder
1	tsp	baking soda
½	tsp	salt
½	cup	pecans or other nuts chopped

Preparation

- Preheat oven to 350°F. Coat one 9 x 5 x 3 inch loaf pan with cooking spray and flour
- Combine water and dates in a mixing bowl. Let stand until cool.
- Beat egg substitute and sugar together and then add to dates.
- Sift dry ingredients, stir well into date mixture.
- Add pecans, stirring well.
- Place in bread pan and bake 1 hour. Let cool in pan on wire rack.

The Settlement Cookbook

Category: Desserts/Bread

English Muffin Loaf

Makes 2 loaves. ~ 15 slices each.

Ingredients:

2	cups	skim milk, warmed to 120°F
½	cup	water, warmed to 120°F.
2	pkgs	dry yeast
3-6	cups	flour
1	Tbsp	sugar
1	tsp	salt, optional or use less
¼	tsp	baking soda

Preparation:

- Mix milk, water, and yeast together.
- Add 3 cups flour, sugar, salt (if used) and baking soda, mixing well.
- Then stir in 3 more cups of flour, adding more to achieve dough consistency. (Use whole wheat flour for variation.)
- Knead until well mixed.
- Oil 2 loaf pans, using corn or olive oil.
- Sprinkle bottom of pans with corn meal.
- Divide into the two loaf pans. Sprinkle tops with corn meal.
- Let rise 45 minutes then bake at 400°F for 25 min.
- Makes great toast for breakfast.

Thanks to: Marlene Gritts

Category: Breads

Nutrition Facts
Serving Size 1 slice (about 15 slices/loaf) (46g)
Servings Per Container 30

Amount Per Serving

Calories 100 — Calories from Fat 5

% Daily Value*

Total Fat 0g	0%
Saturated Fat 0g	0%
Trans Fat 0g	
Cholesterol 0mg	0%
Sodium 95mg	4%
Total Carbohydrate 21g	7%
Dietary Fiber 1g	4%
Sugars 1g	
Protein 3g	

Vitamin A 0% • Vitamin C 0%
Calcium 2% • Iron 6%

*Percent Daily Values are based on a 2,000 calorie diet. Your daily values may be higher or lower depending on your calorie needs:

		Calories:	2,000	2,500
Total Fat	Less than		65g	80g
Saturated Fat	Less than		20g	25g
Cholesterol	Less than		300mg	300mg
Sodium	Less than		2,400mg	2,400mg
Total Carbohydrate			300g	375g
Dietary Fiber			25g	30g

Calories per gram:
Fat 9 • Carbohydrate 4 • Protein 4

FLAXSEED PANCAKES

These pancakes have a delicious, nutty flavor. They are high in fiber and loaded with nutrients. Serve them with pureed canned fruit for even more good nutrition and flavor.

Makes 12 pancakes

Ingredients:

1	cup	whole wheat flour
½	cup	all purpose flour
½	cup	oatmeal
¼	cup	ground flax seeds (OR substitute wheat germ)
2	tsp	baking powder
¼	tsp	baking soda
2	cups	skim milk
1	tsp	vanilla extract

Fruit syrup:

1	cup	canned peaches (in water)

Nutrition Facts
Serving Size 1 pancake (84g)
Servings Per Container 12

Amount Per Serving

Calories 100   Calories from Fat 15

% Daily Value*

Total Fat 1.5g	2%
Saturated Fat 0g	0%
Trans Fat 0g	
Cholesterol 0mg	0%
Sodium 135mg	6%
Total Carbohydrate 19g	6%
Dietary Fiber 2g	8%
Sugars 2g	
Protein 4g	

| Vitamin A 2% | • | Vitamin C 2% |
| Calcium 8% | • | Iron 6% |

*Percent Daily Values are based on a 2,000 calorie diet. Your daily values may be higher or lower depending on your calorie needs:

		Calories:	2,000	2,500
Total Fat		Less than	65g	80g
Saturated Fat		Less than	20g	25g
Cholesterol		Less than	300mg	300mg
Sodium		Less than	2,400mg	2,400mg
Total Carbohydrate			300g	375g
Dietary Fiber			25g	30g

Calories per gram:
   Fat 9 • Carbohydrate 4 • Protein 4

Preparation:

- Combine dry ingredients in a large mixing bowl.
- Add milk and vanilla extract and mix well.
- Lightly spray a large nonstick pan with cooking oil spray.
- Heat over medium-high heat.
- Spoon ¼ cup of pancake batter in the pan for each pancake.
- Cook until the batter bubbles, and then flip the pancake over with a spatula. Cook until golden brown and firm in the center.
- **Fruit syrup:** Drain fruit, reserving the juice. Puree peaches, adding the juice as needed.
- Warm and serve as syrup over the pancakes.

Thanks to: Jill Burns, R.D.

Category: Breads

French Toast

Imagine healthy French toast! Top with fruit or fruit spread or sugar-free syrup.

Makes 4 slices

Ingredients:

3		egg whites
½	cup	non-fat milk
1½	tsp	sugar
½	tsp	vanilla extract
4	slices	wheat bread
		vegetable oil spray
		cinnamon to taste

Preparation:

- Whisk all ingredients together.
- Quickly dip whole wheat bread into mixture.
- Brown in nonstick skillet, over medium heat, using vegetable oil spray if needed,.
- Serve hot.

Thanks to: Dianne Hyson, R.D.

Category: Breads

Nutrition Facts

Serving Size 1 slice (89g)
Servings Per Container 4

Amount Per Serving

Calories 110   Calories from Fat 15

	% Daily Value*
Total Fat 1.5g	2%
Saturated Fat 0g	0%
Trans Fat 0g	
Cholesterol 0mg	0%
Sodium 220mg	9%
Total Carbohydrate 17g	6%
Dietary Fiber 2g	8%
Sugars 4g	
Protein 7g	

Vitamin A 2% • Vitamin C 0%
Calcium 4% • Iron 0%

*Percent Daily Values are based on a 2,000 calorie diet. Your daily values may be higher or lower depending on your calorie needs:

	Calories:	2,000	2,500
Total Fat	Less than	65g	80g
Saturated Fat	Less than	20g	25g
Cholesterol	Less than	300mg	300mg
Sodium	Less than	2,400mg	2,400mg
Total Carbohydrate		300g	375g
Dietary Fiber		25g	30g

Calories per gram:
Fat 9 • Carbohydrate 4 • Protein 4

FRESH APPLE COFFEE CAKE

Filled and topped with cinnamon spiced apples, this big cake is a satisfying close to a simple meal.   Fat-free mayonnaise is the secret to the moist texture.

Makes 16 servings
Prep. time ~20 min, plus ~ 1 hour to cool
Baking time: 1 to 1¼ hours

Ingredients:

4	large	apples, (e.g. Golden Delicious, Granny Smith) (~ 2 lbs)
⅓	cup	orange juice
1½	tsp	ground cinnamon
3	cups	flour
2	tsp	baking powder
½	tsp	salt
2	cup	granulated sugar
1	cup	fat-free mayonnaise
½	cup	skim milk
2½	tsp	vanilla extract
¾	cup	egg substitute
1		egg white (2 Tbsp)
⅔	cup	brown sugar, packed.

Nutrition Facts
Serving Size 1/16 recipe (158g)
Servings Per Container 16

Amount Per Serving

Calories 270   Calories from Fat 5

% Daily Value*

Total Fat 1g — 2%
   Saturated Fat 0g — 0%
   Trans Fat 0g
Cholesterol 0mg — 0%
Sodium 300mg — 13%
Total Carbohydrate 64g — 21%
   Dietary Fiber 2g — 8%
   Sugars 42g
Protein 4g

Vitamin A 2% • Vitamin C 8%
Calcium 4% • Iron 8%

*Percent Daily Values are based on a 2,000 calorie diet. Your daily values may be higher or lower depending on your calorie needs:

		Calories:	2,000	2,500
Total Fat	Less than		65g	80g
Saturated Fat	Less than		20g	25g
Cholesterol	Less than		300mg	300mg
Sodium	Less than		2,400mg	2,400mg
Total Carbohydrate			300g	375g
Dietary Fiber			25g	30g

Calories per gram:
   Fat 9 • Carbohydrate 4 • Protein 4

Preparation:

- Coat a 9 or 10 inch tube pan with cooking spray.
- Peel, core, and coarsely chop apples. Place in medium-sized bowl.
- Mix in orange juice and cinnamon and set aside.
- Stir flour, baking, powder and salt together in a medium bowl and set aside.
- Beat sugar, mayonnaise, milk and vanilla extract together in a large bowl, until well blended.
- Beat in egg substitute and egg white.
- Add flour mixture to egg mixture; stir to blend thoroughly.
- Pour half the batter into prepared pan and top with half the apples.
- Pour remaining batter evenly over apples; top with remaining apples. Sprinkle evenly with brown sugar.
- Bake in 350°F oven for 1 to 1¼ hours until the center of cake springs back when lightly pressed.
- Let cool in pan on a rack for about 1 hour.
- Run a long, thin knife around sides of pan and tube. Carefully invert cake onto rack; lift off pan. Then carefully turn cake over onto a serving plate.

Thanks to: Laurie Crider-Vanpal, Group 29, from Sunset Healthy Heart Cook Book
Category: Breads

Hot Quinoa Breakfast Cereal

Another healthful alternative to oatmeal. You can freeze extra servings in individual containers to microwave on busy mornings.

Serve 4

Ingredients:

1	cup	quinoa
2	cups	water
½	cup	apples, thinly sliced
⅓	cup	raisins
½	tsp	ground cinnamon
		milk or cream
		brown sugar

Preparation:

- Rinse quinoa and add to water; bring to a boil.
- Reduce heat; simmer for 5 minutes.
- Add apples, raisins and cinnamon; simmer until water is absorbed.
- Serve with milk or cream and sweeten to taste with honey or brown sugar.

Nutrition Facts

Serving Size 1/4 recipe (206g)
Servings Per Container 4

Amount Per Serving

Calories 240 — Calories from Fat 25

% Daily Value*

Total Fat 3g	5%
Saturated Fat 0g	0%
Trans Fat 0g	
Cholesterol 0mg	0%
Sodium 10mg	0%
Total Carbohydrate 53g	18%
Dietary Fiber 12g	48%
Sugars 10g	
Protein 7g	

Vitamin A 2% • Vitamin C 2%
Calcium 20% • Iron 20%

*Percent Daily Values are based on a 2,000 calorie diet. Your daily values may be higher or lower depending on your calorie needs:

	Calories:	2,000	2,500
Total Fat	Less than	65g	80g
Saturated Fat	Less than	20g	25g
Cholesterol	Less than	300mg	300mg
Sodium	Less than	2,400mg	2,400mg
Total Carbohydrate		300g	375g
Dietary Fiber		25g	30g

Calories per gram:
Fat 9 • Carbohydrate 4 • Protein 4

Category: Cereal

Source: *CDKitchen*

Joe's Special Frittata

Just like the famous "Joe's Special" served in San Francisco.

6 servings

Ingredients:

2	cups	TVP granules
2½	cups	boiling water
2	tsp	Better than Bouillon, vegetable base
¼	tsp	nutmeg
¼	tsp	oregano
2	med	onions, chopped (1½ cups)
½	lb	mushrooms
1	tsp	olive oil
10	oz	chopped spinach, fresh or frozen (if frozen, thawed, water squeezed out
2	cups	egg substitute

Nutrition Facts
Serving Size 1/6 recipe (340g)
Servings Per Container 6

Amount Per Serving

Calories 200   Calories from Fat 10

% Daily Value*

- Total Fat 1.5g — 2%
-   Saturated Fat 0g — 0%
-   Trans Fat 0g
- Cholesterol 0mg — 0%
- Sodium 450mg — 19%
- Total Carbohydrate 19g — 6%
-   Dietary Fiber 8g — 32%
-   Sugars 8g
- Protein 28g

Vitamin A 120% • Vitamin C 8%
Calcium 25% • Iron 35%

*Percent Daily Values are based on a 2,000 calorie diet. Your daily values may be higher or lower depending on your calorie needs:

	Calories:	2,000	2,500
Total Fat	Less than	65g	80g
Saturated Fat	Less than	20g	25g
Cholesterol	Less than	300mg	300mg
Sodium	Less than	2,400mg	2,400mg
Total Carbohydrate		300g	375g
Dietary Fiber		25g	30g

Calories per gram:
  Fat 9 • Carbohydrate 4 • Protein 4

Preparation:

- Soak TVP in boiling water with bouillon and spices for 10 minutes or until thoroughly softened.
- Sauté onion until soft and slightly browned.
- Add mushrooms and cook on medium heat until all moisture is dissipated.
- Add spinach and heat until limp.
- Just before serving, add egg substitute, stir into mixture and cook until eggs are set.

Thanks to: Doug Cort, Ph.D.

Category: Meat and Egg Substitutes

MUSELIX

Mix the yogurts together if making multiple servings. If only making a single serving, take ¼ to ½ cup of cereal mix and combine with one carton of yogurt.

6 servings

Ingredients:

2		apples, grated (include skin)
1	cup	oats (regular, not instant)
1	cup	bran
½	cup	raisins
16	oz	non-fat lemon yogurt
16	oz	non-fat strawberry yogurt
16	oz	non-fat raspberry yogurt
		dash of lemon extract

Preparation:

- Combine apples, oats, bran and raisins. Combine yogurts and add lemon extract, if desired. Stir in grains and fruit..

Thanks to: Dianne Hyson, R.D.

Category: Cereals

Nutrition Facts

Serving Size 1/6 recipe (338g)
Servings Per Container 6

Amount Per Serving

Calories 300 Calories from Fat 10

% Daily Value*

Total Fat 1g	2%
Saturated Fat 0g	0%
Trans Fat 0g	
Cholesterol 5mg	2%
Sodium 140mg	6%
Total Carbohydrate 66g	22%
Dietary Fiber 9g	36%
Sugars 42g	
Protein 14g	

Vitamin A 10% • Vitamin C 20%
Calcium 40% • Iron 10%

*Percent Daily Values are based on a 2,000 calorie diet. Your daily values may be higher or lower depending on your calorie needs:

		Calories:	2,000	2,500
Total Fat	Less than		65g	80g
Saturated Fat	Less than		20g	25g
Cholesterol	Less than		300mg	300mg
Sodium	Less than		2,400mg	2,400mg
Total Carbohydrate			300g	375g
Dietary Fiber			25g	30g

Calories per gram:
Fat 9 • Carbohydrate 4 • Protein 4

Oatmeal Navy Bean Muffins

Beans make an excellent fat substitute. Puree them first.

Makes 12 muffins

Ingredients:

1	cup	rolled oats
1	cup	non-fat buttermilk (use skim milk with 1 Tbsp lemon juice to make 1 cup)
¼	cup	egg substitute
½	cup	firmly packed light brown sugar
½	cup	cooked navy beans (pureed)
1	cup	all-purpose flour
½	tsp	salt
1	tsp	baking powder
½	tsp	baking soda
½	cup	dried currants

Nutrition Facts
Serving Size (66g)
Servings Per Container

Amount Per Serving
Calories 150 — Calories from Fat 5

% Daily Value*
- Total Fat 0.5g — 1%
-   Saturated Fat 0g — 0%
-   Trans Fat 0g
- Cholesterol 0mg — 0%
- Sodium 220mg — 9%
- Total Carbohydrate 31g — 10%
-   Dietary Fiber 3g — 12%
-   Sugars 14g
- Protein 5g

Vitamin A 2% • Vitamin C 2%
Calcium 4% • Iron 8%

*Percent Daily Values are based on a 2,000 calorie diet. Your daily values may be higher or lower depending on your calorie needs:

	Calories:	2,000	2,500
Total Fat	Less than	65g	80g
Saturated Fat	Less than	20g	25g
Cholesterol	Less than	300mg	300 mg
Sodium	Less than	2,400mg	2,400mg
Total Carbohydrate		300g	375g
Dietary Fiber		25g	30g

Calories per gram:
Fat 9 • Carbohydrate 4 • Protein 4

Preparation:

- Combine oats and buttermilk in a large bowl, and let stand 1 hour.
- Preheat oven to 400°F. Spray 12 medium muffin cups with non-stick cooking spray.
- Add egg, sugar and pureed beans to oat mixture, stirring until just combined.
- Sift flour, salt, baking powder and baking soda into another large bowl. Add to oat mixture, stirring until just combined. Fold in currants.
- Divide batter evenly among prepared muffin cups. Bake muffins in middle of oven until golden and a tester comes out clean (usually about 20 minutes).

Thanks to: Debbie Lucus, R.D.

Category: Breads

Oatmeal Pumpkin Muffins

A fall favorite. Top with pumpkin butter.

Makes 12 muffins

Topping:

¼	cup	rolled oats
1	Tbsp	brown sugar, firmly packed
⅛	tsp	pumpkin pie spice

Muffins:

1	cup	rolled oats (whirl in blender until a fine powder)
1½	cups	all-purpose flour
½	cup	brown sugar, firmly packed
2	tsp	baking powder
1½	tsp	pumpkin pie spice
½	tsp	baking soda
½	tsp	salt (optional)
¼	cup	walnuts, chopped (optional)
¾	cup	light soy milk (or skimmed milk)
1	cup	canned pumpkin
¼	cup	unsweetened applesauce

Nutrition Facts
Serving Size 1 muffin (79g)
Servings Per Container 12

Amount Per Serving
Calories 160   Calories from Fat 25

% Daily Value*
- Total Fat 2.5g — 4%
- Saturated Fat 0g — 0%
- Trans Fat 0g
- Cholesterol 0mg — 0%
- Sodium 250mg — 10%
- Total Carbohydrate 31g — 10%
- Dietary Fiber 2g — 8%
- Sugars 12g
- Protein 4g

Vitamin A 50% • Vitamin C 0%
Calcium 6% • Iron 8%

*Percent Daily Values are based on a 2,000 calorie diet. Your daily values may be higher or lower depending on your calorie needs:

	Calories:	2,000	2,500
Total Fat	Less than	65g	80g
Saturated Fat	Less than	20g	25g
Cholesterol	Less than	300mg	300mg
Sodium	Less than	2,400mg	2,400mg
Total Carbohydrate		300g	375g
Dietary Fiber		25g	30g

Calories per gram:
Fat 9 • Carbohydrate 4 • Protein 4

Preparation:

- Preheat oven to 400°F. Spray 12 medium muffin cups with non-stick cooking spray or line with paper baking cups.
- Mix topping ingredients in small bowl and set aside.
- Combine oats, flour, sugar, baking powder, pumpkin pie spice, baking soda, salt, and walnuts in a large bowl and mix well.
- In separate bowl, mix milk, canned pumpkin and applesauce.
- Add wet ingredients to the dry and mix until just moistened. Don't over mix!
- Fill muffin cups until almost full.
- Sprinkle muffins with topping before baking.
- Bake 22-25 minutes until no dent is left when a muffin center is gently poked with a finger.
- Cool for 5 minutes in pan on a wire rack.

Category: Breads

Oil Free Muffins

Makes 12 muffins.

Ingredients:

2¼	cups	oat bran cereal
1	Tbsp	baking powder
¼	cup	brown sugar
½	cup	dried fruit (raisins, dates, prunes)
1¼	cup	skim milk
2		egg whites
2	Tbsp	corn syrup

Preparation:

- Preheat the oven to 425°F.
- Mix the dry ingredients in a large bowl.
- Mix the milk, egg whites, and corn syrup together and blend with dry ingredients.
- Line muffin pans with paper baking cups, and fill with batter divided equally.
- Bake 13-15 minutes.
- Test for doneness with a toothpick.
- Note: This oil-free recipe requires a bit less baking time than the recipe for basic muffins.

Source: *The 8-Week Cholesterol Cure*

Category: Breads

Nutrition Facts

Serving Size 1 muffin (56g)
Servings Per Container 12

Amount Per Serving

Calories 90	Calories from Fat 5

	% Daily Value*
Total Fat 0.5g	1%
Saturated Fat 0g	0%
Trans Fat 0g	
Cholesterol 0mg	0%
Sodium 190mg	8%
Total Carbohydrate 21g	7%
Dietary Fiber 1g	4%
Sugars 12g	
Protein 3g	

Vitamin A 2%	•	Vitamin C 2%
Calcium 8%	•	Iron 15%

*Percent Daily Values are based on a 2,000 calorie diet. Your daily values may be higher or lower depending on your calorie needs:

	Calories:	2,000	2,500
Total Fat	Less than	65g	80g
Saturated Fat	Less than	20g	25g
Cholesterol	Less than	300mg	300mg
Sodium	Less than	2,400mg	2,400mg
Total Carbohydrate		300g	375g
Dietary Fiber		25g	30g

Calories per gram:
  Fat 9 • Carbohydrate 4 • Protein 4

ORANGE CRANBERRY BREAD

This low-fat citrus bread is the perfect companion for morning coffee. You'll never believe it has less than half a gram of fat per serving.

Makes 1 loaf. ~ 15 slices

Ingredients:

2¼	cups	all-purpose flour
2	tsp	baking powder
1	tsp	baking soda
¼	tsp	salt
1¼	cups	granulated sugar
½	cup	unsweetened applesauce
3		egg whites
1	cup	fresh cranberries, chopped,
OR		
½	cup	dried cranberries (raisins also work well)
2	tsp	grated orange peel
¼	cup	orange juice
1	tsp	vanilla extract

Preparation:

- Preheat oven to 350°F.
- Spray a 9 x 5 x 3 inch loaf pan with vegetable oil cooking spray.
- Combine flour, baking powder, baking soda and salt in a large bowl; set aside.
- Mix together remaining ingredients in another large bowl.
- Add flour mixture; stir gently to blend. Pour batter into pan.
- Bake 50 minutes or until cake tester inserted in center comes out clean.
- Remove bread from oven. Place on wire rack. Cool 10 minutes and serve warm.

Source: *Mott's*

Category: Breads

Overnight Coffee Cake

Make the night before and bake first thing in the morning. Great when you have guests.

Serves 18

Topping:

½	cup	brown sugar, packed
1	tsp	ground cinnamon
¼	cup	walnuts, chopped

Cake Ingredients:

2	cups	flour
1½	tsp	baking powder
1	tsp	baking soda
¼	tsp	salt
1½	tsp	ground nutmeg
½	cup	unsweetened applesauce
½	cup	non-fat plain yogurt
1	cup	sugar
½	cup	egg substitute
8	oz	fat-free sour cream

Preparation:

- Coat a 9 by 13 inch baking pan with vegetable oil cooking spray.
- Mix together and set aside the topping ingredients in a small bowl.
- Combine flour, baking powder, baking soda, salt and nutmeg and set aside.
- Beat applesauce, yogurt, and sugar in a large mixer bowl until light and fluffy.
- Add egg substitute slowly, beating well.
- Add sour cream, beat just until incorporated.
- Using wooden spoon, stir in flour mixture just until patches of white disappear.
- Spread the batter in prepared pan using a rubber spatula to smooth top.
- Sprinkle topping evenly over batter. Cover and refrigerate overnight.
- Uncover coffee cake and bake at 350°F for 30-35 minutes until lightly browned and wooden pick inserted in center comes out clean.
- Cool slightly on wire rack before cutting.

Category: Breads

Nutrition Facts

Serving Size 2x3 inch rectangle (66g)
Servings Per Container 18

Amount Per Serving

Calories 150 Calories from Fat 10

	% Daily Value*
Total Fat 1.5g	2%
Saturated Fat 0g	0%
Trans Fat 0g	
Cholesterol 0mg	0%
Sodium 190mg	8%
Total Carbohydrate 32g	11%
Dietary Fiber 1g	4%
Sugars 19g	
Protein 3g	

Vitamin A 2%	•	Vitamin C 0%	
Calcium 4%	•	Iron 4%	

*Percent Daily Values are based on a 2,000 calorie diet. Your daily values may be higher or lower depending on your calorie needs:

		Calories:	2,000	2,500
Total Fat		Less than	65g	80g
Saturated Fat		Less than	20g	25g
Cholesterol		Less than	300mg	300mg
Sodium		Less than	2,400mg	2,400mg
Total Carbohydrate			300g	375g
Dietary Fiber			25g	30g

Calories per gram:
Fat 9 • Carbohydrate 4 • Protein 4

OVERNIGHT OATMEAL

This makes enough for the family, or to get an individual through the week. It freezes well, too.

Makes 6 servings

Ingredients:

3	cups	skim milk
1½	cups	steel cut oats
½	cup	packed dark brown sugar
¾	tsp	salt

Topping:

2		apples, chopped
2	Tbsp	packed dark-brown sugar
3	Tbsp	dried cranberries or raisins
3	Tbsp	walnuts, chopped

Preparation:

- Coat a slow cooker with vegetable oil cooking spray.
- Combine milk, 3 cups water, the oats, ¼ cup of the brown sugar and the salt in slow cooker.
- Cover and cook overnight on LOW for 9 ½ -10 hours.
- Uncover and stir in remaining ¼ cup brown sugar. Set aside.
- Topping: Coat a large nonstick skillet with nonstick cooking spray and place over medium heat.
- Add apples and cook 4 minutes, stirring occasionally.
- Add brown sugar, 1 Tbsp water and dried cranberries.
- Cook 1 minute.
- Remove from heat and stir in nuts.
- Stir oatmeal in slow cooker until smooth.
- Spoon about a cup into a bowl and add a few tablespoons of the topping.
- Serve warm.

Thanks to: Debbie Lucus, R.D.

Category: Cereals

Nutrition Facts

Serving Size 1/6 recipe (249g)
Servings Per Container 6

Amount Per Serving

Calories 280   Calories from Fat 35

% Daily Value*

Total Fat 4g	6%
Saturated Fat 0.5g	3%
Trans Fat 0g	
Cholesterol 0mg	0%
Sodium 350mg	15%
Total Carbohydrate 57g	19%
Dietary Fiber 4g	16%
Sugars 40g	
Protein 8g	

Vitamin A 6% • Vitamin C 6%
Calcium 20% • Iron 8%

*Percent Daily Values are based on a 2,000 calorie diet. Your daily values may be higher or lower depending on your calorie needs:

		Calories:	2,000	2,500
Total Fat	Less than		65g	80g
Saturated Fat	Less than		20g	25g
Cholesterol	Less than		300mg	300mg
Sodium	Less than		2,400mg	2,400mg
Total Carbohydrate			300g	375g
Dietary Fiber			25g	30g

Calories per gram:
  Fat 9 • Carbohydrate 4 • Protein 4

QUICKIE QUESADILLAS

The banana gives a nice sweet contrast to the bite of the peppers and sprouts.

Makes 6 servings. ~¼ tortilla each

Ingredients:

12		corn or low-fat flour tortillas
6	oz	fat-free Monterey Jack, cheddar, or soy cheese
2	Tbsp	chopped fresh cilantro or parsley
2		jalapeno peppers, minced
OR		
1	can	diced green chilies (4oz)
1	cup	alfalfa sprouts
2	med	bananas, sliced into thin circles

Preparation:

- Sprinkle all ingredients on 6 tortillas.
- Top with second tortilla.
- Heat in microwave until cheese melts, about 45 seconds.
- Cut tortilla into quarters.
- Serve with salsa.

Nutrition Facts
Serving Size 1/4 tortilla (42g)
Servings Per Container 24

Amount Per Serving
Calories 80   Calories from Fat 10

% Daily Value*
Total Fat 1g — 2%
  Saturated Fat 0g — 0%
  Trans Fat 0g
Cholesterol 0mg — 0%
Sodium 210mg — 9%
Total Carbohydrate 14g — 5%
  Dietary Fiber 1g — 4%
  Sugars 3g
Protein 4g

Vitamin A 2% • Vitamin C 4%
Calcium 10% • Iron 0%

*Percent Daily Values are based on a 2,000 calorie diet. Your daily values may be higher or lower depending on your calorie needs:

	Calories:	2,000	2,500
Total Fat	Less than	65g	80g
Saturated Fat	Less than	20g	25g
Cholesterol	Less than	300mg	300mg
Sodium	Less than	2,400mg	2,400mg
Total Carbohydrate		300g	375g
Dietary Fiber		25g	30g

Calories per gram:
  Fat 9 • Carbohydrate 4 • Protein 4

Alternatively, the tortilla could be baked in 350°F oven for 10 -15 minutes if desired.

From Dean Ornish, Eat More, Weigh Less

Category: Mexican

SMOOTHIES

See suggestions below for a wide variety of flavor options.

Makes 2 servings

Ingredients:

1	cup	frozen or fresh fruit
1		banana
½	cup	100% fruit juice

Add one of the following:

1	cup	flavored fat-free yogurt
½	cup	tofu
1	cup	skim milk or soymilk

Preparation:

- Combine fruit and juice in blender container. Add yogurt or tofu or milk.
- Blend all ingredients.
- If your fruit is not frozen, you may use ice cubes.

Variations:

a) Tropical Twist (pineapple, banana, mango)

b) Berries Blast (mixed berries, grape juice)

c) Crazy Creation (strawberries, banana, small cooked sweet potato)

d) Orange Freeze (6oz orange juice concentrate, 1 cup water, 1 cup non-fat milk, 1 tsp vanilla, ice)

e) Pumpkin Pie (pumpkin, vanilla yogurt, pumpkin pie spice)

f) Blue Moon Shake (chocolate soy milk, frozen blueberries)

Thanks to: Jill Burns, R.D.

Category: Miscellaneous

Nutrition Facts

Serving Size 1/2 recipe (302g)
Servings Per Container 2

Amount Per Serving

Calories 190	Calories from Fat 5

	% Daily Value*
Total Fat 0g	0%
Saturated Fat 0g	0%
Trans Fat 0g	
Cholesterol 5mg	2%
Sodium 80mg	3%
Total Carbohydrate 43g	14%
Dietary Fiber 5g	20%
Sugars 29g	
Protein 7g	

Vitamin A 35%	•	Vitamin C 60%
Calcium 20%	•	Iron 6%

*Percent Daily Values are based on a 2,000 calorie diet. Your daily values may be higher or lower depending on your calorie needs:

	Calories:	2,000	2,500
Total Fat	Less than	65g	80g
Saturated Fat	Less than	20g	25g
Cholesterol	Less than	300mg	300mg
Sodium	Less than	2,400mg	2,400mg
Total Carbohydrate		300g	375g
Dietary Fiber		25g	30g

Calories per gram:
Fat 9 • Carbohydrate 4 • Protein 4

Sourdough Oatmeal Bread

Superb for morning toast, soup dunking or a guilty pleasure PB&J. Has a truly impressive quantity of oats, so it fits in well for cardiovascular health. It's a high-density loaf that needs plenty of fermentation time.

Makes 1 loaf. ~ 15 slices

Ingredients:

¼	cup	steel-cut oats
¾	cup	boiling water
⅞	cup	warm water/soy/almond milk
2	Tbsp	honey (less if using milk)
1	cup	rolled oats
2	Tbsp	steel-cut oats
1	Tbsp	malted barley flour
2	Tbsp	vital gluten
3¾	cups	bread flour
1¼	cups	sourdough starter
2½	tsp	sea salt
⅛	tsp	ascorbic acid (vitamin C)
OR		
1	Tbsp	orange juice

Nutrition Facts
Serving Size 1 slice (82g)
Servings Per Container 15

Amount Per Serving

Calories 190 — Calories from Fat 15

% Daily Value*

- Total Fat 1.5g — 2%
- Saturated Fat 0g — 0%
- Trans Fat 0g
- Cholesterol 0mg — 0%
- Sodium 480mg — 20%
- Total Carbohydrate 37g — 12%
- Dietary Fiber 2g — 8%
- Sugars 3g
- Protein 7g

Vitamin A 0% • Vitamin C 25%
Calcium 2% • Iron 6%

*Percent Daily Values are based on a 2,000 calorie diet. Your daily values may be higher or lower depending on your calorie needs:

	Calories:	2,000	2,500
Total Fat	Less than	65g	80g
Saturated Fat	Less than	20g	25g
Cholesterol	Less than	300mg	300mg
Sodium	Less than	2,400mg	2,400mg
Total Carbohydrate		300g	375g
Dietary Fiber		25g	30g

Calories per gram:
Fat 9 • Carbohydrate 4 • Protein 4

Preparation:

- Add steel-cut oats to boiling water, cover, low-boil for 15 minutes and cool.
- Dissolve yeast in warm water or milk, add honey and the ascorbic acid. Slowly combine this mixture with the boiled oats and remaining ingredients in a bowl.
- Knead for 10-15 minutes, adding flour as needed (dough should be tactile and almost sticky).
- Place dough in large bowl, cover with plastic wrap and towel. Let rise 4-6 hours or until nearly doubled.
- Remove from bowl, pat down, form into loaf, transfer to an oiled pan, cover with oiled plastic wrap and towel and let rise 90 minutes or until dough nearly doubles again.
- Preheat oven to 475°F. Remove plastic wrap and put loaf in oven, immediately lower temperature to 425°F and bake for 50-58 minutes. Lower temperature to 375°F if top begins to get too brown. Loaf should reach internal temperature of 205°F.
- Do not use a food processor, as the oats will be pulverized and the loaf texture will be inferior. The ascorbic acid will improve dough rise, so strongly consider using that.

Thanks to: Dave Hansen, Group 40

Category: Bread

STUFFED FRENCH TOAST

An impressive brunch dish.

4 servings. Serving size: 1 stuffed bread slice and ¼ cup sauce.

Ingredients:

4	oz	diagonally cut slices French bread (about 1 inch thick)
3	Tbsp	finely chopped dried apricots, divided
½	cup	non-fat ricotta cheese
2	Tbsp	non-fat mozzarella cheese, shredded (½ oz.)
1	tsp	sugar
¼	tsp	vanilla extract
¾	cup	apricot nectar
½	cup	ripe banana, sliced (about 1 small)
½	cup	skim milk
¼	cup	egg substitute
		vegetable oil cooking spray

Nutrition Facts
Serving Size 1 slice (179g)
Servings Per Container 4

Amount Per Serving
- Calories 220 — Calories from Fat 5
- Total Fat 0.5g — 1%
- Saturated Fat 0g — 0%
- Trans Fat 0g
- Cholesterol 5mg — 2%
- Sodium 370mg — 15%
- Total Carbohydrate 42g — 14%
- Dietary Fiber 2g — 8%
- Sugars 16g
- Protein 12g
- Vitamin A 20% • Vitamin C 2%
- Calcium 15% • Iron 10%

Preparation:

- Cut a slit through top of each slice of bread to form a pocket. Set aside.
- Combine 1 Tbsp dried apricots, ricotta cheese, mozzarella cheese, sugar, and vanilla in a bowl. Stir well.
- Stuff 2 Tbsp cheese mixture into pocket of each slice of bread. Set aside.
- Make sauce by combining remaining 2 Tbsp apricots and apricot nectar in a small saucepan. Bring to a boil.
- Reduce heat and simmer uncovered for 1 minute. Remove from heat and stir in banana. Set aside and keep warm.
- Combine milk and egg substitute in a large shallow dish. Stir well.
- Place stuffed bread in dish, turning to coat. Let stand until milk mixture is absorbed.
- Coat a large nonstick skillet with cooking spray, and place over medium heat until hot.
- Gently add bread to skillet, and cook 2 minutes.
- Carefully turn bread over, and cook 2 minutes or until browned.
- Serve with warm apricot sauce.

Thanks to: Grant Garrison, Group 2

Source: Cooking Light

Category: Breads

Tofu Scramble

The turmeric gives this scrambled dish the color of eggs. Use any veggies you have on hand.

Serves 2

Ingredients:

½		yellow onion, diced
½		tomato, diced
8	oz	firm tofu
1	tsp	garlic powder
1	tsp	onion powder
½	tsp	liquid smoke (optional)
1	Tbsp	light soy sauce
½	tsp	turmeric
¼	tsp	ground cumin
		salt and pepper to taste

Preparation:

- Sauté onion and tomato until onions are translucent.
- Crumble tofu into large pieces and add to pan with water from tofu package.
- Next add remaining ingredients plus any vegetables you like.
- Reduce heat to medium and cook for 5-7 minutes, stirring frequently and adding a teaspoon of olive oil, if needed.
- Wrap in a warmed flour tortilla with a bit of salsa for a breakfast burrito or top with soy or dairy cheese.

Category: Egg/Meat Substitutes

Thanks to: Debbie Lucus, R.D.

Nutrition Facts

Serving Size 1/2 recipe (257g)
Servings Per Container 2

Amount Per Serving

Calories 170 — Calories from Fat 40

	% Daily Value*
Total Fat 4.5g	7%
Saturated Fat 0g	0%
Trans Fat 0g	
Cholesterol 0mg	0%
Sodium 470mg	20%
Total Carbohydrate 15g	5%
Dietary Fiber 4g	16%
Sugars 4g	
Protein 17g	

Vitamin A 70% • Vitamin C 15%
Calcium 70% • Iron 25%

*Percent Daily Values are based on a 2,000 calorie diet. Your daily values may be higher or lower depending on your calorie needs:

	Calories:	2,000	2,500
Total Fat	Less than	65g	80g
Saturated Fat	Less than	20g	25g
Cholesterol	Less than	300mg	300mg
Sodium	Less than	2,400mg	2,400mg
Total Carbohydrate		300g	375g
Dietary Fiber		25g	30g

Calories per gram:
Fat 9 • Carbohydrate 4 • Protein 4

VEGETABLE OMELET

A good basic recipe for a quick breakfast, lunch or dinner. Substitute any veggies you have on hand, or frozen spinach or peppers.

Serves 2

Ingredients:

1	cup	egg substitute
3	Tbsp	broccoli, finely chopped
3	Tbsp	mushrooms, finely chopped
2	Tbsp	red bell pepper, finely chopped
1		green onion, sliced
		pepper to taste
		canola oil spray

Preparation:

- Spray small 8 inch nonstick skillet.
- Heat skillet to medium-low.
- Pour egg substitute into pan.
- When egg is slightly firm, add vegetables on one half of pan. Allow egg mixture to firm more but not completely, and flip second half over vegetable covered half.
- Heat through until cooked and serve immediately.

Nutrition Facts
Serving Size 1/2 recipe (161g)
Servings Per Container 2

Amount Per Serving

Calories 80   Calories from Fat 10

% Daily Value*

Total Fat 1.5g — 2%
  Saturated Fat 0g — 0%
  Trans Fat 0g
Cholesterol 0mg — 0%
Sodium 260mg — 11%
Total Carbohydrate 4g — 1%
  Dietary Fiber 1g — 4%
  Sugars 3g
Protein 13g

Vitamin A 20% • Vitamin C 35%
Calcium 6% • Iron 15%

*Percent Daily Values are based on a 2,000 calorie diet. Your daily values may be higher or lower depending on your calorie needs:

		Calories:	2,000	2,500
Total Fat	Less than		65g	80g
Saturated Fat	Less than		20g	25g
Cholesterol	Less than		300mg	300mg
Sodium	Less than		2,400mg	2,400mg
Total Carbohydrate			300g	375g
Dietary Fiber			25g	30g

Calories per gram:
  Fat 9 • Carbohydrate 4 • Protein 4

Source: Adapted from The New American Diet

Category: Egg Substitute

Vegetable Quesadillas

Makes 16 quarters

May be served as an entrée or cut into wedges for dipping into salsa or fat-free sour cream.

Ingredients:

1	small	onion, chopped
1	small	zucchini, thinly sliced
1	small	yellow squash, thinly sliced
1	clove	garlic, minced
1	can	fat-free refried beans (15 oz)
½	cup	non-fat cheddar cheese shredded (2 oz)
1	cup	salsa
8		whole wheat tortillas (8 inch diameter) 96% fat-free

Preparation:

- Coat a large skillet with vegetable oil cooking spray and warm over medium-high heat.
- Add onions, zucchini, squash, and garlic. Cook, stirring occasionally, for 7 minutes, or until the vegetables are tender.
- Spread beans evenly over 4 tortillas.
- Spoon the vegetables over the beans and sprinkle with cheese.
- Cover with the remaining tortillas.
- Place a quesadilla in the skillet. Cover, and cook over low heat, turning once, for 5 minutes, or until heated through.
- Repeat with the remaining quesadillas. Cut into wedges.
- Serve with salsa.

Note: These ingredients can be adapted to use the Forman grilling machine, or baked in oven.

Category: Mexican

Nutrition Facts

Serving Size 1 qiarter (89g)
Servings Per Container 16

Amount Per Serving	
Calories 100	Calories from Fat 5

	% Daily Value*
Total Fat 1g	2%
Saturated Fat 0g	0%
Trans Fat 0g	
Cholesterol 0mg	0%
Sodium 420mg	18%
Total Carbohydrate 19g	6%
Dietary Fiber 3g	12%
Sugars 2g	
Protein 5g	

Vitamin A 2%	•	Vitamin C 6%
Calcium 4%	•	Iron 2%

*Percent Daily Values are based on a 2,000 calorie diet. Your daily values may be higher or lower depending on your calorie needs:

	Calories:	2,000	2,500
Total Fat	Less than	65g	80g
Saturated Fat	Less than	20g	25g
Cholesterol	Less than	300mg	300mg
Sodium	Less than	2,400mg	2,400mg
Total Carbohydrate		300g	375g
Dietary Fiber		25g	30g

Calories per gram:
  Fat 9 • Carbohydrate 4 • Protein 4

Yogurt Muffins

Perfect with fruit for a quick breakfast. Extras freeze well.

Makes approximately 12 muffins

Ingredients:

1½	cups	all-purpose flour
¾	cup	sugar
2	tsp	baking powder
1	tsp	baking soda
½	tsp	salt
⅔	cup	plain non-fat yogurt
⅔	cups	skim milk
½	cup	blueberries or grated apple (if desired)

For Streusel topping:

½	tsp	cinnamon
½	cup	brown sugar

Preparation:

- Preheat oven to 400°F.
- Combine flour, sugar, baking powder, baking soda and salt in a large mixing bowl.
- Gently stir in yogurt and milk, blending until dry ingredients are just moistened.
- Fill lightly greased or paper-lined muffin cups ¾ full.
- Bake 18 minutes or until well-browned.
- Serve warm.

- **Streusel Variation:** Mix sugar and cinnamon together.
- Fill muffin cups ½ full with batter; place 1 tsp of sugar-cinnamon mixture on top of each and add batter to fill cups ¾ full.

Source: Dannon

Category: Breads

Nutrition Facts
Serving Size 1 muffin (62g)
Servings Per Container 12

Amount Per Serving

Calories 120   Calories from Fat 0

% Daily Value*

Total Fat 0g	0%
Saturated Fat 0g	0%
Trans Fat 0g	
Cholesterol 0mg	0%
Sodium 310mg	13%
Total Carbohydrate 28g	9%
Dietary Fiber 1g	4%
Sugars 15g	
Protein 3g	

Vitamin A 2%	•	Vitamin C 2%
Calcium 6%	•	Iron 4%

*Percent Daily Values are based on a 2,000 calorie diet. Your daily values may be higher or lower depending on your calorie needs:

		2,000	2,500
Total Fat	Less than	65g	80g
Saturated Fat	Less than	20g	25g
Cholesterol	Less than	300mg	300mg
Sodium	Less than	2,400mg	2,400mg
Total Carbohydrate		300g	375g
Dietary Fiber		25g	30g

Calories per gram:
Fat 9 • Carbohydrate 4 • Protein 4

Nutrition Facts
Serving Size 1 muffin (68g)
Servings Per Container 12

Amount Per Serving

Calories 140   Calories from Fat 0

% Daily Value*

Total Fat 0g	0%
Saturated Fat 0g	0%
Trans Fat 0g	
Cholesterol 0mg	0%
Sodium 310mg	13%
Total Carbohydrate 33g	11%
Dietary Fiber 1g	4%
Sugars 20g	
Protein 3g	

Vitamin A 2%	•	Vitamin C 2%
Calcium 6%	•	Iron 4%

*Percent Daily Values are based on a 2,000 calorie diet. Your daily values may be higher or lower depending on your calorie needs:

		2,000	2,500
Total Fat	Less than	65g	80g
Saturated Fat	Less than	20g	25g
Cholesterol	Less than	300mg	300mg
Sodium	Less than	2,400mg	2,400mg
Total Carbohydrate		300g	375g
Dietary Fiber		25g	30g

Calories per gram:
Fat 9 • Carbohydrate 4 • Protein 4

LUNCH

SALADS

Asian Noodle Salad

Variations: try other crunchy vegetables like jicama, celery, or substitute the soba noodles with cooked angel hair or spaghetti pasta.

Makes 6 servings

Ingredients:

8	oz	soba noodles
¼	cup	sunflower seeds
¼	cup	pine nuts (OR chopped or slivered almonds)
		butter flavored spray
3-6	cups	shredded bok choy (OR other mixed greens) (~2 lb)
5		green onions, thinly sliced
1	can	water chestnuts (5 oz)
12	pods	snow peas, cut into bite-sized pieces

Dressing:

1	Tbsp	olive oil
¼	cup	rice wine vinegar
1	Tbsp	light soy sauce
¼	cup	white sugar (Or Splenda)
1	Tbsp	lemon juice

Nutrition Facts
Serving Size (290g)
Servings Per Container 6

Amount Per Serving

Calories 370   Calories from Fat 130

% Daily Value*

- Total Fat 15g — 23%
- Saturated Fat 1.5g — 8%
- Trans Fat 0g
- Cholesterol 0mg — 0%
- Sodium 610mg — 25%
- Total Carbohydrate 52g — 17%
- Dietary Fiber 11g — 44%
- Sugars 16g
- Protein 12g

Vitamin A 140% • Vitamin C 130%
Calcium 20% • Iron 20%

*Percent Daily Values are based on a 2,000 calorie diet. Your daily values may be higher or lower depending on your calorie needs:

	Calories:	2,000	2,500
Total Fat	Less than	65g	80g
Saturated Fat	Less than	20g	25g
Cholesterol	Less than	300mg	300mg
Sodium	Less than	2,400mg	2,400mg
Total Carbohydrate		300g	375g
Dietary Fiber		25g	30g

Calories per gram:
Fat 9 • Carbohydrate 4 • Protein 4

Preparation:

- Preheat oven to 350°F.
- Cook noodles according to directions. Rinse and drain.
- In a large bowl, mix pasta, sunflower seeds and nuts together. Spray with butter-flavored spray.
- Spread the mixture in a thin layer on a baking sheet and bake 7-10 minutes, stirring occasionally, until evenly toasted (watch closely to avoid burning!). Remove from oven and cool slightly.
- In a large bowl toss together the cooked noodles and nuts mixture with bok choy, green onion, water chestnuts, and snow peas.
- Mix remaining ingredients for dressing and pour over salad and toss to evenly coat.
- Serve immediately, or refrigerate until chilled.

Thanks to: Ginny Goodrow, Group 25

Barley Bean Salad

Barley and beans, good sources of soluble fiber, can help lower your cholesterol. Serve alone or with soup for a satisfying meal

Makes 8 servings

Ingredients:

1½	cups	cooked kidney beans
1½	cups	cooked black-eyed peas
1½	cups	cooked barley
6	Tbsp	parsley, finely chopped
1½	cups	corn kernels
1	med	tomato, diced
½	cup	red onion, diced
1	clove	garlic, minced
1	Tbsp	balsamic vinegar (or more to taste)
½	Tbsp	olive oil
		salt and pepper to taste

Nutrition Facts
Serving Size 1/8 recipe (133g)
Servings Per Container 8

Amount Per Serving

Calories 170   Calories from Fat 15

% Daily Value*

- Total Fat 1.5g — 2%
- Saturated Fat 0g — 0%
- Trans Fat 0g
- Cholesterol 0mg — 0%
- Sodium 30mg — 1%
- Total Carbohydrate 34g — 11%
- Dietary Fiber 7g — 28%
- Sugars 3g
- Protein 6g

Vitamin A 10% • Vitamin C 15%
Calcium 6% • Iron 10%

*Percent Daily Values are based on a 2,000 calorie diet. Your daily values may be higher or lower depending on your calorie needs:

		Calories:	2,000	2,500
Total Fat	Less than		65g	80g
Saturated Fat	Less than		20g	25g
Cholesterol	Less than		300mg	300mg
Sodium	Less than		2,400mg	2,400mg
Total Carbohydrate			300g	375g
Dietary Fiber			25g	30g

Calories per gram:
Fat 9 • Carbohydrate 4 • Protein 4

Preparation:

- Mix all ingredients together in a medium bowl; stir until well combined.

Category: Salads

Basic Pasta Salad

Cold pasta with non-fat yogurt-mayonnaise dressing creates lovely salads. The best pasta to use are elbow macaroni, large or small seashells, corkscrew, trombette, or mostaccioli. Use something that can hold its shape.

Makes 12-14 servings (1 cup each)

Ingredients:

¾	cup	non-fat yogurt, plain
¼	cup	non-fat mayonnaise
2	Tbsp	freshly squeezed lemon juice
⅛	tsp	pepper
1	clove	garlic, minced
1	Tbsp	basil leaves, crushed
1	Tbsp	finely chopped parsley (save a little for garnish)
16	oz	no yolk pasta, (NOTE: dill weed is also very nice added to the above mixture)

Nutrition Facts
Serving Size 1 cup (61g)
Servings Per Container 12-14

Amount Per Serving

Calories 150   Calories from Fat 10

% Daily Value*

Total Fat 1g	2%
Saturated Fat 0g	0%
Trans Fat 0g	
Cholesterol 0mg	0%
Sodium 55mg	2%
Total Carbohydrate 30g	10%
Dietary Fiber 1g	4%
Sugars 3g	
Protein 6g	

Vitamin A 2% • Vitamin C 4%
Calcium 2% • Iron 6%

*Percent Daily Values are based on a 2,000 calorie diet. Your daily values may be higher or lower depending on your calorie needs:

		2,000	2,500
Total Fat	Less than	65g	80g
Saturated Fat	Less than	20g	25g
Cholesterol	Less than	300mg	300mg
Sodium	Less than	2,400mg	2,400mg
Total Carbohydrate		300g	375g
Dietary Fiber		25g	30g

Calories per gram:
Fat 9 • Carbohydrate 4 • Protein 4

Preparation:

- Blend the yogurt, mayonnaise, lemon juice and spices together until creamy.
- Cook the pasta, according to package directions, until just tender. It is wise to undercook pasta slightly for a salad.
- Drain the pasta and rinse under cold water until completely cool. Transfer to a large bowl.
- See other recipes for ingredients to add for variations and mix gently.
- Shortly before serving, add the yogurt mixture to the pasta and gently fold until each piece is coated. It is especially important not to add the dressing too early, or the noodles will absorb the nonfat dressing and the salad will not be creamy.
- If you have any leftover salad, more dressing will need to be added to it.
- After stirring well, garnish the salad with parsley and serve.

Category: Salads

Pasta Salad Italiano

Start with **Basic Pasta Salad,** and add some Latin favorites.

Extra Ingredients:

1	cup	steamed broccoli, finely chopped
2	Tbsp	black olives, sliced
1	cup	fresh red tomatoes, chopped

Add the tomatoes just before serving. Corkscrew shaped pasta work well for this one.

Nutrition Facts
Serving Size 1 cup (95g)
Servings Per Container 12

Amount Per Serving

Calories 160   Calories from Fat 10

% Daily Value*

Total Fat 1g — 2%
  Saturated Fat 0g — 0%
  Trans Fat 0g
Cholesterol 0mg — 0%
Sodium 100mg — 4%
Total Carbohydrate 32g — 11%
  Dietary Fiber 2g — 8%
  Sugars 3g
Protein 6g

Vitamin A 6% • Vitamin C 20%
Calcium 4% • Iron 8%

*Percent Daily Values are based on a 2,000 calorie diet. Your daily values may be higher or lower depending on your calorie needs:

		2,000	2,500
Total Fat	Less than	65g	80g
Saturated Fat	Less than	20g	25g
Cholesterol	Less than	300mg	300mg
Sodium	Less than	2,400mg	2,400mg
Total Carbohydrate		300g	375g
Dietary Fiber		25g	30g

Calories per gram:
  Fat 9 • Carbohydrate 4 • Protein 4

Pasta Salad Party

Start with **Basic Pasta Salad,** and add your favorite vegetables.

Extra Ingredients:

10	oz	frozen peas, uncooked
¼	cup	chopped green onions,
⅛	tsp.	low sodium salt or less, dash of Tabasco sauce.

This is beautiful with seashell pasta. Decorate with parsley and lemon wedges.

Nutrition Facts
Serving Size 1 cup (86g)
Servings Per Container 12

Amount Per Serving

Calories 170   Calories from Fat 10

% Daily Value*

Total Fat 1g — 2%
  Saturated Fat 0g — 0%
  Trans Fat 0g
Cholesterol 0mg — 0%
Sodium 80mg — 3%
Total Carbohydrate 33g — 11%
  Dietary Fiber 3g — 12%
  Sugars 4g
Protein 7g

Vitamin A 6% • Vitamin C 20%
Calcium 4% • Iron 8%

*Percent Daily Values are based on a 2,000 calorie diet. Your daily values may be higher or lower depending on your calorie needs:

		2,000	2,500
Total Fat	Less than	65g	80g
Saturated Fat	Less than	20g	25g
Cholesterol	Less than	300mg	300mg
Sodium	Less than	2,400mg	2,400mg
Total Carbohydrate		300g	375g
Dietary Fiber		25g	30g

Calories per gram:
  Fat 9 • Carbohydrate 4 • Protein 4

Pasta Salad South of the Border

Start with **Basic Pasta Salad** (see page 96), and add some Mexican favorites.

Extra Ingredients:

10	oz	frozen corn, uncooked,
¼	cup	green pepper, chopped
¼	cup	red pepper, chopped
1	cup	carrots, grated
2		green onions, chopped
½	tsp	chili powder

This is great for barbecues.   Use a classic salad macaroni.

Nutrition Facts
Serving Size 1 cup (104g)
Servings Per Container 12

Calories 180 — Calories from Fat 10

- Total Fat 1g — 2%
- Saturated Fat 0g — 0%
- Trans Fat 0g
- Cholesterol 0mg — 0%
- Sodium 65mg — 3%
- Total Carbohydrate 36g — 12%
- Dietary Fiber 2g — 8%
- Sugars 4g
- Protein 6g

Vitamin A 35% • Vitamin C 20%
Calcium 4% • Iron 6%

Black Bean and Mango Salad

This has beautiful color and goes well as a side dish with Mexican food.

Yield: 4 servings

Ingredients:

½	cup	cooked black beans
1½	cups	mango, diced
1	Tbsp	or more lime juice

Preparation:

- Mix all ingredients together.
- Serve cold.

Nutrition Facts
Serving Size 1/4 recipe (130g)
Servings Per Container 4

Calories 120 — Calories from Fat 5

- Total Fat 0.5g — 1%
- Saturated Fat 0g — 0%
- Trans Fat 0g
- Cholesterol 0mg — 0%
- Sodium 0mg — 0%
- Total Carbohydrate 25g — 8%
- Dietary Fiber 7g — 28%
- Sugars 8g
- Protein 6g

Vitamin A 15% • Vitamin C 40%
Calcium 2% • Iron 8%

Black Bean Salad

Avocados are a good source of monounsaturated fat and vitamin E.

6 servings

Ingredients:

2	Tbsp	lime juice
1	Tbsp	olive oil
½	tsp	cumin
3	Tbsp	cilantro, finely chopped
1½	cups	black beans, cooked
3	med	tomatoes, chopped
¼	cup	green onion, chopped
2		avocados, chopped
½	cup	non-fat feta cheese

Preparation:

- Mix together lime juice, olive oil, cumin and cilantro as dressing; set aside.
- Combine beans, tomatoes, green onion, and avocados and toss with dressing.
- Just before serving add cheese.

Thanks to: Laurie Van Crider, group 29

Category: Salads

Nutrition Facts

Serving Size 1/6 recipe (194g)
Servings Per Container 6

Amount Per Serving

Calories 210   Calories from Fat 130

	% Daily Value*
Total Fat 14g	22%
Saturated Fat 3g	15%
Trans Fat 0g	
Cholesterol 5mg	2%
Sodium 170mg	7%
Total Carbohydrate 17g	6%
Dietary Fiber 8g	32%
Sugars 3g	
Protein 7g	

Vitamin A 6% • Vitamin C 35%
Calcium 6% • Iron 8%

*Percent Daily Values are based on a 2,000 calorie diet. Your daily values may be higher or lower depending on your calorie needs:

		Calories:	2,000	2,500
Total Fat		Less than	65g	80g
Saturated Fat		Less than	20g	25g
Cholesterol		Less than	300mg	300mg
Sodium		Less than	2,400mg	2,400mg
Total Carbohydrate			300g	375g
Dietary Fiber			25g	30g

Calories per gram:
 Fat 9 • Carbohydrate 4 • Protein 4

Broccoli Salad

Always a favorite at potlucks!

Makes 8 servings

Ingredients:

Dressing:

1	cup	fat-free mayonnaise
⅓	cup	sugar or Splenda
⅓	cup	flavored vinegar -- red wine, raspberry or pomegranate

Salad:

2	cups	raw broccoli florets
1		red onion, chopped
1		red apple, chopped
2		mandarin oranges, peeled and sectioned
½	cup	dried cranberries

Preparation:
- Mix together dressing ingredients.
- Combine salad ingredients and toss with dressing.

Thanks to: Linda Paumer

Cateogory: Salads

Nutrition Facts

Serving Size 1/8 recipe (147g)
Servings Per Container 8

Amount Per Serving

Calories 120   Calories from Fat 10

% Daily Value*

Total Fat 1g	2%
Saturated Fat 0g	0%
Trans Fat 0g	
Cholesterol 5mg	2%
Sodium 250mg	10%
Total Carbohydrate 29g	10%
Dietary Fiber 3g	12%
Sugars 23g	
Protein 1g	

Vitamin A 10% • Vitamin C 45%
Calcium 2% • Iron 2%

*Percent Daily Values are based on a 2,000 calorie diet. Your daily values may be higher or lower depending on your calorie needs:

	Calories:	2,000	2,500
Total Fat	Less than	65g	80g
Saturated Fat	Less than	20g	25g
Cholesterol	Less than	300mg	300mg
Sodium	Less than	2,400mg	2,400mg
Total Carbohydrate		300g	375g
Dietary Fiber		25g	30g

Calories per gram:
Fat 9 • Carbohydrate 4 • Protein 4

Citrus Pasta Salad

The addition of citrus and fruit contributes to the vitamin C content.

Makes 12 servings

Ingredients:

12	oz	frozen orange juice concentrate with pulp
1	tsp	orange zest (grate off only colored part of rind)
3	Tbsp	sugar-free maple syrup
¼	cup	orange flavored dried cranberries
1	tsp	arrowroot
12	oz	pasta, e.g. spiral noodles, or bow ties
1	can	mandarin orange segments, drained
1	cup	mango, cut in bite-sized pieces
¼	cup	orange flavored dried cranberries

Nutrition Facts

Serving Size 1/12 recipe (106g)
Servings Per Container 12

Amount Per Serving

Calories 190 Calories from Fat 5

% Daily Value*

Total Fat 0g — 0%
 Saturated Fat 0g — 0%
 Trans Fat 0g
Cholesterol 0mg — 0%
Sodium 0mg — 0%
Total Carbohydrate 43g — 14%
 Dietary Fiber 2g — 8%
 Sugars 21g
Protein 4g

Vitamin A 2% • Vitamin C 70%
Calcium 0% • Iron 6%

*Percent Daily Values are based on a 2,000 calorie diet. Your daily values may be higher or lower depending on your calorie needs:

		Calories:	2,000	2,500
Total Fat		Less than	65g	80g
Saturated Fat		Less than	20g	25g
Cholesterol		Less than	300mg	300mg
Sodium		Less than	2,400mg	2,400mg
Total Carbohydrate			300g	375g
Dietary Fiber			25g	30g

Calories per gram:
 Fat 9 • Carbohydrate 4 • Protein 4

Preparation:

- Heat orange juice with orange zest, syrup and dried cranberries in a saucepan over medium heat, allowing the volume to reduce slightly. When partially cool, add arrowroot to desired thickness. Cool overnight to develop flavor.
- When ready to prepare, cook pasta, drain and cool under running water. In a large bowl place the pasta, marinade, mandarin orange segments, mango, and additional dried cranberries. Allow to marinate for several hours.
- Note: put all in gallon ziplock bag to more easily mix the ingredients for marinading.

Thanks to: Mary Davis, Group 32

Category: Salad, Pasta

Confetti Bean Salad

Similar to Cowboy Caviar recipe, but less time consuming to prepare.

Makes 10 small servings ~ (3/4 cup each).

Ingredients:

1½	cups	kidney beans, cooked
1½	cups	garbanzo beans, cooked
1½	cups	tomatoes, diced
1½	cups	green peas, cooked
1½	cups	corn kernels
½	cup	onion, chopped
½	cup	green pepper, chopped

Dressing:

4	Tbsp	red wine vinegar or cider vinegar
1	Tbsp	olive oil
1	clove	garlic, minced
½	tsp	salt
¼	tsp	pepper

Preparation:

- In a small bowl, combine dressing ingredients and blend well.
- In a large bowl, combine the salad ingredients.
- Pour dressing over bean mixture. Toss gently to coat.
- Cover and refrigerate for at least 4 hours.

Double the serving size for main dish.

Thanks to: Ginny Goodrow, Group 25

Category: Salads

Nutrition Facts

Serving Size 3/4 cup (141g)
Servings Per Container 10

Amount Per Serving

Calories 130 — Calories from Fat 20

% Daily Value*

Total Fat 2.5g	4%
Saturated Fat 0g	0%
Trans Fat 0g	
Cholesterol 0mg	0%
Sodium 125mg	5%
Total Carbohydrate 22g	7%
Dietary Fiber 6g	24%
Sugars 4g	
Protein 6g	

Vitamin A 8% • Vitamin C 35%
Calcium 4% • Iron 10%

*Percent Daily Values are based on a 2,000 calorie diet. Your daily values may be higher or lower depending on your calorie needs:

		Calories:	2,000	2,500
Total Fat	Less than		65g	80g
Saturated Fat	Less than		20g	25g
Cholesterol	Less than		300mg	300mg
Sodium	Less than		2,400mg	2,400mg
Total Carbohydrate			300g	375g
Dietary Fiber			25g	30g

Calories per gram:
Fat 9 • Carbohydrate 4 • Protein 4

Cool Green Fruit Salad

A fun twist to your usual fruit salad.

Makes 4 servings

Ingredients:

1		honeydew melon, cubes or melon balls
4	oz	seedless green grapes
2		kiwi, peeled and chopped
1		star fruit (optional), thinly sliced
1		Granny Smith apple, unpeeled, thinly sliced
½	cup	sparkling white sugar free grape juice
1	med	lime: prepare juice and grate peel

Preparation:

- Place all fruit into a bowl, sprinkle with lime juice; toss. Chill.
- Just before serving, spoon grape juice over fruit.
- Garnish with grated lime peel.

Category: Salads

Nutrition Facts

Serving Size 1/4 recipe (470g)
Servings Per Container 4

Amount Per Serving

Calories 200 — Calories from Fat 5

% Daily Value*

Total Fat 1g	2%
Saturated Fat 0g	0%
Trans Fat 0g	
Cholesterol 0mg	0%
Sodium 60mg	3%
Total Carbohydrate 52g	17%
Dietary Fiber 5g	20%
Sugars 44g	
Protein 3g	

Vitamin A 4% • Vitamin C 170%
Calcium 4% • Iron 4%

*Percent Daily Values are based on a 2,000 calorie diet. Your daily values may be higher or lower depending on your calorie needs:

	Calories:	2,000	2,500
Total Fat	Less than	65g	80g
Saturated Fat	Less than	20g	25g
Cholesterol	Less than	300mg	300mg
Sodium	Less than	2,400mg	2,400mg
Total Carbohydrate		300g	375g
Dietary Fiber		25g	30g

Calories per gram:
Fat 9 • Carbohydrate 4 • Protein 4

Cool Meal Potato Salad

A great, cool meal for a hot summer day.

Makes ~ 4 servings

Ingredients:

3		potatoes, peeled, cut into ½ inch cubes
2		hard-boiled eggs (discard yolks)
2	ribs	celery, diced
1		sweet pickle, chopped fine
1	Tbsp	red wine or vinegar
1	tsp	dry onion (or sliced green onion)
		seasoned salt (optional)

Dressing:

½	cup	non-fat mayonnaise
1	tsp	Dijonnaise (or other mustard)
½	tsp	horseradish

Preparation:

- Boil potatoes until tender. Meanwhile put chopped celery and pickle into a small container and refrigerate.
- When potatoes are done, put them in a 1½ quart bowl. Sprinkle with red wine or vinegar and onion. Toss gently together, cover with plastic wrap.
- When bowl is cool, refrigerate until cold.
- When potatoes are cold, chop egg whites and add them with celery and pickle to potatoes. Toss together and add a touch of seasoned salt.
- Dressing: blend together mayonnaise, mustard and horseradish.
- Add the dressing to the potato mixture, sprinkle with paprika, cover bowl with plastic wrap. Return to refrigerator until ready to serve.

Suggestion: Serve this on a hot day with sliced tomatoes, crooked neck squash and zucchini, whole wheat rolls and non-fat chocolate loaf cake.

Thanks to: Lew and Dorothy Watkins (Group 2)

Category: Salads

COPPER CARROT PENNIES

Pretty served in a glass bowl.

Makes 10 servings

Ingredients:

Dressing:

1	can	tomato soup
2	tsp	olive oil
½	cup	water
1	cup	sugar
¾	cup	vinegar
1	tsp	mustard
1	tsp	Worcestershire sauce
		salt and pepper to taste

Salad:

2	lbs	carrots, sliced into 'pennies'
1		green pepper, sliced in rings or smaller
1		onion, sliced in rings or smaller

Preparation:

- Prepare dressing by mixing ingredients together in bowl.
- Boil carrots in salted water until tender (perhaps 5 minutes or so). Drain and cool.
- Layer the carrots with the green pepper and onion in a serving bowl.
- Pour dressing over vegetables.
- Cover and refrigerate.
- Serve cold.

Note: Keeps well. May add cherry tomatoes

Thanks to: Mary Dalzell, Group 22

Category: Salads

Nutrition Facts

Serving Size 1/10 recipe (182g)
Servings Per Container 10

Amount Per Serving

Calories 150	Calories from Fat 10

% Daily Value*

Total Fat 1g	2%
Saturated Fat 0g	0%
Trans Fat 0g	
Cholesterol 0mg	0%
Sodium 190mg	8%
Total Carbohydrate 35g	12%
Dietary Fiber 3g	12%
Sugars 28g	
Protein 1g	

Vitamin A 310%	•	Vitamin C 15%
Calcium 4%	•	Iron 4%

*Percent Daily Values are based on a 2,000 calorie diet. Your daily values may be higher or lower depending on your calorie needs:

		Calories:	2,000	2,500
Total Fat		Less than	65g	80g
Saturated Fat		Less than	20g	25g
Cholesterol		Less than	300mg	300mg
Sodium		Less than	2,400mg	2,400mg
Total Carbohydrate			300g	375g
Dietary Fiber			25g	30g

Calories per gram:
Fat 9 • Carbohydrate 4 • Protein 4

Couscous and Black Bean Salad

Couscous is a quick cooking grain and is versatile as a hot side dish or salad. Choose whole wheat couscous for more fiber.

Makes 4 servings. 1 cup each

Ingredients:

1	large	orange
⅛	tsp	salt
⅔	cup	couscous
1	cup	black beans, cooked
½	cup	red bell pepper, chopped
¼	cup	green onion, chopped
2	Tbsp	fresh parsley, chopped
1	Tbsp	seasoned rice vinegar
1½	tsp	olive oil
¼	tsp	ground cumin

Preparation:

- Grate peel and squeeze juice from orange. Set aside ¼ cup juice.
- To rest of juice, add enough water to make 1 cup.
- Put this liquid in medium saucepan with salt. Bring to a boil and stir in uncooked couscous.
- Remove from heat; cover and let stand 5 minutes.
- Fluff with fork and cool slightly.
- Stir in orange rind, beans, bell pepper, green onion, and parsley.
- Combine reserved orange juice with rice vinegar, oil and cumin for dressing.
- Mix with couscous mixture, tossing well.
- Store in airtight container in refrigerator.

Thanks to: Esther Weinstein, group 35

Category: Rice and Grains, Beans, Salads

Nutrition Facts

Serving Size about 1 cup (125g)
Servings Per Container 4

Amount Per Serving

Calories 190   Calories from Fat 20

	% Daily Value*
Total Fat 2g	3%
Saturated Fat 0g	0%
Trans Fat 0g	
Cholesterol 0mg	0%
Sodium 130mg	5%
Total Carbohydrate 37g	12%
Dietary Fiber 4g	16%
Sugars 5g	
Protein 7g	

Vitamin A 15%	•	Vitamin C 70%
Calcium 4%	•	Iron 8%

*Percent Daily Values are based on a 2,000 calorie diet. Your daily values may be higher or lower depending on your calorie needs:

	Calories:	2,000	2,500
Total Fat	Less than	65g	80g
Saturated Fat	Less than	20g	25g
Cholesterol	Less than	300mg	300mg
Sodium	Less than	2,400mg	2,400mg
Total Carbohydrate		300g	375g
Dietary Fiber		25g	30g

Calories per gram:
  Fat 9 • Carbohydrate 4 • Protein 4

Cowboy Caviar

Can be eaten either as a salad, or as an appetizer.

Makes 6 servings

Ingredients:

Dressing:

2	Tbsp	red wine vinegar
2	tsp	hot sauce (Tabasco)
½	tsp	olive oil
1	clove	garlic, minced
⅛	tsp	pepper

Salad:

1½	cups	black-eyed peas, cooked
1½	cups	corn kernels
⅔	cup	green onions, thinly sliced
⅔	cup	fresh cilantro, chopped
1½	cups	tomatoes, chopped
2	cups	cabbage, finely shredded
		salt to taste.

Nutrition Facts

Serving Size 1/6 recipe (175g)
Servings Per Container 6

Amount Per Serving

Calories 100   Calories from Fat 5

% Daily Value*

Total Fat 0g	0%
Saturated Fat 0g	0%
Trans Fat 0g	
Cholesterol 0mg	0%
Sodium 150mg	6%
Total Carbohydrate 20g	7%
Dietary Fiber 4g	16%
Sugars 6g	
Protein 3g	

Vitamin A 10% • Vitamin C 35%
Calcium 10% • Iron 6%

*Percent Daily Values are based on a 2,000 calorie diet. Your daily values may be higher or lower depending on your calorie needs:

	Calories:	2,000	2,500
Total Fat	Less than	65g	80g
Saturated Fat	Less than	20g	25g
Cholesterol	Less than	300mg	300mg
Sodium	Less than	2,400mg	2,400mg
Total Carbohydrate		300g	375g
Dietary Fiber		25g	30g

Calories per gram:
Fat 9 • Carbohydrate 4 • Protein 4

Preparation:

- In a small bowl, combine dressing ingredients and blend well.
- In a large bowl, combine the salad ingredients.
- Add dressing and toss gently to coat.
- To serve as an appetizer, eliminate the cabbage and eat with baked tortilla chips.

Thanks to: Surang Robinson, Group 18 and Sunset Magazine

Category: Salads

Cranberry Raspberry Jello with Pineapple

Walnuts add considerably to the fat content so take that into consideration when serving and keeping track of added fats.

Makes 18 servings.

Ingredients:

2	pkgs	raspberry gelatin (3 oz each)
1 ¼	cups	boiling water
1	can	crushed pineapple with juice (20 oz)
1	can	whole cranberry sauce (16 oz)
½	cup	chopped walnuts (optional)

Topping:

1	cup	non-fat sour cream
8	oz	non-fat cream cheese

Preparation:

- Follow directions on package, mix gelatin with water, pineapple, cranberry sauce and walnuts.
- Leave in mixing bowl or pour into rectangular pan or mold(s) if desired.
- Refrigerate until set.
- Prepare topping by mixing sour cream and cheese together while warming slightly.
- Topping may be spread on gelatin, then cut into squares OR spooned over individual servings.

Nutrition Facts
Serving Size 1/18 (116g)
Servings Per Container 18

Amount Per Serving

Calories 130   Calories from Fat 20

% Daily Value*

Total Fat 2.5g	4%
Saturated Fat 0g	0%
Trans Fat 0g	
Cholesterol 5mg	2%
Sodium 150mg	6%
Total Carbohydrate 26g	9%
Dietary Fiber 1g	4%
Sugars 20g	
Protein 4g	

Vitamin A 2% • Vitamin C 6%
Calcium 8% • Iron 2%

*Percent Daily Values are based on a 2,000 calorie diet. Your daily values may be higher or lower depending on your calorie needs:

		Calories:	2,000	2,500
Total Fat	Less than		65g	80g
Saturated Fat	Less than		20g	25g
Cholesterol	Less than		300mg	300mg
Sodium	Less than		2,400mg	2,400mg
Total Carbohydrate			300g	375g
Dietary Fiber			25g	30g

Calories per gram:
  Fat 9 • Carbohydrate 4 • Protein 4

Category: Salads

CRANBERRY VELVET SALAD

Just like mom used to make, but without the fat. A great holiday dish.

Makes 10 servings.

Ingredients:

1	large	package raspberry gelatin
2½	cups	hot water
1 lb	can	whole cranberry sauce
1	cup	non-fat sour cream

Dressing:

1	cup	non-fat sour cream
¼	cup	powdered sugar
1	tsp	vanilla extract

Preparation:

- Dissolve gelatin in water and chill until slightly thickened.
- Fold in cranberry sauce and sour cream.
- After re-setting, mix dressing and pour over gelatin.

Category: Salads

Nutrition Facts

Serving Size 1/10 recipe (176g)
Servings Per Container 10

Amount Per Serving

Calories 180 — Calories from Fat 0

% Daily Value*

Total Fat 0g	0%
Saturated Fat 0g	0%
Trans Fat 0g	
Cholesterol 5mg	2%
Sodium 150mg	6%
Total Carbohydrate 43g	14%
Dietary Fiber 1g	4%
Sugars 29g	
Protein 3g	

Vitamin A 2% • Vitamin C 0%

Calcium 6% • Iron 0%

*Percent Daily Values are based on a 2,000 calorie diet. Your daily values may be higher or lower depending on your calorie needs:

		Calories:	2,000	2,500
Total Fat	Less than		65g	80g
Saturated Fat	Less than		20g	25g
Cholesterol	Less than		300mg	300mg
Sodium	Less than		2,400mg	2,400mg
Total Carbohydrate			300g	375g
Dietary Fiber			25g	30g

Calories per gram:
  Fat 9 • Carbohydrate 4 • Protein 4

FANCY COLESLAW

Modifying the 'creamy' dressing with non-fat ingredients allows you to enjoy this traditional favorite without the extra fat.

Makes 12 servings

Ingredients:

1		cabbage, finely chopped
¾	cup	fat-free sour cream
¾	cup	fat-free mayonnaise
2	tsp	celery seed or poppy seed
½	cup	raisins or currants
1	tsp	freshly squeezed lemon juice or 2 tsp vinegar
½	cup	onions, chopped
4	tsp	chives, chopped
2	tsp	parsley, finely chopped
2		apples, cut into small pieces
4		jalapeno peppers, chopped
½	cup	green pepper with seeds, chopped
½	cup	red pepper with seeds, chopped
½	cup	scallions, chopped
½	cup	green olives, quartered (optional)
½	cup	carrots, finely sliced
1	tsp	dry mustard
½	cup	corn, freshly steamed and cooled
½	cup	celery, chopped
12-15		green grapes, halved
		red pepper, chopped, for garnish (optional)
		grape leaves

Nutrition Facts

Serving Size 1/12 recipe (209g)
Servings Per Container 12

Amount Per Serving

Calories 120 — Calories from Fat 15

% Daily Value*

Total Fat 1.5g	2%
Saturated Fat 0g	0%
Trans Fat 0g	
Cholesterol 5mg	2%
Sodium 200mg	8%
Total Carbohydrate 25g	8%
Dietary Fiber 5g	20%
Sugars 13g	
Protein 3g	

Vitamin A 40% • Vitamin C 90%
Calcium 10% • Iron 6%

*Percent Daily Values are based on a 2,000 calorie diet. Your daily values may be higher or lower depending on your calorie needs:

		Calories:	2,000	2,500
Total Fat	Less than		65g	80g
Saturated Fat	Less than		20g	25g
Cholesterol	Less than		300mg	300mg
Sodium	Less than		2,400mg	2,400mg
Total Carbohydrate			300g	375g
Dietary Fiber			25g	30g

Calories per gram:
  Fat 9 • Carbohydrate 4 • Protein 4

Preparation:

- Add all ingredients to the chopped cabbage. Mix well.
- Garnish with chopped red pepper, if desired.
- Serve on grape leaves.

Thanks to: Ray Tolleson

Category: Salads

GARBANZO AND POMEGRANATE SALAD

When pomegranates are in season, get several, remove the arils and freeze them for future recipes.

Makes 8 servings

Dressing:

1	tsp	cumin
⅓	cup	lime or lemon juice
1	Tbsp	sugar
1	Tbsp	fresh cilantro, chopped
¼	tsp	cayenne pepper

Salad:

1½	cups	pomegranate arils
3	cups	garbanzo beans, cooked
1½	cups	cucumber, diced
½	cup	mild onion, chopped

Preparation:

- Mix together dressing ingredients.
- Combine salad ingredients and toss with dressing.
- Add salt and pepper to taste.

Thanks to: Jill Burns, R.D.

Cooking your own beans dramatically improves the sodium content of these recipes.

Nutrition Facts

Serving Size 1/8 recipe (114g)
Servings Per Container 8

Amount Per Serving

Calories 110   Calories from Fat 15

% Daily Value*

Total Fat 1.5g	2%
Saturated Fat 0g	0%
Trans Fat 0g	
Cholesterol 0mg	0%
Sodium 5mg	0%
Total Carbohydrate 21g	7%
Dietary Fiber 5g	20%
Sugars 8g	
Protein 5g	

Vitamin A 0%	•	Vitamin C 15%
Calcium 4%	•	Iron 8%

*Percent Daily Values are based on a 2,000 calorie diet. Your daily values may be higher or lower depending on your calorie needs:

		Calories:	2,000	2,500
Total Fat		Less than	65g	80g
Saturated Fat		Less than	20g	25g
Cholesterol		Less than	300mg	300mg
Sodium		Less than	2,400mg	2,400mg
Total Carbohydrate			300g	375g
Dietary Fiber			25g	30g

Calories per gram:
    Fat 9 • Carbohydrate 4 • Protein 4

Category: Salads

Garbanzo Salad

This is a good, fiber filled side dish.

Makes 10 servings ~ ½ cup each

Ingredients:

1	cup	red onion, finely minced
1	tsp	dried thyme leaves
½	cup	sweet red pepper, chopped
½	cup	dark raisins
3	cups	garbanzo beans, cooked
2	tsp	olive oil (optional)
¼	cup	seasoned rice vinegar
¼	tsp	salt

Preparation:

- Combine all ingredients and refrigerate for 4-6 hours or overnight. Stir once to distribute the marinade.
- Remove from refrigerator for about 1 hour before serving to maximize the flavor.

Category: Salads

Nutrition Facts

Serving Size 1/10 recipe (about 1/2 cup) (80g)
Servings Per Container 10

Amount Per Serving

Calories 120   Calories from Fat 20

% Daily Value*

Total Fat 2g	3%
Saturated Fat 0g	0%
Trans Fat 0g	
Cholesterol 0mg	0%
Sodium 140mg	6%
Total Carbohydrate 21g	7%
Dietary Fiber 4g	16%
Sugars 9g	
Protein 4g	

Vitamin A 4%	•	Vitamin C 20%
Calcium 4%	•	Iron 8%

*Percent Daily Values are based on a 2,000 calorie diet. Your daily values may be higher or lower depending on your calorie needs:

		Calories:	2,000	2,500
Total Fat	Less than		65g	80g
Saturated Fat	Less than		20g	25g
Cholesterol	Less than		300mg	300mg
Sodium	Less than		2,400mg	2,400mg
Total Carbohydrate			300g	375g
Dietary Fiber			25g	30g

Calories per gram:
  Fat 9 • Carbohydrate 4 • Protein 4

Ginger Noodle Salad

Just like your favorite restaurant Asian salad. Using whole wheat noodles adds fiber and the light soy sauce reduces the sodium.

Makes 6 servings

Ingredients:

½	lb	whole wheat noodles, cooked, rinsed, drained
¼	cup	light soy sauce
3	cups	broccoli, steamed, drained
1		red bell pepper, cut into strips
3	cups	mung bean sprouts
2		green onions, thinly sliced

Dressing:

1	tsp	ground ginger
1	tsp	sugar (optional)
1	Tbsp	rice wine vinegar
1	tsp	crushed red pepper
1	tsp	sesame oil (optional)
1	tsp	water

Preparation:

- Combine the cooked noodles with soy sauce; refrigerate for about 2 hours.
- Mix the dressing ingredients together.
- To serve, toss the noodles with the dressing, evenly coat the noodles.
- Add the vegetables and toss the salad.
- Serve warm or cold.

Category: Salads

Nutrition Facts

Serving Size 1/6 recipe (182g)
Servings Per Container 6

Amount Per Serving

Calories 200   Calories from Fat 20

% Daily Value*

Total Fat 2g	3%
Saturated Fat 0g	0%
Trans Fat 0g	
Cholesterol 0mg	0%
Sodium 380mg	16%
Total Carbohydrate 39g	13%
Dietary Fiber 6g	24%
Sugars 8g	
Protein 9g	

Vitamin A 45%	Vitamin C 130%
Calcium 4%	Iron 10%

*Percent Daily Values are based on a 2,000 calorie diet. Your daily values may be higher or lower depending on your calorie needs:

		Calories:	2,000	2,500
Total Fat	Less than		65g	80g
Saturated Fat	Less than		20g	25g
Cholesterol	Less than		300mg	300mg
Sodium	Less than		2,400mg	2,400mg
Total Carbohydrate			300g	375g
Dietary Fiber			25g	30g

Calories per gram:
 Fat 9 • Carbohydrate 4 • Protein 4

GLORIFIED CARROT RAISIN SALAD

Exact amounts of each ingredient are not critical and everyone has individual likes and dislikes and some ingredients you might want in different amounts than those specified. Use your imagination!

Makes 8 servings

Ingredients:

2	cups	carrots, finely sliced
1		green or red pepper, sliced
1	cup	broccoli florets
1	cup	celery, sliced
1	cup	fresh snow peas
1	cup	fresh bean sprouts
½	cup	raisins (soak in 2 Tbsp orange juice to soften)
¼	cup	dried apricots, cut in half
1		sweet apple, diced, unpeeled
1		mandarin orange, sectioned

Dressing:

2	Tbsp	honey
2	Tbsp	frozen orange juice concentrate, undiluted

Preparation:

- Place fruits and vegetables in large bowl.
- To make the dressing, use equal parts honey and orange juice concentrate mixed together.
- Pour the dressing on fruits and vegetables and mix.

Nutrition Facts

Serving Size 1/8 recipe (159g)
Servings Per Container 8

Amount Per Serving

Calories 110   Calories from Fat 5

% Daily Value*

Total Fat 0g	0%
Saturated Fat 0g	0%
Trans Fat 0g	
Cholesterol 0mg	0%
Sodium 40mg	2%
Total Carbohydrate 28g	9%
Dietary Fiber 4g	16%
Sugars 20g	
Protein 2g	

Vitamin A 100%	•	Vitamin C 70%
Calcium 4%	•	Iron 4%

*Percent Daily Values are based on a 2,000 calorie diet. Your daily values may be higher or lower depending on your calorie needs:

		Calories:	2,000	2,500
Total Fat	Less than		65g	80g
Saturated Fat	Less than		20g	25g
Cholesterol	Less than		300mg	300mg
Sodium	Less than		2,400mg	2,400mg
Total Carbohydrate			300g	375g
Dietary Fiber			25g	30g

Calories per gram:
Fat 9 • Carbohydrate 4 • Protein 4

Note: If desired, pour a small amount of lemon juice on apples to prevent browning

Category: Salads

Hearty Barley Salad

The mixture of fruits and vegetables make this dish even more nutritious.

Makes 12 servings ~ ¾ cup each

Ingredients:

2	cups	water
1	cup	barley, uncooked
1½	cups	black beans, cooked
1	can	pineapple chunks in juice, drained (8 oz)
1½	cups	broccoli florets
1	cup	sweet red pepper, chopped
1	cup	green pepper, chopped
1	cup	cantaloupe, cubed
½	cup	celery, chopped

Dressing:

⅓	cup	unsweetened pineapple juice
¼	cup	lime juice
¼	cup	honey
2	Tbsp	Dijon mustard
1½	Tbsp	light soy sauce
¼	tsp	garlic powder
⅛	tsp	dried crushed red pepper

Nutrition Facts

Serving Size 3/4 cup (169g)
Servings Per Container 12

Amount Per Serving

Calories 150   Calories from Fat 5

% Daily Value*

- Total Fat 0g — 0%
- Saturated Fat 0g — 0%
- Trans Fat 0g
- Cholesterol 0mg — 0%
- Sodium 135mg — 6%
- Total Carbohydrate 33g — 11%
- Dietary Fiber 5g — 20%
- Sugars 14g
- Protein 4g

Vitamin A 25% • Vitamin C 80%
Calcium 2% • Iron 6%

*Percent Daily Values are based on a 2,000 calorie diet. Your daily values may be higher or lower depending on your calorie needs:

		Calories:	2,000	2,500
Total Fat		Less than	65g	80g
Saturated Fat		Less than	20g	25g
Cholesterol		Less than	300mg	300mg
Sodium		Less than	2,400mg	2,400mg
Total Carbohydrate			300g	375g
Dietary Fiber			25g	30g

Calories per gram:
Fat 9 • Carbohydrate 4 • Protein 4

Preparation:

- In a medium saucepan, bring water to a boil.
- Add barley, cover, reduce heat, and simmer 30-40 minutes or until barley is tender.
- Remove from heat. Let stand, covered for 5 minutes.
- Then place saucepan with barley in a pan of cold water, and let cool to room temperature.
- Drain barley and combine with other ingredients.
- Mix dressing ingredients, stirring well with a wire whisk.
- Toss lightly with barley. Mix to coat.

Thanks to: Laurie Crider-Vanpal, Group 27

Category: Salads, Rice and Grains

Kasha Southwest Salad

Kasha are buckwheat groats, roasted to bring out a delicious flavor and aroma. It is available in the supermarket with other grains and cereals.

Makes 8 servings

Ingredients:

1	tsp	olive oil
¾	cup	yellow onion, minced
¾	cup	celery, diced
2	cloves	garlic, minced
1½	tsp	ground coriander
1½	tsp	cumin
1	tsp	chili powder
3	cups	kasha, cooked
1½	cups	kidney beans, cooked
1½	cups	tomatoes, chopped
½	cup	corn kernels, cooked
2	Tbsp	parsley, chopped
2	Tbsp	cilantro, chopped
1	jar	salsa, such as "Pace Picante" sauce (16 oz)

Preparation:

- Heat oil in pan. Add onion, celery and garlic.
- Cook about 5 minutes.
- Remove to a large bowl.
- Stir in coriander, cumin, and chili powder.
- Add cooked kasha, kidney beans, tomatoes, corn, parsley and cilantro.
- Mix in salsa until you get desired taste and texture.
- Any remaining sauce can be served on the side.

Note: Concerns with this recipe and sodium content can be addressed by using fresh made salsa rather than jarred.

Thanks to: Mary Trost

Category: Salads

Nutrition Facts

Serving Size 1/8 recipe (238g)
Servings Per Container 8

Amount Per Serving

Calories 140 — Calories from Fat 10

% Daily Value*

Total Fat 1.5g	2%
Saturated Fat 0g	0%
Trans Fat 0g	
Cholesterol 0mg	0%
Sodium 470mg	20%
Total Carbohydrate 28g	9%
Dietary Fiber 8g	32%
Sugars 5g	
Protein 6g	

Vitamin A 15% • Vitamin C 15%
Calcium 4% • Iron 8%

*Percent Daily Values are based on a 2,000 calorie diet. Your daily values may be higher or lower depending on your calorie needs:

	Calories:	2,000	2,500
Total Fat	Less than	65g	80g
Saturated Fat	Less than	20g	25g
Cholesterol	Less than	300mg	300mg
Sodium	Less than	2,400mg	2,400mg
Total Carbohydrate		300g	375g
Dietary Fiber		25g	30g

Calories per gram:
Fat 9 • Carbohydrate 4 • Protein 4

LENTIL SALAD

Lentils aren't just for soup!

Makes 14 servings (½ cup each)

Ingredients:

1½	cups	lentils, uncooked
4	cups	water
2		onions, sliced
1		whole clove
2		bay leaves
2	cloves	garlic, crushed
1	tsp	Tabasco sauce
1	Tbsp	olive oil
½	cup	red wine vinegar
2	cups	celery, chopped
½	cup	fresh parsley, chopped
½	cup	onion, chopped
2		tomatoes, cut in wedges
		salad greens

Nutrition Facts
Serving Size 1/2 cup (95g)
Servings Per Container 14

Amount Per Serving

Calories 100   Calories from Fat 15

% Daily Value*

Total Fat 1.5g	2%
Saturated Fat 0g	0%
Trans Fat 0g	
Cholesterol 0mg	0%
Sodium 20mg	1%
Total Carbohydrate 16g	5%
Dietary Fiber 3g	12%
Sugars 2g	
Protein 6g	

Vitamin A 6% • Vitamin C 15%
Calcium 2% • Iron 10%

*Percent Daily Values are based on a 2,000 calorie diet. Your daily values may be higher or lower depending on your calorie needs:

		Calories:	2,000	2,500
Total Fat	Less than		65g	80g
Saturated Fat	Less than		20g	25g
Cholesterol	Less than		300mg	300mg
Sodium	Less than		2,400mg	2,400mg
Total Carbohydrate			300g	375g
Dietary Fiber			25g	30g

Calories per gram:
Fat 9 • Carbohydrate 4 • Protein 4

Preparation:

- In a large saucepan combine lentils, water, onion slices, clove, bay leaves, garlic, salt and ½ tsp Tabasco sauce.
- Bring to boil, reduce heat and simmer, covered for 30 minutes until lentils are tender. Drain.
- Add oil, vinegar and remaining ½ tsp Tabasco sauce.
- Mix well and let cool.
- After chilling, add celery, parsley and onions.
- Cover and chill several hours.
- Turn into bowl lined with cold greens or onto individual serving plates lined with lettuce.

Source: *Adapted from New American Diet*

Category: Salads

MACARONI SALAD

Very traditional summer favorite.

4 servings

Ingredients:

1	cup	dry small elbow macaroni, cooked and cooled
2	ribs	celery, diced
1	small	onion, diced
¼	med	green pepper, chopped
1		sweet pickle, diced fine
1		boiled egg, chopped (discard yolk)
6		stuffed olives, sliced
1	oz	non-fat cheddar cheese, cut into very small cubes.

Dressing:

½	cup	non-fat mayonnaise
1	tsp	Dijon mustard
½	tsp	horseradish

Preparation:

- Mix macaroni with celery, onion, green pepper, sweet pickle, egg white, olives and cheese.
- Mix dressing ingredients thoroughly and add to salad.
- Add a little seasoned salt if desired.

Thanks to: Lew and Dorothy Watkins, Group 2

Category: Pasta

Nutrition Facts

Serving Size 1/4 recipe (151g)
Servings Per Container 4

Amount Per Serving

Calories 170   Calories from Fat 25

% Daily Value*

Total Fat 2.5g	4%
Saturated Fat 0g	0%
Trans Fat 0g	
Cholesterol 5mg	2%
Sodium 510mg	21%
Total Carbohydrate 30g	10%
Dietary Fiber 3g	12%
Sugars 6g	
Protein 7g	

Vitamin A 6%	•	Vitamin C 20%
Calcium 10%	•	Iron 6%

*Percent Daily Values are based on a 2,000 calorie diet. Your daily values may be higher or lower depending on your calorie needs:

		Calories:	2,000	2,500
Total Fat		Less than	65g	80g
Saturated Fat		Less than	20g	25g
Cholesterol		Less than	300mg	300mg
Sodium		Less than	2,400mg	2,400mg
Total Carbohydrate			300g	375g
Dietary Fiber			25g	30g

Calories per gram:
Fat 9 • Carbohydrate 4 • Protein 4

Oriental Cabbage Slaw

The addition of strawberries sweetens this tasty dish. It is a vitamin C powerhouse!

8 servings

Salad Ingredients:

1		cabbage, chopped
1	lb	bean sprouts
4		oranges
½	cup	strawberries, sliced
1	Tbsp	sesame seeds*

Dressing:

3	oz.	light soy sauce
⅓	cup	vegetable broth (see recipe)
2	Tbsp	rice wine vinegar
1	tsp	sugar
⅓	tsp	garlic powder/fresh garlic
⅓	tsp	black pepper

Preparation:

- Combine cabbage, bean sprouts, oranges, strawberries and sesame seeds.
- Combine dressing ingredients and toss with cabbage slaw.
- Garnish with fresh orange slices.

Nutrition Facts
Serving Size 1/8 recipe (260g)
Servings Per Container 8

Amount Per Serving

Calories 100   Calories from Fat 10

% Daily Value*

Total Fat 1g	2%
Saturated Fat 0g	0%
Trans Fat 0g	
Cholesterol 0mg	0%
Sodium 440mg	18%
Total Carbohydrate 20g	7%
Dietary Fiber 5g	20%
Sugars 11g	
Protein 5g	

Vitamin A 15% • Vitamin C 150%
Calcium 10% • Iron 8%

*Percent Daily Values are based on a 2,000 calorie diet. Your daily values may be higher or lower depending on your calorie needs:

		Calories:	2,000	2,500
Total Fat	Less than		65g	80g
Saturated Fat	Less than		20g	25g
Cholesterol	Less than		300mg	300mg
Sodium	Less than		2,400mg	2,400mg
Total Carbohydrate			300g	375g
Dietary Fiber			25g	30g

Calories per gram:
  Fat 9 • Carbohydrate 4 • Protein 4

* Note: 1 Tbsp of sesame seeds is equivalent to approximately 1 tsp of added fat.

Thanks to: David Smith-Walsh, Executive Chef, University Club

Category: Salads

Pilgrim Corn Salad

Be mindful of those nuts! (added fats). Try wrapping this in lettuce for an appetizer (lettuce wraps).

Makes 8 servings ~ ½ cup

Salad Ingredients:

2½	cups	corn kernels
¾	cup	sweetened, dried cranberries
2	Tbsp	pecans, chopped
2	Tbsp	fresh basil, finely chopped
		fresh basil sprigs for garnish

Dressing:

2	Tbsp	balsamic vinegar
2	tsp	olive oil
1	Tbsp	apricot preserves
1	tsp	Dijon mustard
1	tsp	Worcestershire sauce

Preparation:

- In a medium bowl, mix corn, cranberries and pecans.
- In a small bowl, combine dressing ingredients and beat with wire whisk until smooth.
- Add dressing to corn mixture and stir in basil.
- Toss to coat well. Let stand 10 minutes.
- To serve, stir gently to mix and add garnish.

Nutrition Facts

Serving Size 1/2 cup (62g)
Servings Per Container 8

Amount Per Serving

Calories 110   Calories from Fat 25

% Daily Value*

Total Fat 2.5g	4%
Saturated Fat 0g	0%
Trans Fat 0g	
Cholesterol 0mg	0%
Sodium 25mg	1%
Total Carbohydrate 20g	7%
Dietary Fiber 2g	8%
Sugars 12g	
Protein 1g	

Vitamin A 0% • Vitamin C 2%
Calcium 0% • Iron 2%

*Percent Daily Values are based on a 2,000 calorie diet. Your daily values may be higher or lower depending on your calorie needs:

	Calories:	2,000	2,500
Total Fat	Less than	65g	80g
Saturated Fat	Less than	20g	25g
Cholesterol	Less than	300mg	300mg
Sodium	Less than	2,400mg	2,400mg
Total Carbohydrate		300g	375g
Dietary Fiber		25g	30g

Calories per gram:
Fat 9 • Carbohydrate 4 • Protein 4

Category: Salads

Pomegranate, Mandarin and Kiwi Salad

An excellent way to use fall fruits.

Makes 4 servings

Salad Ingredients:

1½	quarts	mixed salad greens
3		mandarin oranges, peeled and sectioned
2		kiwi, peeled and sliced
¾	cup	pomegranate arils

Dressing:

3	Tbsp	red wine vinegar
1	tsp	olive oil
¼	cup	cranberries, fresh or dried
1	Tbsp	Dijon mustard
1	Tbsp	sugar
1		clove garlic, minced
½	tsp	salt
½	tsp	freshly ground black pepper
2	Tbsp	water

Preparation:

- Combine dressing ingredients in blender or food processor and blend together until smooth.
- Toss mixed greens with dressing.
- Serve on plates, adding fruit on top and sprinkling with pomegranate arils.

Category: Salads

Nutrition Facts

Serving Size 1/4 recipe (270g)
Servings Per Container 4

Amount Per Serving

Calories 160 — Calories from Fat 20

% Daily Value*

Total Fat 2g	3%
Saturated Fat 0g	0%
Trans Fat 0g	
Cholesterol 0mg	0%
Sodium 410mg	17%
Total Carbohydrate 37g	12%
Dietary Fiber 7g	28%
Sugars 28g	
Protein 3g	

Vitamin A 60% • Vitamin C 100%
Calcium 4% • Iron 6%

*Percent Daily Values are based on a 2,000 calorie diet. Your daily values may be higher or lower depending on your calorie needs:

		Calories:	2,000	2,500
Total Fat	Less than		65g	80g
Saturated Fat	Less than		20g	25g
Cholesterol	Less than		300mg	300mg
Sodium	Less than		2,400mg	2,400mg
Total Carbohydrate			300g	375g
Dietary Fiber			25g	30g

Calories per gram:
Fat 9 • Carbohydrate 4 • Protein 4

Quinoa Garden Salad

Quinoa is a gluten-free whole grain that is among the highest protein grains. It cooks much more quickly than traditional rice.

Makes 6 servings

Ingredients:

1	cup	water
½	cup	quinoa, well-rinsed
1	cup	green, yellow, and/or orange bell pepper, chopped
2		tomatoes, chopped
1	cup	garbanzo beans, cooked
½	cup	green onion, chopped
2	Tbsp	fresh parsley, chopped
2	Tbsp	fresh mint, chopped
2	Tbsp	lemon juice
		salt and ground black pepper to taste

Preparation:

- In a small saucepan, combine water and quinoa.
- Bring to a boil; reduce heat.
- Cover and simmer about 15 minutes, or until water is absorbed.
- Remove from heat and set aside.
- In a large bowl, combine pepper, tomatoes, garbanzo beans, green onion, parsley and mint.
- Add the cooked quinoa; mix well.
- Add lemon juice; toss well to mix.
- Season to taste with salt and pepper.
- Cover and refrigerate for 2-4 hours before serving.

Category: Salads

Nutrition Facts

Serving Size 1/6 recipe (171g)
Servings Per Container 6

Amount Per Serving

Calories 120	Calories from Fat 15

	% Daily Value*
Total Fat 2g	3%
Saturated Fat 0g	0%
Trans Fat 0g	
Cholesterol 0mg	0%
Sodium 60mg	3%
Total Carbohydrate 21g	7%
Dietary Fiber 4g	16%
Sugars 3g	
Protein 5g	

Vitamin A 6%	•	Vitamin C 80%
Calcium 4%	•	Iron 10%

*Percent Daily Values are based on a 2,000 calorie diet. Your daily values may be higher or lower depending on your calorie needs:

		Calories:	2,000	2,500
Total Fat		Less than	65g	80g
Saturated Fat		Less than	20g	25g
Cholesterol		Less than	300mg	300mg
Sodium		Less than	2,400mg	2,400mg
Total Carbohydrate			300g	375g
Dietary Fiber			25g	30g

Calories per gram:
Fat 9 • Carbohydrate 4 • Protein 4

Snow Pea Salad with Sesame Dressing

To blanch fresh peas (either shelled or whole edible-pod types), bring water to a boil in a large pan, then add peas. Cook just until they start to turn a brighter green, 15 to 30 seconds, drain immediately. Rinse well under cold running water until cool and drain again.

Makes 4 servings

Ingredients:

1	lb	snow peas, trimmed, blanched and drained
2	tsp	sesame seeds, toasted
1	tsp	sesame oil
3	Tbsp	light soy sauce
1	Tbsp	mirin or dry sherry
2	tsp	white vinegar
2	tsp	sugar
2	tsp	fresh ginger (grated)
½	tsp	hot Chinese mustard
2	Tbsp	green onions, thinly sliced

Preparation:

- Toss the drained snow peas with the toasted sesame seeds.
- In a medium bowl, combine the other ingredients and toss the snow peas with them.
- Cover and chill, at least 1 hour, or up to 1 day.
- Just before serving, mound salad on a platter and sprinkle with sliced green onions.

Category: Salads

Nutrition Facts

Serving Size 1/4 recipe (142g)
Servings Per Container 4

Amount Per Serving

Calories 90 — Calories from Fat 20

% Daily Value*

Total Fat 2g	3%
Saturated Fat 0g	0%
Trans Fat 0g	
Cholesterol 0mg	0%
Sodium 400mg	17%
Total Carbohydrate 14g	5%
Dietary Fiber 3g	12%
Sugars 9g	
Protein 5g	

Vitamin A 25%	•	Vitamin C 110%	
Calcium 6%	•	Iron 15%	

*Percent Daily Values are based on a 2,000 calorie diet. Your daily values may be higher or lower depending on your calorie needs:

		Calories:	2,000	2,500
Total Fat	Less than		65g	80g
Saturated Fat	Less than		20g	25g
Cholesterol	Less than		300mg	300mg
Sodium	Less than		2,400mg	2,400mg
Total Carbohydrate			300g	375g
Dietary Fiber			25g	30g

Calories per gram:
 Fat 9 • Carbohydrate 4 • Protein 4

Spinach Salad with Pears

A great combination of fall fruits and veggies.

Makes 4 servings

Ingredients:

1	tsp	finely shredded orange peel
½	cup	orange juice
½	cup	seasoned rice vinegar
2		firm ripe pears
⅔	cup	red onions, thinly sliced
1	lb	spinach leaves

Preparation:

- Combine orange peel, juice, and vinegar for dressing.
- Core and slice pears and onion into the dressing.
- Just before serving, pour dressing over spinach and mix gently.

Variation: Add mandarin oranges or sliced strawberries instead of pears.

Category: Salads

Nutrition Facts

Serving Size 1/4 recipe (317g)
Servings Per Container 4

Amount Per Serving

Calories 150 — Calories from Fat 5

% Daily Value*

Total Fat 0.5g	1%
Saturated Fat 0g	0%
Trans Fat 0g	
Cholesterol 0mg	0%
Sodium 470mg	20%
Total Carbohydrate 36g	12%
Dietary Fiber 7g	28%
Sugars 23g	
Protein 4g	

Vitamin A 210% • Vitamin C 80%
Calcium 15% • Iron 20%

*Percent Daily Values are based on a 2,000 calorie diet. Your daily values may be higher or lower depending on your calorie needs:

		Calories:	2,000	2,500
Total Fat	Less than		65g	80g
Saturated Fat	Less than		20g	25g
Cholesterol	Less than		300mg	300mg
Sodium	Less than		2,400mg	2,400mg
Total Carbohydrate			300g	375g
Dietary Fiber			25g	30g

Calories per gram:
  Fat 9 • Carbohydrate 4 • Protein 4

Surprise Cole Slaw

Similar to other cole slaws, but fewer ingredients.

10 servings

Ingredients:

1	med	head napa cabbage
1	med	purple onion (or Candy Sweet white onion), thinly sliced
2	cups	seedless grapes, red or green, whole or halved

Dressing:

1	cup	non-fat mayonnaise
2	Tbsp	sugar
2	Tbsp	seasoned rice vinegar
		salt and pepper to taste

Preparation

- Mix together dressing ingredients.
- Cut cabbage in half and thinly slice or shred into a large bowl.
- Add onion and grapes.
- Add dressing and toss. Refrigerate at least one hour before serving.

Thanks to: Jerre Schermerhorn, Group 29

Category: Salads

Nutrition Facts
Serving Size 1/10 recipe (167g)
Servings Per Container 10

Amount Per Serving

Calories 80 Calories from Fat 5

% Daily Value*

Total Fat 1g	2%
Saturated Fat 0g	0%
Trans Fat 0g	
Cholesterol 5mg	2%
Sodium 240mg	10%
Total Carbohydrate 16g	5%
Dietary Fiber 2g	8%
Sugars 12g	
Protein 2g	

Vitamin A 25% • Vitamin C 50%
Calcium 6% • Iron 0%

*Percent Daily Values are based on a 2,000 calorie diet. Your daily values may be higher or lower depending on your calorie needs:

		Calories:	2,000	2,500
Total Fat	Less than		65g	80g
Saturated Fat	Less than		20g	25g
Cholesterol	Less than		300mg	300mg
Sodium	Less than		2,400mg	2,400mg
Total Carbohydrate			300g	375g
Dietary Fiber			25g	30g

Calories per gram:
   Fat 9 • Carbohydrate 4 • Protein 4

Winter Red Cabbage Salad

This is a fruity cole slaw. The dried fruit increases the fiber content and adds even more color to the red of the cabbage.

Makes 6 servings

Ingredients:

1½	lb	red cabbage, thinly sliced
½	tsp	black pepper, freshly ground
¼	cup	cider vinegar
8		dried apricots, diced
8	dried	calimyrna figs, diced
3	Tbsp	golden raisins
2		Granny Smith apples, unpeeled cored, julienned
1½	tsp	olive oil
2	Tbsp	balsamic vinegar
½	tsp	brown sugar
½	tsp	cumin
		pepper to taste
¼	cup	chopped walnuts

Nutrition Facts

Serving Size 1/6 (233g)
Servings Per Container 6

Amount Per Serving

Calories 180 — Calories from Fat 30

% Daily Value*

- Total Fat 3g — 5%
-   Saturated Fat 0g — 0%
-   Trans Fat 0g
- Cholesterol 0mg — 0%
- Sodium 35mg — 1%
- Total Carbohydrate 37g — 12%
-   Dietary Fiber 6g — 24%
-   Sugars 22g
- Protein 3g

Vitamin A 35% • Vitamin C 110%
Calcium 8% • Iron 10%

*Percent Daily Values are based on a 2,000 calorie diet. Your daily values may be higher or lower depending on your calorie needs:

	Calories:	2,000	2,500
Total Fat	Less than	65g	80g
Saturated Fat	Less than	20g	25g
Cholesterol	Less than	300mg	300mg
Sodium	Less than	2,400mg	2,400mg
Total Carbohydrate		300g	375g
Dietary Fiber		25g	30g

Calories per gram:
Fat 9 • Carbohydrate 4 • Protein 4

Preparation:

- In a large bowl, combine cabbage, pepper and cider vinegar. Toss well.
- Cover and store overnight in refrigerator. Drain.
- Add apricots, figs raisins, and apples and toss well.
- Drizzle oil over top and toss.
- Then add balsamic vinegar and toss again.
- Add to taste brown sugar, cumin, pepper.
- Toss and taste, adjusting flavor with more vinegar, cumin, sugar or pepper.
- Add walnuts just before serving.

Thanks to: Will Yoshimoto, Group 33.

Category: Salads

SANDWICHES

FALAFEL SANDWICH

Traditional filling for pocket or pita bread in the Middle East...try it, you'll like it!

Makes 4 servings

Falafel Ingredients:

1	cup	falafel mix*
¾	cup	water
2		pita breads, cut into 4 halves
		alfalfa sprouts,
		tomatoes chopped,
		lettuce shredded
		any other chopped vegetable as desired

Yogurt Dressing:

1	cup	plain non-fat yogurt or sour cream
1	Tbsp	freshly squeezed lemon juice
1	Tbsp	parsley, chopped

Nutrition Facts

Serving Size 1/2 pita (205g)
Servings Per Container 4

Amount Per Serving

Calories 250   Calories from Fat 40

% Daily Value*

Total Fat 4g	6%
Saturated Fat 0g	0%
Trans Fat 0g	
Cholesterol 0mg	0%
Sodium 760mg	32%
Total Carbohydrate 45g	15%
Dietary Fiber 3g	12%
Sugars 6g	
Protein 11g	

Vitamin A 10%	•	Vitamin C 20%
Calcium 15%	•	Iron 15%

*Percent Daily Values are based on a 2,000 calorie diet. Your daily values may be higher or lower depending on your calorie needs:

		Calories:	2,000	2,500
Total Fat	Less than		65g	80g
Saturated Fat	Less than		20g	25g
Cholesterol	Less than		300mg	300mg
Sodium	Less than		2,400mg	2,400mg
Total Carbohydrate			300g	375g
Dietary Fiber			25g	30g

Calories per gram:
    Fat 9 • Carbohydrate 4 • Protein 4

Preparation:

- Preheat oven to 350°F.
- Mix instant falafel and water. Let stand for 10 minutes.
- Make into tablespoon-sized patties or balls.
- Place on nonstick cookie sheet and bake for 10 minutes on each side for patties or for 20 minutes if shaped into balls.
- While hot, place in sliced pita bread and top with yogurt dressing and desired vegetable garnish.

- **Yogurt Dressing:** Combine all ingredients. Makes 1 cup.

*Falafel mix is found in many supermarkets (one 10-ounce package usually contains 2 cups dry mix). The mix should list ingredients including garbanzo beans and yellow peas, wheat germ, onion, parsley, herbs, spices, salt and baking soda. Make sure that fat is <u>not</u> included.

Thanks to: Dianne Hyson, R.D.

Category: Sandwiches

GRILLED CHEESE WITH TOMATO AND BASIL

A more sophisticated grilled cheese. Try different whole grain breads and vary the flavor of cheese.

Makes 1 sandwich

Ingredients:

		I Can't Believe It's Not Butter Spray
2	slices	whole wheat bread
1	slice	fat-free cheese or soy cheese such as Veggie Slices
1-2	slices	tomato
		fresh basil leaves

Preparation:

- Spray outside of bread with butter spray.
- Fill inside with cheese, tomato, and basil.
- Top with remaining slice of bread, sprayed side up.
- Place sandwich in medium warm pan.
- Cook until desired darkness, flipping sides.

Category: Sandwiches

Nutrition Facts

Serving Size (177g)
Servings Per Container

Amount Per Serving

Calories 250 Calories from Fat 30

% Daily Value*

Total Fat 3g — 5%
 Saturated Fat 0g — 0%
 Trans Fat 0g
Cholesterol 5mg — 2%
Sodium 520mg — 22%
Total Carbohydrate 50g — 17%
 Dietary Fiber 15g — 60%
 Sugars 9g
Protein 20g

Vitamin A 15% • Vitamin C 10%
Calcium 35% • Iron 15%

*Percent Daily Values are based on a 2,000 calorie diet. Your daily values may be higher or lower depending on your calorie needs:

	Calories:	2,000	2,500
Total Fat	Less than	65g	80g
Saturated Fat	Less than	20g	25g
Cholesterol	Less than	300mg	300mg
Sodium	Less than	2,400mg	2,400mg
Total Carbohydrate		300g	375g
Dietary Fiber		25g	30g

Calories per gram:
 Fat 9 • Carbohydrate 4 • Protein 4

Herbed Cottage Cheese Sandwich Spread

Use this spread with vegetables on your favorite bread or roll, or as a dip with vegetables. Make ahead of time to let flavors blend.

Makes 2½ cups of spread

Ingredients:

1¼	cups	non-fat cottage cheese
¼	cup	non-fat plain yogurt
½	tsp	sugar
1	tsp	freshly squeezed lemon juice
2	Tbsp	onion, chopped
¼	cup	carrot, chopped
¼	cup	celery, chopped
	dash	Worcestershire sauce
	dash	seasoning salt
	dash	celery salt
1	Tbsp	fresh chopped basil (or more to taste)

Preparation:

- Place the cottage cheese, sugar, and lemon juice in a blender and blend until smooth.
- Scrape mixture out of the blender and into a bowl.
- Stir in the vegetables, Worcestershire sauce and other seasonings.

Category: Sandwiches

Nutrition Facts

Serving Size 1/2 cup (447g)
Servings Per Container 5

Amount Per Serving

Calories 260 — Calories from Fat 0

% Daily Value*

Total Fat 0g	0%
Saturated Fat 0g	0%
Trans Fat 0g	
Cholesterol 15mg	5%
Sodium 1210mg	50%
Total Carbohydrate 30g	10%
Dietary Fiber 2g	8%
Sugars 20g	
Protein 36g	

Vitamin A 110% • Vitamin C 15%
Calcium 25% • Iron 2%

*Percent Daily Values are based on a 2,000 calorie diet. Your daily values may be higher or lower depending on your calorie needs:

	Calories:	2,000	2,500
Total Fat	Less than	65g	80g
Saturated Fat	Less than	20g	25g
Cholesterol	Less than	300mg	300mg
Sodium	Less than	2,400mg	2,400mg
Total Carbohydrate		300g	375g
Dietary Fiber		25g	30g

Calories per gram:
Fat 9 • Carbohydrate 4 • Protein 4

HOT VEGETABLE HERO

You won't miss meat with the variety of veggies in this healthy sandwich.

Makes 4 servings

Ingredients:

1	loaf	French or Italian bread (8 oz)
1	large	yellow onion, sliced thin
2	med	carrots, peeled and sliced thin
½	med	sweet red pepper, cored, seeded, and sliced thin
1	med	zucchini (about ½ lb), sliced thin
1	cup	unsalted tomato sauce
½	tsp	dried oregano
½	tsp	black pepper
4	oz	non-fat cheese, sliced
		non-fat cooking spray

Nutrition Facts

Serving Size 1/4 recipe (287g)
Servings Per Container 4

Amount Per Serving

Calories 330   Calories from Fat 5

% Daily Value*

Total Fat 0g	0%
Saturated Fat 0g	0%
Trans Fat 0g	
Cholesterol 5mg	2%
Sodium 730mg	30%
Total Carbohydrate 63g	21%
Dietary Fiber 6g	24%
Sugars 11g	
Protein 19g	

Vitamin A 150% • Vitamin C 60%
Calcium 30% • Iron 20%

*Percent Daily Values are based on a 2,000 calorie diet. Your daily values may be higher or lower depending on your calorie needs:

		Calories:	2,000	2,500
Total Fat	Less than		65g	80g
Saturated Fat	Less than		20g	25g
Cholesterol	Less than		300mg	300mg
Sodium	Less than		2,400mg	2,400mg
Total Carbohydrate			300g	375g
Dietary Fiber			25g	30g

Calories per gram:
Fat 9 • Carbohydrate 4 • Protein 4

Preparation:

- Preheat the broiler.
- Slice the bread in half lengthwise and scoop out and discard the soft center.
- Place the halves, cut side up, on a baking sheet and broil 4 inches from the heat for 1 minute or until lightly toasted. Set aside.
- In a heavy 10 inch skillet, sauté onion in vegetable oil spray and water, as needed, for 5 minutes or until soft.
- Stir in the carrots, red pepper and zucchini, and cook, covered for 8-10 minutes or until the carrots are tender.
- Add the tomato sauce, oregano, and black pepper, and simmer, uncovered, for 2 minutes.
- Spoon the vegetable mixture into the bottom half of the bread, top with the cheese, and place under the broiler 4 inches from the heat.
- Broil for 1 minute or until the cheese has melted.
- Transfer to a cutting board and top with the toasted upper half.
- **Cut into 4 sandwiches.**

Category: Sandwiches

Pita Pizza

This recipe makes one pita. Double or triple it for company.

1 serving

Ingredients:

1		whole wheat pita bread
2	Tbsp	fat-free spaghetti sauce (add oregano if desired)
2	Tbsp	green pepper, finely chopped
2	Tbsp	mushrooms, finely chopped
2	Tbsp	onion, finely chopped
2		black olives, sliced (optional)
2	Tbsp	non-fat grated cheese (~½ oz.)
		other desired vegetables (tomatoes, broccoli, etc.)

Nutrition Facts

Serving Size 1 pita (166g)
Servings Per Container 1

Amount Per Serving

Calories 260   Calories from Fat 35

% Daily Value*

Total Fat 3.5g	5%
Saturated Fat 1g	5%
Trans Fat 0g	
Cholesterol 5mg	2%
Sodium 660mg	28%
Total Carbohydrate 47g	16%
Dietary Fiber 6g	24%
Sugars 2g	
Protein 14g	

Vitamin A 6%   •   Vitamin C 40%
Calcium 15%   •   Iron 20%

*Percent Daily Values are based on a 2,000 calorie diet. Your daily values may be higher or lower depending on your calorie needs:

		Calories:	2,000	2,500
Total Fat	Less than		65g	80g
Saturated Fat	Less than		20g	25g
Cholesterol	Less than		300mg	300mg
Sodium	Less than		2,400mg	2,400mg
Total Carbohydrate			300g	375g
Dietary Fiber			25g	30g

Calories per gram:
  Fat 9 • Carbohydrate 4 • Protein 4

Preparation:

- Preheat oven to 425°F.
- Spread sauce on one side of unsliced pita bread.
- Sprinkle green peppers, mushrooms, onions, and black olives over sauce.
- Sprinkle cheese over vegetables.
- Place on ungreased pizza pan or cookie sheet.
- Bake 5-10 minutes or until done.

Directions for Microwave: Prepare as for oven. Microwave on medium high until warm. Roll up and eat.

Source: *New American Diet*

Category: Breads

Zucchini Pizza

A great low carbohydrate pizza using zucchini for the crust.

Makes 6 servings

Ingredients:

2	cups	zucchini, grated
1	cup	non-fat mozzarella cheese, grated, divided
1	cup	non-fat cheddar cheese, grated, divided
3		egg whites (medium), beaten
2	Tbsp	flour
¼	tsp	dried basil
⅛	tsp	black pepper
½	cup	unsalted tomato sauce
¼	cup	mushrooms, sliced thin
¼	cup	onion, chopped
¼	tsp	oregano
¼	tsp	garlic
¼	tsp	thyme
		vegetable oil cooking spray

Nutrition Facts

Serving Size 1/6 recipe (147g)
Servings Per Container 6

Amount Per Serving

Calories 100   Calories from Fat 5

% Daily Value*

Total Fat 0g	0%
Saturated Fat 0g	0%
Trans Fat 0g	
Cholesterol 5mg	2%
Sodium 280mg	12%
Total Carbohydrate 9g	3%
Dietary Fiber 1g	4%
Sugars 3g	
Protein 15g	

Vitamin A 20% • Vitamin C 20%
Calcium 35% • Iron 4%

*Percent Daily Values are based on a 2,000 calorie diet. Your daily values may be higher or lower depending on your calorie needs:

		Calories:	2,000	2,500
Total Fat	Less than		65g	80g
Saturated Fat	Less than		20g	25g
Cholesterol	Less than		300mg	300mg
Sodium	Less than		2,400mg	2,400mg
Total Carbohydrate			300g	375g
Dietary Fiber			25g	30g

Calories per gram:
  Fat 9 • Carbohydrate 4 • Protein 4

Preparation:

- Preheat oven to 350°F.
- Combine zucchini with 2 tablespoons of the mozzarella cheese, egg whites, flour, basil and black pepper.
- Spread mixture in 9 inch quiche pan, sprayed with vegetable oil cooking spray.
- Bake 20 minutes.
- Then, place under broiler and broil 3 minutes. Remove from broiler and return oven to 350°F.
- Top pizza evenly with tomato sauce, onion, mushrooms, remaining mozzarella and cheddar cheese, and spices.
- Bake 5-10 minutes.

Thanks to: Sharon Myers, R.N.

Category: Sandwiches

SOUPS

ALL VEGETABLE CHILI

Soaking the wheat berries overnight will help them cook faster.

Serves 6   ~ ¾ cup each

Ingredients:

½	cup	wheat berries
1	large	garlic clove, minced
2	large	red onions, chopped
2	medium	carrots, chopped or sliced
1		red bell pepper, chopped into 1inch pieces
1		green bell pepper, chopped into 1 inch pieces
2	lb	plum tomatoes, chopped
1	can	tomato paste (6 oz)
2	tsp	dried oregano
1	tsp	ground cumin
½	tsp	cayenne pepper
4	Tbsp	chili powder
3	cups	cooked kidney beans

Preparation:

- Place wheat berries in small saucepan, cover with water and boil until soft.
- Sauté garlic and onions in 3 Tbsp of water.
- Combine all ingredients in a large pot and simmer for 30 minutes.

Thanks to: Bob and Claire Ingels, Group 1

Category: Soups

Nutrition Facts

Serving Size about 3/4 cup (440g)
Servings Per Container 6

Amount Per Serving

Calories 260   Calories from Fat 15

	% Daily Value*
Total Fat 1.5g	2%
Saturated Fat 0g	0%
Trans Fat 0g	
Cholesterol 0mg	0%
Sodium 350mg	15%
Total Carbohydrate 53g	18%
Dietary Fiber 15g	60%
Sugars 14g	
Protein 13g	

Vitamin A 160%   •   Vitamin C 130%
Calcium 8%   •   Iron 30%

*Percent Daily Values are based on a 2,000 calorie diet. Your daily values may be higher or lower depending on your calorie needs:

	Calories:	2,000	2,500
Total Fat	Less than	65g	80g
Saturated Fat	Less than	20g	25g
Cholesterol	Less than	300mg	300mg
Sodium	Less than	2,400mg	2,400mg
Total Carbohydrate		300g	375g
Dietary Fiber		25g	30g

Calories per gram:
  Fat 9   •   Carbohydrate 4   •   Protein 4

Asparagus and Potato Bisque

Using skim milk and non-fat yogurt, you get a 'creamy' soup without the extra fat and calories.

Makes 6 servings ~ ¾ cup each.

Ingredients:

1	large	potato, peeled and chopped
1	small	onion, chopped
1½	cups	water or non-fat vegetable stock
1	lb	fresh asparagus
2	tsp	lemon juice
1	cup	skim milk
½	cup	non-fat plain yogurt
		pinch nutmeg
		salt and freshly ground pepper

Preparation:

- In saucepan, combine potato, onion and water or stock; cover and simmer until potato is nearly tender, 5 to 10 minutes.
- Cut asparagus into about 1½ inch lengths. Add to potato mixture; cover and simmer for 5 minutes or until asparagus is tender.
- Using slotted spoon, remove asparagus tips and let cool in cold water to prevent further cooking. Drain and reserve for garnish.
- In food processor or blender, puree asparagus-potato mixture; add lemon juice.
- Pour into bowl; cover and refrigerate until chilled.
- Stir in milk and yogurt; season with salt, pepper and nutmeg to taste.
- Serve cold or reheat.
- Garnish each serving with reserved asparagus tips.

Source: The Lighthearted Cookbook

Category: Soups

Nutrition Facts

Serving Size about 3/4 cup each (258g)

Servings Per Container 6

Amount Per Serving

Calories 70	Calories from Fat 0

	% Daily Value*
Total Fat 0g	0%
Saturated Fat 0g	0%
Trans Fat 0g	
Cholesterol 0mg	0%
Sodium 35mg	1%
Total Carbohydrate 16g	5%
Dietary Fiber 3g	12%
Sugars 6g	
Protein 5g	

Vitamin A 15%	•	Vitamin C 25%
Calcium 10%	•	Iron 10%

*Percent Daily Values are based on a 2,000 calorie diet. Your daily values may be higher or lower depending on your calorie needs:

	Calories:	2,000	2,500
Total Fat	Less than	65g	80g
Saturated Fat	Less than	20g	25g
Cholesterol	Less than	300mg	300mg
Sodium	Less than	2,400mg	2,400mg
Total Carbohydrate		300g	375g
Dietary Fiber		25g	30g

Calories per gram:
 Fat 9 • Carbohydrate 4 • Protein 4

BLACK BEAN AND RICE SOUP

You can substitute 2 cans of black beans, but use low sodium beans and rinse before using to keep the sodium low.

Makes 6 servings ~ 6 cups

Ingredients:

3	cups	black beans cooked
3	cups	water
½	tsp	dried oregano
1	tsp	garlic powder
2	tsp	hot pepper sauce
3	cups	brown rice, cooked
½	cup	chopped onion to garnish (optional)

Preparation:

- Blend beans with liquid in blender until smooth.
- Pour into large saucepan.
- Stir in water, oregano, garlic powder and hot pepper sauce. Bring to a boil.
- Stir in rice.
- Reduce heat, cover and simmer 5 minutes.
- Remove from heat.
- Let stand 5 minutes.
- Serve with chopped onions, if desired.

Thanks to: Lew and Dorothy Watkins, Group 2

Category: Soups

Nutrition Facts

Serving Size 1 cup (266g)
Servings Per Container 6

Amount Per Serving

Calories 290	Calories from Fat 15

	% Daily Value*
Total Fat 2g	3%
Saturated Fat 0g	0%
Trans Fat 0g	
Cholesterol 0mg	0%
Sodium 50mg	2%
Total Carbohydrate 58g	19%
Dietary Fiber 9g	36%
Sugars 1g	
Protein 12g	

Vitamin A 0%	•	Vitamin C 4%
Calcium 4%	•	Iron 15%

*Percent Daily Values are based on a 2,000 calorie diet. Your daily values may be higher or lower depending on your calorie needs:

	Calories:	2,000	2,500
Total Fat	Less than	65g	80g
Saturated Fat	Less than	20g	25g
Cholesterol	Less than	300mg	300mg
Sodium	Less than	2,400mg	2,400mg
Total Carbohydrate		300g	375g
Dietary Fiber		25g	30g

Calories per gram:
    Fat 9 • Carbohydrate 4 • Protein 4

Black Bean Soup

This is a great quick soup.

Makes 4 servings

Ingredients:

1	cup	jarred fresh tomato salsa
3	cups	black beans, cooked
2	cups	vegetable broth (see page 384)

Preparation:

- Heat salsa in a large saucepan, medium heat, stirring frequently, 5 minutes.
- Stir in black beans and broth.
- Heat to boiling, reduce heat to low, cover and simmer 15 minutes.
- Cool slightly.
- Ladle half the soup into a food processor or blender and puree.
- Return the puree to the pot and reheat.
- Serve, garnishing with spoonfuls of fat-free sour cream or non-fat plain yogurt and additional salsa.

Other possible additions: add a cooked potato, in chunks, to the to-be-pureed mixture. Add cooked corn to be heated at the end. Add lime juice or 1-2 tablespoons dry sherry to each bowl.

Real Simple, November 2003

Category: Soups

Nutrition Facts

Serving Size 1/4 recipe (303g)
Servings Per Container 4

Amount Per Serving

Calories 170   Calories from Fat 10

	% Daily Value*
Total Fat 1g	2%
Saturated Fat 0g	0%
Trans Fat 0g	
Cholesterol 0mg	0%
Sodium 380mg	16%
Total Carbohydrate 35g	12%
Dietary Fiber 11g	44%
Sugars 5g	
Protein 11g	

Vitamin A 100% • Vitamin C 70%
Calcium 8% • Iron 25%

*Percent Daily Values are based on a 2,000 calorie diet. Your daily values may be higher or lower depending on your calorie needs:

	Calories:	2,000	2,500
Total Fat	Less than	65g	80g
Saturated Fat	Less than	20g	25g
Cholesterol	Less than	300mg	300mg
Sodium	Less than	2,400mg	2,400mg
Total Carbohydrate		300g	375g
Dietary Fiber		25g	30g

Calories per gram:
  Fat 9 • Carbohydrate 4 • Protein 4

BROCCOLI SOUP

Broccoli is an excellent source of vitamin C and fiber; carrots provide beta carotene, a phytochemical that acts as an antioxidant to reduce risk of heart disease.

Makes 8 servings

Ingredients:

3	quarts	vegetable broth (see page 384)
4	cups	broccoli, chopped with stems (~2 bunches)
4	med	carrots, diced
1	large	russet potato, diced
¼	large	red onion, diced
1	heart	celery, diced
1	sprig	rosemary (6-8 inches long)
1	tsp	white pepper
¼	cup	Madeira
		cooking spray

Preparation:

- Place broccoli, carrots, and potato in broth. Bring to a boil, cover and reduce to simmer until tender (about ½ hour).
- Drain vegetables and reserve liquid. Set aside to cool.
- Sauté separately red onion and celery heart. Allow to cool.
- In a portion of the reserved liquid, puree all vegetables, a little at a time, in a blender and return to soup kettle.
- Use a little liquid to grind leaves of rosemary. Add rosemary, white pepper and Madeira to broth.
- Heat to boiling. Stir and reduce heat to low for 5 minutes to allow flavors to blend while covered.
- Serve hot or refrigerate to serve chilled with a garnish of your choice.

Nutrition Facts

Serving Size 1/8 recipe (619g)
Servings Per Container 8

Amount Per Serving

Calories 180 — Calories from Fat 10

% Daily Value*

- Total Fat 1.5g — 2%
- Saturated Fat 0g — 0%
- Trans Fat 0g
- Cholesterol 0mg — 0%
- Sodium 190mg — 8%
- Total Carbohydrate 38g — 13%
- Dietary Fiber 10g — 40%
- Sugars 11g
- Protein 8g

Vitamin A 420% • Vitamin C 300%
Calcium 25% • Iron 40%

*Percent Daily Values are based on a 2,000 calorie diet. Your daily values may be higher or lower depending on your calorie needs:

		Calories: 2,000	2,500
Total Fat	Less than	65g	80g
Saturated Fat	Less than	20g	25g
Cholesterol	Less than	300mg	300mg
Sodium	Less than	2,400mg	2,400mg
Total Carbohydrate		300g	375g
Dietary Fiber		25g	30g

Calories per gram:
Fat 9 • Carbohydrate 4 • Protein 4

Thanks to: Lyn & Jim Livingston, Group 8

Category: Soup

C & W Green Pea Soup

C&W is a brand of frozen vegetables commonly found in California supermarkets. Fresh vegetables would certainly work too or other brands of frozen ones.

Makes 10 servings ~ ¾ cup each

Ingredients:

3	cups	chicken flavored broth
4	cups	C&W frozen petite peas thawed
1		potato, peeled & cut into cubes
1		onion, diced
10	oz	C&W frozen chopped spinach, thawed
1½	Tbsp	margarine
1½	Tbsp	flour
1½	cups	skim milk
¾	tsp	marjoram
⅛	tsp	ground pepper
½	cup	fat-free Parmesan cheese

Preparation:

- In medium saucepan, combine broth, peas, potato, onion and spinach.
- Bring to a boil; reduce heat and simmer 15 minutes.
- Let cool slightly.
- Puree in blender or food processor in batches; set aside.
- Melt margarine in a large saucepan. Add flour and cook 1 minute, stirring constantly. Add vegetable puree and milk, marjoram, and ground pepper. Cook over medium heat until hot and thickened. Stir in Parmesan cheese and cook one more minute.
- Top with chopped fresh parsley and serve.

Category: Soups

Nutrition Facts

Serving Size 3/4 cup (223g)
Servings Per Container 10

Amount Per Serving

Calories 130   Calories from Fat 20

% Daily Value*

Total Fat 2g	3%
Saturated Fat 0g	0%
Trans Fat 0g	
Cholesterol 0mg	0%
Sodium 540mg	23%
Total Carbohydrate 18g	6%
Dietary Fiber 3g	12%
Sugars 6g	
Protein 8g	

Vitamin A 25%	•	Vitamin C 10%
Calcium 15%	•	Iron 8%

*Percent Daily Values are based on a 2,000 calorie diet. Your daily values may be higher or lower depending on your calorie needs:

		Calories:	2,000	2,500
Total Fat	Less than		65g	80g
Saturated Fat	Less than		20g	25g
Cholesterol	Less than		300mg	300mg
Sodium	Less than		2,400mg	2,400mg
Total Carbohydrate			300g	375g
Dietary Fiber			25g	30g

Calories per gram:
Fat 9 • Carbohydrate 4 • Protein 4

Campfire Vegetable Bean Pasta Soup

This is as great by the campfire as it is on the stovetop. Each serving provides a serving of vegetables and almost 40% of your daily fiber.

Makes 6 servings

Ingredients:

1	cup	onion, chopped
2		garlic cloves, minced
3	cups	fat-free chicken-flavored broth, reduced sodium
1½	cups	water
1½	cups	garbanzo beans, cooked
1½	cups	red kidney beans, cooked
2	tsp	curry powder
¼	tsp	salt
1	cup	carrots, sliced (2 large carrots)
¾	cup	small pasta shells
1	cup	zucchini, half-moon slices
¼	cup	couscous (a quick-cooking semolina)
6	oz	spinach
1-2	Tbsp	fresh lemon juice

Preparation:

- Coat large Dutch oven/soup pot with cooking spray. Heat over medium-high heat. Add onion and garlic.
- Cook, stirring, 2 minutes. (Add splash of broth as needed to prevent sticking or browning).
- Add broth, water, beans, curry powder, and salt. Bring to a boil.
- Add carrots, lower heat and simmer for 5 minutes.
- Add pasta shells and simmer 5 more minutes. Add zucchini, couscous, and spinach.
- Simmer for 5 more minutes, stirring occasionally until couscous and pasta are tender.
- Stir in lemon juice. Adjust salt to taste.

Nutrition Facts

Serving Size 1/6 recipe (414g)
Servings Per Container 6

Amount Per Serving

Calories 240 — Calories from Fat 15

	% Daily Value*
Total Fat 2g	3%
Saturated Fat 0g	0%
Trans Fat 0g	
Cholesterol 0mg	0%
Sodium 460mg	19%
Total Carbohydrate 42g	14%
Dietary Fiber 9g	36%
Sugars 6g	
Protein 12g	

Vitamin A 100% • Vitamin C 20%
Calcium 10% • Iron 20%

*Percent Daily Values are based on a 2,000 calorie diet. Your daily values may be higher or lower depending on your calorie needs:

		Calories:	2,000	2,500
Total Fat	Less than		65g	80g
Saturated Fat	Less than		20g	25g
Cholesterol	Less than		300mg	300mg
Sodium	Less than		2,400mg	2,400mg
Total Carbohydrate			300g	375g
Dietary Fiber			25g	30g

Calories per gram:
Fat 9 • Carbohydrate 4 • Protein 4

Category: Soups

CAN OPENER CHILI

Weigh the convenience of this off-the-pantry shelf recipe against the sodium content of those canned products. Be sure to watch your salt level on other items.

Makes 6 servings

Ingredients:

1	can	fat-free refried (15 oz) pinto beans (use 2 cans if you like it thicker)
1	can	kidney beans (15 oz) (use 2 cans if you like beans)
1	can	diced tomatoes (28 oz)
1	can	diced green chiles (4oz)
1	packet	chili seasoning mix
1	jar	salsa (optional)
1	tsp	garlic powder
1	tsp	onion powder
¼	tsp	ground black pepper

Preparation:

- Combine all ingredients in a large pot and simmer for an hour or more.

Thanks to: Iris Ridenour, Group 2

Category: Soups

Nutrition Facts

Serving Size 1/6 recipe (377g)
Servings Per Container 6

Amount Per Serving

Calories 200   Calories from Fat 10

% Daily Value*

Total Fat 1g	2%
Saturated Fat 0g	0%
Trans Fat 0g	
Cholesterol 0mg	0%
Sodium 1360mg	57%
Total Carbohydrate 37g	12%
Dietary Fiber 7g	28%
Sugars 8g	
Protein 9g	

Vitamin A 15%	•	Vitamin C 50%
Calcium 6%	•	Iron 15%

*Percent Daily Values are based on a 2,000 calorie diet. Your daily values may be higher or lower depending on your calorie needs:

		Calories:	2,000	2,500
Total Fat	Less than		65g	80g
Saturated Fat	Less than		20g	25g
Cholesterol	Less than		300mg	300mg
Sodium	Less than		2,400mg	2,400mg
Total Carbohydrate			300g	375g
Dietary Fiber			25g	30g

Calories per gram:
  Fat 9 • Carbohydrate 4 • Protein 4

CHILI MOLE

Choose low sodium broth and pasta sauce to reduce the sodium content.

Makes 10 servings

Ingredients:

1	cup	onion, chopped
1	cup	celery, chopped (2 stalks)
1		green pepper, chopped (1/2 cup)
28	oz	pasta sauce with garlic
1		bay leaf
4½	cups	pinto beans, cooked
1	4 oz	can Ortega fire roasted green chiles, diced
3	Tbsp	unsweetened cocoa
1	Tbsp	chili powder
1	Tbsp	oregano, dried
1½	tsp	nutmeg, ground
1	tsp	allspice
2	Tbsp	cumin
1	tsp	pepper
1½	cup	fat-free chicken flavored broth
12	oz	veggie ground round

Preparation:

- Spray Dutch oven or large pot with nonfat cooking spray.
- Sauté gently onion, celery, and green pepper.
- Add remaining ingredients except for veggie ground round and simmer slowly 20 minutes.
- Add veggie ground round and simmer 5 minutes more only.
- If mixture becomes too thick, thin with V8 juice or similar.

Thanks to: Phyllis and Walter Quinn, Group 25

Category: Soups

Nutrition Facts

Serving Size 1/10 recipe (329g)
Servings Per Container 10

Amount Per Serving

Calories 220   Calories from Fat 10

% Daily Value*

Total Fat 1g	2%
Saturated Fat 0g	0%
Trans Fat 0g	
Cholesterol 0mg	0%
Sodium 930mg	39%
Total Carbohydrate 34g	11%
Dietary Fiber 11g	44%
Sugars 5g	

Protein 15g

Vitamin A 20%	•	Vitamin C 25%
Calcium 10%	•	Iron 30%

*Percent Daily Values are based on a 2,000 calorie diet. Your daily values may be higher or lower depending on your calorie needs:

	Calories:	2,000	2,500
Total Fat	Less than	65g	80g
Saturated Fat	Less than	20g	25g
Cholesterol	Less than	300mg	300mg
Sodium	Less than	2,400mg	2,400mg
Total Carbohydrate		300g	375g
Dietary Fiber		25g	30g

Calories per gram:
 Fat 9 • Carbohydrate 4 • Protein 4

Chili Rico

Makes 6 servings ~ 7 ½ cups of chili.

Ingredients:

1	med	onion, chopped
2	cloves	garlic, minced
3	cups	tomatoes, coarsely chopped
3	cups	kidney beans, cooked
1½	cups	corn kernels
½	cup	Pace Picante Sauce
1½	tsp	ground cumin
1	tsp	oregano leaves, crushed
1	tsp	unsweetened cocoa
½	tsp	cinnamon
1		red or green bell pepper, cut into ½ inch pieces
		cooking spray

Optional toppings:

fat-free sour cream
green onions, chopped

Preparation:

- Cook onion and garlic in cooking spray in large saucepan or Dutch oven until onion is tender but not brown.
- Add remaining ingredients except red pepper and optional toppings; bring to a boil. Reduce heat, cover and simmer 20 minutes.
- Stir in red pepper, continue to simmer uncovered 5 minutes or until desired consistency.
- Ladle into bowls; top as desired and serve with additional picante sauce.

Thanks to: Iris Ridenour, Group 2

Category: Soups

Nutrition Facts

Serving Size 1/6 recipe (about 1 cup) (308g)
Servings Per Container 6

Amount Per Serving

Calories 180   Calories from Fat 5

% Daily Value*

Total Fat 1g	2%
Saturated Fat 0g	0%
Trans Fat 0g	
Cholesterol 0mg	0%
Sodium 370mg	15%
Total Carbohydrate 36g	12%
Dietary Fiber 8g	32%
Sugars 8g	
Protein 9g	

Vitamin A 8% • Vitamin C 70%
Calcium 10% • Iron 15%

*Percent Daily Values are based on a 2,000 calorie diet. Your daily values may be higher or lower depending on your calorie needs:

		Calories:	2,000	2,500
Total Fat	Less than		65g	80g
Saturated Fat	Less than		20g	25g
Cholesterol	Less than		300mg	300mg
Sodium	Less than		2,400mg	2,400mg
Total Carbohydrate			300g	375g
Dietary Fiber			25g	30g

Calories per gram:
Fat 9 • Carbohydrate 4 • Protein 4

COLD TOMATO YOGURT SOUP

Substituting Greek yogurt would add more protein and a little thicker consistency.

Makes 4 servings ~ 1 cup

Ingredients:

2		green onions cut into 2-inch pieces
2½	cups	tomatoes, peeled and chopped (about 1 lb)
16	oz	fat-free yogurt, plain
1	Tbsp	sugar
1	Tbsp	fresh basil, minced
¼	tsp	salt
2	drops	hot sauce

Preparation:

- Using a food processor or blender puree all the ingredients.
- Cover and chill.
- To serve, ladle into individual soup bowls.

Category: Soups

Nutrition Facts

Serving Size 1 cup (231g)
Servings Per Container 4

Amount Per Serving

Calories 100 — Calories from Fat 0

% Daily Value*

Total Fat 0g	0%
Saturated Fat 0g	0%
Trans Fat 0g	
Cholesterol 5mg	2%
Sodium 270mg	11%
Total Carbohydrate 17g	6%
Dietary Fiber 2g	8%
Sugars 15g	
Protein 8g	

Vitamin A 30% • Vitamin C 25%

Calcium 20% • Iron 2%

*Percent Daily Values are based on a 2,000 calorie diet. Your daily values may be higher or lower depending on your calorie needs:

		Calories:	2,000	2,500
Total Fat	Less than		65g	80g
Saturated Fat	Less than		20g	25g
Cholesterol	Less than		300mg	300mg
Sodium	Less than		2,400mg	2,400mg
Total Carbohydrate			300g	375g
Dietary Fiber			25g	30g

Calories per gram:
Fat 9 • Carbohydrate 4 • Protein 4

CORN CHOWDER

This is a great low fat version of Mimi's fat-laden soup.

Makes 4 servings

Ingredients:

1	large	onion chopped
2	stalks	celery, chopped
½		green, red or yellow bell pepper, chopped
1	Tbsp	flour (or cornstarch)
½	tsp	paprika
1	cup	fat-free chicken broth,
2	cups	corn kernels
1	cup	skim milk
¼	tsp	ground black pepper
1-2	medium	carrots, chopped

Preparation:

- Steam onions, celery, carrots and peppers 5 minute, until soft.
- Blend in flour (or cornstarch) and paprika.
- Cook, stirring for 3 minutes.
- Gradually stir in chicken broth. Cook and stir constantly until mixture thickens (about 3-5 minutes).
- Add corn, cover and cook 5 minutes. Add milk and black pepper.
- Heat but DO NOT BOIL.
- Serve with herbed croutons added to serving bowl, if desired.

Thanks to: Nan Hoy

Category: Soups

Nutrition Facts

Serving Size 1/4 recipe (315g)
Servings Per Container 4

Amount Per Serving

Calories 140 — Calories from Fat 5

% Daily Value*

Total Fat 0.5g	1%
Saturated Fat 0g	0%
Trans Fat 0g	
Cholesterol 0mg	0%
Sodium 180mg	8%
Total Carbohydrate 27g	9%
Dietary Fiber 4g	16%
Sugars 10g	
Protein 6g	

Vitamin A 130% • Vitamin C 40%
Calcium 10% • Iron 2%

*Percent Daily Values are based on a 2,000 calorie diet. Your daily values may be higher or lower depending on your calorie needs:

		Calories:	2,000	2,500
Total Fat	Less than		65g	80g
Saturated Fat	Less than		20g	25g
Cholesterol	Less than		300mg	300mg
Sodium	Less than		2,400mg	2,400mg
Total Carbohydrate			300g	375g
Dietary Fiber			25g	30g

Calories per gram:
Fat 9 • Carbohydrate 4 • Protein 4

Debbie's Taco Soup

Another convenient recipe adapted from Weight Watchers, needing careful attention to sodium content if that is an issue for you. Substituting fresh for canned ingredients can help there.

Makes 12 servings

Ingredients:

1	pkg	taco seasoning
1	pkg	Harvest Burger Crumbles
1	med	onion, chopped
3	cans	Mexican chili beans
1	can	stewed tomatoes (15 oz)
1	pkg	frozen corn (6 oz) OR canned equivalent.
1½	cups	water
1	can	chili peppers (4.5 oz)
1	pkg	dry ranch dressing mix

Preparation:

- Mix ingredients together, heat and serve.

TVP Substitute: Substitute for the Harvest Burger Crumbles, ⅓- ½ cup Textured Soy Protein granules. Increase the water to about 2 cups to compensate for the rehydration of the TVP.

Thanks to: Debbie Lucus, R.D.

Category: Soups

Nutrition Facts

Serving Size 1/12 recipe (239g)
Servings Per Container 12

Amount Per Serving

Calories 210 — Calories from Fat 0

% Daily Value*

Total Fat 0g	0%
Saturated Fat 0g	0%
Trans Fat 0g	
Cholesterol 0mg	0%
Sodium 670mg	28%
Total Carbohydrate 31g	10%
Dietary Fiber 8g	32%
Sugars 6g	
Protein 8g	

Vitamin A 6%	•	Vitamin C 15%
Calcium 10%	•	Iron 10%

*Percent Daily Values are based on a 2,000 calorie diet. Your daily values may be higher or lower depending on your calorie needs:

		Calories:	2,000	2,500
Total Fat		Less than	65g	80g
Saturated Fat		Less than	20g	25g
Cholesterol		Less than	300mg	300mg
Sodium		Less than	2,400mg	2,400mg
Total Carbohydrate			300g	375g
Dietary Fiber			25g	30g

Calories per gram:
 Fat 9 • Carbohydrate 4 • Protein 4

Garbanzo Stew

Curry, turmeric and other Indian spices are being studied for their health benefits, including anti-inflammatory properties.

Makes 8 servings ~ ½ cup/serving

Ingredients:

1	tsp	olive oil
1	cup	onion, finely chopped
4	cups	tomato, chopped (about 1 ½ lbs.)
1	tsp	sugar
1	tsp	curry powder
½	tsp	salt
¼	tsp	ground turmeric
⅛	tsp	ground red pepper
3	cups	garbanzo beans, cooked
½	tsp	garam masala* or mixture of spices (see below)
¼	cup	fresh cilantro, chopped

Nutrition Facts

Serving Size 1/8 recipe (163g)
Servings Per Container 8

Amount Per Serving

Calories 120   Calories from Fat 20

% Daily Value*

- Total Fat 2g — 3%
  - Saturated Fat 0g — 0%
  - Trans Fat 0g
- Cholesterol 0mg — 0%
- Sodium 150mg — 6%
- Total Carbohydrate 20g — 7%
  - Dietary Fiber 5g — 20%
  - Sugars 6g
- Protein 6g

Vitamin A 15% • Vitamin C 25%
Calcium 4% • Iron 10%

*Percent Daily Values are based on a 2,000 calorie diet. Your daily values may be higher or lower depending on your calorie needs:

	Calories:	2,000	2,500
Total Fat	Less than	65g	80g
Saturated Fat	Less than	20g	25g
Cholesterol	Less than	300mg	300mg
Sodium	Less than	2,400mg	2,400mg
Total Carbohydrate		300g	375g
Dietary Fiber		25g	30g

Calories per gram:
Fat 9 • Carbohydrate 4 • Protein 4

Preparation:

- Coat large sauce pan with oil. Heat pan over medium heat.
- Sauté onion for 5 minutes or until tender.
- Stir in tomato, sugar, curry powder, salt, turmeric, ground red pepper and cook 8 minutes or until thick.
- Stir in garbanzo beans and garam masala. Cook for 5 minutes or until thoroughly heated.
- Sprinkle each serving with 1 Tbsp chopped cilantro.

*Garam masala is a mixture of ground spices such as cloves, cinnamon, cardamom, coriander, cumin, nutmeg and black peppercorns and can be found in spices section of larger supermarkets.

From Bharti Kirchner, a specialist in Indian cuisine, from Cooking Light Magazine

Category: Soups

KALE AND POTATO SOUP

Kale isn't just used to line the salad bar. It is a great source of folate, iron, and fiber.

Makes 6 servings

Ingredients:

4	med		potatoes, peeled and diced
1	med		onion, peeled and coarsely chopped
2	cups		kale leaves
2-3			garlic cloves, peeled
1	tsp		salt
1½	tsp		olive oil
⅛	tsp		black pepper, freshly ground

Preparation:

- Kale should be coarsely chopped, discard center ribs.
- In a large pot, combine vegetables and cover with water.
- Bring to a boil.
- Cover, lower heat, and simmer very gently for 1 hour and 15 minutes (or less), or until kale is quite tender.
- In as many batches as necessary, pour the soup into the container of an electric blender and blend until you have a smooth texture.
- Pour soup back into soup pot and taste for seasonings.
- Add more water if the soup seems too thick.
- Just before serving, add oil and black pepper.

Category: Soups

Nutrition Facts

Serving Size 1/6 recipe (124g)
Servings Per Container 6

Amount Per Serving	
Calories 100	Calories from Fat 10

	% Daily Value*
Total Fat 1.5g	2%
Saturated Fat 0g	0%
Trans Fat 0g	
Cholesterol 0mg	0%
Sodium 400mg	17%
Total Carbohydrate 21g	7%
Dietary Fiber 2g	8%
Sugars 2g	
Protein 2g	

Vitamin A 45%	•	Vitamin C 45%
Calcium 4%	•	Iron 4%

*Percent Daily Values are based on a 2,000 calorie diet. Your daily values may be higher or lower depending on your calorie needs:

	Calories:	2,000	2,500
Total Fat	Less than	65g	80g
Saturated Fat	Less than	20g	25g
Cholesterol	Less than	300mg	300mg
Sodium	Less than	2,400mg	2,400mg
Total Carbohydrate		300g	375g
Dietary Fiber		25g	30g

Calories per gram:
  Fat 9 • Carbohydrate 4 • Protein 4

Kidney Bean Gumbo

Okra and beans both provide soluble fiber, the type of fiber that can lower cholesterol.

6 servings ~ 1½ cups each.

Ingredients:

1½	cups	okra
1	cup	onion, chopped
3	cloves	garlic, minced
1	tsp	olive oil
½	cup	celery, diced
1	cup	green pepper, chopped
3	cups	tomatoes, chopped
		pepper to taste
		cayenne to taste
1	tsp	thyme leaves
1	cup	peas
1½	cups	kidney beans, cooked

Preparation:

- Cook okra in boiling water until tender.
- Drain and set aside.
- Sauté onion and garlic until onion is soft and golden.
- Add celery and green pepper and cook until tender.
- Add tomatoes and heat to boiling. Reduce heat.
- Add pepper, cayenne, and thyme and simmer for 45 minutes.
- Add cooked okra, peas, and beans.
- Cook for a few minutes longer, until peas are done. Be sure to not overcook vegetables.
- Serve over rice.

Category: Soups

Nutrition Facts

Serving Size 1 1/2 cups (267g)
Servings Per Container 6

Amount Per Serving

Calories 120 — Calories from Fat 10

	% Daily Value*
Total Fat 1g	2%
Saturated Fat 0g	0%
Trans Fat 0g	
Cholesterol 0mg	0%
Sodium 25mg	1%
Total Carbohydrate 22g	7%
Dietary Fiber 9g	36%
Sugars 6g	
Protein 7g	

Vitamin A 25%	•	Vitamin C 80%
Calcium 8%	•	Iron 10%

*Percent Daily Values are based on a 2,000 calorie diet. Your daily values may be higher or lower depending on your calorie needs:

		Calories:	2,000	2,500
Total Fat	Less than		65g	80g
Saturated Fat	Less than		20g	25g
Cholesterol	Less than		300mg	300mg
Sodium	Less than		2,400mg	2,400mg
Total Carbohydrate			300g	375g
Dietary Fiber			25g	30g

Calories per gram:
 Fat 9 • Carbohydrate 4 • Protein 4

Lentil Stew

Lentils are in the bean family, but don't need to be pre-soaked.

Makes 8 servings

Ingredients:

1½	quarts	water for stock
2	cups	lentils
1	tsp	dried basil
1		onion, chopped
2		carrots, sliced or grated
1	can	stewed tomatoes
1	oz	Lipton onion soup mix
1	cup	TVP or veggie ground round
½	cup	vegetable broth (see page 384 or use canned)
2	Tbsp	vinegar

Preparation:

- In large pot, heat water and add lentils, basil, onion, carrots, tomatoes, and soup mix.
- Cook 30 minutes.
- Soak TVP in boiling fat-free chicken broth until hydrated and add to soup pot.
- Add vinegar just before serving.

Thanks to: George & Ilya Kross, Group 7

Category: Soups

Nutrition Facts

Serving Size 1/8 recipe (346g)
Servings Per Container 8

Amount Per Serving

Calories 250   Calories from Fat 10

	% Daily Value*
Total Fat 1.5g	2%
Saturated Fat 0g	0%
Trans Fat 0g	
Cholesterol 0mg	0%
Sodium 430mg	18%
Total Carbohydrate 40g	13%
Dietary Fiber 9g	36%
Sugars 6g	
Protein 19g	

Vitamin A 70%	•	Vitamin C 25%
Calcium 10%	•	Iron 35%

*Percent Daily Values are based on a 2,000 calorie diet. Your daily values may be higher or lower depending on your calorie needs:

	Calories:	2,000	2,500
Total Fat	Less than	65g	80g
Saturated Fat	Less than	20g	25g
Cholesterol	Less than	300mg	300mg
Sodium	Less than	2,400mg	2,400mg
Total Carbohydrate		300g	375g
Dietary Fiber		25g	30g

Calories per gram:
Fat 9 • Carbohydrate 4 • Protein 4

Lentil Soup

Who doesn't love a steaming bowl of lentil soup on a cold night? By using fresh ingredients and spices, the sodium is kept to a moderate level.

Makes 10 servings

Ingredients:

3	cups	green lentils
7	cups	water or stock
1	tsp	salt
2	tsp	minced garlic
1	cup	onion, chopped
1	cup	celery, minced
1	cup	carrot, chopped
1	tsp	olive oil
1½	cups	fresh tomatoes, chopped
2	Tbsp	dry red wine
2	Tbsp	lemon juice
1½	Tbsp	molasses or brown sugar
1	Tbsp	wine vinegar
4		scallions, chopped (½ cup)
		Optional: fine herbs, such as thyme, oregano, or basil
		ground black pepper to taste

Nutrition Facts

Serving Size 1/10 recipe (297g)
Servings Per Container 10

Amount Per Serving

Calories 230 — Calories from Fat 15

% Daily Value*

- Total Fat 2g — 3%
-   Saturated Fat 0g — 0%
-   Trans Fat 0g
- Cholesterol 0mg — 0%
- Sodium 260mg — 11%
- Total Carbohydrate 41g — 14%
-   Dietary Fiber 7g — 28%
-   Sugars 4g
- Protein 15g

Vitamin A 50% • Vitamin C 15%
Calcium 4% • Iron 25%

*Percent Daily Values are based on a 2,000 calorie diet. Your daily values may be higher or lower depending on your calorie needs:

		Calories:	2,000	2,500
Total Fat	Less than		65g	80g
Saturated Fat	Less than		20g	25g
Cholesterol	Less than		300mg	300mg
Sodium	Less than		2,400mg	2,400mg
Total Carbohydrate			300g	375g
Dietary Fiber			25g	30g

Calories per gram:
  Fat 9 • Carbohydrate 4 • Protein 4

Preparation:

- In large pot, simmer the lentils, water, and salt, covered, for 3-4 hours.
- Sauté garlic, onion, celery and carrots in oil. Add to lentils.
- Continue to simmer on low heat.
- Add pepper, tomatoes, wine, lemon juice, molasses or brown sugar, wine vinegar and herbs (if using) about 30 minutes before serving.
- Sprinkle extra vinegar and freshly chopped scallions onto each serving.

Thanks to: Lance & Valerie McIntyre, Group 1

Category: Soups

LENTIL SWEET POTATO STEW

This recipe will become a favorite-a tasty combination of lentils and sweet potatoes, perfect for Fall.

Makes 4 servings

Ingredients:

1	tsp	olive oil
3	cloves	garlic, minced (1½ teaspoons)
1		onion, minced (¾ cup)
3	tsp	curry powder
1	tsp	fresh ginger, finely grated
1	fresh	jalapeno pepper, seeded & minced
1	cup	dried lentils
2		sweet potatoes, peeled & cubed
2		tomatoes, chopped, including juice
4	cups	fat-free vegetable stock
1	cup	non-fat yogurt, plain (or non-fat sour cream)
¼	cup	fresh cilantro or parsley, chopped
		salt to taste

Nutrition Facts

Serving Size 1/4 recipe (578g)
Servings Per Container 4

Amount Per Serving

Calories 370   Calories from Fat 30

% Daily Value*

Total Fat 3.5g	5%
Saturated Fat 0.5g	3%
Trans Fat 0g	
Cholesterol 0mg	0%
Sodium 180mg	8%
Total Carbohydrate 65g	22%
Dietary Fiber 13g	52%
Sugars 16g	
Protein 21g	

Vitamin A 260% • Vitamin C 180%
Calcium 30% • Iron 50%

*Percent Daily Values are based on a 2,000 calorie diet. Your daily values may be higher or lower depending on your calorie needs:

	Calories:	2,000	2,500
Total Fat	Less than	65g	80g
Saturated Fat	Less than	20g	25g
Cholesterol	Less than	300mg	300mg
Sodium	Less than	2,400mg	2,400mg
Total Carbohydrate		300g	375g
Dietary Fiber		25g	30g

Calories per gram:
  Fat 9 • Carbohydrate 4 • Protein 4

Preparation:

- Heat a large soup pot over medium-high heat, add oil, garlic, onion, curry powder, ginger, and jalapeno pepper.
- Sauté until mixture is fragrant, about 4 minutes.
- Add lentils, sweet potatoes, tomatoes, and broth. Add salt to taste.
- Bring to a boil, reduce the heat to medium, cover loosely, and let the soup simmer until the lentils are tender, about 30 minutes.
- Just before serving, swirl in yogurt and cilantro.

Source: *Sacramento Bee*

Category: Soups

Lu's Tortilla Soup

This is a nice twist on the popular restaurant version that usually contains chicken. If you miss the meat, try adding vegetarian chicken strips available in the health food section at most grocery stores.

Makes 6 servings

Ingredients:

4	cups	fat-free chicken broth
2 ½	cups	corn kernels (hominy)
3	cups	chunky enchilada sauce (see page 368)
1 ½	cups	black beans, cooked
1 ½	cups	red kidney beans, cooked
1	can	green chiles (4 oz), diced
½	cup	green onion, diced
½	cup	cilantro, finely diced
2	cloves	garlic, crushed
1	Tbsp	crushed oregano leaves
2	tsp	ground cumin
6		corn tortillas, cut into strips
		fat-free jack cheese, shredded (optional)

Preparation:

- In a large soup pot, mix together broth, enchilada sauce, beans, cilantro and oregano.
- In another pan which has been lightly sprayed, sauté garlic, green onion, cumin, hominy and diced green chiles until soft.
- Add to soup pot. Let this mixture come to a fast boil, lower heat and simmer for about an hour.
- Add half of tortilla strips to soup, immediately before serving.
- With each individual serving, add fresh tortilla strips, and, if desired, sprinkle with shredded jack cheese.

Also delicious with a dollop of fat-free sour cream on top instead of the cheese.

Thanks to: Lu Crowe, Group 14

Category: Soups

Nutrition Facts

Serving Size 1/6 recipe (639g)
Servings Per Container 6

Amount Per Serving

Calories 320   Calories from Fat 25

% Daily Value*

Total Fat 2.5g	4%
Saturated Fat 0g	0%
Trans Fat 0g	
Cholesterol 0mg	0%
Sodium 590mg	25%
Total Carbohydrate 59g	20%
Dietary Fiber 14g	56%
Sugars 9g	
Protein 17g	

Vitamin A 50%	•	Vitamin C 45%
Calcium 10%	•	Iron 20%

*Percent Daily Values are based on a 2,000 calorie diet. Your daily values may be higher or lower depending on your calorie needs:

		Calories:	2,000	2,500
Total Fat	Less than		65g	80g
Saturated Fat	Less than		20g	25g
Cholesterol	Less than		300mg	300mg
Sodium	Less than		2,400mg	2,400mg
Total Carbohydrate			300g	375g
Dietary Fiber			25g	30g

Calories per gram:
Fat 9 • Carbohydrate 4 • Protein 4

ROASTED RED PEPPER AND SWEET POTATO SOUP

This is packed with vitamins A and C and a good substitute for the higher sodium versions available commercially. Use fresh tomatoes to reduce sodium even further.

Makes 6 servings

Ingredients:

1	med	red bell pepper, seeded
½	med	onion, chopped
1	med	sweet potato, peeled and cubed
2	cloves	garlic, peeled (1 tsp)
1	cup	pinto beans, cooked
1	cup	diced canned tomatoes, with herbs
2	cups	vegetable broth (see page 384)

Garnish:

fat-free croutons
fat-free Parmesan cheese.

Preparation:

- Roast pepper in oven at 450°F for 15-20 min, until skin is blackened.
- Cool and remove skin (rub between paper towels) and cut into strips.
- Spray a large stockpot with vegetable oil cooking spray and brown onion over medium heat.
- Add the pepper strips and the remaining ingredients to pot.
- Bring to boil, reduce heat, cover and simmer for 90 min.
- Purée soup in blender until smooth.
- Garnish with croutons and cheese.

Thanks to: Anne Dunn Group 21

Category: Soups

Nutrition Facts

Serving Size 1/6 recipe (233g)
Servings Per Container 6

Amount Per Serving

Calories 100   Calories from Fat 5

% Daily Value*

Total Fat 0g	0%
Saturated Fat 0g	0%
Trans Fat 0g	
Cholesterol 0mg	0%
Sodium 250mg	10%
Total Carbohydrate 19g	6%
Dietary Fiber 5g	20%
Sugars 5g	
Protein 4g	

Vitamin A 100%   •   Vitamin C 90%
Calcium 6%   •   Iron 15%

*Percent Daily Values are based on a 2,000 calorie diet. Your daily values may be higher or lower depending on your calorie needs:

	Calories:	2,000	2,500
Total Fat	Less than	65g	80g
Saturated Fat	Less than	20g	25g
Cholesterol	Less than	300mg	300mg
Sodium	Less than	2,400mg	2,400mg
Total Carbohydrate		300g	375g
Dietary Fiber		25g	30g

Calories per gram:
Fat 9   •   Carbohydrate 4   •   Protein 4

Speedy TVP Stew

This recipe lends itself to oven, stove top, crockpot or microwave cooking. Cook slowly on stove top until veggies are tender. Check occasionally and stir so that it does not dry out and burn!

Serves 8

Ingredients:

1	cup	water
1	cup	red wine OR bouillon
1⅓	cups	TVP (chunks or strips, beef or unflavored)
1	pkg	McCormick Beef Stew Bag'n'seasoning mix
1	med	onion diced (¾ cup)
5	cups	fresh veggies cut into bite-sized pieces (e.g. carrots, potatoes, celery, leeks, and mushrooms)

OR

1	pkg	frozen vegetables for stew (24 oz)
8	oz	unsalted tomato sauce
¼	cup	flour

Preparation:

- Heat water and wine to near boiling.
- Add TVP and seasoning mix.
- Place vegetables in cooking bag.
- Mix tomato sauce, flour and any liquid from the TVP, in large measuring cup until smooth.
- Place TVP and tomato sauce into bag with veggies and mix well.
- Place all in a 9 x13 inch pan.
- Tie bag, spread contents evenly. Puncture bag with 4 small holes.
- Cook in microwave as directed by frozen veggie directions, 15-20 minutes.
- OR
- Cook in 350°F oven for 35 minutes.
- Check for flavor when cooked. Add salt, pepper, etc, to taste.
- If mixture is runny, mix ¼ cup flour with some cold liquid and add, stirring well to thicken so the tasty broth will stick to the solids.

Nutrition Facts

Serving Size 1/8 recipe (208g)
Servings Per Container 8

Amount Per Serving

Calories 170 — Calories from Fat 0

% Daily Value*

Total Fat 0g	0%
Saturated Fat 0g	0%
Trans Fat 0g	
Cholesterol 0mg	0%
Sodium 110mg	5%
Total Carbohydrate 24g	8%
Dietary Fiber 5g	20%
Sugars 8g	
Protein 11g	

Vitamin A 35%	•	Vitamin C 15%
Calcium 8%	•	Iron 15%

*Percent Daily Values are based on a 2,000 calorie diet. Your daily values may be higher or lower depending on your calorie needs:

	Calories:	2,000	2,500
Total Fat	Less than	65g	80g
Saturated Fat	Less than	20g	25g
Cholesterol	Less than	300mg	300mg
Sodium	Less than	2,400mg	2,400mg
Total Carbohydrate		300g	375g
Dietary Fiber		25g	30g

Calories per gram:
Fat 9 • Carbohydrate 4 • Protein 4

- Serve. (Many tasters are convinced that stews are best reheated after being left overnight in the refrigerator)

Alternate methods:

Oven and without cooking bag: Spray 9 x 13 inch pan with cooking spray. Arrange all ingredients. Adjust liquid (wine, bouillon) volume so TVP chunks are covered. Cover pan loosely with foil or lid, allowing steam to escape. Cook in 375° F oven. After 20 minutes, check if potatoes and carrots are cooked.

Crockpot: Use standard technique, stewing for several hours, remembering that lengthy cooking does seem to improve flavor.

Thanks to: Ginny Goodrow, Group 25

Category: Soups

Spring Asparagus Soup

Different from the 'creamy' version.

Makes 6 servings ~ 1 cup each

Ingredients:

2	large	shallots, coarsely chopped (½ cup)
2	stalks	celery, coarsely chopped
1	lb	asparagus cut into 1 inch pieces (tough ends discarded)
6	cups	vegetable broth (page 384)
⅓	cup	uncooked rice
1	pinch	nutmeg
		salt, pepper, to taste

Preparation:

- Spray stockpot with vegetable oil cooking spray and sauté shallots and celery.
- Add asparagus, broth and rice and bring to a boil.
- Reduce heat and simmer until asparagus is tender and rice is cooked, about 15-20 minutes.
- Season with salt and pepper to taste, and a pinch of nutmeg.
- Purée until smooth.
- Garnish with Italian parsley.

Category: Soups

Nutrition Facts

Serving Size 1/6 recipe (about 1 cup) (413g)
Servings Per Container 6

Amount Per Serving	
Calories 130	Calories from Fat 5
	% Daily Value*
Total Fat 1g	2%
Saturated Fat 0g	0%
Trans Fat 0g	
Cholesterol 0mg	0%
Sodium 105mg	4%
Total Carbohydrate 27g	9%
Dietary Fiber 6g	24%
Sugars 6g	
Protein 6g	

Vitamin A 210%	•	Vitamin C 150%
Calcium 15%	•	Iron 35%

*Percent Daily Values are based on a 2,000 calorie diet. Your daily values may be higher or lower depending on your calorie needs:

		Calories:	2,000	2,500
Total Fat	Less than		65g	80g
Saturated Fat	Less than		20g	25g
Cholesterol	Less than		300mg	300mg
Sodium	Less than		2,400mg	2,400mg
Total Carbohydrate			300g	375g
Dietary Fiber			25g	30g

Calories per gram:
  Fat 9 • Carbohydrate 4 • Protein 4

Sweet and Sour Soup

Quick and easy. Similar to your favorite Chinese restaurant.

Makes 4 servings ~ 1 cup each

Ingredients:

4	cups	vegetable broth (see page 384)
⅓	cup	vinegar
¼	cup	ketchup
2	oz	black mushrooms
3	Tbsp	sugar
2		green onions, chopped as garnish
2	Tbsp	cilantro, chopped as garnish (optional)

Preparation:

- Heat broth in stockpot.
- Add remaining ingredients, heat thoroughly, garnish and serve.

Thanks to: David Smith-Walsh

Category: Soups

Nutrition Facts

Serving Size 1/4 recipe (about 1 cup) (364g)

Servings Per Container 4

Amount Per Serving

Calories 110 — Calories from Fat 5

	% Daily Value*
Total Fat 1g	2%
Saturated Fat 0g	0%
Trans Fat 0g	
Cholesterol 0mg	0%
Sodium 250mg	10%
Total Carbohydrate 26g	9%
Dietary Fiber 5g	20%
Sugars 15g	
Protein 4g	

Vitamin A 200% • Vitamin C 140%
Calcium 15% • Iron 25%

*Percent Daily Values are based on a 2,000 calorie diet. Your daily values may be higher or lower depending on your calorie needs:

		Calories:	2,000	2,500
Total Fat	Less than		65g	80g
Saturated Fat	Less than		20g	25g
Cholesterol	Less than		300mg	300mg
Sodium	Less than		2,400mg	2,400mg
Total Carbohydrate			300g	375g
Dietary Fiber			25g	30g

Calories per gram:
Fat 9 • Carbohydrate 4 • Protein 4

Sweet Potato Jalapeno Soup with Tomatillo Cream

This might seem like a lot of work, but it doesn't take too long to prepare and is well worth the effort.

Makes 10 cups

Ingredients:

2	med	leeks, white part only, cleaned and finely chopped
1	clove	garlic, minced
¼	tsp	cumin, ground
3	lbs	sweet potatoes or yams, peeled, cut into 2 inch. pieces (about 6 medium)
6-7	cups	vegetable broth (see page 384)
1	small	jalapeno chile, seeded and chopped
½	tsp	salt (optional)
¼	tsp	white pepper
2	Tbsp	fresh lime juice
1	tsp	brown sugar (optional)
½	cup	corn kernels

Tomatillo Cream:

½	cup	non-fat plain yogurt (or non-fat sour cream)
2	Tbsp	tomatillo salsa (green salsa)
1	Tbsp	cilantro, finely chopped
¼	tsp	salt (optional)

Nutrition Facts
Serving Size 1/10 recipe (about 3/4 cup) (480g)
Servings Per Container 10

Amount Per Serving

Calories 260   Calories from Fat 5

% Daily Value*

- Total Fat 0.5g — 1%
- Saturated Fat 0g — 0%
- Trans Fat 0g
- Cholesterol 0mg — 0%
- Sodium 370mg — 15%
- Total Carbohydrate 59g — 20%
- Dietary Fiber 11g — 44%
- Sugars 19g
- Protein 8g

Vitamin A 670% • Vitamin C 170%
Calcium 15% • Iron 25%

*Percent Daily Values are based on a 2,000 calorie diet. Your daily values may be higher or lower depending on your calorie needs:

		Calories:	2,000	2,500
Total Fat		Less than	65g	80g
Saturated Fat		Less than	20g	25g
Cholesterol		Less than	300mg	300mg
Sodium		Less than	2,400mg	2,400mg
Total Carbohydrate			300g	375g
Dietary Fiber			25g	30g

Calories per gram:
Fat 9 • Carbohydrate 4 • Protein 4

Preparation:

- In a large soup pot, sauté leeks in vegetable oil cooking spray for 6 minutes or until softened.
- Add garlic and cumin and cook for another minute.
- Add sweet potatoes, broth, jalapeno, salt and pepper. Simmer covered for 20-25 minutes or until sweet potatoes are very tender.
- Purée the soup in the pan with a hand beater or use a food processor or blender.
- Add an additional cup of broth if the soup is too thick.
- Return the soup to the pot and bring it to a simmer.
- Add lime juice, brown sugar, and corn kernels.
- Cook for 3 minutes more. Taste for seasoning.

- In a small bowl, combine yogurt, salsa and cilantro as tomatillo cream.
- To serve: ladle the soup into bowls.
- Garnish with a tablespoon of the tomatillo cream, a sprinkling of corn kernels, chopped cilantro (1 tsp) and a squeeze (1 tsp) of fresh lime juice.

You can prepare this soup up to 3 days ahead, but the tomatillo cream and garnish need to be prepared within an hour or so of serving.

Thanks to: Jill Burns, R.D.
Category: Soups

SWEET POTATO STEW

Makes 4 - 6 servings

Ingredients:

2	large	sweet potatoes (about 2 lbs)
1	cup	onion chopped (1 medium)
1	Tbsp	chili powder
1	cup	orange juice (use calcium fortified for added nutrition)
1	Tbsp	honey (optional)
1½	cup	black beans, cooked
1	Tbsp	light butter, softened (optional)
2	Tbsp	flour
¼	cup	almond slivers, toasted (optional)

Preparation:

- Peel and cut sweet potatoes into 1 inch chunks.
- Put in a large microwave safe bowl with onion, chili powder, orange juice, and honey (if used).
- Cover, microwave on high for 20 minutes until potatoes are soft but hold their shape.
- Add beans, blend together.
- Mix together butter substitute and flour. Add to stew and mix.
- Microwave on high for about 5 minutes or until beans are heated through and stew has thickened slightly.
- Sprinkle with almond slivers

Thanks to: Jill Burns R.D.

Category: Soups and Stews

Nutrition Facts
Serving Size 1/6 recipe (260g)
Servings Per Container 6

Amount Per Serving

Calories 230   Calories from Fat 20

% Daily Value*

Total Fat 2.5g	4%
Saturated Fat 0g	0%
Trans Fat 0g	
Cholesterol 0mg	0%
Sodium 200mg	8%
Total Carbohydrate 48g	16%
Dietary Fiber 9g	36%
Sugars 16g	
Protein 7g	

Vitamin A 150%   •   Vitamin C 60%
Calcium 6%   •   Iron 10%

*Percent Daily Values are based on a 2,000 calorie diet. Your daily values may be higher or lower depending on your calorie needs:

	Calories:	2,000	2,500
Total Fat	Less than	65g	80g
Saturated Fat	Less than	20g	25g
Cholesterol	Less than	300mg	300mg
Sodium	Less than	2,400mg	2,400mg
Total Carbohydrate		300g	375g
Dietary Fiber		25g	30g

Calories per gram:
Fat 9 • Carbohydrate 4 • Protein 4

Winter Vegetable Soup

A good way to use your vegetable drawer odds and ends. Hominy can be found in the canned bean or Mexican section at your grocery store.

Makes 10-12 servings " Should serve a crowd"

Ingredients:

1	cup	TVP bacon bits
4	cups	vegetable broth (see page 384), divided
1½	cups	onions, coarsely chopped
4	large	carrots, peeled and chopped
4-5		celery stalks, with tops, chopped
2	tsp	minced garlic
2	cups	broccoli stems, OR, kale OR cabbage, chopped
3-4		potatoes, peeled and chopped into ½ inch pieces
3	cups	tomatoes, chopped
1	can	white hominy, drained and rinsed (29 oz)
3	cups	black beans, cooked
½	cup	parsley, chopped

Nutrition Facts

Serving Size 1/12 recipe (400g)
Servings Per Container 12

Amount Per Serving

Calories 210   Calories from Fat 15

% Daily Value*

Total Fat 1.5g	2%
Saturated Fat 0g	0%
Trans Fat 0g	
Cholesterol 0mg	0%
Sodium 230mg	10%
Total Carbohydrate 41g	14%
Dietary Fiber 11g	44%
Sugars 9g	
Protein 12g	

Vitamin A 170% • Vitamin C 110%
Calcium 15% • Iron 25%

*Percent Daily Values are based on a 2,000 calorie diet. Your daily values may be higher or lower depending on your calorie needs:

		Calories:	2,000	2,500
Total Fat		Less than	65g	80g
Saturated Fat		Less than	20g	25g
Cholesterol		Less than	300mg	300mg
Sodium		Less than	2,400mg	2,400mg
Total Carbohydrate			300g	375g
Dietary Fiber			25g	30g

Calories per gram:
Fat 9 • Carbohydrate 4 • Protein 4

Preparation:

- Put TVP in bowl with 2 cups of vegetable broth; set aside to hydrate.
- In a large pot, sauté onions, carrots, celery, garlic, and broccoli stems in vegetable oil cooking spray (canola or olive oil).
- Turn and stir until steaming.
- Add hydrated TVP bacon bits, remainder of broth, potatoes, tomatoes, hominy, beans and parsley.
- Heat well, stirring occasionally, until potatoes are done.
- Taste and adjust seasonings.
- If needed, thicken with Instant Potato buds or flakes.

Thanks to: Phyllis and Walter Quinn, group 25

Category: Soups and Stews

DINNER

BEANS

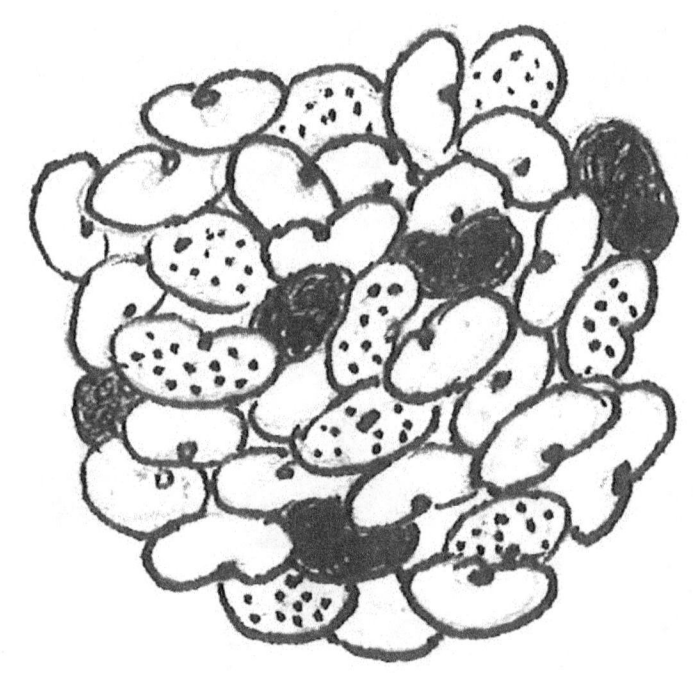

BAKED BEANS PLYMOUTH-STYLE

The addition of molasses and apple make these beans similar to baked beans. Generally, a serving is ½ cup, full of fiber and protein.

Makes 6 servings

Ingredients:

1	med	onion, chopped
2	med	apples, grated
½	tsp	salt
2	tsp	dry mustard
1	can	unsalted tomato sauce (8 oz)
1	cup	water
2	Tbsp	molasses
8	cups	beans, cooked and drained (great northern, navy or small red beans work well OR use canned beans

Preparation:

- Preheat oven to 350°F.
- Coat large covered casserole with nonstick spray.
- Sauté onion in cooking spray for 3 minutes.
- Add apples, cook over low heat, keeping tightly covered for 5 minutes.
- Mix well in large casserole with other ingredients.
- Bake covered with lid or foil for 45 minutes.

Category: Beans

Nutrition Facts

Serving Size (413g)
Servings Per Container

Amount Per Serving

Calories 420   Calories from Fat 20

% Daily Value*

Total Fat 2g	3%
Saturated Fat 0g	0%
Trans Fat 0g	
Cholesterol 0mg	0%
Sodium 200mg	8%
Total Carbohydrate 82g	27%
Dietary Fiber 28g	112%
Sugars 14g	
Protein 21g	

Vitamin A 4% • Vitamin C 20%
Calcium 20% • Iron 35%

*Percent Daily Values are based on a 2,000 calorie diet. Your daily values may be higher or lower depending on your calorie needs:

		Calories:	2,000	2,500
Total Fat	Less than		65g	80g
Saturated Fat	Less than		20g	25g
Cholesterol	Less than		300mg	300mg
Sodium	Less than		2,400mg	2,400mg
Total Carbohydrate			300g	375g
Dietary Fiber			25g	30g

Calories per gram:
 Fat 9 • Carbohydrate 4 • Protein 4

Barbecue Bean Casserole

Using a combination of beans makes this a little different than traditional BBQ beans. Beans are a good source of cholesterol lowering soluble fiber.

Makes 8 servings

Ingredients:

4½	cups	beans, cooked (mix your choice of kidney, red, cannelloni, garbanzo, pinto)
¾	cup	barbecue sauce
2	Tbsp	brown sugar (optional)
½	Tbsp	dry mustard
2	Tbsp	minced onion

Preparation:

- Rinse and drain the beans, combine in saucepan or casserole with remaining ingredients.
- Simmer on stove top over low heat for 15 to 60 minutes (longer time yields better flavor).
- Or, bake them in a 350°F oven for 30 to 60 minutes; uncover the last 15 minutes to thicken the sauce.

Thanks to: Laurie Crider-Vanpal, Group 29

Category: Beans

Nutrition Facts

Serving Size 1/8 recipe (114g)
Servings Per Container 8

Amount Per Serving

Calories 180   Calories from Fat 10

% Daily Value*

Total Fat 1.5g	2%
Saturated Fat 0g	0%
Trans Fat 0g	
Cholesterol 0mg	0%
Sodium 200mg	8%
Total Carbohydrate 35g	12%
Dietary Fiber 7g	28%
Sugars 11g	
Protein 8g	

Vitamin A 2%	•	Vitamin C 4%
Calcium 4%	•	Iron 10%

*Percent Daily Values are based on a 2,000 calorie diet. Your daily values may be higher or lower depending on your calorie needs:

		Calories:	2,000	2,500
Total Fat	Less than		65g	80g
Saturated Fat	Less than		20g	25g
Cholesterol	Less than		300mg	300mg
Sodium	Less than		2,400mg	2,400mg
Total Carbohydrate			300g	375g
Dietary Fiber			25g	30g

Calories per gram:
  Fat 9 • Carbohydrate 4 • Protein 4

CAJUN PINTO BEANS

For a Latin or New Orleans flair.

Makes 8 servings

Ingredients:

2	cups	dry pinto beans (do not soak)
5	cups	water
1½	large	onion, chopped (1½ cups)
1	Tbsp	garlic powder
2	tsp	paprika
¼	tsp	cayenne flakes or pepper
1-2		bay leaves, remove before serving
1	Tbsp	crushed dry parsley
3	stalks	celery, chopped fine
⅓	cup	green bell pepper, chopped

Preparation:

- Wash beans to ensure they are clean.
- Put all ingredients into a soup pot and bring to a boil.
- Reduce heat and simmer at least 2½ hours.

Thanks to: Abbott and Norma Thibodeaux

Nutrition Facts
Serving Size 1/8 recipe (259g)
Servings Per Container 8

Amount Per Serving

Calories 190 — Calories from Fat 5

% Daily Value*

- Total Fat 1g — 2%
  - Saturated Fat 0g — 0%
  - Trans Fat 0g
- Cholesterol 0mg — 0%
- Sodium 35mg — 1%
- Total Carbohydrate 35g — 12%
  - Dietary Fiber 9g — 36%
  - Sugars 3g
- Protein 11g

Vitamin A 8% • Vitamin C 20%
Calcium 8% • Iron 15%

*Percent Daily Values are based on a 2,000 calorie diet. Your daily values may be higher or lower depending on your calorie needs:

	Calories:	2,000	2,500
Total Fat	Less than	65g	80g
Saturated Fat	Less than	20g	25g
Cholesterol	Less than	300mg	300mg
Sodium	Less than	2,400mg	2,400mg
Total Carbohydrate		300g	375g
Dietary Fiber		25g	30g

Calories per gram:
Fat 9 • Carbohydrate 4 • Protein 4

Category: Beans

Classic Baked Beans

"Classic Baked Beans" says it all. Tasty, but allow several hours of cooking time.

Makes 8 serving ~ 1 cup each

Ingredients:

1	lb	navy beans, uncooked
3	Tbsp	brown sugar
½	tsp	salt or less
1	tsp	dry mustard
½	cup	dark molasses
½	cup	ketchup
2		onions, cut into quarters

Preparation:

- Wash the beans and soak overnight in enough water to cover them. Drain.
- Place in a saucepan and cover with water. Simmer, covered, 1-2 hours.
- Preheat oven to 325°F.
- Mix the brown sugar, salt, mustard, molasses and ketchup with beans and remaining liquid.
- Place onion quarters in the bottom of a 2 quart casserole. Pour in the beans.
- Add enough boiling water to cover beans.
- Cover casserole; place in oven and bake for 5-6 hours, adding more water as needed.

Nutrition Facts

Serving Size 1 cup (136g)
Servings Per Container 8

Amount Per Serving

Calories 290   Calories from Fat 10

% Daily Value*

Total Fat 1g	2%
Saturated Fat 0g	0%
Trans Fat 0g	
Cholesterol 0mg	0%
Sodium 330mg	14%
Total Carbohydrate 60g	20%
Dietary Fiber 15g	60%
Sugars 27g	
Protein 13g	

Vitamin A 2%	•	Vitamin C 8%
Calcium 20%	•	Iron 35%

*Percent Daily Values are based on a 2,000 calorie diet. Your daily values may be higher or lower depending on your calorie needs:

		Calories:	2,000	2,500
Total Fat	Less than		65g	80g
Saturated Fat	Less than		20g	25g
Cholesterol	Less than		300mg	300mg
Sodium	Less than		2,400mg	2,400mg
Total Carbohydrate			300g	375g
Dietary Fiber			25g	30g

Calories per gram:
 Fat 9 • Carbohydrate 4 • Protein 4

Category: Beans

CURRIED GARBANZO BEANS AND POTATOES

This dish is similar to the Indian version. You can prepare in advance and put in the oven when you get home from work.

Makes 6 servings

Ingredients:

2	tsp	olive oil or cooking spray
1	cup	red or yellow pepper, diced
½	cup	onion, finely chopped
4	tsp	flour
1	tsp	curry powder
½	tsp	salt
½	tsp	ground cumin
½	tsp	pepper
2	cups	water
1¾	cups	round red potatoes, diced unpeeled
1	cup	Granny Smith apples, partially peeled, diced
1	cup	green peas
1½	cups	garbanzo beans, cooked

Nutrition Facts

Serving Size 1/6 recipe (250g)
Servings Per Container 6

Amount Per Serving

Calories 170 Calories from Fat 25

% Daily Value*

Total Fat 3g	5%
Saturated Fat 0g	0%
Trans Fat 0g	
Cholesterol 0mg	0%
Sodium 210mg	9%
Total Carbohydrate 29g	10%
Dietary Fiber 7g	28%
Sugars 8g	
Protein 6g	

Vitamin A 20% • Vitamin C 90%
Calcium 4% • Iron 15%

*Percent Daily Values are based on a 2,000 calorie diet. Your daily values may be higher or lower depending on your calorie needs:

		Calories:	2,000	2,500
Total Fat		Less than	65g	80g
Saturated Fat		Less than	20g	25g
Cholesterol		Less than	300mg	300mg
Sodium		Less than	2,400mg	2,400mg
Total Carbohydrate			300g	375g
Dietary Fiber			25g	30g

Calories per gram:
Fat 9 • Carbohydrate 4 • Protein 4

Preparation:

- Preheat oven to 350°F.
- Heat oil or cooking spray in a large nonstick skillet over medium heat.
- Add bell pepper and onion, sauté for 6 minutes or until tender.
- Sprinkle with flour and the next 4 ingredients. Stir well and cook for an additional 30 seconds.
- Add potatoes, apples, peas and garbanzo beans together with water. (You may not need all of the water depending upon the consistency you like.)
- Pour into baking dish and bake for 35 - 40 minutes.
- Serve over rice.

Thanks to: Bob and Pat Curley, Group 3

Category: Beans

DAVE'S HEARTY BURRITO

This recipe makes good use of several things you could have created from recipes in this collection. Very easy meal once you get all your ingredients created.

Makes 1 serving

Ingredients:

1		homemade tortilla (see page 213) or fat-free flour tortilla
¼	cup	fat-free refried beans (see page 174 or commercial brand)
2	Tbsp	fat-free cheddar cheese (divided)
¼	cup	Spanish rice (see page 267) or other cooked rice
2	Tbsp	tomatillo sauce (see page 383)

Preparation:

- Fill homemade tortilla with beans, 1 Tbsp cheese, and rice.
- Roll and top with tomatillo sauce, 1 Tbsp cheese and bake at 350°F for 10 minutes.

Thanks to: David Smith-Walsh

Category: Beans, Mexican

Nutrition Facts

Serving Size 1 burrito (230g)
Servings Per Container 1

Amount Per Serving

Calories 250	Calories from Fat 15

% Daily Value*

Total Fat 1.5g	2%
Saturated Fat 0g	0%
Trans Fat 0g	
Cholesterol 5mg	2%
Sodium 370mg	15%
Total Carbohydrate 52g	17%
Dietary Fiber 8g	32%
Sugars 4g	
Protein 13g	

Vitamin A 40%	•	Vitamin C 50%
Calcium 20%	•	Iron 20%

*Percent Daily Values are based on a 2,000 calorie diet. Your daily values may be higher or lower depending on your calorie needs:

		Calories:	2,000	2,500
Total Fat	Less than		65g	80g
Saturated Fat	Less than		20g	25g
Cholesterol	Less than		300mg	300mg
Sodium	Less than		2,400mg	2,400mg
Total Carbohydrate			300g	375g
Dietary Fiber			25g	30g

Calories per gram:
   Fat 9 • Carbohydrate 4 • Protein 4

LAZY BAKED BEANS

When you need that baked bean fix, but don't want to bother with cooking your own beans and are willing to grab cans from the cupboard.

Makes 8 servings

Ingredients:

2	cans	vegetarian baked beans in tomato sauce (16 oz)
½	cup	onion, chopped
¼	cup	green pepper, chopped
3	Tbsp	brown sugar
1	Tbsp	molasses
2	tsp	Worcestershire sauce
¼	tsp	dry mustard
¼	tsp	pepper

Preparation:

- Preheat oven to 400°F.
- Mix ingredients well, place in ovenproof dish, cover and bake for about 45 minutes, stirring occasionally.

Thanks to: Dianne Hyson, R.D.

Category: Beans

Nutrition Facts

Serving Size 1/8 recipe (137g)
Servings Per Container 8

Amount Per Serving

Calories 140   Calories from Fat 5

% Daily Value*

Total Fat 0g	0%
Saturated Fat 0g	0%
Trans Fat 0g	
Cholesterol 0mg	0%
Sodium 440mg	18%
Total Carbohydrate 29g	10%
Dietary Fiber 6g	24%
Sugars 15g	
Protein 5g	

Vitamin A 6%	•	Vitamin C 10%
Calcium 4%	•	Iron 15%

*Percent Daily Values are based on a 2,000 calorie diet. Your daily values may be higher or lower depending on your calorie needs:

		Calories:	2,000	2,500
Total Fat	Less than		65g	80g
Saturated Fat	Less than		20g	25g
Cholesterol	Less than		300mg	300mg
Sodium	Less than		2,400mg	2,400mg
Total Carbohydrate			300g	375g
Dietary Fiber			25g	30g

Calories per gram:
  Fat 9 • Carbohydrate 4 • Protein 4

LAZY BAKED BEANS WITH PINEAPPLE

Follow above recipe but add a 20 oz can of crushed pineapple including juice, and a bit of liquid smoke if desired. Simmer in crockpot for at least 3-4 hours. Always better the next day, even cold.

Makes 8 servings

Variation from: Ginny Goodrow, group 25:

Nutrition Facts

Serving Size 1/8 recipe (166g)
Servings Per Container 8

Amount Per Serving

Calories 160	Calories from Fat 5

% Daily Value*

Total Fat 0.5g	1%
Saturated Fat 0g	0%
Trans Fat 0g	
Cholesterol 0mg	0%
Sodium 440mg	18%
Total Carbohydrate 34g	11%
Dietary Fiber 6g	24%
Sugars 19g	
Protein 5g	

Vitamin A 6%	•	Vitamin C 15%
Calcium 6%	•	Iron 15%

*Percent Daily Values are based on a 2,000 calorie diet. Your daily values may be higher or lower depending on your calorie needs:

		Calories:	2,000	2,500
Total Fat	Less than		65g	80g
Saturated Fat	Less than		20g	25g
Cholesterol	Less than		300mg	300mg
Sodium	Less than		2,400mg	2,400mg
Total Carbohydrate			300g	375g
Dietary Fiber			25g	30g

Calories per gram:
Fat 9 • Carbohydrate 4 • Protein 4

Lentils with Spinach

Lentils are quick to cook compared to other dried beans. Adding spinach increases the vitamin C, folate, and fiber.

Makes 4 servings

Ingredients:

1	quart	water
½	cup	lentils
1		carrot, finely chopped (½ cup)
¼		onion, finely chopped (½ cup)
1	dried	bay leaf
1	tsp	olive oil
8	oz	spinach cut into ½ inch pieces
		coarse salt and freshly ground pepper to taste,

Preparation:

- In a large saucepan, combine water, lentils, carrot, onion, bay leaf, salt and pepper.
- Bring to a boil. Lower the heat and simmer, partially covered, until the lentils are soft (15-20 minutes).
- Drain, discarding bay leaf.
- Use a paper towel to wipe out any water from the saucepan, add oil.
- Return pan to medium heat.
- Stir in lentils, vegetables and spinach.
- Cook, stirring occasionally, until spinach is wilted (about 2 minutes).
- Taste, adjust seasoning if desired.
- Use a slotted spoon to transfer to serving bowl.

Category: Beans

Nutrition Facts

Serving Size 1/4 recipe (357g)
Servings Per Container 4

Amount Per Serving

Calories 120	Calories from Fat 20

	% Daily Value*
Total Fat 2g	3%
Saturated Fat 0g	0%
Trans Fat 0g	
Cholesterol 0mg	0%
Sodium 70mg	3%
Total Carbohydrate 20g	7%
Dietary Fiber 5g	20%
Sugars 2g	
Protein 8g	

Vitamin A 170%	•	Vitamin C 30%
Calcium 8%	•	Iron 20%

*Percent Daily Values are based on a 2,000 calorie diet. Your daily values may be higher or lower depending on your calorie needs:

		Calories:	2,000	2,500
Total Fat		Less than	65g	80g
Saturated Fat		Less than	20g	25g
Cholesterol		Less than	300mg	300mg
Sodium		Less than	2,400mg	2,400mg
Total Carbohydrate			300g	375g
Dietary Fiber			25g	30g

Calories per gram:
  Fat 9 • Carbohydrate 4 • Protein 4

REFRIED BEANS

Make your own! Contain less salt than the canned ones. If this is below your salt threshold, add a little Lite Salt.

Makes 4 cups

Ingredients:

1½	cups	pinto beans, uncooked
¼	cup	onion, chopped
2	cloves	garlic, minced
1	tsp	ground cumin
		vegetable oil spray

Preparation:

- Soak beans overnight in water.
- The next day boil beans in 6 cups fresh water until tender (2-3 hours).
- Drain and save some liquid.
- Sauté onions and garlic in vegetable oil cooking spray until clear.
- Add a little water if vegetables stick.
- Mash half of the beans, and add to onion and garlic.
- Continue to sauté for 10 minutes, stirring frequently.
- Allow some of the mashed beans to brown. Add cumin. Add remaining beans and continue cooking until they are warmed through.
- Water or liquid from beans may be added to keep the beans soft and mushy.

Nutrition Facts

Serving Size makes 4 cups (224g)
Servings Per Container

Amount Per Serving

Calories 380   Calories from Fat 5

% Daily Value*

Total Fat 0g	0%
Saturated Fat 0g	0%
Trans Fat 0g	
Cholesterol 0mg	0%
Sodium 95mg	4%
Total Carbohydrate 135g	45%
Dietary Fiber 85g	340%
Sugars 6g	
Protein 43g	

Vitamin A 0% • Vitamin C 4%
Calcium 2% • Iron 4%

*Percent Daily Values are based on a 2,000 calorie diet. Your daily values may be higher or lower depending on your calorie needs:

		2,000	2,500
Total Fat	Less than	65g	80g
Saturated Fat	Less than	20g	25g
Cholesterol	Less than	300mg	300mg
Sodium	Less than	2,400mg	2,400mg
Total Carbohydrate		300g	375g
Dietary Fiber		25g	30g

Calories per gram:
 Fat 9 • Carbohydrate 4 • Protein 4

Source: *Adapted from New American Diet*

Category: Beans

Soft Lentils

Baking these lentils will give you time to put together the rest of dinner while they cook.

Makes 8 servings

Ingredients:

1	tsp	olive oil
3	cups	minced onions
1½	tsp	salt
1	cup	tomatoes, roasted and minced
OR		
1	cup	canned tomatoes, diced
1	tsp	brown sugar
1	tsp	balsamic vinegar
8	cups	lentils, well cooked (see note below)
		black pepper to taste

Nutrition Facts

Serving Size 1/8 recipe (191g)
Servings Per Container 8

Amount Per Serving

Calories 370   Calories from Fat 25

% Daily Value*

- Total Fat 2.5g — 4%
- Saturated Fat 0g — 0%
- Trans Fat 0g
- Cholesterol 0mg — 0%
- Sodium 520mg — 22%
- Total Carbohydrate 65g — 22%
- Dietary Fiber 12g — 48%
- Sugars 4g
- Protein 25g

Vitamin A 4% • Vitamin C 20%
Calcium 6% • Iron 40%

*Percent Daily Values are based on a 2,000 calorie diet. Your daily values may be higher or lower depending on your calorie needs:

	Calories:	2,000	2,500
Total Fat	Less than	65g	80g
Saturated Fat	Less than	20g	25g
Cholesterol	Less than	300mg	300mg
Sodium	Less than	2,400mg	2,400mg
Total Carbohydrate		300g	375g
Dietary Fiber		25g	30g

Calories per gram:
Fat 9 • Carbohydrate 4 • Protein 4

Preparation:

- Preheat oven to 350°F.
- Lightly spray a shallow 9 x 13 inch casserole dish with vegetable oil.
- Heat oil in a large, deep skillet or Dutch oven. Cook onions and salt, covered, over low heat for about 30 minutes, stirring often. Add water when it gets dry.
- Add tomatoes, cover and cook for another 15-20 minutes, stirring frequently.
- Stir in brown sugar, vinegar and lentils; add pepper to taste.
- Transfer to prepared baking pan, cover tightly with foil, and bake for about 45 minutes, or until heated through.
- Serve hot, topped with a scattering of sliced green olives if desired.

NOTE: to get 8 cups of cooked lentils, begin with 4 cups dried. Rinse well, place in a pot with 10 cups of water, bring to boil, and then simmer until very soft (20 minutes for red lentils, 30-40 minutes for green or French lentils). If you have more than 8 cups, the extra lentils can be saved to add to vegetable soup, salad, or cooked grains.

Category: Beans

BREADS

Baking Mix

Use this baking mix as your base for the following biscuit recipe. Similar to Bisquick.

Ingredients:

7	cups	flour
2	cups	oat bran
4	Tbsp	baking powder
2	tsp	baking soda
1 ⅓	cups	non-fat dry powdered milk

Preparation:

- Mix all ingredients in a very large bowl.
- Store in an airtight container and use in recipes calling for Baking Mix.

Nutrition Facts

Serving Size (1224g)
Servings Per Container

Amount Per Serving

Calories 4150   Calories from Fat 200

% Daily Value*

Total Fat 22g	34%
Saturated Fat 4g	20%
Trans Fat 0g	
Cholesterol 0mg	0%
Sodium 8270mg	345%
Total Carbohydrate 879g	293%
Dietary Fiber 53g	212%
Sugars 51g	
Protein 159g	

Vitamin A 0% • Vitamin C 30%
Calcium 290% • Iron 290%

*Percent Daily Values are based on a 2,000 calorie diet. Your daily values may be higher or lower depending on your calorie needs:

		2,000	2,500
Total Fat	Less than	65g	80g
Saturated Fat	Less than	20g	25g
Cholesterol	Less than	300mg	300mg
Sodium	Less than	2,400mg	2,400mg
Total Carbohydrate		300g	375g
Dietary Fiber		25g	30g

Calories per gram:
  Fat 9 • Carbohydrate 4 • Protein 4

Note: Serving size refers to entire recipe.

BISCUITS

Makes 8 servings

Ingredients:

1⅓	cup	baking mix (see page 177)
⅛	tsp	salt
½	cup	water

Topping:

1½	tsp	sugar
	pinch	cinnamon

Preparation:
- Preheat oven to 375°F.
- Prepare baking pan with cooking spray.
- Mix ingredients together and form biscuits.
- Use a bit of mix or flour to keep dough from sticking to board while cutting.
- Sprinkle with cinnamon sugar mixture to imitate browning.
- Bake for about 10 minutes - don't overcook.

Thanks to: Ginny Goodrow

Category: Breads

Nutrition Facts

Serving Size 1/8 recipe (36g)
Servings Per Container 8

Amount Per Serving

Calories 70   Calories from Fat 5

% Daily Value*

Total Fat 0g	0%
Saturated Fat 0g	0%
Trans Fat 0g	
Cholesterol 0mg	0%
Sodium 170mg	7%
Total Carbohydrate 15g	5%
Dietary Fiber 1g	4%
Sugars 2g	
Protein 3g	

Vitamin A 0% • Vitamin C 0%
Calcium 4% • Iron 4%

*Percent Daily Values are based on a 2,000 calorie diet. Your daily values may be higher or lower depending on your calorie needs:

		Calories:	2,000	2,500
Total Fat	Less than		65g	80g
Saturated Fat	Less than		20g	25g
Cholesterol	Less than		300mg	300mg
Sodium	Less than		2,400mg	2,400mg
Total Carbohydrate			300g	375g
Dietary Fiber			25g	30g

Calories per gram:
Fat 9 • Carbohydrate 4 • Protein 4

CORNBREAD

Cornbread is one of the easiest quick breads to modify. This is straight from the Alber's cornmeal box with substitutions of the higher fat ingredients. Add some diced green chiles for a Mexican flair or some corn kernels for more texture.

Makes 18 servings

Ingredients:

2	cups	flour
2	cups	cornmeal
⅞	cup	sugar (1 cup less 2 Tbsp)
2	Tbsp	baking powder
2	tsp	salt
½	cup	applesauce, unsweetened
½	cup	egg substitute
2	cups	non-fat milk

Preparation:

- Preheat oven to 400°F. Coat 9 x 13 inch pan with butter-flavored cooking spray.
- In a large bowl, mix flour, cornmeal, sugar, baking powder and salt.
- In separate bowl, mix together applesauce, egg substitute, and milk.
- Add wet ingredients to dry ingredients; mix until smooth. Pour into prepared pan.
- Bake for 25 min.
- Turn oven to broil, and brown top of cornbread, watching carefully.

Category: Breads

Nutrition Facts

Serving Size 1/18 recipe (80g)
Servings Per Container 18

Amount Per Serving

Calories 160   Calories from Fat 5

% Daily Value*

Total Fat 0.5g	1%
Saturated Fat 0g	0%
Trans Fat 0g	
Cholesterol 0mg	0%
Sodium 470mg	20%
Total Carbohydrate 34g	11%
Dietary Fiber 1g	4%
Sugars 12g	
Protein 4g	

Vitamin A 2%	•	Vitamin C 0%	
Calcium 8%	•	Iron 8%	

*Percent Daily Values are based on a 2,000 calorie diet. Your daily values may be higher or lower depending on your calorie needs:

		Calories:	2,000	2,500
Total Fat		Less than	65g	80g
Saturated Fat		Less than	20g	25g
Cholesterol		Less than	300mg	300mg
Sodium		Less than	2,400mg	2,400mg
Total Carbohydrate			300g	375g
Dietary Fiber			25g	30g

Calories per gram:
  Fat 9 • Carbohydrate 4 • Protein 4

Honey Cornbread

If you can't find non-fat buttermilk, make your own by combining 1 tablespoon of an acid (lemon juice or vinegar) to every cup of skim milk. Let sit in refrigerator for 5 minutes before using.

Makes 16 servings

Ingredients:

1	cup	yellow cornmeal
OR		
¾	cup	cornmeal + ¼ cup bran
1	cup	whole wheat flour
½	tsp	sea salt
1	tsp	baking powder
1	tsp	baking soda
¼	cup	honey
1	tsp	egg substitute, whipped
1⅞	cups	non-fat buttermilk
1	tsp	canola oil
2	cups	fresh or frozen corn kernels (optional)

Preparation:

- Preheat oven to 375° F. Spray 8 x 8 inch pan with vegetable oil spray.
- Combine dry ingredients.
- Stir in liquid ingredients.
- Stir in corn.
- Do not overmix. Batter must be a little lumpy.
- Pour into prepared pan.
- Bake 30 minutes without corn or 55 minutes with corn until toothpick inserted in center comes out clean.
- Cool slightly and cut in 2 inch squares.
- Batter can be prepared hours in advance and refrigerated (covered) in the pan until one half hour before baking.

Thanks to: Hazel and Russell Schanrock, Group 1

Category: Breads

Nutrition Facts

Serving Size 2x2 inch square (66g)
Servings Per Container 16

Amount Per Serving

Calories 100   Calories from Fat 10

% Daily Value*

Total Fat 1g	2%
Saturated Fat 0g	0%
Trans Fat 0g	
Cholesterol 0mg	0%
Sodium 220mg	9%
Total Carbohydrate 20g	7%
Dietary Fiber 2g	8%
Sugars 6g	
Protein 3g	

| Vitamin A 2% | • | Vitamin C 0% |
| Calcium 4% | • | Iron 4% |

*Percent Daily Values are based on a 2,000 calorie diet. Your daily values may be higher or lower depending on your calorie needs:

		Calories:	2,000	2,500
Total Fat	Less than		65g	80g
Saturated Fat	Less than		20g	25g
Cholesterol	Less than		300mg	300mg
Sodium	Less than		2,400mg	2,400mg
Total Carbohydrate			300g	375g
Dietary Fiber			25g	30g

Calories per gram:
Fat 9 • Carbohydrate 4 • Protein 4

Honey Wheat Bread

Add ingredients per the order suggested in your bread maker.

Makes 1 loaf ~ 15 slices

Ingredients:

¾	cup	water
1	Tbsp	water
½	cup	non-fat cottage cheese
¼	cup	honey
1	Tbsp	canola oil
2	cups	white bread flour
1	cup	wheat flour
1	Tbsp	sugar
1½	tsp	salt
2¼	tsp	dry yeast
2	egg	whites

Preparation:

- Combine water, cottage cheese, honey and oil and heat until warmed.
- Add to these warmed ingredients flours, sugar, salt, dry yeast and egg whites.
- Put in bread machine and push start button.

Thanks to: Elizabeth and Robert Sagehorn, Group 3

Category: Breads

Nutrition Facts

Serving Size 1 slice (60g)
Servings Per Container 15

Amount Per Serving

Calories 130   Calories from Fat 15

% Daily Value*

Total Fat 1.5g	2%
Saturated Fat 0g	0%
Trans Fat 0g	
Cholesterol 0mg	0%
Sodium 270mg	11%
Total Carbohydrate 25g	8%
Dietary Fiber 1g	4%
Sugars 6g	
Protein 5g	

Vitamin A 0%   •   Vitamin C 0%

Calcium 2%   •   Iron 2%

*Percent Daily Values are based on a 2,000 calorie diet. Your daily values may be higher or lower depending on your calorie needs:

		Calories:	2,000	2,500
Total Fat	Less than		65g	80g
Saturated Fat	Less than		20g	25g
Cholesterol	Less than		300mg	300mg
Sodium	Less than		2,400mg	2,400mg
Total Carbohydrate			300g	375g
Dietary Fiber			25g	30g

Calories per gram:
Fat 9   •   Carbohydrate 4   •   Protein 4

Honey Wheat Rolls

These are well worth the effort. Using the bread machine to mix the dough saves time.

Makes 16 dinner rolls (2 oz each)

Ingredients:

2	tsp	active dry yeast
1	cup	water
¼	cup	honey
¼	cup	egg substitute
2¾	cup	bread flour
1¼	cup	wheat flour
1	tsp	sea salt

Preparation:

- If using a bread machine, mix on dough cycle.
- If preparing by hand, mix ingredients and knead for 10 minutes, then place in an un-oiled bowl, cover, and let rise until doubled (75-90 minutes).
- Divide into 16 parts.
- Roll each piece into an elongated, pencil-like strand.
- Hold one end of the strand, and coil the remainder around it, tucking the outside end under the newly-formed swirl (so the rolls will rise vertically rather than spreading horizontally).
- Place rolls 2 inches apart on floured baking sheet, cover, and let rise until doubled in size (about 30-45 min).
- Bake at 350° F for 12-18 minutes until lightly browned on top.

Nutrition Facts
Serving Size 1 roll (58g)
Servings Per Container 16

Amount Per Serving

Calories 140 — Calories from Fat 5

% Daily Value*

Total Fat 0.5g	1%
Saturated Fat 0g	0%
Trans Fat 0g	
Cholesterol 0mg	0%
Sodium 180mg	8%
Total Carbohydrate 28g	9%
Dietary Fiber 2g	8%
Sugars 4g	
Protein 5g	

Vitamin A 0%	•	Vitamin C 0%
Calcium 0%	•	Iron 4%

*Percent Daily Values are based on a 2,000 calorie diet. Your daily values may be higher or lower depending on your calorie needs:

		Calories:	2,000	2,500
Total Fat	Less than		65g	80g
Saturated Fat	Less than		20g	25g
Cholesterol	Less than		300mg	300mg
Sodium	Less than		2,400mg	2,400mg
Total Carbohydrate			300g	375g
Dietary Fiber			25g	30g

Calories per gram:
Fat 9 • Carbohydrate 4 • Protein 4

Thanks to: Dave Hansen, Group 40

Category: Breads

INDIAN CORN BREAD

The addition of pumpkin makes this a nice fall treat.

16 servings

Ingredients:

¾	cup	corn meal
¾	cup	white sugar
1	cup	all purpose flour
2	tsp	baking powder
1	tsp	cinnamon
⅛	tsp	nutmeg
⅛	tsp	cloves
⅛	tsp	salt
1	cup	pumpkin
¼	cup	egg substitute
½	cup	nonfat milk

Preparation:

- Preheat oven to 350°F.
- Mix all ingredients in a large bowl.
- Blend well.
- Pour into 9 inch loaf pan.
- Bake for 45 minutes.

Thanks to: Russell and Hazel Schanrock, Group 1

Category: Breads

Nutrition Facts

Serving Size 1/16 recipe (47g)
Servings Per Container 16

Amount Per Serving

Calories 100   Calories from Fat 5

% Daily Value*

Total Fat 0g	0%
Saturated Fat 0g	0%
Trans Fat 0g	
Cholesterol 0mg	0%
Sodium 100mg	4%
Total Carbohydrate 22g	7%
Dietary Fiber 1g	4%
Sugars 10g	
Protein 2g	

Vitamin A 40% • Vitamin C 0%
Calcium 2% • Iron 4%

*Percent Daily Values are based on a 2,000 calorie diet. Your daily values may be higher or lower depending on your calorie needs:

		Calories:	2,000	2,500
Total Fat	Less than		65g	80g
Saturated Fat	Less than		20g	25g
Cholesterol	Less than		300mg	300mg
Sodium	Less than		2,400mg	2,400mg
Total Carbohydrate			300g	375g
Dietary Fiber			25g	30g

Calories per gram:
  Fat 9 • Carbohydrate 4 • Protein 4

Low Fat Pizza

This is an excellent veggie pizza. The dough can be thrown together quickly, but you can also pick up refrigerated uncooked pizza dough at most stores and it is often available in whole wheat (not the Pillsbury variety, which is higher in fat).

Makes 10 servings

Pizza Dough Ingredients:

1	cup	very warm water
1	pkg	dry yeast
1	tsp	sugar
1	tsp	salt
2 - 2 ½	cups	flour
2	Tbsp	cornmeal
		vegetable oil cooking spray

Topping:

½	cup	tomato paste to cover dough
½	cup	onion, chopped
¼	cup	fresh basil, chopped
¼	cup	oregano, chopped
½	cup	green pepper, sliced
½	cup	mushrooms, sliced
½	cup	fat-free mozzarella cheese, grated
½	cup	tomatoes, sliced
½	lb	veggie pepperoni

Preparation:

- Preheat oven to 425°F.
- Make a dough that is easy to handle, using water, yeast, sugar, salt and flour. Pat dough into a 12 inch pizza pan that has been sprayed with vegetable oil spray and sprinkled with corn meal.
- Paint dough with tomato paste.
- Sauté onions, basil and oregano for 2-3 minutes.
- Add sliced green peppers and sauté for about another 4 minutes.
- Layer the dough with mushrooms, fat-free mozzarella cheese, sliced tomatoes, sautéed mixture, more cheese and top with veggie pepperoni.
- Bake for 20 minutes. Delicious!

Nutrition Facts

Serving Size 1/10 recipe (131g)
Servings Per Container 10

Amount Per Serving

Calories 190 — Calories from Fat 5

	% Daily Value*
Total Fat 0.5g	1%
Saturated Fat 0g	0%
Trans Fat 0g	
Cholesterol 0mg	0%
Sodium 270mg	11%
Total Carbohydrate 33g	11%
Dietary Fiber 4g	16%
Sugars 3g	
Protein 13g	

Vitamin A 8% • Vitamin C 15%
Calcium 8% • Iron 20%

*Percent Daily Values are based on a 2,000 calorie diet. Your daily values may be higher or lower depending on your calorie needs:

		Calories:	2,000	2,500
Total Fat	Less than		65g	80g
Saturated Fat	Less than		20g	25g
Cholesterol	Less than		300mg	300mg
Sodium	Less than		2,400mg	2,400mg
Total Carbohydrate			300g	375g
Dietary Fiber			25g	30g

Calories per gram:
Fat 9 • Carbohydrate 4 • Protein 4

Topping Notes: Ingredient amounts are approximations only and can be adjusted or omitted to taste. Daiya Vegan cheese melts well if you want to try that.

Thanks to: Ken Martin, Group 7

Category: Breads

Stout Bread

An earthy, dark loaf, named for the heavy, strongly flavored ale that is the only liquid.

Makes 1 loaf, ~ 15 slices (servings)

Ingredients:

1½	tsp	active yeast
9	oz	Guinness Stout
¾	cup	wheat flour
½	cup	rye starter
3	cup	bread flour
2	tsp	sea salt
¾	cup	rye flour

Preparation:

- Add yeast to stout, set aside.
- Measure remaining ingredients into food processor/bowl.
- Slowly add ale, mix/knead, adding more if needed.
- Dough should be soft and pliable.
- In food processor, knead 45-60 seconds; in mixer or by hand, knead 10 minutes.
- Form dough into ball, place in bowl, cover with plastic wrap and towel, let rise 4-12 hours (dough will not rise much).
- Put baking stone in oven, with shallow pan below, preheat oven to 475°F.
- Remove dough from bowl, pat-down, fold and form into round/football shape.
- Sprinkle cloth-lined basket with rye flour, put dough in basket (top-down), cover, let rise 45 minutes.
- Remove loaf from basket, diagonally slash loaf top 8 times, put in oven, add cup of water to pan for steam, lower temp to 425°F, and bake 46-50 min.
- Crust will be deep brown.

Rye starter is a sourdough starter, equal parts water and rye flour and a pinch of yeast, aged and fed (with water and rye flour) for 72 hours at room temperature.

Thanks to: Dave Hansen, group 40

Category: Breads

Nutrition Facts

Serving Size 1 slice (68g)
Servings Per Container 15

Amount Per Serving

Calories 160   Calories from Fat 5

% Daily Value*

Total Fat 0.5g	1%
Saturated Fat 0g	0%
Trans Fat 0g	
Cholesterol 0mg	0%
Sodium 380mg	16%
Total Carbohydrate 31g	10%
Dietary Fiber 2g	8%
Sugars 0g	
Protein 5g	

Vitamin A 0% • Vitamin C 0%
Calcium 0% • Iron 10%

*Percent Daily Values are based on a 2,000 calorie diet. Your daily values may be higher or lower depending on your calorie needs:

	Calories:	2,000	2,500
Total Fat	Less than	65g	80g
Saturated Fat	Less than	20g	25g
Cholesterol	Less than	300mg	300mg
Sodium	Less than	2,400mg	2,400mg
Total Carbohydrate		300g	375g
Dietary Fiber		25g	30g

Calories per gram:
Fat 9 • Carbohydrate 4 • Protein 4

EGG / MEAT SUBSTITUTES

Regarding the taste of TVP (textured vegetable protein)
Some find TVP burdened with the slight taste of cardboard. To eliminate this undesirable flavor, Group 18 Support Person, Joanie Bach, devised this simple procedure.

Boil the TVP in 2-3 times volume of water for 35 minutes. Drain in a strainer. Rinse well with running water. Return to pan, add equal volume of flavored liquid (broth, wine, lots of spices), simmer for 15 minutes. Let stand. Use in recipes as meat. Not as tasty as the real thing, nor quite as good as newer, ready-to-use products but there is the advantage that TVP is very cheap, stores 'forever' on shelf, and is still nutritious.

Those who are impatient are happy with a speedier method: boil for 5 minutes, rinse well, add a flavor-filled liquid and then proceed to cook the hydrated, softened TVP with other flavorful ingredients (marinara sauce, beef stew seasoning, sweet and sour, pizza sauce, etc.)

Baked Golden Tofu Dumplings with Saucy Dip

Peanut butter makes this a higher fat recipe.

Makes 4 servings

Ingredients:

8	oz	extra-firm tofu
1	tsp	natural peanut butter
1	Tbsp	tamari sauce
3		scallions, chopped
OR		
¼	cup	green onions, chopped
1	small	green or red pepper, chopped (½ cup)
2	med	celery stalks, chopped
8	med	mushrooms, diced
3		water chestnuts, diced
1	med	sprig parsley, minced (1 tablespoon)

Saucy Dipping Sauce:

¾	cup	apple juice
2	tsp	maple syrup or brown sugar
1-2	tsp	tamari sauce
1-2	tsp	apple cider vinegar
½	tsp	ginger, grated (optional)
2	cloves	garlic, pressed
1-2	tsp	arrowroot powder (or cornstarch)
1-2	tsp	water

Nutrition Facts
Serving Size 1/4 recipe (216g)
Servings Per Container 4

Amount Per Serving

Calories 130   Calories from Fat 35

% Daily Value*

Total Fat 4g	6%
Saturated Fat 0g	0%
Trans Fat 0g	
Cholesterol 0mg	0%
Sodium 590mg	25%
Total Carbohydrate 17g	6%
Dietary Fiber 2g	8%
Sugars 10g	
Protein 7g	

Vitamin A 6%	Vitamin C 35%
Calcium 15%	Iron 10%

*Percent Daily Values are based on a 2,000 calorie diet. Your daily values may be higher or lower depending on your calorie needs:

		Calories: 2,000	2,500
Total Fat	Less than	65g	80g
Saturated Fat	Less than	20g	25g
Cholesterol	Less than	300mg	300mg
Sodium	Less than	2,400mg	2,400mg
Total Carbohydrate		300g	375g
Dietary Fiber		25g	30g

Calories per gram:
Fat 9 • Carbohydrate 4 • Protein 4

Preparation:

- Preheat oven to 375°F.
- Mash tofu with a fork or potato masher until broken up.
- Add other ingredients and mix well.
- Form the tofu mixture into golf ball sized dumplings. Place on cookie sheet sprayed with vegetable oil cooking spray.
- Rinse hands in cold water periodically to keep dumplings from clinging.
- Bake in oven for 30 minutes or until golden brown.
- Mix together ingredients for Saucy Dip.
- Serve dumplings on a bed of steamed kale with a small dish of sauce on the side.

Category: Meat Substitutes

Lentil and Kale Loaf

Any dark green leafy vegetable could be used here, but kale is a nutrition powerhouse!

Makes 8 servings

Ingredients:

2	cups	lentils, cooked
1	cup	kale, boiled and chopped
1	cup	fat-free cheddar cheese
½	cup	fat-free cottage cheese
½	cup	fat-free yogurt
1	cup	bread crumbs
2	Tbsp	wheat germ
2	tsp	light soy sauce
3		egg whites, beaten

Preparation:

- Preheat oven to 350°F.
- Mix all ingredients in a large bowl.
- Put mixture in loaf pan.
- Sprinkle bread crumbs on top.
- Bake for 1 hour or until done.

Thanks to: Surang Robinson, Group 18

Category: Meat and Egg Substitute

Nutrition Facts

Serving Size 1/8 recipe (156g)
Servings Per Container 8

Amount Per Serving

Calories 170   Calories from Fat 10

% Daily Value*

Total Fat 1g	2%
Saturated Fat 0g	0%
Trans Fat 0g	
Cholesterol 5mg	2%
Sodium 420mg	18%
Total Carbohydrate 24g	8%
Dietary Fiber 6g	24%
Sugars 4g	
Protein 15g	

Vitamin A 50%   •   Vitamin C 10%
Calcium 20%   •   Iron 6%

*Percent Daily Values are based on a 2,000 calorie diet. Your daily values may be higher or lower depending on your calorie needs:

		Calories:	2,000	2,500
Total Fat	Less than		65g	80g
Saturated Fat	Less than		20g	25g
Cholesterol	Less than		300mg	300mg
Sodium	Less than		2,400mg	2,400mg
Total Carbohydrate			300g	375g
Dietary Fiber			25g	30g

Calories per gram:
Fat 9   •   Carbohydrate 4   •   Protein 4

Maple Brandy Meat Substitute

This recipe will make you think you are eating honey-baked ham. You can use a variety of meat substitutes, including vegetarian 'strips', rehydrated chunks of TVP, or extra firm Tofu or Seitan.

Makes 4 servings

Ingredients:

12	oz	beef meat substitute
3	Tbsp	brown sugar
¼	tsp	ground cloves
¼	tsp	ground cinnamon
¼	cup	maple syrup
1	Tbsp	brandy

Preparation:

- Put all ingredients in ziplock bag and marinate for two hours.
- Drain, saving liquid.
- Place meat substitute in a sauté pan and heat through.
- Add marinade.
- Reduce heat and simmer for about 5 minutes.
- Thicken if necessary with 1 tsp cornstarch in 2 tsp water.
- Serve as an entrée; a great substitute for holiday dinners.

Thanks to: Frankie Christopher, Group 23

Category: Meat Substitute

Nutrition Facts

Serving Size 1/4 recipe (119g)
Servings Per Container 4

Amount Per Serving

Calories 190   Calories from Fat 0

% Daily Value*

Total Fat 0g	0%
Saturated Fat 0g	0%
Trans Fat 0g	
Cholesterol 0mg	0%
Sodium 420mg	18%
Total Carbohydrate 30g	10%
Dietary Fiber 5g	20%
Sugars 22g	
Protein 15g	

Vitamin A 0% • Vitamin C 0%
Calcium 10% • Iron 25%

*Percent Daily Values are based on a 2,000 calorie diet. Your daily values may be higher or lower depending on your calorie needs:

		Calories:	2,000	2,500
Total Fat		Less than	65g	80g
Saturated Fat		Less than	20g	25g
Cholesterol		Less than	300mg	300mg
Sodium		Less than	2,400mg	2,400mg
Total Carbohydrate			300g	375g
Dietary Fiber			25g	30g

Calories per gram:
Fat 9 • Carbohydrate 4 • Protein 4

Nan's Stroganoff

Makes 8 servings

Ingredients:

2	cups	vegetable broth (see page 384)
2	cups	TVP chunks (Textured Vegetable Protein)
3	lbs	onions, finely chopped
2	lbs	fresh mushrooms, sliced
1	can	fat-free tomato soup (10 oz)
1	can	tomato paste (6 oz)
1	cup	fat-free sour cream
1	Tbsp	Worcestershire sauce

Preparation:

- To hydrate TVP, bring liquid to a boil.
- Stir in TVP and let stand for at least 10 minutes.
- Sauté together onions and mushrooms in large saucepan, using vegetable oil cooking spray.
- When onions are cooked through, add soup, tomato paste, sour cream and Worcestershire sauce. Blend well.
- Add TVP last to avoid overcooking.
- Serve with rice or noodles (yolkless of course).

Thanks: to Nan Chorman, Group 31

Category: Meat Substitute

Nutrition Facts

Serving Size 1/8 recipe (472g)
Servings Per Container 8

Amount Per Serving

Calories 250 — Calories from Fat 5

% Daily Value*

Total Fat 0.5g	1%
Saturated Fat 0g	0%
Trans Fat 0g	
Cholesterol 5mg	2%
Sodium 280mg	12%
Total Carbohydrate 43g	14%
Dietary Fiber 10g	40%
Sugars 18g	
Protein 20g	

Vitamin A 60% • Vitamin C 70%
Calcium 25% • Iron 30%

*Percent Daily Values are based on a 2,000 calorie diet. Your daily values may be higher or lower depending on your calorie needs:

		Calories:	2,000	2,500
Total Fat		Less than	65g	80g
Saturated Fat		Less than	20g	25g
Cholesterol		Less than	300mg	300mg
Sodium		Less than	2,400mg	2,400mg
Total Carbohydrate			300g	375g
Dietary Fiber			25g	30g

Calories per gram:
  Fat 9 • Carbohydrate 4 • Protein 4

Quick and Easy Stroganoff

Like traditional stroganoff without the guilt. You could also use the Cream Sauce recipe (see page 370) in place of the sauce mix and sour cream to save sodium, but you might want to add some garlic with the onions for more seasoning.

Makes 8 servings

Ingredients:

8	oz	yolkless noodles
1	cup	TVP beef chunks or other soy meat substitute
2	cups	water
½	med	onion, cut in thin slices
½	cup	mushrooms, sliced
1	pkg	McCormick Beef Stroganoff Sauce Mix
1	cup	fat-free sour cream OR non-fat plain yogurt

Preparation:

- Cook non-fat noodles as directed.
- Meanwhile hydrate TVP by microwaving it for 2 minutes with 1 cup water.
- Let sit for 10 minutes or until chunks are soft. Drain.
- Sauté onions and mushrooms in a large skillet, coated with vegetable oil spray.
- Add 1 cup water and seasoning.
- Stir in hydrated TVP.
- Cover and simmer for 10 minutes.
- Remove from heat and stir in sour cream or yogurt.
- Serve over noodles.

Category: Meat Substitute

Nutrition Facts

Serving Size 1/8 recipe (151g)
Servings Per Container 8

Amount Per Serving

Calories 160	Calories from Fat 0

% Daily Value*

Total Fat 0g	0%
Saturated Fat 0g	0%
Trans Fat 0g	
Cholesterol 5mg	2%
Sodium 570mg	24%
Total Carbohydrate 28g	9%
Dietary Fiber 3g	12%
Sugars 3g	
Protein 10g	

Vitamin A 2%	•	Vitamin C 2%
Calcium 10%	•	Iron 15%

*Percent Daily Values are based on a 2,000 calorie diet. Your daily values may be higher or lower depending on your calorie needs:

		Calories:	2,000	2,500
Total Fat		Less than	65g	80g
Saturated Fat		Less than	20g	25g
Cholesterol		Less than	300mg	300mg
Sodium		Less than	2,400mg	2,400mg
Total Carbohydrate			300g	375g
Dietary Fiber			25g	30g

Calories per gram:
  Fat 9 • Carbohydrate 4 • Protein 4

Sloppy Joes

Textured vegetable protein (TVP) is just dehydrated soy flour. Rehydrate per directions and you will have the protein and texture of meat without the cholesterol and saturated fat. You need to spice it up in each recipe you use as TVP does not have a lot of flavor.

Makes 8 servings

Ingredients:

8	large	Kaiser or hard rolls, split
1	tsp	olive oil
2	cloves	garlic, minced
1	med	onion, chopped
1		green pepper, chopped
2	cups	TVP granules mixed with 1⅓ cups hot water
1	can	tomato paste (6 oz)
½	cup	water
1	tsp	dried oregano
¼	cup	ketchup
¼	tsp	cayenne pepper
1	tsp	Worcestershire sauce
1	Tbsp	honey (optional)
		Lettuce, shredded

Preparation:

- Heat a skillet, add the oil, and when it is hot sauté quickly the garlic, onions, peppers, and TVP.
- Mix the tomato paste with the water and seasonings and stir into the pan.
- Bring to a boil, taste and add salt if desired.
- Sauce should be thick but spreadable; add a little more water if needed.
- Split the buns in half, toasting if desired.
- Spoon sauce on bottom half of bun, pile on lettuce and top with remaining half.

Nutrition Facts
Serving Size 1 sandwich (231g)
Servings Per Container 8

Amount Per Serving

Calories 300 — Calories from Fat 30

% Daily Value*

- Total Fat 3g — 5%
  - Saturated Fat 0g — 0%
  - Trans Fat 0g
- Cholesterol 0mg — 0%
- Sodium 480mg — 20%
- Total Carbohydrate 49g — 16%
  - Dietary Fiber 8g — 32%
  - Sugars 12g
- Protein 19g

Vitamin A 50% • Vitamin C 35%
Calcium 15% • Iron 30%

*Percent Daily Values are based on a 2,000 calorie diet. Your daily values may be higher or lower depending on your calorie needs:

	Calories:	2,000	2,500
Total Fat	Less than	65g	80g
Saturated Fat	Less than	20g	25g
Cholesterol	Less than	300mg	300mg
Sodium	Less than	2,400mg	2,400mg
Total Carbohydrate		300g	375g
Dietary Fiber		25g	30g

Calories per gram:
Fat 9 • Carbohydrate 4 • Protein 4

Source: *The TVP Cookbook, by Dorothy R. Bates*

Category: Meat Substitutes

SOUTHWEST SURPRISE

If you cook this in your cast iron skillet on the stove, you can move the same pan to the oven and save dirtying another pan. Cooking in a cast iron skillet increases the iron in your recipe.

Makes 15 servings

Ingredients :

12	oz	vegetarian sausage, such as Gimme Lean
1	med	onion, peeled and coarsely chopped
1½	cups	tomatoes, chopped
1½	cups	corn kernels
2½	cups	tomato sauce, unsalted
1	can	tomato paste (6 oz)
¼	cup	red wine
1	tsp	chili powder
1	cup	fat-free cheddar cheese, shredded, OR Veggie Shreds
1	pkg	Krusteaz Honey Cornbread Muffin Mix (15 oz)
1	cup	skim milk
¼	cup	egg substitute OR 2 egg whites

Nutrition Facts
Serving Size 1/15 (194g)
Servings Per Container 15

Amount Per Serving
Calories 250 Calories from Fat 45

% Daily Value*
- Total Fat 5g — 8%
- Saturated Fat 0.5g — 3%
- Trans Fat 0g
- Cholesterol 0mg — 0%
- Sodium 550mg — 23%
- Total Carbohydrate 38g — 13%
- Dietary Fiber 5g — 20%
- Sugars 8g
- Protein 14g

Vitamin A 10% • Vitamin C 15%
Calcium 25% • Iron 15%

*Percent Daily Values are based on a 2,000 calorie diet. Your daily values may be higher or lower depending on your calorie needs:

	Calories:	2,000	2,500
Total Fat	Less than	65g	80g
Saturated Fat	Less than	20g	25g
Cholesterol	Less than	300mg	300mg
Sodium	Less than	2,400mg	2,400mg
Total Carbohydrate		300g	375g
Dietary Fiber		25g	30g

Calories per gram:
Fat 9 • Carbohydrate 4 • Protein 4

Preparation:

- Preheat oven to 400°F. Coat a 13 x 9 inch baking pan with nonstick cooking spray and set aside.
- In a large skillet, combine vegetarian sausage, onion, tomatoes, corn, tomato sauce, tomato paste, red wine and chili powder.
- Cook mixture over medium-high heat until hot and bubbly.
- Pour into prepared pan and sprinkle with ½ cup of the shredded cheese.
- In a medium bowl, stir together milk, egg whites and muffin mix until the dry ingredients are just moistened.
- Spread over mixture in pan and sprinkle with remaining ½ cup of cheese.
- Bake for 25 to 30 minutes or until cornbread is golden brown and a toothpick inserted in the center comes out clean.

Source: Raley's

Category: Meat Substitutes

SPECIAL K COTTAGE CHEESE LOAF

A convincing substitute for the comfort food, meat loaf.

Makes 8 servings (2 x 4 inch square)

Ingredients:

½	cup	egg substitute
¼	cup	applesauce, unsweetened
2	tsp	Better than Boullion, vegetable base
¼	cup	onion, chopped
¼	cup	nuts (walnuts, pecans). chopped
¼	cup	skim milk
16	oz	fat-free cottage cheese
3	cups	Special K Cereal, uncrushed.

Preparation:

- Preheat over to 350°F.
- Mix thoroughly all ingredients.
- Spray 8 inch square pan with vegetable oil cooking spray.
- Pat mixture evenly in pan,
- Bake for about 1 hr.

May top with a tomato sauce or ketchup. Can also double recipe, using a 9 x 13 inch pan.

Thanks to: Alice Hill, Group 22

Category: Meat Substitutes

Nutrition Facts

Serving Size 2x4 inch square (114g)
Servings Per Container 8

Amount Per Serving	
Calories 130	Calories from Fat 25

	% Daily Value*
Total Fat 2.5g	4%
Saturated Fat 0g	0%
Trans Fat 0g	
Cholesterol 5mg	2%
Sodium 510mg	21%
Total Carbohydrate 15g	5%
Dietary Fiber 1g	4%
Sugars 6g	
Protein 12g	

Vitamin A 10%	•	Vitamin C 15%
Calcium 8%	•	Iron 20%

*Percent Daily Values are based on a 2,000 calorie diet. Your daily values may be higher or lower depending on your calorie needs:

	Calories:	2,000	2,500
Total Fat	Less than	65g	80g
Saturated Fat	Less than	20g	25g
Cholesterol	Less than	300mg	300mg
Sodium	Less than	2,400mg	2,400mg
Total Carbohydrate		300g	375g
Dietary Fiber		25g	30g

Calories per gram:
 Fat 9 • Carbohydrate 4 • Protein 4

Spicy Bean and Lentil Loaf

Another faux meatloaf. This one is high in fiber from the beans and lentils.

Makes 6 servings

Ingredients:

1	med	onion, finely chopped (¾ cup)
1	clove	garlic, crushed (1 tsp)
2	stalks	celery, finely chopped
1½	cups	red kidney beans, cooked
1½	cups	lentils, cooked
¼	cup	egg whites
1	med	carrot, coarsely grated
½	cup	fat-free cheddar cheese, finely grated
1	cup	whole wheat bread crumbs
1	Tbsp	tomato paste
1	Tbsp	ketchup
1	tsp	chili powder

Preparation:

- Preheat the oven to 350°F. Spray a 2 lb loaf pan with vegetable oil cooking spray.
- Place onion, garlic, and celery in oil-sprayed saucepan.
- Cook gently for 5 minutes, stirring occasionally. Remove the pan from heat and cool slightly.
- Put beans, lentils, and egg whites in a blender or food processor with the onion mixture and process until smooth.
- Transfer the mixture to a bowl, add and mix in carrot, cheese, bread crumbs, tomato paste, ketchup and chili powder. Mix well.
- Spoon the mixture into the prepared loaf pan and level the surface.
- Bake for about 1 hour.

Category: Meat Substitutes

Nutrition Facts

Serving Size 1/6 recipe (229g)
Servings Per Container 6

Amount Per Serving	
Calories 200	Calories from Fat 5

	% Daily Value*
Total Fat 0.5g	1%
Saturated Fat 0g	0%
Trans Fat 0g	
Cholesterol 0mg	0%
Sodium 330mg	14%
Total Carbohydrate 34g	11%
Dietary Fiber 10g	40%
Sugars 6g	
Protein 15g	

Vitamin A 50%	•	Vitamin C 8%	
Calcium 10%	•	Iron 10%	

*Percent Daily Values are based on a 2,000 calorie diet. Your daily values may be higher or lower depending on your calorie needs:

	Calories:	2,000	2,500
Total Fat	Less than	65g	80g
Saturated Fat	Less than	20g	25g
Cholesterol	Less than	300mg	300mg
Sodium	Less than	2,400mg	2,400mg
Total Carbohydrate		300g	375g
Dietary Fiber		25g	30g

Calories per gram:
Fat 9 • Carbohydrate 4 • Protein 4

STUFFED GREEN PEPPERS

Any color bell pepper will do. Red, yellow and orange peppers have a milder, sweeter flavor than green. All bell peppers have more vitamin C than an orange.

Makes 6 servings, ½ pepper each

Ingredients:

3	large	green bell peppers
6	oz	vegetarian ground round
1	cup	unsalted tomato sauce
⅛	tsp	thyme
½	cup	coarse, dry bread crumbs
1	tsp	salt
¼	tsp	pepper
2	Tbsp	onion, chopped
2	Tbsp	dry sherry OR fat-free broth

Preparation:

- Heat oven to 350°F.
- Wash bell peppers, cut cap with stem and remove seeds and membranes.
- In large saucepan, cook peppers for 5 minutes in boiling water. Drain.
- Mix in a bowl meat substitute, tomato sauce, thyme, bread crumbs, salt, pepper, onion and sherry.
- Stuff peppers lightly with mixture.
- Stand upright in a small baking dish.
- Bake covered (foil or lid) 45 minutes.
- Uncover and bake 15 minutes more.

Thanks to: Dave Paquette, Group 27

Category: Meat Substitutes

Nutrition Facts
Serving Size 1/2 pepper (164g)
Servings Per Container 6

Amount Per Serving

Calories 160   Calories from Fat 5

% Daily Value*

Total Fat 0g	0%
Saturated Fat 0g	0%
Trans Fat 0g	
Cholesterol 0mg	0%
Sodium 440mg	18%
Total Carbohydrate 21g	7%
Dietary Fiber 7g	28%
Sugars 8g	
Protein 16g	

Vitamin A 10% • Vitamin C 120%
Calcium 10% • Iron 25%

*Percent Daily Values are based on a 2,000 calorie diet. Your daily values may be higher or lower depending on your calorie needs:

		Calories:	2,000	2,500
Total Fat	Less than		65g	80g
Saturated Fat	Less than		20g	25g
Cholesterol	Less than		300mg	300mg
Sodium	Less than		2,400mg	2,400mg
Total Carbohydrate			300g	375g
Dietary Fiber			25g	30g

Calories per gram:
Fat 9 • Carbohydrate 4 • Protein 4

Stuffed Portobello Mushrooms

Prep time: 15 min   Cook time: 15 min

Makes 2 servings

We take these to cook quickly when we are guests at homes of carnivores. We take some extra to share and the hosts learn that our heart-healthy diet includes delicious entrées.

Ingredients:

2	4 inch	Portobello mushrooms
½	tsp	olive oil
½	Tbsp	red wine vinegar
1	tsp	thyme, fresh minced OR ¼ tsp dried
1	large	clove garlic, minced (1 tsp)
½	Tbsp	olive oil
¼	cup	red bell pepper, minced,
1	clove	garlic, minced
¾	cup	fresh bread crumbs
½	Tbsp	green onion minced
1	Tbsp	parsley minced
1	tsp	fresh thyme, minced (OR ¼ tsp dried)
½	cup	non-fat Monterey Jack cheese, grated
		salt, pepper to taste.

Nutrition Facts

Serving Size 1 mushroom (334g)
Servings Per Container 2

Amount Per Serving

Calories 220   Calories from Fat 40

% Daily Value*

Total Fat 4.5g	7%
Saturated Fat 0.5g	3%
Trans Fat 0g	
Cholesterol 5mg	2%
Sodium 840mg	35%
Total Carbohydrate 22g	7%
Dietary Fiber 4g	16%
Sugars 9g	
Protein 22g	

Vitamin A 25% • Vitamin C 60%
Calcium 80% • Iron 10%

*Percent Daily Values are based on a 2,000 calorie diet. Your daily values may be higher or lower depending on your calorie needs:

		Calories:	2,000	2,500
Total Fat		Less than	65g	80g
Saturated Fat		Less than	20g	25g
Cholesterol		Less than	300mg	300mg
Sodium		Less than	2,400mg	2,400mg
Total Carbohydrate			300g	375g
Dietary Fiber			25g	30g

Calories per gram:
  Fat 9 • Carbohydrate 4 • Protein 4

Preparation:

- Wipe mushrooms clean with damp paper towel and discard stems.
- Whisk together oil, vinegar, thyme, garlic and any salt and pepper in a small bowl.
- Spoon mixture evenly over gills of mushroom caps.
- **Stuffing:** Heat ½ tsp oil in a small skillet, on medium heat and sauté pepper 3 minutes.
- Add garlic and sauté 1 min to release fragrance.
- Remove from heat and blend in bread crumbs.
- Stir in green onion, parsley, and thyme. When cool, stir in cheese.
- Put mushroom caps, gills side up, on a baking sheet; drizzle with unabsorbed vinaigrette.
- Divide the stuffing evenly among the caps and press it into place, covering the gills.
- Cook in hot oven or on grill until they are tender and stuffing is crisp, about 10 minutes.

Thanks to: Ginny Goodrow, Group 25

TEMPEH TACO SALAD

Tempeh is a soy-based protein-rich product available to vegetarian cuisine, with a complex, savory flavor, full of depth and culinary potential. Depending on how it is cooked and seasoned, it can taste meaty, nutty, earthy, smoky or even sweet. A little goes a long way, as tempeh is rich and substantial. It is firm in texture, has a slightly nutty flavor, and mushroom aroma. Tempeh can be found in natural food stores and sometimes in the frozen foods section of a market, usually in half-inch-thick cakes.

6 servings

Ingredients:

6	oz	fresh tempeh, cubed
2	Tbsp	taco seasoning mix
½	cup	water
¾	cup	fat-free sour cream
4	cups	mixed lettuce or romaine
1	large	tomato, chopped
½	med	red onion, chopped
1½	cups	black, pinto or kidney beans, cooked
¼	cup	fat-free cheese or soy cheese shreds

Preparation:

- In a medium skillet, combine tempeh, 1 Tbsp taco seasoning mix and water.
- Break up tempeh until crumbly and cook for 5-10 minutes, until the water is absorbed and tempeh heated thoroughly.
- In a small bowl, combine remaining 1 Tbsp seasoning mix and sour cream.
- In a large bowl, toss tempeh, sour cream mixture with lettuce, tomato, onion, and beans. Sprinkle cheese on top.
- Serve with baked tortilla chips.

Thanks to: Jill Burns, R.D.

Category: Meat Substitutes

Nutrition Facts

Serving Size 1/6 recipe (209g)
Servings Per Container 6

Amount Per Serving

Calories 180   Calories from Fat 30

% Daily Value*

Total Fat 3.5g	5%
Saturated Fat 0.5g	3%
Trans Fat 0g	
Cholesterol 5mg	2%
Sodium 280mg	12%
Total Carbohydrate 24g	8%
Dietary Fiber 5g	20%
Sugars 2g	
Protein 13g	

Vitamin A 60% • Vitamin C 10%
Calcium 10% • Iron 10%

*Percent Daily Values are based on a 2,000 calorie diet. Your daily values may be higher or lower depending on your calorie needs:

		Calories:	2,000	2,500
Total Fat	Less than		65g	80g
Saturated Fat	Less than		20g	25g
Cholesterol	Less than		300mg	300mg
Sodium	Less than		2,400mg	2,400mg
Total Carbohydrate			300g	375g
Dietary Fiber			25g	30g

Calories per gram:
Fat 9 • Carbohydrate 4 • Protein 4

Tofu Stir Fry

For even firmer tofu, place tofu block on a plate, with another plate on top of the block. Put your cast iron skillet, or another heavy object on top and let sit about 30 minutes. The water will be pressed out. If that is too much trouble, they do sell tofu presses, and some tofus, such as Wildwood brand, have very little water content.

Makes 6 servings

Ingredients:

12	oz	extra firm lite tofu
⅓	cup	light soy sauce
1	Tbsp	honey
2	tsp	balsamic vinegar
2	Tbsp	fresh ginger, grated
2	tsp	garlic, minced
½	tsp	toasted sesame oil
½	tsp	olive oil
1	bunch	green onions, cut into 1 inch pieces
6	cups	vegetables, chopped (broccoli, asparagus, cabbage, snow peas, bean sprouts, etc)

Preparation:

- Preheat oven to 400°F.
- Spray non stick baking pan with vegetable oil cooking spray.
- Place tofu in pan in single layer.
- Mix together in small bowl or measuring cup soy sauce, honey, vinegar, ginger, garlic, and sesame oil.
- Pour half of soy sauce mixture over tofu; bake 30 minutes.
- Sauté in skillet or wok for 1 minute green onions in ½ tsp oil.
- Add chopped vegetables to skillet or wok with remaining soy sauce mixture.
- Stir fry for 5 more minutes.
- Add cooked tofu, toss lightly and serve.

Category: Meat Substitutes

Nutrition Facts

Serving Size 1/6 recipe (212g)
Servings Per Container 6

Amount Per Serving

Calories 120   Calories from Fat 25

	% Daily Value*
Total Fat 3g	5%
Saturated Fat 0g	0%
Trans Fat 0g	
Cholesterol 0mg	0%
Sodium 510mg	21%
Total Carbohydrate 17g	6%
Dietary Fiber 4g	16%
Sugars 8g	
Protein 10g	

Vitamin A 40% • Vitamin C 140%
Calcium 30% • Iron 15%

*Percent Daily Values are based on a 2,000 calorie diet. Your daily values may be higher or lower depending on your calorie needs:

	Calories:	2,000	2,500
Total Fat	Less than	65g	80g
Saturated Fat	Less than	20g	25g
Cholesterol	Less than	300mg	300mg
Sodium	Less than	2,400mg	2,400mg
Total Carbohydrate		300g	375g
Dietary Fiber		25g	30g

Calories per gram:
Fat 9 • Carbohydrate 4 • Protein 4

TVP and Tofu Loaf

Another faux-meatloaf, but now using TVP and tofu, to increase protein content.

Makes 8 servings

Ingredients:

1	cup	vegetable broth (see page 384)
1	cup	TVP granules
8	oz	extra firm, lite tofu
1	cup	quick oats
OR		
½	cup	oats with ½ cup whole wheat flour
2	slices	fresh bread
¾	cup	fat-free cottage cheese
OR		
½	cup	cottage cheese and ½ cup non-fat grated cheddar cheese
½	cup	onion, chopped
1	cup	mushrooms, chopped
½	cup	wheat germ (optional)
1		red pepper, toasted or grilled, slivered
1	large	carrot, shredded
⅓	cup	parsley, chopped
½	cup	ketchup
2		egg whites, slightly beaten
2	tsp	dry mustard
½	tsp	sea salt
1	Tbsp	light soy sauce
2	tsp	ground black pepper

Topping:

½	cup	ketchup
2	tsp	dried mustard
OR		
		chopped parsley and bread crumbs).

Nutrition Facts

Serving Size 1/8 recipe (1 inch slice) (227g)
Servings Per Container 8

Amount Per Serving

Calories 230   Calories from Fat 30

% Daily Value*

Total Fat 3.5g	5%
Saturated Fat 0g	0%
Trans Fat 0g	
Cholesterol 0mg	0%
Sodium 920mg	38%
Total Carbohydrate 32g	11%
Dietary Fiber 7g	28%
Sugars 15g	
Protein 18g	

Vitamin A 60% • Vitamin C 40%
Calcium 20% • Iron 25%

*Percent Daily Values are based on a 2,000 calorie diet. Your daily values may be higher or lower depending on your calorie needs:

		Calories:	2,000	2,500
Total Fat	Less than		65g	80g
Saturated Fat	Less than		20g	25g
Cholesterol	Less than		300mg	300mg
Sodium	Less than		2,400mg	2,400mg
Total Carbohydrate			300g	375g
Dietary Fiber			25g	30g

Calories per gram:
   Fat 9 • Carbohydrate 4 • Protein 4

Preparation: (Preheat oven to 375°F).

- Heat broth to near boiling, stir in TVP granules   Let stand 10 minutes to completely soften.
- Mix tofu, oats, and bread crumbs together well.
- Stir in cottage cheese.

- Spin bread in blender to make fine crumb; add to mixture.
- Stir in all remaining ingredients.
- Put mixture in vegetable oil cooking sprayed 9 x 6 inch loaf pan
- Top with mixture of <u>either</u> ketchup and mustard OR parsley and bread crumbs.
- Bake for 1 hour or until firm.

Thanks to: Surang Robinson, Group 18

TVP Loaf

Loaf can be served with Tomato Sauce or Mushroom Gravy. Leftovers can be sliced for sandwiches or a cold cut platter.

Makes 8 servings, each serving ~ 1 inch slice

Ingredients:

3	cups	TVP granules
2½	cups	boiling water
¼	cup	ketchup
1	tsp	basil
½	cup	onion, finely chopped
¾	cup	unbleached or whole wheat flour
1	tsp	salt
¼	tsp	ground black pepper
½	tsp	garlic powder
½	tsp	each oregano and marjoram (optional)
½	cup	fresh parsley, finely minced

Preparation:
- Mix TVP in a large bowl with water, ketchup and basil.
- Let stand for 10 minutes.
- Sauté onion until soft in vegetable cooking oil sprayed pan.
- Add onions to the rehydrated TVP and stir in flour, spices and seasonings.
- Spray a loaf or bread pan with vegetable oil cooking spray.
- Pack mixture in tightly, smoothing top.
- Bake 350°F about 45 minutes.
- If loaf begins to get too brown on top, cover with foil.
- After removing from oven, let stand in pan 10 minutes, then run a knife around edges to loosen and turn loaf out onto a platter.

Nutrition Facts

Serving Size 1 inch slice (145g)
Servings Per Container 8

Amount Per Serving

Calories 180 — Calories from Fat 0

	% Daily Value*
Total Fat 0g	0%
Saturated Fat 0g	0%
Trans Fat 0g	
Cholesterol 0mg	0%
Sodium 390mg	16%
Total Carbohydrate 23g	8%
Dietary Fiber 7g	28%
Sugars 7g	
Protein 20g	

Vitamin A 8%	•	Vitamin C 10%	
Calcium 15%	•	Iron 30%	

*Percent Daily Values are based on a 2,000 calorie diet. Your daily values may be higher or lower depending on your calorie needs:

	Calories:	2,000	2,500
Total Fat	Less than	65g	80g
Saturated Fat	Less than	20g	25g
Cholesterol	Less than	300mg	300mg
Sodium	Less than	2,400mg	2,400mg
Total Carbohydrate		300g	375g
Dietary Fiber		25g	30g

Calories per gram:
　Fat 9 • Carbohydrate 4 • Protein 4

- Garnish with lemon slices and sprigs of parsley.

Thanks to: Jerre Schermerhorn, Group 29, from Dorothy R. Bates TVP Cookbook

Category: Meat Substitutes

VEGETARIAN LOAF

This loaf is more bread and vegetable based, so a bit higher in carbs and not quite as high in fiber and protein.

Makes ~ 15 slices

Ingredients:

1	loaf	sourdough French bread (~1 ½ lb)
½	cup	onion, chopped
2	med	zucchini, sliced
1	cup	corn kernels
1	tsp	olive oil
2		tomatoes, diced
¼	cup	green chiles, minced
1	Tbsp	chili powder
1½	Tbsp	cumin

Preparation:

- Preheat oven to 325 °F
- Cut ½ inch lengthwise off top of French bread. Set aside.
- Scoop out dough portion of bottom half of loaf.
- Sauté onions, zucchini and corn in oil until tender.
- Add tomatoes and green chilis with seasonings.
- When tender, remove from heat and fill loaf cavity.
- Replace top and wrap loaf in foil.
- Bake 15 minutes.
- Cut loaf into 2 inch length portions.
- Serve on bed of shredded lettuce.
- Garnish with carrot sticks, pineapple slices, and a scoop of cottage cheese.

Nutrition Facts

Serving Size 1/15 loaf (85g)
Servings Per Container 15

Amount Per Serving

Calories 200   Calories from Fat 5

% Daily Value*

Total Fat 0.5g	1%
Saturated Fat 0g	0%
Trans Fat 0g	
Cholesterol 0mg	0%
Sodium 430mg	18%
Total Carbohydrate 41g	14%
Dietary Fiber 2g	8%
Sugars 3g	
Protein 7g	

Vitamin A 4%	•	Vitamin C 8%
Calcium 2%	•	Iron 15%

*Percent Daily Values are based on a 2,000 calorie diet. Your daily values may be higher or lower depending on your calorie needs:

		Calories:	2,000	2,500
Total Fat	Less than		65g	80g
Saturated Fat	Less than		20g	25g
Cholesterol	Less than		300mg	300mg
Sodium	Less than		2,400mg	2,400mg
Total Carbohydrate			300g	375g
Dietary Fiber			25g	30g

Calories per gram:
   Fat 9 • Carbohydrate 4 • Protein 4

Thanks to: Lonnie Gee, Nutrition Student

Category: Vegetables

MEXICAN FOOD

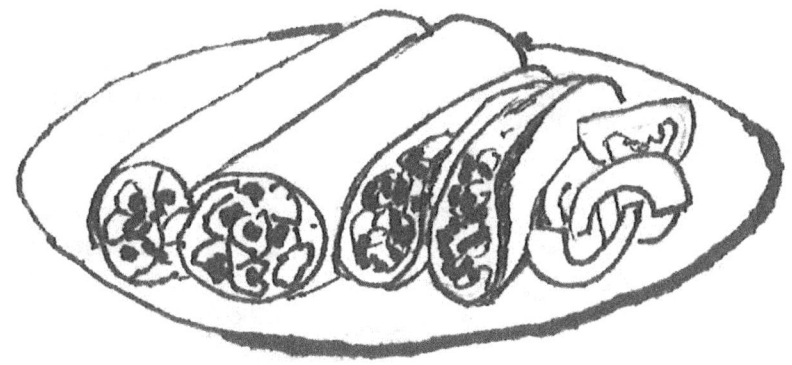

    Mexican foods lend themselves easily to vegetarian modification. They are often high in fiber from beans and corn and make use of a multitude of fresh vegetables. Beware of using high sodium canned items and go easy on the cheese. Non-fat cheeses can be used as well as vegetarian cheeses that use soy, rice, or nuts as a base. Be creative and let your taste buds savor all the Latin flavors.

Bean and Corn Enchiladas

Using homemade enchilada sauce reduces the sodium in this dish.

Makes 16 enchiladas

Ingredients:

½		green bell pepper, chopped
½	cup	scallions, chopped
⅓	cup	water
2	cups	pinto beans, cooked
1	cup	corn kernels
3	tsp	green chiles, diced (canned or fresh)
2	tsp	garlic, minced
2	tsp	ground cumin
16	corn	tortillas
4	cups	chunky enchilada sauce (see page 368)
4	oz	non-fat cheddar cheese, grated for top (optional)
		fresh cilantro or parsley sprigs for garnish (optional)

Nutrition Facts

Serving Size 1 enchilada (232g)
Servings Per Container 16

Amount Per Serving

Calories 140   Calories from Fat 15

% Daily Value*

- **Total Fat** 1.5g — 2%
-   Saturated Fat 0g — 0%
-   Trans Fat 0g
- **Cholesterol** 0mg — 0%
- **Sodium** 280mg — 12%
- **Total Carbohydrate** 26g — 9%
-   Dietary Fiber 5g — 20%
-   Sugars 5g
- **Protein** 6g

Vitamin A 25% • Vitamin C 30%
Calcium 10% • Iron 8%

*Percent Daily Values are based on a 2,000 calorie diet. Your daily values may be higher or lower depending on your calorie needs:

		Calories:	2,000	2,500
Total Fat	Less than		65g	80g
Saturated Fat	Less than		20g	25g
Cholesterol	Less than		300mg	300mg
Sodium	Less than		2,400mg	2,400mg
Total Carbohydrate			300g	375g
Dietary Fiber			25g	30g

Calories per gram:
  Fat 9 • Carbohydrate 4 • Protein 4

Preparation:

- Preheat over to 375°F.
- Sauté the green pepper and scallions in the water until softened, about 5 minutes.
- Mix the beans, corn, chiles, garlic, and cumin in a bowl. Add the sautéed vegetables. Mix.
- Steam the tortillas for 1 minute or wrap them in a cloth and heat in the microwave on high for 1 minute.
- Dip the tortillas in heated chunky enchilada sauce, being careful not to soak them.
- Spoon about ¼ cup of the bean mixture on each, and roll up.
- Place in a non-stick, 13 x 9 inch baking pan, seam side down.
- Bake for 15-20 minutes, or until bubbly.
- Remove from the oven and cover with the remaining sauce.
- Garnish with grated non-fat cheese. Return to oven until cheese begins to soften.
- Add sprigs of fresh cilantro or parsley if desired.
- Serve at once.

Thanks to: Kitty Oulicky, Group 5

Category: Mexican, Beans

Butternut Squash Enchiladas

This fun dish helps to incorporate winter squash in your diet. Any winter squash can be used. They are typically high in fiber and vitamin A. They are more starchy than summer squash, so contain more carbohydrates. If you are short on time, you can buy pre-cut winter squash in the frozen food section (but much more costly than using fresh).

Makes 10 servings

Ingredients:

1	med	butternut squash
8	oz.	fat-free cream cheese
½	cup	green onions, chopped
10		corn or low-fat flour tortillas
2	cups	chunky enchilada sauce (see page 368) or favorite salsa

Preparation:

- Peel and chop butternut squash; boil or steam in microwave until tender.
- Preheat oven to 350°F.
- Mash squash as you would for mashed potatoes (without the butter or milk!).
- Blend in the cream cheese and green onions.
- Fill each tortilla with squash mixture; place in in casserole dish.
- Top enchiladas with sauce or salsa.
- Bake for 15-20 minutes until heated.

Thanks to: Jill Burns, R.D.

Category: Mexican

Nutrition Facts

Serving Size 1/10 recipe (215g)
Servings Per Container 10

Amount Per Serving

Calories 130 — Calories from Fat 10

% Daily Value*

Total Fat 1.5g	2%
Saturated Fat 0g	0%
Trans Fat 0g	
Cholesterol 5mg	2%
Sodium 260mg	11%
Total Carbohydrate 24g	8%
Dietary Fiber 5g	20%
Sugars 5g	
Protein 6g	

Vitamin A 50% • Vitamin C 20%
Calcium 10% • Iron 6%

*Percent Daily Values are based on a 2,000 calorie diet. Your daily values may be higher or lower depending on your calorie needs:

		Calories:	2,000	2,500
Total Fat	Less than		65g	80g
Saturated Fat	Less than		20g	25g
Cholesterol	Less than		300mg	300mg
Sodium	Less than		2,400mg	2,400mg
Total Carbohydrate			300g	375g
Dietary Fiber			25g	30g

Calories per gram:
Fat 9 • Carbohydrate 4 • Protein 4

Chile Relleno Casserole

Chiles rellenos are typically stuffed with high-fat cheese, battered, and fried. You won't miss them in this dish.

Makes 4 servings

Ingredients:

1	cup	brown rice, cooked
2	cups	fat-free refried beans (see page 174)
½	cup	salsa
½	cup	taco sauce
1	can	whole green chiles (7oz)
4	oz	non-fat cheese, grated
½	tsp	garlic powder
1	Tbsp	chives or green onions, minced
		vegetable cooking spray

Preparation:

- Lightly spray a large, deep casserole dish.
- Mix beans and rice with ¼ cup each of salsa and taco sauce.
- Place half of this mixture on the bottom of the dish and set aside.
- Slit the canned chiles lengthwise and remove all of the seeds and cut off the stem ends. Rinse under cold water. Slice peppers lengthwise.
- Preheat oven to 350°F.
- Lay peppers on rice mixture; layer cheese on top. Cover this with the remaining rice-bean mixture.
- Combine remaining taco sauce and salsa with spices and green onions. Pour this mixture over top. Bake for 30 minutes.

Thanks to: Debbie Garduno, R.N. and Kurt Basgall

Category: Mexican

Nutrition Facts

Serving Size 1/4 recipe (280g)
Servings Per Container 4

Amount Per Serving

Calories 270 — Calories from Fat 5

% Daily Value*

Total Fat 0.5g	1%
Saturated Fat 0g	0%
Trans Fat 0g	
Cholesterol 5mg	2%
Sodium 1130mg	47%
Total Carbohydrate 44g	15%
Dietary Fiber 8g	32%
Sugars 5g	
Protein 18g	

Vitamin A 6%	•	Vitamin C 30%
Calcium 30%	•	Iron 15%

*Percent Daily Values are based on a 2,000 calorie diet. Your daily values may be higher or lower depending on your calorie needs:

		Calories:	2,000	2,500
Total Fat	Less than		65g	80g
Saturated Fat	Less than		20g	25g
Cholesterol	Less than		300mg	300mg
Sodium	Less than		2,400mg	2,400mg
Total Carbohydrate			300g	375g
Dietary Fiber			25g	30g

Calories per gram:
  Fat 9 • Carbohydrate 4 • Protein 4

Chile Relleno Tofu Casserole

Another way to enjoy your chiles rellenos.

Makes 8 servings

Ingredients:

12	oz	extra firm light tofu
1½	cup	non-fat white cheese, shredded (6 oz)
2	cans	whole green chiles (7oz each)
6	large	egg whites
½	cup	egg substitute
⅔	cup	non-fat milk
1	cup	flour
1	tsp	baking powder
1¼	cup	fat-free cheddar cheese, shredded (5 oz)
1	jar	favorite salsa (15 oz)

Preparation:

- Preheat oven to 375°F.
- Coat a shallow 2½ to 3 quart casserole with non-stick spray.
- In medium bowl, coarsely mash tofu with a fork or blender and drain if necessary. Mix in cheese.
- Cut a slit down the side and remove all the seeds from chiles.
- Equally fill chiles with tofu mixture and arrange side by side in baking pan.
- In a bowl, whip egg whites and egg substitute on high speed until thick and foamy. Add in milk, flour, and baking powder and mix until smooth. Fold in about half of the shredded cheese.
- Pour this egg mixture over chiles. Sprinkle with remaining cheddar cheese.
- Bake, uncovered, until top is a rich, golden brown (25 - 30 minutes).
- To serve: scatter top with sliced black olives (optional) and accompany with the warmed sauce/salsa.

Thanks to: Ginny Goodrow, Group 25

Category: Mexican

Nutrition Facts

Serving Size 1/8 recipe (261g)
Servings Per Container 8

Amount Per Serving

Calories 210   Calories from Fat 10

% Daily Value*

Total Fat 1.5g	2%
Saturated Fat 0g	0%
Trans Fat 0g	
Cholesterol 5mg	2%
Sodium 1150mg	48%
Total Carbohydrate 24g	8%
Dietary Fiber 2g	8%
Sugars 4g	
Protein 22g	

Vitamin A 30%	•	Vitamin C 20%
Calcium 60%	•	Iron 10%

*Percent Daily Values are based on a 2,000 calorie diet. Your daily values may be higher or lower depending on your calorie needs:

		2,000	2,500
Total Fat	Less than	65g	80g
Saturated Fat	Less than	20g	25g
Cholesterol	Less than	300mg	300mg
Sodium	Less than	2,400mg	2,400mg
Total Carbohydrate		300g	375g
Dietary Fiber		25g	30g

Calories per gram:
  Fat 9 • Carbohydrate 4 • Protein 4

Chile Rellenos con no Manteca

Increasing the veggies and using less cheese reduce the calories in this recipe.

10 servings

Ingredients:

½	large	red onion
¼	cup	cilantro
8	oz	artichokes hearts (if canned, water-packed)
1	tsp	chili powder
3	cups	non-fat cottage cheese
1	can	Anaheim chiles (mild) (7 oz)
2	cans	S & W Mexican tomatoes (15 oz)
1	pkg	frozen broccoli, corn, and red pepper (16 oz)
¼	cup	non-fat cheddar & mozarella cheese, shredded

Preparation:

- Preheat oven to 350°F.
- Chop onion, cilantro and artichokes very fine in a food processor or blender. Set aside.
- Blend the cottage cheese until smooth.
- Add the chopped onion, cilantro and artichoke hearts and ½ teaspoon chili powder to the cottage cheese and stir. Remove mixture from food processor or blender.
- Place both cans of tomatoes and ½ teaspoon chili powder into the blender or food processor and blend until smooth.
- Spread this mixture in the bottom of a 9 x 13 inch baking dish. Sprinkle the mixed vegetables over the tomato mixture.
- Drain the chiles, slit open on one side and remove all seeds. Stuff each chili with several tablespoons of the cottage cheese mixture and place on the tomato mixture in the baking dish.
- Sprinkle cheese over the top and bake for 30 minutes.
- This dish may be frozen and heated in the microwave.

Thanks to: Karen Bishop Johnson, Group 4

Category: Mexican

Nutrition Facts

Serving Size 1/10 recipe (256g)
Servings Per Container 10

Amount Per Serving

Calories 130 — Calories from Fat 5

% Daily Value*

Total Fat 0.5g	1%
Saturated Fat 0g	0%
Trans Fat 0g	
Cholesterol 5mg	2%
Sodium 690mg	29%
Total Carbohydrate 20g	7%
Dietary Fiber 3g	12%
Sugars 9g	
Protein 12g	

Vitamin A 15% • Vitamin C 40%
Calcium 8% • Iron 4%

*Percent Daily Values are based on a 2,000 calorie diet. Your daily values may be higher or lower depending on your calorie needs:

		Calories: 2,000	2,500
Total Fat	Less than	65g	80g
Saturated Fat	Less than	20g	25g
Cholesterol	Less than	300mg	300mg
Sodium	Less than	2,400mg	2,400mg
Total Carbohydrate		300g	375g
Dietary Fiber		25g	30g

Calories per gram:
Fat 9 • Carbohydrate 4 • Protein 4

Easy Enchiladas

A quick meal for a crowd.

12 servings

Ingredients:

2	cups	chunky enchilada sauce (see page 368)
12		corn tortillas
1½	cups	fat-free chicken or beef broth
15	oz	fat-free ricotta cheese
1	cup	green onions, chopped
½	cup	fat-free cheese, grated

Preparation:

- Preheat oven to 350°F.
- Heat sauce in a saucepan.
- Heat broth in a skillet.
- Dip tortillas, one at a time, in broth to make them pliable.
- Put in baking pan and fill with ricotta cheese and onions.
- Roll and repeat this until tortillas are used.
- Pour sauce on top to cover all.
- Garnish with fat-free cheese and bake until cheese melts.

Note: To reduce sodium even further, you could skip the broth dipping and soften the tortillas wrapped in a moist towel in the microwave.

Thanks to: Lilly and Oscar Gallegos, Group 8

Category: Mexican

Nutrition Facts

Serving Size 1 enchilada1 (199g)
Servings Per Container 12

Amount Per Serving

Calories 120 — Calories from Fat 10

% Daily Value*

- Total Fat 1g — 2%
- Saturated Fat 0g — 0%
- Trans Fat 0g
- Cholesterol 5mg — 2%
- Sodium 210mg — 9%
- Total Carbohydrate 19g — 6%
- Dietary Fiber 3g — 12%
- Sugars 4g
- Protein 8g

Vitamin A 20% • Vitamin C 15%
Calcium 15% • Iron 4%

*Percent Daily Values are based on a 2,000 calorie diet. Your daily values may be higher or lower depending on your calorie needs:

	Calories:	2,000	2,500
Total Fat	Less than	65g	80g
Saturated Fat	Less than	20g	25g
Cholesterol	Less than	300mg	300mg
Sodium	Less than	2,400mg	2,400mg
Total Carbohydrate		300g	375g
Dietary Fiber		25g	30g

Calories per gram:
Fat 9 • Carbohydrate 4 • Protein 4

Enchilada Casserole

Similar to Easy Enchiladas, but you don't have to get your hands dirty rolling the enchiladas.

12 servings

Ingredients:

¼	cup	onions, chopped
3	cups	chunky enchilada sauce (see page 368)
1	pkg	Taco Seasoning mix
¾	cup	fat-free cottage cheese
½	cup	non-fat cheese, shredded (VeggieShreds melts nicely)
1	cup	spinach, chopped (or frozen, thawed, drained)
12		corn tortillas
¾	cup	veggie ground round (or other meat substitute)

Preparation:

- Preheat oven to 350°F.
- In a nonstick pan sprayed with nonstick cooking spray sauté onions. Add tomatoes and simmer 15 minutes.
- Add taco seasoning and simmer another 10 minutes and set aside.
- In a bowl, mix together cottage cheese, shredded cheese, and spinach. Set aside.
- Coat casserole dish with nonstick cooking spray.
- Spread just enough tomato sauce to coat bottom of dish.
- Tear 6 tortillas into 2 inch pieces and layer on the bottom of dish.
- Add meat substitute to the remaining tomato sauce.
- Cover tortilla pieces with half of this sauce mixture.
- Next, layer with half of cheese and spinach mixture.
- Repeat the layers: 6 corn tortillas, tomato and "meat" sauce, cheese and spinach mixture.
- Bake about 20 min.

Nutrition Facts

Serving Size 1/12 recipe (212g)
Servings Per Container 12

Amount Per Serving

Calories 140   Calories from Fat 10

% Daily Value*

Total Fat 1g	2%
Saturated Fat 0g	0%
Trans Fat 0g	
Cholesterol 0mg	0%
Sodium 490mg	20%
Total Carbohydrate 23g	8%
Dietary Fiber 4g	16%
Sugars 5g	
Protein 7g	

Vitamin A 30%	•	Vitamin C 20%
Calcium 8%	•	Iron 6%

*Percent Daily Values are based on a 2,000 calorie diet. Your daily values may be higher or lower depending on your calorie needs:

		Calories:	2,000	2,500
Total Fat	Less than		65g	80g
Saturated Fat	Less than		20g	25g
Cholesterol	Less than		300mg	300mg
Sodium	Less than		2,400mg	2,400mg
Total Carbohydrate			300g	375g
Dietary Fiber			25g	30g

Calories per gram:
  Fat 9 • Carbohydrate 4 • Protein 4

Category: Mexican

Homemade Tortillas

These are so easy to make, you'll never buy them again. You can pick up a tortilla press for less than $20.

Makes 8

Flour Tortillas

Ingredients:

2	cups	flour
1	cup	water
1	tsp	baking powder
½	tsp	salt
1	tsp	olive oil

Preparation:

- Combine ingredients, knead for 5 minutes, roll into small balls, then roll out thin.
- Toast in a nonstick frying pan. Cast iron pan works best.

Nutrition Facts

Serving Size 1 tortilla (62g)
Servings Per Container 8

Amount Per Serving

Calories 120   Calories from Fat 10

% Daily Value*

Total Fat 1g	2%
Saturated Fat 0g	0%
Trans Fat 0g	
Cholesterol 0mg	0%
Sodium 220mg	9%
Total Carbohydrate 24g	8%
Dietary Fiber 1g	4%
Sugars 0g	
Protein 3g	

Vitamin A 0% • Vitamin C 0%
Calcium 2% • Iron 8%

*Percent Daily Values are based on a 2,000 calorie diet. Your daily values may be higher or lower depending on your calorie needs:

		Calories:	2,000	2,500
Total Fat	Less than		65g	80g
Saturated Fat	Less than		20g	25g
Cholesterol	Less than		300mg	300mg
Sodium	Less than		2,400mg	2,400mg
Total Carbohydrate			300g	375g
Dietary Fiber			25g	30g

Calories per gram:
  Fat 9 • Carbohydrate 4 • Protein 4

Corn Tortilla

Makes 8 servings

Ingredients:

1½	cups	masa harina
1	cup	water + 1 Tbsp
½	tsp	salt

Preparation:

- Combine ingredients and knead for 30 seconds.
- Let stand, covered, for 15 minutes.
- Divide into 8 balls.
- Place each ball between 2 sheets of plastic wrap and press.

Category: Mexican

Thanks to: David Smith-Walsh, Chef, University Club UCDavis

Nutrition Facts

Serving Size 1/8 recipe (54g)
Servings Per Container 8

Amount Per Serving

Calories 80 — Calories from Fat 5

	% Daily Value*
Total Fat 1g	2%
Saturated Fat 0g	0%
Trans Fat 0g	
Cholesterol 0mg	0%
Sodium 150mg	6%
Total Carbohydrate 16g	5%
Dietary Fiber 2g	8%
Sugars 0g	
Protein 2g	

Vitamin A 0% • Vitamin C 0%
Calcium 4% • Iron 8%

*Percent Daily Values are based on a 2,000 calorie diet. Your daily values may be higher or lower depending on your calorie needs:

	Calories:	2,000	2,500
Total Fat	Less than	65g	80g
Saturated Fat	Less than	20g	25g
Cholesterol	Less than	300mg	300mg
Sodium	Less than	2,400mg	2,400mg
Total Carbohydrate		300g	375g
Dietary Fiber		25g	30g

Calories per gram:
  Fat 9 • Carbohydrate 4 • Protein 4

HUARACHES

These are high in fiber and iron. If using low sodium products, add more spices.

Makes 4 servings

Prep and cooking time: about 40 minutes

Ingredients:

1	lb	mushroom, quartered
1	6 oz	onion, thinly sliced
2	cloves	garlic, minced
½	tsp	dried oregano
2	cups	dehydrated masa flour (corn tortilla flour)
1	tsp	baking powder
¼	tsp	salt
1¾	cups	low sodium, fat-free chicken broth
1½	cups	fat-free refried beans (see page 174)
2	cups	cabbage, shredded (½ cup each serving)
½	cup	tomato or green tomatillo salsa (2 Tbsp each)
¼	cup	crumbled fat-free feta cheese (1 Tbsp each)
¼	cup	non-fat sour cream (1 Tbsp each)
		salt and pepper to taste

Nutrition Facts

Serving Size 1/4 recipe (445g)
Servings Per Container 4

Amount Per Serving

Calories 360 Calories from Fat 25

% Daily Value*

Total Fat 3g	5%
Saturated Fat 0g	0%
Trans Fat 0g	
Cholesterol 0mg	0%
Sodium 770mg	32%
Total Carbohydrate 71g	24%
Dietary Fiber 15g	60%
Sugars 7g	
Protein 25g	

Vitamin A 2%	•	Vitamin C 30%
Calcium 15%	•	Iron 25%

*Percent Daily Values are based on a 2,000 calorie diet. Your daily values may be higher or lower depending on your calorie needs:

		Calories:	2,000	2,500
Total Fat	Less than		65g	80g
Saturated Fat	Less than		20g	25g
Cholesterol	Less than		300mg	300mg
Sodium	Less than		2,400mg	2,400mg
Total Carbohydrate			300g	375g
Dietary Fiber			25g	30g

Calories per gram:
  Fat 9 • Carbohydrate 4 • Protein 4

Preparation:

- **Prepare Mushroom Topping:** In a 10 to 12 inch nonstick frying pan over high heat, sauté mushrooms, onion, garlic with the oregano, stirring frequently. Cook until mushrooms brown, 12 to 15 minutes. Add salt and pepper to taste. Should make 2 cups.
- **Prepare sole of Huaraches (masa dough):** In a bowl, mix masa, baking powder, salt and broth. Stir together until dough holds together well, adding a little water if needed.
- Divide the dough into 4 equal portions. Shape each portion into a 6 inch log on a sheet of waxed paper. Pat each log into a ⅛ inch thick oval about 4 x 8 inches. (If shaped ahead, stack with waxed paper, wrap airtight, and refrigerate for up to 2 hours.)

- Place a griddle or 2 large frying pans over medium-high heat. When pan is hot, flip masa dough onto pan and peel off paper. Cook about 3 minutes until bottom of each masa is light brown. Use a wide spatula to turn huaraches over.
- **Making Huaraches:** With dough still on griddle, spread ¼ of the refried beans over each huarache and then cover with ¼ of the Mushroom Topping. Continue cooking for 2-3 minutes until huarache bottoms are lightly browned. With a wide spatula, transfer to plates.
- Top huaraches equally with layers of cabbage, salsa, crumbled cheese and sour cream.
- Note: If they are too large to easily turn on the griddle, make them half as big and divide toppings equally.

Category: Mexican

Mexican Lasagna

This recipe has been modified over time from a Cooking Light recipe. It is quick and easy and always a crowd pleaser.

Makes 8 servings

Ingredients:

1½	cups	pink, pinto, or black beans, cooked
1½	cups	tomatoes, chopped
1	can	green chiles, chopped (4-oz)
2	cups	corn kernels
2		green onions, minced
½	tsp	ground cumin
½	tsp	dried oregano
8		corn tortillas (see page 214)
1½	cups	fat-free Monterey Jack cheese, grated

Nutrition Facts

Serving Size 1/8 recipe (166g)
Servings Per Container 8

Amount Per Serving

Calories 180   Calories from Fat 10

% Daily Value*

Total Fat 1.5g	2%
Saturated Fat 0g	0%
Trans Fat 0g	
Cholesterol 0mg	0%
Sodium 240mg	10%
Total Carbohydrate 29g	10%
Dietary Fiber 6g	24%
Sugars 4g	
Protein 11g	

Vitamin A 10% • Vitamin C 10%
Calcium 35% • Iron 6%

*Percent Daily Values are based on a 2,000 calorie diet. Your daily values may be higher or lower depending on your calorie needs:

	Calories:	2,000	2,500
Total Fat	Less than	65g	80g
Saturated Fat	Less than	20g	25g
Cholesterol	Less than	300mg	300mg
Sodium	Less than	2,400mg	2,400mg
Total Carbohydrate		300g	375g
Dietary Fiber		25g	30g

Calories per gram:
Fat 9 • Carbohydrate 4 • Protein 4

Preparation:

- Preheat oven to 400°F.
- Combine and mix thoroughly beans, tomatoes, chiles, corn, green onion, and oregano.
- Spray 2 quart casserole or baking dish with vegetable oil cooking spray.
- Line baking dish with 4 tortillas, overlapping.
- Spread half of bean mixture on top of tortillas.

- Sprinkle with half cheese. Repeat.
- Bake 12-15 minutes or until cheese is bubbly.
- Let stand 1-2 minutes, then cut into squares to serve.
- Top with non-fat yogurt or sour cream.

Thanks to: Debbie Lucus, R.D.

Category: Mexican

MILLET APPLESAUCE ENCHILADAS

Millet is another whole grain to add to your repertoire. It is gluten-free and looks a little like bird seed before cooking. You can use it in most any recipe where you would use rice.

Makes 12 servings

Ingredients:

½	cup	whole millet
1½	cups	water
1½	cups	applesauce, unsweetened
1	cup	non-fat cottage cheese
⅓	cup	red onions, chopped
15	oz	unsalted tomato sauce (see pages 371, 380, 383).
1	Tbsp	chili powder
12		corn tortillas (see page 214)
1½	cups	refried beans (see page 174)

Preparation:

- Preheat oven to 350°F.
- Spread the millet in a baking pan and place in oven for 10 minutes or until lightly browned.
- Bring water to a boil in a sauccpan; add the toasted millet, cover, and cook over low heat for 25 minutes.
- Combine the cooked millet with the applesauce, cottage cheese and chopped onions in a bowl, mixing well.
- Combine tomato sauce with chili powder. Spread a thin layer of this sauce in a 10 x 14 inch nonstick baking pan.

Nutrition Facts

Serving Size 1 enchilada (162g)
Servings Per Container 12

Amount Per Serving

Calories 140   Calories from Fat 10

% Daily Value*

Total Fat 1.5g	2%
Saturated Fat 0g	0%
Trans Fat 0g	
Cholesterol 0mg	0%
Sodium 95mg	4%
Total Carbohydrate 30g	10%
Dietary Fiber 6g	24%
Sugars 7g	
Protein 6g	

Vitamin A 8%	•	Vitamin C 8%
Calcium 2%	•	Iron 4%

*Percent Daily Values are based on a 2,000 calorie diet. Your daily values may be higher or lower depending on your calorie needs:

		Calories:	2,000	2,500
Total Fat	Less than		65g	80g
Saturated Fat	Less than		20g	25g
Cholesterol	Less than		300mg	300mg
Sodium	Less than		2,400mg	2,400mg
Total Carbohydrate			300g	375g
Dietary Fiber			25g	30g

Calories per gram:
Fat 9 • Carbohydrate 4 • Protein 4

- Heat two tortillas in the oven for about a minute, or until softened; remove them and heat another two while filling the first ones.
- Spread a thin layer of refried beans on each softened tortilla, top with about 2-3 Tbsp millet and cottage cheese mixture, roll, and place seam side down in the pan.
- Repeat this procedure with the remaining tortillas.
- Pour the remaining sauce over the enchiladas. Bake uncovered for 30 minutes.
- Serve with non-fat or fat-free sour cream, salsa or additional applesauce, if desired.

Thanks to: Bill McPoil and Gail Miata

Category: Mexican

MUSHROOM QUESADILLAS

Adding veggies increases the nutrients in this typically high fat cheese dish.

Makes 6 servings

Ingredients:

8	oz	fresh mushrooms, sliced
½	med	onion, thinly sliced and separated into rings
1	tsp	garlic, minced
3	Tbsp	fresh cilantro, chopped
3	8 inch	whole wheat flour tortillas (96% fat-free)
6	Tbsp	non-fat pepper-jack cheese, shredded

Preparation:

- Coat a large skillet with vegetable oil cooking spray.
- Cook mushroom, onions, garlic for 5 to 7 minutes until tender.
- Stir in cilantro and remove from heat.
- Place mushroom mixture on half of each tortilla.
- Sprinkle evenly with cheese.
- Fold the other half of each tortilla over cheese.
- Place on baking sheet and bake in oven at 350°F for about 5 minutes.
- Cut in half and serve warm with salsa, if desired.

Nutrition Facts

Serving Size 1/2 tortilla (81g)
Servings Per Container 6

Amount Per Serving

Calories 90	Calories from Fat 10

	% Daily Value*
Total Fat 1g	2%
Saturated Fat 0g	0%
Trans Fat 0g	
Cholesterol 0mg	0%
Sodium 220mg	9%
Total Carbohydrate 14g	5%
Dietary Fiber 2g	8%
Sugars 3g	
Protein 5g	

Vitamin A 2%	•	Vitamin C 4%
Calcium 10%	•	Iron 2%

*Percent Daily Values are based on a 2,000 calorie diet. Your daily values may be higher or lower depending on your calorie needs:

	Calories:	2,000	2,500
Total Fat	Less than	65g	80g
Saturated Fat	Less than	20g	25g
Cholesterol	Less than	300mg	300mg
Sodium	Less than	2,400mg	2,400mg
Total Carbohydrate		300g	375g
Dietary Fiber		25g	30g

Calories per gram:
Fat 9 • Carbohydrate 4 • Protein 4

Category: Mexican

Source: *American Heart Association Quick & Easy Cookbook, 1995*

Tamale TVP Pie

This hearty dish represents all the best of Mexican foods.

Makes 6 servings

Ingredients:

½	med	onion, finely chopped
½	cup	celery, finely chopped
½	cup	green pepper, finely chopped
¼	cup	textured vegetable protein (TVP)
OR		
1	pkg	veggie ground round
½	cup	water
1½	cups	tomatoes, chopped
8	oz	tomato sauce, unsalted (see pages 371, 380 and 383)
1¼	cups	corn kernels
2	tsp	chili powder
½	cup	yellow corn meal
1	cup	water
2	oz	ripe olives (optional)
¾	cup	non-fat cheddar cheese
2	oz	**olives for garnish**
		vegetable oil cooking spray

Nutrition Facts

Serving Size 1/6 recipie (250g)
Servings Per Container 6

Amount Per Serving

Calories 150   Calories from Fat 25

% Daily Value*

Total Fat 3g	5%
Saturated Fat 0g	0%
Trans Fat 0g	
Cholesterol 5mg	2%
Sodium 280mg	12%
Total Carbohydrate 24g	8%
Dietary Fiber 5g	20%
Sugars 6g	
Protein 9g	

Vitamin A 20% • Vitamin C 40%
Calcium 20%   • Iron 10%

*Percent Daily Values are based on a 2,000 calorie diet. Your daily values may be higher or lower depending on your calorie needs:

	Calories:	2,000	2,500
Total Fat	Less than	65g	80g
Saturated Fat	Less than	20g	25g
Cholesterol	Less than	300mg	300mg
Sodium	Less than	2,400mg	2,400mg
Total Carbohydrate		300g	375g
Dietary Fiber		25g	30g

Calories per gram:
   Fat 0 • Carbohydrate 4 • Protein 4

Preparation:

- Spray a 12 inch skillet with vegetable oil cooking spray.
- Sauté onion, celery and green pepper.
- When vegetables are beginning to soften, add TVP and ½ cup water.
- Stir frequently.
- Add tomatoes, tomato sauce and corn.
- Add chili powder, mix well and bring to a boil.
- Mix together corn meal, and 1 cup water.
- Add corn meal mixture to skillet mixture, stirring constantly.

- Taste and add salt if necessary. Let thicken a little.
- Add olives, if desired. Spray 11 x 8 inch baking pan with vegetable oil cooking spray.
- Pour mixture into pan, cover and bake for 1 hour in a 350°F oven.
- Remove from oven and sprinkle with cheddar cheese.
- Return to oven for about 5 minutes or until cheese melts.
- Garnish with other half of olives, if desired.

Thanks to: Lew and Dorothy Watkins, Group 2

Note: Remember to count those tasty olives as added fat! Five to seven small olives is equivalent to 1 teaspoon of added fat.

Category: Mexican

TAMALE VEGETABLE PIE

In this version of tamale pie, adding **egg** white to the crust adds protein missing from meat or meat substitute.

Makes 6 servings

Filling:

2	cups	tomatoes, chopped
2	cups	corn, frozen
1½	cups	pinto beans, cooked
½	cup	green chiles, chopped
⅓	cup	green bell pepper, chopped
⅓	cup	onion, chopped
½	tsp	ground cumin
½	tsp	chili powder
¼	tsp	dried cilantro leaves
¼	tsp	oregano leaves
¼	tsp	garlic powder

Crust:

¼	cup	yellow cornmeal
½	cup	flour
1	tsp	baking powder
1	Tbsp	sugar
¼	tsp	salt
½	cup	skim milk
¼	cup	egg substitute
1	tsp	olive oil
		fresh red or jalapeno peppers as needed for garnish

Nutrition Facts

Serving Size 1/6 recipe (234g)
Servings Per Container 6

Amount Per Serving

Calories 210 Calories from Fat 15

% Daily Value*

Total Fat 2g	3%
Saturated Fat 0g	0%
Trans Fat 0g	
Cholesterol 0mg	0%
Sodium 230mg	10%
Total Carbohydrate 41g	14%
Dietary Fiber 7g	28%
Sugars 8g	
Protein 9g	

Vitamin A 20%	•	Vitamin C 110%
Calcium 8%	•	Iron 15%

*Percent Daily Values are based on a 2,000 calorie diet. Your daily values may be higher or lower depending on your calorie needs:

		Calories:	2,000	2,500
Total Fat		Less than	65g	80g
Saturated Fat		Less than	20g	25g
Cholesterol		Less than	300mg	300mg
Sodium		Less than	2,400mg	2,400mg
Total Carbohydrate			300g	375g
Dietary Fiber			25g	30g

Calories per gram:
  Fat 9 • Carbohydrate 4 • Protein 4

Preparation:

- Preheat oven to 350°F.
- In a 3 quart saucepan, combine the filling ingredients.
- Cook over medium heat, stirring occasionally, 10 to 15 minutes, or until mixture is very hot and flavors are blended.
- Cover to keep warm; set aside.
- For the crust, in a small mixing bowl, combine cornmeal, flour, baking powder, sugar and salt. Add milk, egg substitute and oil, mix just until blended.
- Spoon filling into a 9 inch round cake dish.
- Spoon crust batter over filling.
- Sprinkle top with paprika, if desired.
- Bake 30 to 40 minutes.
- Garnish with peppers, if desired.

Category: Mexican

PASTA

Broccoli Lasagna Rolls

Rolling the lasagna noodles ensures portion control and thereby helps reduce calories and carbohydrates in this typically calorie-laden dish.

Makes 6 servings

Ingredients:

Sauce:

¼	cup	green pepper, chopped
1	tsp	fresh parsley, finely chopped
½	tsp	marjoram leaves
½	tsp	thyme leaves
1	tsp	oregano leaves
1	tsp	basil leaves
1	bay	leaf
2	cups	unsalted tomato sauce (see page 371, 380, 383)
¼	cup	water
6		spinach or plain lasagna noodles, yolkless
		vegetable cooking spray

Filling:

3	cups	broccoli, cooked finely chopped
1	cup	non-fat cottage cheese
2	Tbsp	non-fat grated cheese
½	tsp	nutmeg
1	tsp	cayenne pepper (or to taste)

Nutrition Facts

Serving Size 1/6 recipe (204g)
Servings Per Container 6

Amount Per Serving

Calories 170   Calories from Fat 10

% Daily Value*

Total Fat 1g	2%
Saturated Fat 0g	0%
Trans Fat 0g	
Cholesterol 0mg	0%
Sodium 200mg	8%
Total Carbohydrate 31g	10%
Dietary Fiber 3g	12%
Sugars 8g	
Protein 11g	

Vitamin A 20% • Vitamin C 90%
Calcium 8% • Iron 15%

*Percent Daily Values are based on a 2,000 calorie diet. Your daily values may be higher or lower depending on your calorie needs:

		Calories:	2,000	2,500
Total Fat		Less than	65g	80g
Saturated Fat		Less than	20g	25g
Cholesterol		Less than	300mg	300mg
Sodium		Less than	2,400mg	2,400mg
Total Carbohydrate			300g	375g
Dietary Fiber			25g	30g

Calories per gram:
   Fat 9 • Carbohydrate 4 • Protein 4

Preparation:

- Sauce: Heat cooking spray in medium-sized pan. Add green peppers, parsley, spices and bay leaf. Sauté over very low heat, being careful not to burn spices.
- Add tomato sauce and water. Simmer 2-3 hours. Remove bay leaf.
- About ½ hour before sauce will be finished, cook lasagna noodles according to package directions. Set aside.
- Make filling. Finely chop cooked broccoli and place in a medium-sized bowl. Add cottage cheese, non-fat cheese, seasonings and mix well.
- Preheat oven to 350°F. Spread filling evenly over cooked noodles.

- Carefully roll noodles up. Place in non-stick baking dish. Cover with sauce and bake for about 20 minutes.

Source: Adapted from New American Diet

Category: Pasta

Cottage Cheese Stuffed Manicotti

Simple to fix. The manicotti shells do not need to be precooked!

Makes 5 servings

Ingredients:

Tomato Sauce:

1	clove	garlic, minced
1	tsp	olive oil
2	cups	tomato sauce, unsalted
3	cups	tomatoes, chopped
1	½ tsp	oregano leaves
1	Tbsp	parsley, chopped

Filling:

1	cup	non-fat cottage cheese
1	cup	drained cooked spinach
3	Tbsp	non-fat cheese, freshly grated
2		egg whites
¼	cup	parsley, chopped
1	tsp	garlic powder
8	oz	manicotti shells, uncooked (15 pieces)
1	cup	water
		dash pepper

Nutrition Facts

Serving Size 1/5 recipe (341g)
Servings Per Container 5

Amount Per Serving

Calories 300 — Calories from Fat 25

% Daily Value*

Total Fat 2.5g	4%
Saturated Fat 0.5g	3%
Trans Fat 0g	
Cholesterol 5mg	2%
Sodium 290mg	12%
Total Carbohydrate 52g	17%
Dietary Fiber 5g	20%
Sugars 12g	
Protein 17g	

Vitamin A 45% • Vitamin C 60%
Calcium 10% • Iron 15%

*Percent Daily Values are based on a 2,000 calorie diet. Your daily values may be higher or lower depending on your calorie needs:

		2,000	2,500
Total Fat	Less than	65g	80g
Saturated Fat	Less than	20g	25g
Cholesterol	Less than	300mg	300mg
Sodium	Less than	2,400mg	2,400mg
Total Carbohydrate		300g	375g
Dietary Fiber		25g	30g

Calories per gram:
Fat 9 • Carbohydrate 4 • Protein 4

Preparation:

- To prepare sauce: Sauté garlic in olive oil.
- Add tomato sauce and tomatoes slowly. Stir in oregano and parsley. Bring to boil and simmer covered for 20 minutes to 2 hours, stirring occasionally.
- Combine filling ingredients and stuff uncooked manicotti shells using small butter knife.

- Preheat oven to 375°F.
- Pour 2 cups tomato sauce into bottom of a 9 x 13 inch casserole dish.
- Arrange stuffed manicotti shells in a single layer over sauce side by side.
- Cover shells with remaining 3 cups sauce and pour 1 cup water over sauce.
- Cover dish with foil and bake for 50 minutes.
- Remove foil and bake another 10 minutes.

Category: Pasta

Fettuccine with Cottage Cheese Alfredo Sauce

This is a great twist on the usual high fat, creamy sauce. Using cottage cheese increases the protein and calcium.

Makes 6 servings

Ingredients:

1½	cups	non-fat cottage cheese
3	Tbsp	skim milk
½	cup	red (or yellow) bell pepper, chopped
1	clove	garlic, minced
½	cup	peas, frozen
⅛	tsp	pepper
8	oz	(dry weight) fettuccine cooked and drained
2	Tbsp	non-fat Parmesan cheese, grated
1	Tbsp	fresh basil, snipped

Preparation:

- Blend cottage cheese and milk in a blender until smooth.
- In 2 quart saucepan cook pepper and garlic in 1 or 2 Tbsp of water until just tender.
- Over medium heat add milk mixture, peas, and seasonings until heated through. Be careful not to boil.
- Toss with hot pasta.
- Sprinkle with Parmesan and basil.

Nutrition Facts

Serving Size 1/6 recipe (136g)
Servings Per Container 6

Amount Per Serving

Calories 200 — Calories from Fat 5

% Daily Value*

- Total Fat 0.5g — 1%
  - Saturated Fat 0g — 0%
  - Trans Fat 0g
- Cholesterol 5mg — 2%
- Sodium 260mg — 11%
- Total Carbohydrate 36g — 12%
  - Dietary Fiber 2g — 8%
  - Sugars 6g
- Protein 14g

Vitamin A 15% • Vitamin C 30%
Calcium 8% • Iron 10%

*Percent Daily Values are based on a 2,000 calorie diet. Your daily values may be higher or lower depending on your calorie needs:

		Calories:	2,000	2,500
Total Fat	Less than		65g	80g
Saturated Fat	Less than		20g	25g
Cholesterol	Less than		300mg	300mg
Sodium	Less than		2,400mg	2,400mg
Total Carbohydrate			300g	375g
Dietary Fiber			25g	30g

Calories per gram:
Fat 9 • Carbohydrate 4 • Protein 4

Thanks to: Bill and Joann Lannon

Category: Pasta

Jane's No-Boil Lasagna

The no-cook noodles make assembly a breeze.

Makes 18 servings

Ingredients:

15	oz	non-fat Ricotta cheese
½	cup	fat-free Parmesan cheese
½	cup	egg substitute
2	jars	fat-free pasta sauce (26 oz)
1	lb	package no-cook lasagna noodles
1	lb	fat-free mozzarella cheese, grated
1	pkg	spinach, frozen (10 oz), thawed with extra liquid squeezed out
1	cup	parsley, chopped

Preparation:

- Preheat oven to 350°F. Prepare 13 x 9 inch baking pan with cooking spray.
- In a bowl, combine ricotta and Parmesan cheese with egg substitute.
- To assemble, spread 1 cup sauce on bottom of pan.
- Layer, in order, half of each noodles, ricotta mixture, pasta sauce, mozzarella.
- Then, arrange one package of spinach over all.
- Repeat the layers, noodles, ricotta, sauce, cheese.
- Top with chopped parsley.
- Cover tightly with lid or foil.
- Bake 1 hour or until hot and bubbly.
- Let stand covered 15 minutes before serving.

Nutrition Facts

Serving Size 1/18 recipe (185g)
Servings Per Container 18

Amount Per Serving

Calories 220   Calories from Fat 10

% Daily Value*

Total Fat 1g	2%
Saturated Fat 0g	0%
Trans Fat 0g	
Cholesterol 5mg	2%
Sodium 490mg	20%
Total Carbohydrate 32g	11%
Dietary Fiber 3g	12%
Sugars 6g	
Protein 19g	

Vitamin A 60% • Vitamin C 20%
Calcium 40% • Iron 15%

*Percent Daily Values are based on a 2,000 calorie diet. Your daily values may be higher or lower depending on your calorie needs:

		Calories:	2,000	2,500
Total Fat	Less than		65g	80g
Saturated Fat	Less than		20g	25g
Cholesterol	Less than		300mg	300mg
Sodium	Less than		2,400mg	2,400mg
Total Carbohydrate			300g	375g
Dietary Fiber			25g	30g

Calories per gram:
Fat 9 • Carbohydrate 4 • Protein 4

Note: You can substitute a can of stewed tomatoes with a pinch of Italian seasoning for one jar of sauce. If you have trouble finding fat-free Parmesan, a reasonable substitution is a reduced fat Italian cheese blend.

Thanks to: Jane Hue, group 28

Category: Pasta

Linguine with Lentils

Any dark green leafy vegetable could be used in this recipe (spinach, kale, mustard greens, rainbow chard). The greens add vitamin A, C, and folate, as well as fiber.

Makes 10 servings

Ingredients:

3	cups	vegetable broth (see page 384)
1	cup	lentils, rinsed and drained
1	tsp	cumin seeds
1	lb.	Swiss chard, well rinsed
1	Tbsp	olive oil
1		onion, chopped
2	cloves	garlic, minced
½	tsp	crushed red pepper flakes
8	oz	dry linguine (try whole wheat)
4	oz.	fat-free cream cheese, diced

Nutrition Facts

Serving Size 1/10 recipe (205g)
Servings Per Container 10

Amount Per Serving

Calories 210 — Calories from Fat 25

% Daily Value*

Total Fat 2.5g	4%
Saturated Fat 0g	0%
Trans Fat 0g	
Cholesterol 0mg	0%
Sodium 200mg	8%
Total Carbohydrate 36g	12%
Dietary Fiber 5g	20%
Sugars 4g	
Protein 12g	

Vitamin A 120% • Vitamin C 70%
Calcium 10% • Iron 25%

*Percent Daily Values are based on a 2,000 calorie diet. Your daily values may be higher or lower depending on your calorie needs:

		Calories:	2,000	2,500
Total Fat	Less than		65g	80g
Saturated Fat	Less than		20g	25g
Cholesterol	Less than		300mg	300mg
Sodium	Less than		2,400mg	2,400mg
Total Carbohydrate			300g	375g
Dietary Fiber			25g	30g

Calories per gram:
Fat 9 • Carbohydrate 4 • Protein 4

Preparation:

- Bring 2 cups of broth to a boil.
- Add lentils and cumin seeds.
- Reduce heat, cover, and simmer until lentils are tender (about 30 minutes). Drain; pour into a bowl.
- Cut off and discard coarse stem ends of chard; cut stems and leaves crosswise into 1 inch wide strips.
- To lentil pan, add oil, chard (stems only), onion, garlic, and red pepper flakes.
- Cook over medium heat, stirring often, until onion is lightly browned (about 15 minutes).
- Add chard leaves; cook, stirring until limp (about 3 minutes).
- Add lentils and 1 cup broth; cook uncovered, until hot (about 3 minutes)
- Cook pasta until *al dente*.
- Drain and pour into a bowl.
- Add lentil mixture and cheese; mix lightly to blend.
- Season with pepper.

Category: Pasta

MACARONI & CHEESE

Cheese mixture burns very easily when cooked on stovetop. To avoid this, the recipe uses the microwave.

Makes 6 servings

Ingredients:

12	oz	macaroni or pasta of choice
2	cups	skim milk
1	Tbsp	flour
½	tsp	salt
12	oz	fat-free singles sharp cheddar cheese
		dash pepper

Preparation:

- Preheat oven to 350°F.
- Cook macaroni per package instructions.
- Cut cheese into pieces to aid in melting.
- Stir together milk, flour, salt, pepper, and cheese in a microwaveable container.
- Microwave about 2 minutes, until cheese is melted.
- Mix cheese sauce with pasta.
- Bake 40 minutes.

Category: Pasta

Nutrition Facts

Serving Size 1/6 recipe (197g)
Servings Per Container 6

Amount Per Serving

Calories 330 — Calories from Fat 10

	% Daily Value*
Total Fat 1.5g	2%
Saturated Fat 0g	0%
Trans Fat 0g	
Cholesterol 10mg	3%
Sodium 800mg	33%
Total Carbohydrate 48g	16%
Dietary Fiber 2g	8%
Sugars 6g	
Protein 29g	

Vitamin A 20%	•	Vitamin C 0%
Calcium 60%	•	Iron 10%

*Percent Daily Values are based on a 2,000 calorie diet. Your daily values may be higher or lower depending on your calorie needs:

		Calories:	2,000	2,500
Total Fat	Less than		65g	80g
Saturated Fat	Less than		20g	25g
Cholesterol	Less than		300mg	300mg
Sodium	Less than		2,400mg	2,400mg
Total Carbohydrate			300g	375g
Dietary Fiber			25g	30g

Calories per gram:
  Fat 9 • Carbohydrate 4 • Protein 4

Pasta al Pesto

This is dryer than regular pesto, but packed with all the flavor and considerably less fat! Pinenuts, however, still count as an added fat and approximately 1 Tbsp nuts = 1 tsp fat.

Makes 5 servings

Ingredients:

1	tsp	olive oil
8-12	cloves	garlic, minced
3	Tbsp	pinenuts, finely chopped (optional)
1		large bunch fresh basil
½	lb	whole wheat spaghetti or other yolkless pasta
4	Tbsp	non-fat mozzarella cheese, grated (4 oz)

Preparation:

- In a small, heavy skillet, gently heat oil and sauté minced garlic and chopped nuts for 6-8 minutes, until garlic is barely golden.
- Remove from heat.
- Wash basil. Pick leaves from stems to yield 3-4 cups of basil leaves.
- Chop the leaves into thin strips. Toss with oil and garlic in skillet, but do not heat until just before serving.
- Grate the mozzarella cheese.
- Ten minutes before serving time, drop spaghetti into rapidly boiling water and cook according to package directions.
- Cook until just tender. Drain well.
- Toss with pesto sauce, sprinkle with mozzarella and serve.

Nutrition Facts

Serving Size 1/5 recipe (around 1 cup) (98g)
Servings Per Container 5

Amount Per Serving

Calories 220　　Calories from Fat 30

　　　　　　　　　　　　　　% Daily Value*

Total Fat 3.5g	5%
Saturated Fat 0g	0%
Trans Fat 0g	
Cholesterol 0mg	0%
Sodium 60mg	3%
Total Carbohydrate 40g	13%
Dietary Fiber 8g	32%
Sugars 0g	
Protein 10g	

Vitamin A 35%　•　Vitamin C 15%
Calcium 15%　•　Iron 15%

*Percent Daily Values are based on a 2,000 calorie diet. Your daily values may be higher or lower depending on your calorie needs:

	Calories:	2,000	2,500
Total Fat	Less than	65g	80g
Saturated Fat	Less than	20g	25g
Cholesterol	Less than	300mg	300mg
Sodium	Less than	2,400mg	2,400mg
Total Carbohydrate		300g	375g
Dietary Fiber		25g	30g

Calories per gram:
　Fat 9　•　Carbohydrate 4　•　Protein 4

Note: To make a creamy pesto sauce, combine this recipe and nonfat cream sauce (see page 370)

Thanks to: Michele Lites, R.D.

Category: Pasta

PASTA PRIMAVERA

This recipe is a good way to increase your intake of veggies and fiber. The white sauce is low in fat, so overall a very good combination.

Makes 6 servings

Ingredients:

12	oz	whole wheat spaghetti or linguine
2	cups	broccoli, cut into 1 inch pieces
12	oz	mushrooms, each cut in half
1	tsp	olive oil
1		small onion, minced
1		small carrot, julienned
1		small red pepper, cut into ¼ inch thick strips
1	can	evaporated skim milk (8 oz)
½	cup	vegetable broth (see page 384)
1½	tsp	cornstarch
½	tsp	salt (optional)
2	cloves	garlic, minced
1	med	tomato, seeded and diced
3	Tbsp	fat-free mozzarella cheese
2	Tbsp	parsley, minced

Nutrition Facts

Serving Size 1/6 recipe (276g)
Servings Per Container 6

Amount Per Serving

Calories 290   Calories from Fat 20

% Daily Value*

Total Fat 2g	3%
Saturated Fat 0g	0%
Trans Fat 0g	
Cholesterol 0mg	0%
Sodium 300mg	13%
Total Carbohydrate 57g	19%
Dietary Fiber 9g	36%
Sugars 9g	
Protein 16g	

Vitamin A 70%	•	Vitamin C 100%
Calcium 20%	•	Iron 20%

*Percent Daily Values are based on a 2,000 calorie diet. Your daily values may be higher or lower depending on your calorie needs:

		Calories:	2,000	2,500
Total Fat	Less than		65g	80g
Saturated Fat	Less than		20g	25g
Cholesterol	Less than		300mg	300mg
Sodium	Less than		2,400mg	2,400mg
Total Carbohydrate			300g	375g
Dietary Fiber			25g	30g

Calories per gram:
   Fat 9   •   Carbohydrate 4   •   Protein 4

Preparation:

- In a saucepan, prepare spaghetti as label directs; drain.
- Return spaghetti to saucepan; keep warm.
- Heat broccoli pieces to boiling in one inch of water, in a 2 quart saucepan, over high heat.
- Reduce heat to low; cover and simmer 2-3 minutes, stirring occasionally, until broccoli is tender-crisp; drain.
- While broccoli is cooking, in a 12 inch skillet, heat oil (high heat) and cook mushrooms, onion, and carrot, stirring frequently, until vegetables are golden and tender-crisp. Add red pepper strips and cook, stirring, until tender.
- Mix together evaporated skim milk, vegetable broth, cornstarch and salt in a separate bowl and add to skillet.

- Heat to boiling for 1 minute.
- Add diced tomato, cheese, parsley, broccoli, and spaghetti, tossing to coat well; heat thoroughly.

Source: Good Housekeeping

Category: Pasta

PASTA WITH MOCK CREAM SAUCE

Ricotta and milk are another good combination to make a creamy sauce. The orange squash and green spinach are beautiful together.

Makes 8 servings

Ingredients:

1	lb	tubular pasta (e.g. penne)
1		butternut squash
½	cup	fat-free ricotta cheese
¼	cup	skim milk
1	med	onion, chopped
1	clove	garlic, minced (½ tsp)
10	oz	fresh spinach
		salt and pepper to taste

Preparation:

- Cook pasta according to package directions. Drain and set aside.
- Place squash in baking dish, cut sides down.
- Cook in oven at 350°F for 30 minutes (or microwave on high 5-6 minutes).
- Scoop out squash from rind and put in food processor (or blender).
- Add ricotta cheese and milk. Blend until creamy. Add more milk if need to thin.
- Add salt and pepper to taste.
- Sauté onion and garlic until soft in oil-sprayed pan.
- Add spinach and cook until wilted.
- Toss together pasta, cream sauce and sautéed spinach and enjoy.

Thanks to: Terry Lavirgne, Group 29

Category: Pasta

Nutrition Facts

Serving Size 1/8 recipe (159g)
Servings Per Container 8

Amount Per Serving

Calories 250 — Calories from Fat 15

	% Daily Value*
Total Fat 1.5g	2%
Saturated Fat 1g	5%
Trans Fat 0g	
Cholesterol 5mg	2%
Sodium 125mg	5%
Total Carbohydrate 49g	16%
Dietary Fiber 4g	16%
Sugars 6g	
Protein 11g	

Vitamin A 70% • Vitamin C 20%
Calcium 10% • Iron 15%

*Percent Daily Values are based on a 2,000 calorie diet. Your daily values may be higher or lower depending on your calorie needs:

	Calories:	2,000	2,500
Total Fat	Less than	65g	80g
Saturated Fat	Less than	20g	25g
Cholesterol	Less than	300mg	300mg
Sodium	Less than	2,400mg	2,400mg
Total Carbohydrate		300g	375g
Dietary Fiber		25g	30g

Calories per gram:
Fat 9 • Carbohydrate 4 • Protein 4

Pasta with Spinach and Beans

This is an interesting combination of pasta, beans, and veggies that makes a colorful, nutritious dish.

Makes 6 servings

Ingredients:

8	oz	penne, rotini, or other pasta
1	tsp	olive oil
1		green pepper, chopped
2		cloves garlic, minced (1 tsp)
1½	cups	unsalted white, navy or cannellini beans, cooked
1½	cups	tomatoes, chopped
10	oz	spinach, frozen chopped thawed, squeezed dry (OR chard)
¼	cup	sun-dried tomatoes, chopped and reconstituted
2	Tbsp	fresh oregano, chopped
2	Tbsp	fresh basil, chopped
		dash hot-pepper sauce
		salt and black pepper to taste.

Nutrition Facts

Serving Size 1/6 recipe (229g)
Servings Per Container 6

Amount Per Serving

Calories 230   Calories from Fat 25

% Daily Value*

Total Fat 2.5g	4%
Saturated Fat 0g	0%
Trans Fat 0g	
Cholesterol 0mg	0%
Sodium 120mg	5%
Total Carbohydrate 44g	15%
Dietary Fiber 7g	28%
Sugars 5g	
Protein 11g	

Vitamin A 130% • Vitamin C 50%
Calcium 10% • Iron 20%

*Percent Daily Values are based on a 2,000 calorie diet. Your daily values may be higher or lower depending on your calorie needs:

		Calories:	2,000	2,500
Total Fat	Less than		65g	80g
Saturated Fat	Less than		20g	25g
Cholesterol	Less than		300mg	300mg
Sodium	Less than		2,400mg	2,400mg
Total Carbohydrate			300g	375g
Dietary Fiber			25g	30g

Calories per gram:
  Fat 9 • Carbohydrate 4 • Protein 4

Preparation:

- Cook pasta in a large pot of boiling water for 10 to 12 minutes, or until tender, and drain well.
- While pasta is cooking, in a large non-stick frying pan over medium heat, using olive oil, sauté green pepper and garlic for 3 minutes or until peppers are slightly wilted.
- Add beans, tomatoes, spinach, sun-dried tomatoes, and oregano and simmer for 10 minutes.
- Add cooked pasta and basil and other seasonings. Toss to mix.

Thanks to: Jerre Schermerhorn, Group 29

Category: Pasta

PAULINE'S MACARONI & CHEESE

This is so good you will want to have seconds, but be careful. Even though low in fat, it is a hearty dish, high in carbohydrates.

Makes 8 servings

Ingredients:

1	lb	elbow macaroni
1	cup	soy cheddar cheese
1	cup	fat–free soy mozzarella style cheese
⅓	cup	Smart Squeeze nonfat margarine spread
½	cup	egg whites
1	cup	evaporated fat-free milk

Preparation:

- Bring water to a boil in a large pot.
- Add macaroni, and cook for 10 minutes or until done.
- Drain and place in large bowl.
- Add and stir in remaining ingredients, one ingredient at a time. Bake at 350°F for 25 to 30 minutes.
- Let cool before serving.

Thanks to: Pauline Mitchell, Group 25

Category: Pasta

Nutrition Facts

Serving Size 1/8 recipe (143g)
Servings Per Container 8

Amount Per Serving

Calories 280	Calories from Fat 20

	% Daily Value*
Total Fat 2.5g	4%
Saturated Fat 0g	0%
Trans Fat 0g	
Cholesterol 0mg	0%
Sodium 370mg	15%
Total Carbohydrate 51g	17%
Dietary Fiber 2g	8%
Sugars 6g	
Protein 18g	

Vitamin A 4%	•	Vitamin C 0%
Calcium 10%	•	Iron 10%

*Percent Daily Values are based on a 2,000 calorie diet. Your daily values may be higher or lower depending on your calorie needs:

	Calories:	2,000	2,500
Total Fat	Less than	65g	80g
Saturated Fat	Less than	20g	25g
Cholesterol	Less than	300mg	300mg
Sodium	Less than	2,400mg	2,400mg
Total Carbohydrate		300g	375g
Dietary Fiber		25g	30g

Calories per gram:
 Fat 9 • Carbohydrate 4 • Protein 4

STUFFED SHELLS

Very tasty, and well worth the effort to stuff the shells yourself.

Makes 9 servings ~ 3 x 3 inch square

Ingredients:

12-15		jumbo pasta shells (16 oz)
16	oz.	non-fat ricotta cheese
OR		
16	oz	non-fat cottage cheese
4	oz.	non-fat mozzarella cheese, grated
¼	cup	egg substitute
1	Tbsp	parsley, chopped
¼	tsp	salt
⅛	tsp	pepper
¼	tsp	nutmeg
16	oz	vegetable marinara sauce (see page 385 or use other fat free marinara sauce

Nutrition Facts

Serving Size 3x3 inch square (171g)
Servings Per Container 9

Amount Per Serving

Calories 260   Calories from Fat 10

	% Daily Value*
Total Fat 1g	2%
Saturated Fat 0g	0%
Trans Fat 0g	
Cholesterol 5mg	2%
Sodium 290mg	12%
Total Carbohydrate 44g	15%
Dietary Fiber 2g	8%
Sugars 6g	
Protein 18g	

Vitamin A 25%	•	Vitamin C 10%
Calcium 30%	•	Iron 10%

*Percent Daily Values are based on a 2,000 calorie diet. Your daily values may be higher or lower depending on your calorie needs:

		Calories:	2,000	2,500
Total Fat	Less than		65g	80g
Saturated Fat	Less than		20g	25g
Cholesterol	Less than		300mg	300mg
Sodium	Less than		2,400mg	2,400mg
Total Carbohydrate			300g	375g
Dietary Fiber			25g	30g

Calories per gram:
 Fat 9 • Carbohydrate 4 • Protein 4

Preparation:

- Preheat oven to 350°F.
- Boil shells in sufficient water to allow easy movement.
- Cook 9 minutes; drain.
- Rinse with cold water for easy handling.
- Drain and separate.
- Meanwhile, mix together cheeses, egg substitute, parsley, salt, pepper and nutmeg.
- Fill the cooked shells with cheese mixture. (A butter spreader makes this an easy job.)
- Cover the bottom of a 9 x 9 inch square pan with some of the sauce.
- Arrange filled shells in single layer in the pan.
- Pour remaining sauce over the shells and bake covered for 30 minutes, until bubbling.

Note: If using cottage cheese, whirl it until smooth in a food processor or blender. If doubling the recipe, use a 13 x 9 inch pan.

Thanks to: Lew and Dorothy Watkins, Group 2

Category: Pasta

Vegetable Lasagna

A creamy lasagna, packed with protein.

Makes 12 servings

Ingredients:

16	oz	lasagna noodles (curly-edged)
1	pkg.	spinach, frozen chopped (10 oz.)
1	cup	fontina cheese, shredded (4 oz.)
1	cup	carrot, shredded
1	cup	zucchini, shredded
3	cups	non-fat ricotta cheese (24 oz.)
2		egg whites, lightly beaten
1	med	onion, chopped
1	tsp	olive oil
2	Tbsp	flour
¼	tsp	ground nutmeg
1	cup	vegetable broth (see page 384)
½	cup	non-fat Parmesan cheese, grated
		vegetable oil cooking spray

Nutrition Facts

Serving Size 3 x 3 inch square (203g)
Servings Per Container 12

Amount Per Serving

Calories 270 Calories from Fat 40

	% Daily Value*
Total Fat 4.5g	7%
Saturated Fat 2g	10%
Trans Fat 0g	
Cholesterol 15mg	5%
Sodium 270mg	11%
Total Carbohydrate 38g	13%
Dietary Fiber 2g	8%
Sugars 6g	
Protein 19g	

Vitamin A 70% • Vitamin C 15%
Calcium 35% • Iron 10%

*Percent Daily Values are based on a 2,000 calorie diet. Your daily values may be higher or lower depending on your calorie needs:

		Calories:	2,000	2,500
Total Fat	Less than		65g	80g
Saturated Fat	Less than		20g	25g
Cholesterol	Less than		300mg	300mg
Sodium	Less than		2,400mg	2,400mg
Total Carbohydrate			300g	375g
Dietary Fiber			25g	30g

Calories per gram:
  Fat 9 • Carbohydrate 4 • Protein 4

Preparation:

- Preheat oven to 350°F.
- Cook lasagna according to package directions; drain. (Separate lasagna and lay flat on wax paper or aluminum foil to keep pieces from sticking together as they cool.)
- Press water from thawed spinach. Combine with fontina cheese, carrot, zucchini, and 2 ½ cups of the ricotta cheese and the egg whites.
- Place layer of lasagna on bottom of 13 x 9 inch baking dish that has been sprayed with vegetable oil cooking spray.
- Spread with ½ of the cheese mixture.
- Repeat layers, ending with lasagna.
- Sauté onion in oil until tender. Add flour and nutmeg.
- Stir in broth and remaining ricotta.
- Cook and stir until mixture comes to a boil.
- Spoon over lasagna.
- Sprinkle with Parmesan cheese.

- Cover with aluminum foil and bake for 45 min.
- Uncover and broil about 2-3 minutes or until lightly browned.

Thanks to: *Gil Kalmar, Group 12*

Category: Pasta

ZUCCHINI LASAGNA

Use the roasted tomato herb sauce in this recipe, or another low-fat, low salt alternative.

Makes 6 servings

Ingredients:

1½	cups	roasted tomato herb sauce (see page 380)
6		lasagna noodles
8	oz	non-fat ricotta or non-fat cottage cheese
½	cup	egg substitute
½	tsp	ground nutmeg
4	med	zucchini, sliced lengthwise in ⅛ inch strips
4	oz	non-fat mozzarella cheese, grated
		vegetable oil cooking spray
		pepper to taste

Preparation:

- Cook lasagna noodles, drain, and cool.
- Preheat oven to 350°F.
- Spray a 9 x 9 inch square pan with vegetable oil cooking spray.
- Spoon in about one Tbsp of the tomato sauce.
- Arrange lasagna noodles so that the bottom of the pan is covered.
- In a bowl, mix together ricotta (or cottage) cheese with the egg substitute, salt, nutmeg and pepper.
- Spoon about half the cheese mixture onto the noodles.
- Arrange zucchini slices on top; sprinkle with ⅓ of the mozzarella; spoon some of the sauce over.
- Repeat for another layer and sprinkle remaining mozzarella on top.
- Cover with foil and bake about 45 minutes, or until bubbly throughout.

Nutrition Facts

Serving Size 1/6 recipe (243g)
Servings Per Container 6

Amount Per Serving

Calories 200   Calories from Fat 10

% Daily Value*

Total Fat 1g	2%
Saturated Fat 0g	0%
Trans Fat 0g	
Cholesterol 5mg	2%
Sodium 270mg	11%
Total Carbohydrate 31g	10%
Dietary Fiber 3g	12%
Sugars 8g	
Protein 17g	

Vitamin A 50% • Vitamin C 30%
Calcium 25% • Iron 10%

*Percent Daily Values are based on a 2,000 calorie diet. Your daily values may be higher or lower depending on your calorie needs:

		Calories:	2,000	2,500
Total Fat		Less than	65g	80g
Saturated Fat		Less than	20g	25g
Cholesterol		Less than	300mg	300mg
Sodium		Less than	2,400mg	2,400mg
Total Carbohydrate			300g	375g
Dietary Fiber			25g	30g

Calories per gram:
  Fat 9 • Carbohydrate 4 • Protein 4

- Freeze any leftovers for another meal.

Thanks to: Lew and Dorothy Watkins, Group 2

Category: Pasta

POTATOES

CHIPOTLE MASHED SWEET POTATOES

Chipotle chiles come canned in adobo sauce. For this recipe, you only need two and others can be reserved for another use. They freeze well so that will make them easy to save.

Yield: 10 servings, ~ ½ cup each

Ingredients:

2½	lbs	sweet potatoes, peeled, cubed
½	cup	evaporated fat-free milk
5	squirts	I Can't Believe It's Not Butter Spray (optional)
2	Tbsp	lime juice
2		chipotle chiles
¼	cup	brown sugar, packed
¼	tsp	salt
½	tsp	ground cinnamon
¼	tsp	ground cinnamon

Preparation:

- Boil sweet potatoes until tender. Drain and return potatoes to pan.
- Mash to desired consistency with milk, butter spray and lime juice.
- Cook for 2 minutes, stirring constantly.
- Remove chiles from can and chop. Stir chopped chiles into potato mixture with brown sugar, salt and cinnamon. Sprinkle with additional cinnamon.

Category: Potatoes

Nutrition Facts

Serving Size 1/10 recipe, about 1/2 cup (141g)
Servings Per Container 10

Amount Per Serving

Calories 120   Calories from Fat 0

% Daily Value*

Total Fat 0g	0%
Saturated Fat 0g	0%
Trans Fat 0g	
Cholesterol 0mg	0%
Sodium 160mg	7%
Total Carbohydrate 28g	9%
Dietary Fiber 4g	16%
Sugars 13g	
Protein 3g	

Vitamin A 110% • Vitamin C 30%
Calcium 6% • Iron 4%

*Percent Daily Values are based on a 2,000 calorie diet. Your daily values may be higher or lower depending on your calorie needs:

		Calories:	2,000	2,500
Total Fat	Less than		65g	80g
Saturated Fat	Less than		20g	25g
Cholesterol	Less than		300mg	300mg
Sodium	Less than		2,400mg	2,400mg
Total Carbohydrate			300g	375g
Dietary Fiber			25g	30g

Calories per gram:
 Fat 9 • Carbohydrate 4 • Protein 4

Cottage Style Twice Baked Potatoes

A healthy, twice-baked potato--yum. Cottage cheese provides protein and calcium.

Makes 8 servings ~ ½ potato each

Ingredients:

4		medium potatoes
1	cup	non-fat cottage cheese
½	cup	skim milk or non-fat buttermilk
1	Tbsp	onion, minced
½	tsp	reduced sodium "salt" or less
		dash pepper
		paprika
		parsley, chopped

Preparation:

- Preheat oven to 400°F.
- Scrub potatoes. Make shallow slits around the middle as if you were cutting the potatoes in half lengthwise. Bake until done, 30-60 minutes, depending on size of potato.
- Cut hot potatoes in half lengthwise. Scoop out potatoes, leaving skins intact for stuffing.
- With wire whisk, beat scooped-out potato with remaining ingredients, except paprika and parsley, until fluffy.
- Pile mixture back into skins. Sprinkle with paprika and parsley.
- Bake 10 minutes more or until just golden.

Nutrition Facts

Serving Size 1/2 potato (122g)
Servings Per Container 8

Amount Per Serving

Calories 80 — Calories from Fat 0

% Daily Value*

Total Fat 0g	0%
Saturated Fat 0g	0%
Trans Fat 0g	
Cholesterol 0mg	0%
Sodium 260mg	11%
Total Carbohydrate 16g	5%
Dietary Fiber 2g	8%
Sugars 4g	

Protein 6g

Vitamin A 2%	•	Vitamin C 25%
Calcium 4%	•	Iron 4%

*Percent Daily Values are based on a 2,000 calorie diet. Your daily values may be higher or lower depending on your calorie needs:

		Calories:	2,000	2,500
Total Fat		Less than	65g	80g
Saturated Fat		Less than	20g	25g
Cholesterol		Less than	300mg	300mg
Sodium		Less than	2,400mg	2,400mg
Total Carbohydrate			300g	375g
Dietary Fiber			25g	30g

Calories per gram:
Fat 9 • Carbohydrate 4 • Protein 4

Category: Potatoes

Cranberry Glazed Sweet Potatoes

Perfect for the holiday table. A good substitute for the usually high-fat sweet potatoes.

Makes 8 servings ~ ¾ cup each

Ingredients:

6	med	sweet potatoes, peeled, cut into 1 inch pieces (about 2 lb)
½	cup	brown sugar, firmly packed
¼	cup	orange juice
½	tsp	salt
1	cup	whole-berry cranberry sauce

Preparation:

- Place sweet potatoes in a covered 2 quart casserole dish and microwave at HIGH for 10 minutes, or until tender.
- Combine brown sugar, orange juice and salt in a 2-cup glass measuring cup. Microwave HIGH 3 minutes, stirring every minute.
- Add to sweet potatoes in casserole dish with cranberry sauce and toss gently to mix.
- Microwave on HIGH 10 minutes, or until heated through, basting with sauce twice during cooking.
- Garnish with orange rind, if desired.

Thanks to: Debbie Lucus, R.D.

Category: Potatoes

Nutrition Facts

Serving Size 3/4 cup (170g)
Servings Per Container 8

Amount Per Serving

Calories 200   Calories from Fat 0

% Daily Value*

Total Fat 0g	0%
Saturated Fat 0g	0%
Trans Fat 0g	
Cholesterol 0mg	0%
Sodium 220mg	9%
Total Carbohydrate 50g	17%
Dietary Fiber 4g	16%
Sugars 27g	
Protein 2g	

Vitamin A 320% • Vitamin C 8%
Calcium 4% • Iron 4%

*Percent Daily Values are based on a 2,000 calorie diet. Your daily values may be higher or lower depending on your calorie needs:

		Calories:	2,000	2,500
Total Fat	Less than		65g	80g
Saturated Fat	Less than		20g	25g
Cholesterol	Less than		300mg	300mg
Sodium	Less than		2,400mg	2,400mg
Total Carbohydrate			300g	375g
Dietary Fiber			25g	30g

Calories per gram:
Fat 9 • Carbohydrate 4 • Protein 4

Easy Pineapple Yam Bake

Quick and easy.

Makes 16 servings

Ingredients:

2	cans	yams in light syrup (28 z oz each)
1	can	pineapple chunks (20 oz)
1	cup	pineapple juice (reserved from cans).
1	Tbsp	cornstarch
2	cups	mini-marshmallows

Preparation:

- Preheat oven to 350°F. Coat 8 x 8 inch baking pan with non-stick spray.
- Drain and place yams and pineapple in baking pan.
- Microwave the reserved pineapple juice for 1 minute, then whisk in cornstarch.
- Pour over pineapple-yams.
- Sprinkle marshmallows over top.
- Bake for 20 minutes or until lightly browned.

Thanks to: Jeff Biggurl, Group 29

Category: Potatoes

Nutrition Facts

Serving Size 1/16 recipe (157g)
Servings Per Container 16

Amount Per Serving

Calories 160   Calories from Fat 5

	% Daily Value*
Total Fat 0g	0%
Saturated Fat 0g	0%
Trans Fat 0g	
Cholesterol 0mg	0%
Sodium 45mg	2%
Total Carbohydrate 37g	12%
Dietary Fiber 3g	12%
Sugars 16g	
Protein 2g	

Vitamin A 180%   •   Vitamin C 25%

Calcium 2%   •   Iron 6%

*Percent Daily Values are based on a 2,000 calorie diet. Your daily values may be higher or lower depending on your calorie needs:

		Calories:	2,000	2,500
Total Fat	Less than		65g	80g
Saturated Fat	Less than		20g	25g
Cholesterol	Less than		300mg	300mg
Sodium	Less than		2,400mg	2,400mg
Total Carbohydrate			300g	375g
Dietary Fiber			25g	30g

Calories per gram:
   Fat 9   •   Carbohydrate 4   •   Protein 4

New Potatoes and Peas

Using the cream sauce recipe from this collection in this recipe allows you good control of all your ingredients.

Makes 8 servings

Ingredients:

3	lbs	new white potatoes
2½	cups	cream sauce (see page 370)
1	pkg	petite whole onions, frozen (10 oz)
1	pkg	green peas, frozen

Preparation:

- Cook potatoes in saucepan of salted water until tender:
- Drain, cut into quarters.
- Add the potatoes to sauce and stir in onions and peas.
- Stir, heat and serve.

Thanks to: Phyllis Merrick, group 26

Category: Potatoes

Nutrition Facts

Serving Size 1/8 recipe (348g)
Servings Per Container 8

Amount Per Serving

Calories 180 — Calories from Fat 5

% Daily Value*

Total Fat 0g	0%
Saturated Fat 0g	0%
Trans Fat 0g	
Cholesterol 0mg	0%
Sodium 670mg	28%
Total Carbohydrate 33g	11%
Dietary Fiber 5g	20%
Sugars 8g	
Protein 8g	

Vitamin A 25% • Vitamin C 35%
Calcium 15% • Iron 8%

*Percent Daily Values are based on a 2,000 calorie diet. Your daily values may be higher or lower depending on your calorie needs:

		Calories:	2,000	2,500
Total Fat	Less than		65g	80g
Saturated Fat	Less than		20g	25g
Cholesterol	Less than		300mg	300mg
Sodium	Less than		2,400mg	2,400mg
Total Carbohydrate			300g	375g
Dietary Fiber			25g	30g

Calories per gram:
Fat 9 • Carbohydrate 4 • Protein 4

OVEN BAKED FRENCH FRIES

This would be equally as good using sweet potatoes.

Makes 6 servings

Ingredients:

4	med	potatoes, unpeeled
1½	tsp	canola oil
1	tsp	paprika
1	tsp	garlic powder
1	tsp	Cajun spice
½	tsp	salt or less

Preparation:

- Preheat oven to 450°F.
- Wash potatoes and then cut into strips or lengthwise, about ½ inch thick.
- While preparing, keep strips in bowl of ice water to crisp.
- Drain and pat dry on paper towels.
- Return to bowl and sprinkle with oil.
- Put in bag and shake or mix with hands to distribute oil evenly over potatoes.
- Bake on a baking sheet until golden brown and tender, about 30 to 40 minutes, turning frequently.
- Sprinkle generously with spices, lightly with salt.

Category: Potatoes

Nutrition Facts

Serving Size 1/6 recipe (102g)
Servings Per Container 6

Amount Per Serving

Calories 80	Calories from Fat 10

	% Daily Value*
Total Fat 1g	2%
Saturated Fat 0g	0%
Trans Fat 0g	
Cholesterol 0mg	0%
Sodium 190mg	8%
Total Carbohydrate 18g	6%
Dietary Fiber 2g	8%
Sugars 2g	
Protein 3g	

Vitamin A 4%	•	Vitamin C 30%
Calcium 2%	•	Iron 4%

*Percent Daily Values are based on a 2,000 calorie diet. Your daily values may be higher or lower depending on your calorie needs:

	Calories:	2,000	2,500
Total Fat	Less than	65g	80g
Saturated Fat	Less than	20g	25g
Cholesterol	Less than	300mg	300mg
Sodium	Less than	2,400mg	2,400mg
Total Carbohydrate		300g	375g
Dietary Fiber		25g	30g

Calories per gram:
  Fat 9 • Carbohydrate 4 • Protein 4

Roasted New Potatoes with Garlic

This is a good side dish. Roasting the potatoes brings out the flavor and cooking the garlic cloves at the same time saves energy. While roasting these, you might also wrap some other garlic heads in foil and throw in the oven too, for future use. They freeze well.

Prep time: 20 minutes. Cooking time: 40 minutes

Makes 4 servings

Ingredients:

1	lb	tiny red potatoes
1	head	garlic, cloves separated but not peeled
1	tsp	olive oil
½	tsp	salt
¼	tsp	black pepper

Preparation:

- Preheat oven to 350°F.
- Coat 9 x 13 inch baking pan with vegetable oil cooking spray.
- Wash but do not peel potatoes. Cut in half.
- In the pan arrange potatoes in a single layer.
- Tuck garlic among the potatoes.
- Spray lightly with olive oil.
- Salt and pepper to taste.
- Bake for 30 to 40 minutes or until potatoes are tender and garlic is soft.
- Squeeze garlic from peels onto potatoes.
- Mix together and serve.

Source: *Sacramento Bee*

Category: Potatoes

Nutrition Facts

Serving Size 1/4 recipe (123g)
Servings Per Container 4

Amount Per Serving

	% Daily Value*
Calories 100 Calories from Fat 10	
Total Fat 1.5g	2%
Saturated Fat 0g	0%
Trans Fat 0g	
Cholesterol 0mg	0%
Sodium 310mg	13%
Total Carbohydrate 21g	7%
Dietary Fiber 2g	8%
Sugars 2g	
Protein 3g	

Vitamin A 0%   •   Vitamin C 20%
Calcium 2%   •   Iron 6%

*Percent Daily Values are based on a 2,000 calorie diet. Your daily values may be higher or lower depending on your calorie needs:

	Calories:	2,000	2,500
Total Fat	Less than	65g	80g
Saturated Fat	Less than	20g	25g
Cholesterol	Less than	300mg	300mg
Sodium	Less than	2,400mg	2,400mg
Total Carbohydrate		300g	375g
Dietary Fiber		25g	30g

Calories per gram:
  Fat 9   •   Carbohydrate 4   •   Protein 4

Roasted New Potatoes with Rosemary

When a potato is harvested young, it is called a new potato. The skin is thin and fragile. New potatoes are low in starch and high in moisture. They may be referred to as waxy potatoes.

Makes 8 servings

Ingredients:

2	lbs	small red new potatoes
1	tsp	dried rosemary leaves
¼	tsp	black pepper

Preparation:

- Preheat oven to 450°F
- Coat a baking dish lightly with vegetable oil cooking spray.
- Scrub potatoes and cut into halves or quarters and place in pan.
- Sprinkle with rosemary and pepper.
- Bake 50 minutes or until potatoes are tender.
- Stir once or twice during baking.

Source: *S. Schlesinger, 500 Fat-Free Recipes*

Category: Potatoes

Nutrition Facts

Serving Size 1/8 recipe (114g)
Servings Per Container 8

Amount Per Serving

Calories 80 — Calories from Fat 0

% Daily Value*

Total Fat 0g	0%
Saturated Fat 0g	0%
Trans Fat 0g	
Cholesterol 0mg	0%
Sodium 20mg	1%
Total Carbohydrate 18g	6%
Dietary Fiber 2g	8%
Sugars 1g	
Protein 2g	

Vitamin A 0% • Vitamin C 15%
Calcium 2% • Iron 4%

*Percent Daily Values are based on a 2,000 calorie diet. Your daily values may be higher or lower depending on your calorie needs:

		Calories:	2,000	2,500
Total Fat	Less than		65g	80g
Saturated Fat	Less than		20g	25g
Cholesterol	Less than		300mg	300mg
Sodium	Less than		2,400mg	2,400mg
Total Carbohydrate			300g	375g
Dietary Fiber			25g	30g

Calories per gram:
Fat 9 • Carbohydrate 4 • Protein 4

Roasted Sweet Potatoes

These can be so wonderfully flavorful, that you may find that the usual additions - marshmallows, butter, brown sugar - are not needed.

Makes 4 servings

Ingredients:

1	lb	sweet potatoes
1	tsp	olive oil

Preparation:

- Preheat oven 400°F.
- Wash and scrub medium-sized sweet potatoes.
- Dry and coat lightly with oil.
- Cut a small piece off one end OR half way through baking, puncture with fork as a safety valve to prevent bursting.
- Bake 40 minutes or so.

Source: *Joy of Cooking*

Category: Potatoes

Nutrition Facts

Serving Size 1/4 recipe (115g)
Servings Per Container 4

Amount Per Serving

Calories 100	Calories from Fat 10

	% Daily Value*
Total Fat 1g	2%
Saturated Fat 0g	0%
Trans Fat 0g	
Cholesterol 0mg	0%
Sodium 60mg	3%
Total Carbohydrate 20g	7%
Dietary Fiber 3g	12%
Sugars 6g	
Protein 2g	

Vitamin A 100%	•	Vitamin C 25%
Calcium 2%	•	Iron 4%

*Percent Daily Values are based on a 2,000 calorie diet. Your daily values may be higher or lower depending on your calorie needs:

		Calories:	2,000	2,500
Total Fat		Less than	65g	80g
Saturated Fat		Less than	20g	25g
Cholesterol		Less than	300mg	300mg
Sodium		Less than	2,400mg	2,400mg
Total Carbohydrate			300g	375g
Dietary Fiber			25g	30g

Calories per gram:
  Fat 9 • Carbohydrate 4 • Protein 4

SOUTHERN SWEET POTATOES

A lighter version of a holiday favorite.

Makes 10 servings

Ingredients:

1	can	sweet potatoes, drained (29 oz)
⅔	cup	brown sugar, firmly packed
4	Tbsp	flour
½	tsp	ground cinnamon
1	tsp	butter substitute
⅓	cup	pineapple juice
1	tsp	vanilla extract
⅓	cup	dried cranberries
⅓	cup	crushed pineapple
½	cup	miniature marshmallows (optional)

Preparation:

- Preheat oven to 350°F.
- Place sweet potatoes, crushed pineapple and cranberries in a large, flat casserole dish.
- In small mixing bowl, add and mix sugar, flour, cinnamon, butter substitute, pineapple juice, and vanilla extract, in order listed.
- Pour this pineapple mixture over the sweet potatoes.
- Top with marshmallows.
- Bake, uncovered, for 20-30 minutes.

Thanks to: Michele Lites, R.D.

Category: Vegetables

Nutrition Facts

Serving Size 1/10 recipe (123g)
Servings Per Container 10

Amount Per Serving

Calories 170 Calories from Fat 0

% Daily Value*

Total Fat 0g	0%
Saturated Fat 0g	0%
Trans Fat 0g	
Cholesterol 0mg	0%
Sodium 105mg	4%
Total Carbohydrate 42g	14%
Dietary Fiber 2g	8%
Sugars 25g	
Protein 2g	

Vitamin A 130% • Vitamin C 40%
Calcium 4% • Iron 6%

*Percent Daily Values are based on a 2,000 calorie diet. Your daily values may be higher or lower depending on your calorie needs:

		Calories:	2,000	2,500
Total Fat	Less than		65g	80g
Saturated Fat	Less than		20g	25g
Cholesterol	Less than		300mg	300mg
Sodium	Less than		2,400mg	2,400mg
Total Carbohydrate			300g	375g
Dietary Fiber			25g	30g

Calories per gram:
　Fat 9 • Carbohydrate 4 • Protein 4

Two Potato Casserole

Similar to scalloped potatoes, this version has extra nutrition from spinach and sweet potatoes. Look at the vitamins C and A!

Makes 8 servings

Ingredients:

4	large	baking potatoes (about 2 pounds)
4	med	sweet potatoes (about 2 pounds)
1	tsp	olive oil
1	small	onion, chopped
3	Tbsp	all purpose flour
½	tsp	salt
¼	tsp	coarsely ground black pepper
2 ½	cups	evaporated skimmed milk
2	pkg	spinach, frozen chopped thawed and squeezed dry (10 oz)

Preparation:

- In 8 quart saucepan, over high heat, place unpeeled baking potatoes and sweet potatoes in enough water to cover and heat to boiling.
- Reduce heat to low, cover and simmer 20-30 minutes until potatoes are just fork tender but not soft (depending on size of sweet potatoes, they may cook faster than baking potatoes). Drain.
- Cool potatoes until easy to handle.
- Peel baking and sweet potatoes; cut in 1 inch thick slices.
- Preheat oven to 375°F.
- In 2 quart saucepan over medium heat, cook onion in olive oil until tender, about 5 minutes.
- Stir in flour, salt and pepper until blended.
- With wire whisk, gradually stir in milk and cook, stirring constantly, until sauce boils and thickens.
- In a 1 quart casserole dish, lightly spray cooking oil and arrange half of the potato slices; top with all the spinach, pour half of the sauce on top.
- Repeat with remaining potatoes and sauce. Cover casserole and bake 30 minutes.

Nutrition Facts

Serving Size 1/8 recipe (391g)
Servings Per Container 8

Amount Per Serving

Calories 270	Calories from Fat 5

	% Daily Value*
Total Fat 1g	2%
Saturated Fat 0g	0%
Trans Fat 0g	
Cholesterol 5mg	2%
Sodium 400mg	17%
Total Carbohydrate 55g	18%
Dietary Fiber 7g	28%
Sugars 19g	
Protein 13g	

Vitamin A 150%	•	Vitamin C 70%
Calcium 35%	•	Iron 15%

*Percent Daily Values are based on a 2,000 calorie diet. Your daily values may be higher or lower depending on your calorie needs:

	Calories:	2,000	2,500
Total Fat	Less than	65g	80g
Saturated Fat	Less than	20g	25g
Cholesterol	Less than	300mg	300mg
Sodium	Less than	2,400mg	2,400mg
Total Carbohydrate		300g	375g
Dietary Fiber		25g	30g

Calories per gram:
Fat 9 • Carbohydrate 4 • Protein 4

- Uncover and bake 15 minutes longer or until casserole is hot and bubbly and top is browned..

Thanks to: Hazel & Russell Schanrock, (Group 1)

Category: Potatoes

RICE & GRAINS

BARLEY AND MUSHROOM PILAF

This is a nice alternative to rice or potatoes. Can be varied by adding chopped celery or green onion, chopped fresh dill, thyme or basil. It's nice for a buffet and can be prepared in advance.

Makes 8 servings

Ingredients:

1	tsp	canola oil
1	med	onion, chopped
½	lb	mushrooms, sliced
1	cup	pearl barley
3	cups	hot chicken stock, fat-free
¼	cup	fresh parsley, chopped
		freshly ground pepper

Preparation:

- Preheat oven to 350°F.
- In non-stick skillet, sauté onion and cook for about 2 minutes or until softened.
- Add mushrooms and cook, stirring occasionally, for 5 minutes.
- Transfer mixture to 11 x 7 inch baking dish; add barley and chicken stock.
- Bake, covered, for 1 hour; uncover and bake for 10 minutes longer (or bake in 325°F oven for 1 ½ hours).
- Stir in parsley and pepper to taste.

Category: Rice & Grains

Nutrition Facts

Serving Size 1/8 recipe (164g)
Servings Per Container 8

Amount Per Serving

Calories 120 — Calories from Fat 10

	% Daily Value*
Total Fat 1g	2%
Saturated Fat 0g	0%
Trans Fat 0g	
Cholesterol 0mg	0%
Sodium 150mg	6%
Total Carbohydrate 22g	7%
Dietary Fiber 5g	20%
Sugars 2g	
Protein 6g	

Vitamin A 4% • Vitamin C 8%
Calcium 2% • Iron 6%

*Percent Daily Values are based on a 2,000 calorie diet. Your daily values may be higher or lower depending on your calorie needs:

		Calories: 2,000	2,500
Total Fat	Less than	65g	80g
Saturated Fat	Less than	20g	25g
Cholesterol	Less than	300mg	300mg
Sodium	Less than	2,400mg	2,400mg
Total Carbohydrate		300g	375g
Dietary Fiber		25g	30g

Calories per gram:
Fat 9 • Carbohydrate 4 • Protein 4

Couscous with Veggies

Couscous is the easiest grain imaginable. Just mix with boiling water/broth and let sit for 5 minutes. Don't forget to fluff after 5 minutes, or it will get lumpy.

Makes 6 servings

Ingredients:

2	cups	fat-free broth
10	oz	couscous (1½ cups)
1	cup	green beans (leftovers)
1	cup	corn kernels
1	cup	bok choy shredded

Preparation:

- Bring broth to a boil in medium-sized saucepan.
- Stir in couscous and vegetables.
- Cover and remove from heat.
- Let stand 5 minutes; fluff with fork.

Thanks to: Phyllis Quinn, group 25

Category: Rice and Grains

Nutrition Facts

Serving Size 1/6 recipe (217g)
Servings Per Container 6

Amount Per Serving

Calories 220 Calories from Fat 10

% Daily Value*

Total Fat 1g	2%
Saturated Fat 0g	0%
Trans Fat 0g	
Cholesterol 0mg	0%
Sodium 330mg	14%
Total Carbohydrate 44g	15%
Dietary Fiber 4g	16%
Sugars 2g	
Protein 7g	

Vitamin A 25% • Vitamin C 25%
Calcium 4% • Iron 6%

*Percent Daily Values are based on a 2,000 calorie diet. Your daily values may be higher or lower depending on your calorie needs:

		Calories:	2,000	2,500
Total Fat	Less than		65g	80g
Saturated Fat	Less than		20g	25g
Cholesterol	Less than		300mg	300mg
Sodium	Less than		2,400mg	2,400mg
Total Carbohydrate			300g	375g
Dietary Fiber			25g	30g

Calories per gram:
 Fat 9 • Carbohydrate 4 • Protein 4

CURRIED RICE AND SWEET POTATOES

If you enjoy curry, this team of rice and sweet potatoes makes a great side dish. By including apples, raisins, and peas you have a variety of nutrients in one dish. Be mindful of how much added fat those walnuts contribute though.

Makes 6 servings

Ingredients:

½	cup	onion, chopped
½	tsp	garlic, minced
2	cups	water
1	cup	dry brown rice
2	cups	sweet potatoes, peeled and diced
1	cup	peeled and chopped apple (e.g. Granny Smith)
1	cup	peas, cooked
⅓	cup	golden raisins
½	cup	walnuts, toasted
1	tsp	curry powder
		salt to taste

Preparation:

- In a pot coated with non-stick cooking spray, sauté onion and garlic until tender.
- Add water and bring to a boil. Stir in rice and sweet potatoes.
- Cover, reduce heat, and simmer 15 minutes or until the liquid is absorbed.
- Carefully stir in remaining ingredients and heat.

Thanks to: Debbie Lucus, R.D.

Category: Rice & Grains

Nutrition Facts

Serving Size 1/6 recipe (235g)
Servings Per Container 6

Amount Per Serving

Calories 290 — Calories from Fat 70

% Daily Value*

Total Fat 8g	12%
Saturated Fat 1g	5%
Trans Fat 0g	
Cholesterol 0mg	0%
Sodium 50mg	2%
Total Carbohydrate 50g	17%
Dietary Fiber 6g	24%
Sugars 12g	
Protein 7g	

Vitamin A 140% • Vitamin C 10%
Calcium 4% • Iron 10%

*Percent Daily Values are based on a 2,000 calorie diet. Your daily values may be higher or lower depending on your calorie needs:

		Calories:	2,000	2,500
Total Fat		Less than	65g	80g
Saturated Fat		Less than	20g	25g
Cholesterol		Less than	300mg	300mg
Sodium		Less than	2,400mg	2,400mg
Total Carbohydrate			300g	375g
Dietary Fiber			25g	30g

Calories per gram:
  Fat 9 • Carbohydrate 4 • Protein 4

CURRY SPICED COUSCOUS

Curry spice is a combination of multiple spices. In this recipe, you can use prepared curry, or mix the spices on your own as described.

Makes 8 servings

Preparation time: about 15 min. Cooking time: about 15 min.

Ingredients:

1	tsp	olive oil (or spray with Pam)
1	large	onion, chopped
1	cup	carrots, chopped
1	tsp	ground coriander
½	tsp	ground cumin
½	tsp	ground ginger
¼	tsp	ground cinnamon

OR

2¼	tsp	curry or garam masala spices
3⅓	cups	vegetable broth (see page 384)
2	cups	couscous
½	cup	dried apricots, chopped
½	cup	golden raisins
⅓	cup	cilantro, chopped
		salt and pepper to taste

Preparation:

- Heat oil in a 5 to 6 quart pan over medium high heat.
- Add onion and carrots, cook until soft (about 8 minutes) stirring often.
- If pan appears dry, add water, 1 Tbsp at a time. Stir in spices.
- Add vegetable broth and bring to a boil over high heat.
- Stir in couscous and fruit.
- Cover and remove from heat. Let stand until liquid has been absorbed (about 5 minutes).
- Fluff couscous with a fork; season to taste with salt and pepper. Stir in cilantro.

Thanks to: Laurie Crider-Vanpal, Group 29

Category: Rice & Grains

Nutrition Facts

Serving Size 1/8 recipe (219g)
Servings Per Container 8

Amount Per Serving

Calories 260 Calories from Fat 10

% Daily Value*

Total Fat 1.5g	2%
Saturated Fat 0g	0%
Trans Fat 0g	
Cholesterol 0mg	0%
Sodium 55mg	2%
Total Carbohydrate 56g	19%
Dietary Fiber 6g	24%
Sugars 13g	
Protein 8g	

Vitamin A 140%	•	Vitamin C 60%
Calcium 8%	•	Iron 15%

*Percent Daily Values are based on a 2,000 calorie diet. Your daily values may be higher or lower depending on your calorie needs:

	Calories:	2,000	2,500
Total Fat	Less than	65g	80g
Saturated Fat	Less than	20g	25g
Cholesterol	Less than	300mg	300mg
Sodium	Less than	2,400mg	2,400mg
Total Carbohydrate		300g	375g
Dietary Fiber		25g	30g

Calories per gram:
Fat 9 • Carbohydrate 4 • Protein 4

Garbanzo Bulgur and Tomato Pilaf

Bulgur and cracked wheat are other whole grains that require minimal cooking time. This classic Greek dish is easy to prepare and can be made as many as 2 days ahead

Makes 6 servings

Ingredients:

1	cup	bulgur, uncooked or cracked wheat
1	cup	boiling water
½	tsp	salt
1½	cups	garbanzo beans, cooked
1	cup	plum tomatoes, diced
1	cup	scallions, sliced (white and light green parts)
½	cup	flat-leaf parsley, chopped
¼	cup	fresh lemon juice
1	Tbsp	extra-virgin olive oil (or less)
1½	tsp	lemon peel, grated

Preparation:

- In a large bowl, combine bulgur and water, cover and let stand 30 minutes.
- Fluff bulgur with fork. Add remaining ingredients.
- Stir well.
- Serve chilled or at room temperature.

Category: Rice & Grains

Nutrition Facts

Serving Size 1/6 recipe (162g)
Servings Per Container 6

Amount Per Serving

Calories 170   Calories from Fat 35

% Daily Value*

Total Fat 3.5g	**5%**
Saturated Fat 0g	0%
Trans Fat 0g	
Cholesterol 0mg	**0%**
Sodium 210mg	**9%**
Total Carbohydrate 30g	**10%**
Dietary Fiber 8g	32%
Sugars 3g	
Protein 7g	

Vitamin A 15% • Vitamin C 30%
Calcium 4% • Iron 10%

*Percent Daily Values are based on a 2,000 calorie diet. Your daily values may be higher or lower depending on your calorie needs:

		Calories:	2,000	2,500
Total Fat	Less than		65g	80g
Saturated Fat	Less than		20g	25g
Cholesterol	Less than		300mg	300mg
Sodium	Less than		2,400mg	2,400mg
Total Carbohydrate			300g	375g
Dietary Fiber			25g	30g

Calories per gram:
  Fat 9 • Carbohydrate 4 • Protein 4

Lemon Rice with Spinach and Red Bell Pepper

Adding lemon juice or rind to many dishes gives a fresh flavor without adding more sodium.

Makes 8 servings

Ingredients:

⅓	cup	onion, chopped
1	tsp	olive oil
1	cup	long grain rice
½	tsp	salt
2½	cups	water
1	cup	spinach, chopped
2	Tbsp	fresh lemon juice
1		red bell pepper chopped (about ½ cup)

Preparation:

- In a medium saucepan sauté onion in olive oil until soft.
- Mix in rice and salt.
- Add water and bring to a boil. Reduce heat to low and cover pan.
- After 15 minutes, stir spinach and lemon juice into rice.
- Cook for 10 minutes more or until liquid is completely absorbed.
- Mix in red pepper and serve.

Category: Rice and Grains

Nutrition Facts

Serving Size 1/2 cup (121g)
Servings Per Container 8

Amount Per Serving

Calories 90	Calories from Fat 5

	% Daily Value*
Total Fat 0.5g	1%
Saturated Fat 0g	0%
Trans Fat 0g	
Cholesterol 0mg	0%
Sodium 150mg	6%
Total Carbohydrate 19g	6%
Dietary Fiber 0g	0%
Sugars 1g	
Protein 2g	

Vitamin A 15%	•	Vitamin C 25%
Calcium 0%	•	Iron 4%

*Percent Daily Values are based on a 2,000 calorie diet. Your daily values may be higher or lower depending on your calorie needs:

		Calories:	2,000	2,500
Total Fat		Less than	65g	80g
Saturated Fat		Less than	20g	25g
Cholesterol		Less than	300mg	300mg
Sodium		Less than	2,400mg	2,400mg
Total Carbohydrate			300g	375g
Dietary Fiber			25g	30g

Calories per gram:
    Fat 9 • Carbohydrate 4 • Protein 4

Meatless Jambalaya

Jambalaya, a traditional Creole dish, is a spicy mix of tomatoes, rice, peppers, onion. The spices evoke the flavor of Italian sausage without the calories or fat.

Makes 6 servings

Ingredients:

½	cup	onion, coarsely chopped
½	cup	green bell pepper, coarsely chopped
2	cloves	garlic, minced
2	cups	water
1½	cups	tomatoes, chopped
1	can	tomato sauce, unsalted (8-oz)
⅛	tsp	fennel seed, crushed
½	tsp	dried Italian seasoning
¼	tsp	ground red pepper (cayenne)
1	cup	long-grain white rice, uncooked regular
1½	cups	red or kidney beans, cooked

Preparation:

- Heat large skillet over medium high heat until hot. Spray with vegetable cooking oil.
- Add onion, bell pepper, and garlic, and cook 3-5 minutes until crisp-tender.
- Stir in water, tomatoes, tomato sauce, fennel seed, Italian seasoning, and ground red pepper and bring to a boil.
- Add rice. Reduce heat to low; cover and simmer 20-30 minutes until rice is tender, stirring occasionally.
- Then stir in beans and cover; simmer an additional 5-10 minutes or until thoroughly heated, stirring occasionally.

Thanks to: Sue Fincher, Group 27

Category: Rice and Grains

Nutrition Facts

Serving Size 1/6 recipe (456g)
Servings Per Container 6

Amount Per Serving

Calories 270 — Calories from Fat 5

	% Daily Value*
Total Fat 0g	0%
Saturated Fat 0g	0%
Trans Fat 0g	
Cholesterol 0mg	0%
Sodium 730mg	30%
Total Carbohydrate 58g	19%
Dietary Fiber 10g	40%
Sugars 8g	
Protein 11g	

Vitamin A 8% • Vitamin C 40%
Calcium 10% • Iron 20%

*Percent Daily Values are based on a 2,000 calorie diet. Your daily values may be higher or lower depending on your calorie needs:

	Calories:	2,000	2,500
Total Fat	Less than	65g	80g
Saturated Fat	Less than	20g	25g
Cholesterol	Less than	300mg	300mg
Sodium	Less than	2,400mg	2,400mg
Total Carbohydrate		300g	375g
Dietary Fiber		25g	30g

Calories per gram:
Fat 9 • Carbohydrate 4 • Protein 4

POLENTA

Serve a marinara sauce over these tasty squares.

Makes 15 servings ~ 3 x 3 inch squares

Ingredients:

1	cup	cornmeal
½	cup	cheese, nonfat grated
½	cup	water
¼	tsp	salt
¼	tsp	black pepper

Preparation:

- Combine all ingredients in a saucepan, bring to a boil and cook for 10 minutes.
- Pour onto a foil lined 15 x 9 inch pan.
- Spread out to 1½ inch thickness.
- Allow to cool.
- Broil until toasted.
- Cut into squares.

Category: Rice and Grains

Nutrition Facts

Serving Size 3x3 inch square (20g)
Servings Per Container 15

Amount Per Serving

Calories 35 — Calories from Fat 5

% Daily Value*

Total Fat 0g	0%
Saturated Fat 0g	0%
Trans Fat 0g	
Cholesterol 0mg	0%
Sodium 70mg	3%
Total Carbohydrate 7g	2%
Dietary Fiber 1g	4%
Sugars 0g	
Protein 2g	

Vitamin A 0% • Vitamin C 0%
Calcium 4% • Iron 2%

*Percent Daily Values are based on a 2,000 calorie diet. Your daily values may be higher or lower depending on your calorie needs:

		Calories:	2,000	2,500
Total Fat	Less than		65g	80g
Saturated Fat	Less than		20g	25g
Cholesterol	Less than		300mg	300mg
Sodium	Less than		2,400mg	2,400mg
Total Carbohydrate			300g	375g
Dietary Fiber			25g	30g

Calories per gram:
Fat 9 • Carbohydrate 4 • Protein 4

QUINOA STUFFED PEPPERS

Any grain could be used in this recipe, but quinoa cooks relatively quickly and bumps up the protein and fiber.

Makes 8 servings ~ ½ pepper each

Ingredients:

1	cup	quinoa
2	cups	water
4	large	green peppers or 6 medium
1	med	onion, diced
½	lb	fresh mushrooms, sliced
1	can	diced tomatoes, drained, (save the juice) (28oz)
2	cloves	garlic, crushed
12	oz	jar Mexican salsa
2	Tbsp	dry sherry
10	oz	mozzarella cheese, fat-free shredded

Preparation:

- Preheat oven to 325°F.
- Rinse quinoa thoroughly in a small strainer and drain.
- Place grain and water in a 1½ quart saucepan,. Bring to boil, reduce to simmer, cover and cook until all water is absorbed (10-15 minutes).
- When done, the grain appears translucent and the germ ring is visible. Set aside.
- Cut off stem end, remove seeds and membranes from peppers. Steam until soft but not limp.
- Treat a large skillet with vegetable oil cooking spray, and sauté onion and mushrooms.
- Add tomatoes, garlic and salsa and cook over medium heat for 10 minutes.
- Add sherry and simmer 10 more minutes.
- Fold in quinoa.
- Place peppers in baking dish and fill with quinoa mixture.
- This will take about half of the mixture.
- Thin remainder with the reserved tomato juice and pour around the peppers.
- Sprinkle cheese over peppers.

Nutrition Facts

Serving Size 1/2 pepper (386g)
Servings Per Container 8

Amount Per Serving

Calories 200   Calories from Fat 15

	% Daily Value*
Total Fat 1.5g	2%
Saturated Fat 0g	0%
Trans Fat 0g	
Cholesterol 10mg	3%
Sodium 1010mg	42%
Total Carbohydrate 31g	10%
Dietary Fiber 5g	20%
Sugars 10g	
Protein 14g	

Vitamin A 25%	•	Vitamin C 140%
Calcium 30%	•	Iron 10%

*Percent Daily Values are based on a 2,000 calorie diet. Your daily values may be higher or lower depending on your calorie needs:

		Calories:	2,000	2,500
Total Fat	Less than		65g	80g
Saturated Fat	Less than		20g	25g
Cholesterol	Less than		300mg	300mg
Sodium	Less than		2,400mg	2,400mg
Total Carbohydrate			300g	375g
Dietary Fiber			25g	30g

Calories per gram:
   Fat 9 • Carbohydrate 4 • Protein 4

Rice Casserole

Using brown rice would add more fiber. This is a good dish for leftover rice from a previous meal.

Makes 6 servings

Ingredients:

0	onion	chopped (¼ cup)
¼	cup	water
6	mushrooms	sliced
3	cups	cooked rice
1	can	chopped green chiles (4 oz)
1 ½	cups	cream sauce (see page 370)
2	cloves	garlic, minced
1	tsp	ground cumin
½	tsp	salt
1	cup	fat-free sour cream

Preparation:

- Preheat oven to 375°F.
- Sauté onions in water for 3 minutes.
- Add mushrooms and sauté 3 more minutes.
- Combine all ingredients in bowl and mix well.
- Place in baking pan and bake for 30 minutes.

Thanks to: Lilly Gallegos, Group 8

Category: Rice and Grains

(Previous recipe continued:)

- Bake for 30-35 minutes.

Category: Rice and Grains

Nutrition Facts

Serving Size 1/6 recipe (241g)
Servings Per Container 6

Amount Per Serving

Calories 200   Calories from Fat 5

% Daily Value*

Total Fat 0g	0%
Saturated Fat 0g	0%
Trans Fat 0g	
Cholesterol 5mg	2%
Sodium 510mg	21%
Total Carbohydrate 38g	13%
Dietary Fiber 1g	4%
Sugars 5g	
Protein 8g	

Vitamin A 6% • Vitamin C 2%
Calcium 20% • Iron 8%

*Percent Daily Values are based on a 2,000 calorie diet. Your daily values may be higher or lower depending on your calorie needs:

		Calories:	2,000	2,500
Total Fat	Less than		65g	80g
Saturated Fat	Less than		20g	25g
Cholesterol	Less than		300mg	300mg
Sodium	Less than		2,400mg	2,400mg
Total Carbohydrate			300g	375g
Dietary Fiber			25g	30g

Calories per gram:
  Fat 9 • Carbohydrate 4 • Protein 4

RICE PAPER WRAPPED SALAD ROLLS

This is the Vietnamese fajita and is traditionally served with shrimp and pork. You may, however, use just about anything in the filling. Lively and flavorful, these rolls may be served with black bean sauce or Vietnamese dipping sauce.

Makes 6 servings as appetizers.

Ingredients:

2	oz.	pressed tofu, sliced ¼ inch thick and 2 inches long
1	oz.	dried black mushrooms, ¼ cup julienned carrots
2	cups	hot water
¼	cup	yellow onions, thinly sliced
1	cup	cooked rice vermicelli
4		butter or romaine lettuce leaves, halved lengthwise
1	cup	bean sprouts
½	cup	mint leaves
12	sprigs	cilantro (optional)
6	sheets	round rice paper, 12 inches in diameter (keep extra on hand just in case you tear them)
1	cup	black bean sauce (see page 367) chili paste

Nutrition Facts

Serving Size 4 cut rolls, 1 entire wrap (131g)
Servings Per Container 6

Amount Per Serving

Calories 170   Calories from Fat 15

% Daily Value*

Total Fat 1.5g	2%
Saturated Fat 0g	0%
Trans Fat 0g	
Cholesterol 0mg	0%
Sodium 490mg	20%
Total Carbohydrate 34g	11%
Dietary Fiber 3g	12%
Sugars 10g	
Protein 5g	

Vitamin A 45% • Vitamin C 15%
Calcium 6% • Iron 6%

*Percent Daily Values are based on a 2,000 calorie diet. Your daily values may be higher or lower depending on your calorie needs:

		Calories:	2,000	2,500
Total Fat	Less than		65g	80g
Saturated Fat	Less than		20g	25g
Cholesterol	Less than		300mg	300mg
Sodium	Less than		2,400mg	2,400mg
Total Carbohydrate			300g	375g
Dietary Fiber			25g	30g

Calories per gram:
  Fat 9 • Carbohydrate 4 • Protein 4

Preparation:

- Soak dried mushrooms in 2 cups hot water for 30 minutes, then strain (save liquid) and slice thin.
- In a medium size saucepan, heat the strained mushroom liquid.
- Bring to a vigorous boil, add tofu, mushrooms, carrots and onions.
- Continue cooking for another 2-3 minutes. Remove from heat, strain off liquid, and set aside until cool.
- Refer to figures provided for rice paper techniques on page 264 (A-E).
- Fill a large mixing bowl with warm water. Holding the rice paper with both hands, dip it into the water and turn it until entire sheet is wet and pliable. (See A).

- Spread out flat on damp cheesecloth. Do not let the sheets touch each other.
- You can reinforce the 12 inches rice paper by layering a 6 inch sheet (or extra pieces) of softened rice paper on top (B). (This technique is critical if you are making these 1-2 hours before serving).
- Line the bottom third of rice paper with lettuce leaves, bean sprouts, herbs, noodles and the vegetable mixture.
- Make sure the filling is evenly piled from one edge to another. (B).
- Starting with the edge closest to you, press down on filling with your fingers and use your thumbs to begin rolling the paper over the filling (C).
- After one full turn, stop and fold in the sides (D)
- Continue rolling until filling is completely sealed (E).
- The length should be about 5-6 inches long and about 1 –1 ½ inches wide.
- Place on a plate and cover with a damp cheesecloth until you finish filling the remaining wrappers.
- If you like, cut rolls in 4 equal pieces and serve with black bean sauce (see recipe) dotted with chili paste.
- Place 4 cut rolls (stand them upright) on each appetizer plate.
- Garnish with whole sprigs of cilantro or mint. Serve sauce in separate dish.

These rolls can be filled with any combination of vegetables and made a couple of hours in advance. Store at room temperature in an airtight container lined with damp cheesecloth until needed.
Thanks to: Mai Pham, Lemon Grass Restaurant

Category: Rice and Grains

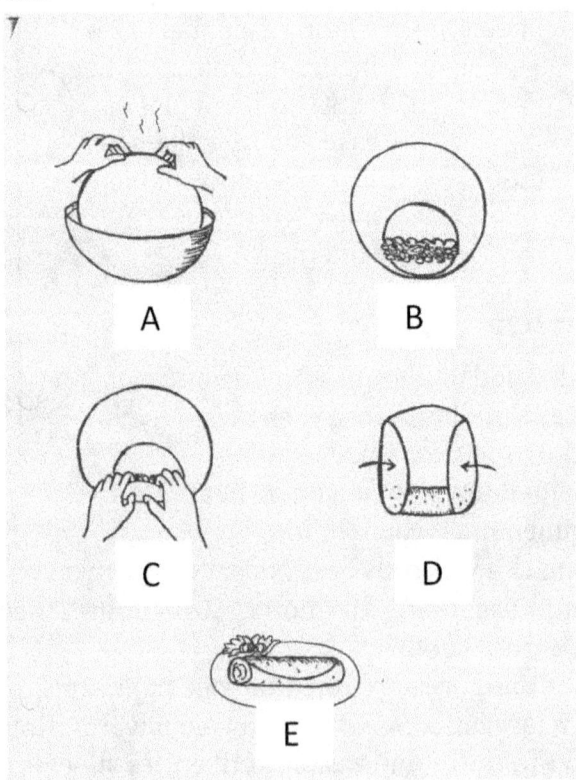

Rice Pilaf

Rice pilafs are deceptively high in fat. Here is one that you can enjoy without all of the added oil.

Makes 4 servings

Ingredients:

⅓	cup	brown rice
⅓	cup	white rice
⅓	cup	bulgur
2	cups	green onions, chopped
½	cup	celery, chopped
⅓	cup	peas
½	cup	egg substitute
		vegetable oil spray

Preparation:

- Steam rice and prepare bulgur according to directions.
- In a nonstick pan, sauté green onion, celery and peas in vegetable spray.
- Cook egg substitute and stir gently until firm.
- Add to rice.

Nutrition Facts

Serving Size 1/4 recipe (148g)
Servings Per Container 4

Amount Per Serving

Calories 200   Calories from Fat 10

% Daily Value*

Total Fat 1.5g	2%
Saturated Fat 0g	0%
Trans Fat 0g	
Cholesterol 0mg	0%
Sodium 95mg	4%
Total Carbohydrate 39g	13%
Dietary Fiber 5g	20%
Sugars 4g	
Protein 7g	

Vitamin A 10% • Vitamin C 25%
Calcium 6% • Iron 15%

*Percent Daily Values are based on a 2,000 calorie diet. Your daily values may be higher or lower depending on your calorie needs:

		Calories:	2,000	2,500
Total Fat	Less than		65g	80g
Saturated Fat	Less than		20g	25g
Cholesterol	Less than		300mg	300mg
Sodium	Less than		2,400mg	2,400mg
Total Carbohydrate			300g	375g
Dietary Fiber			25g	30g

Calories per gram:
 Fat 9 • Carbohydrate 4 • Protein 4

Thanks to: David Smith-Walsh, Executive Chef University Club

Category: Rice & Grains

RISOTTO MOLLYNESE

Adding broccoli and peppers to traditional risotto helps you get more veggies for the day.

Makes 8 servings

Ingredients:

1⅓	cups	fat-free chicken broth
⅔	cup	water
1	cup	long grain rice
½	cup	green pepper, thinly sliced
½	cup	red bell pepper, diced
⅓	cup	dry white wine
1	tsp	Italian herb seasoning
OR		
½	tsp	each dried basil and oregano
⅛	tsp	mill grind black pepper pinch of turmeric or crushed saffron
2	cups	broccoli chopped
6	Tbsp	butter substitute (Molly McButter)

Preparation:

- In a large non-stick saucepan, combine chicken broth and water.
- Bring to a boil.
- Reduce heat; add all ingredients <u>except</u> broccoli and butter substitute.
- Cover and cook over medium-low heat for 20 minutes.
- Stir in broccoli; cover and continue cooking more minutes, until rice is fluffy.
- Remove from heat; stir in butter substitute.
- Serve immediately.

Thanks to: Russell and Hazel Schanrock, Group 1

Category: Rice and Grains

Nutrition Facts

Serving Size 1/8 recipe (about 1/2 cup) (136g)
Servings Per Container 8

Amount Per Serving

Calories 110   Calories from Fat 0

% Daily Value*

Total Fat 0g	0%
Saturated Fat 0g	0%
Trans Fat 0g	
Cholesterol 0mg	0%
Sodium 480mg	20%
Total Carbohydrate 22g	7%
Dietary Fiber 1g	4%
Sugars 1g	
Protein 3g	

Vitamin A 10% • Vitamin C 70%
Calcium 2% • Iron 6%

*Percent Daily Values are based on a 2,000 calorie diet. Your daily values may be higher or lower depending on your calorie needs:

	Calories:	2,000	2,500
Total Fat	Less than	65g	80g
Saturated Fat	Less than	20g	25g
Cholesterol	Less than	300mg	300mg
Sodium	Less than	2,400mg	2,400mg
Total Carbohydrate		300g	375g
Dietary Fiber		25g	30g

Calories per gram:
Fat 9 • Carbohydrate 4 • Protein 4

SOUTHWESTERN RICE

Possible additions: corn; favorite beans. Additional seasoning if desired, garlic powder, chili powder, cumin.

Makes 4 servings

Ingredients:

1	cup	brown rice
½	cup	chopped onion
1 ½	cups	vegetable broth (see page 384)
1	cup	chunky salsa (e.g. Pace mild)
1	cup	water

Preparation:

- Treat a saucepan with vegetable oil cooking spray and sauté rice and onion lightly.
- Add broth, salsa, and water.
- Cover and simmer for about 40 minutes, until rice is done.

Garnish as desired with sliced olives, chopped green onion, cilantro.

Thanks to: Nan Chorman, Group 31

Category : Rice and Grains

Nutrition Facts

Serving Size 1/4 recipe (about 1/2 cup) (301g)
Servings Per Container 4

Amount Per Serving

Calories 220   Calories from Fat 20

% Daily Value*

- Total Fat 2g — 3%
  - Saturated Fat 0g — 0%
  - Trans Fat 0g
- Cholesterol 0mg — 0%
- Sodium 500mg — 21%
- Total Carbohydrate 46g — 15%
  - Dietary Fiber 5g — 20%
  - Sugars 6g
- Protein 5g

Vitamin A 80% • Vitamin C 50%
Calcium 6% • Iron 15%

*Percent Daily Values are based on a 2,000 calorie diet. Your daily values may be higher or lower depending on your calorie needs:

		Calories:	2,000	2,500
Total Fat	Less than		65g	80g
Saturated Fat	Less than		20g	25g
Cholesterol	Less than		300mg	300mg
Sodium	Less than		2,400mg	2,400mg
Total Carbohydrate			300g	375g
Dietary Fiber			25g	30g

Calories per gram:
 Fat 9 • Carbohydrate 4 • Protein 4

SPANISH RICE

This recipe makes good use of the broth and sauce you have made ahead from other recipes in this collection.

Makes 6 servings

Ingredients:

½		tomato, diced (½ cup)
1	med	onion, sliced
1		green bell pepper, chopped
1½	cup	vegetable broth (see page 384)
½	cup	hearty tomato sauce (see page 371)
2	tsp	cumin
½	tsp	chili powder
¼	tsp	garlic powder
¼	tsp	ground black pepper
1	cup	uncooked rice

Preparation:

- Combine all ingredients except rice. Bring to boil.
- Add rice and cover, reduce heat to low, cover for 15 minutes or until rice has absorbed all the liquid.
- Remove from heat.
- Let stand covered 10 minutes before serving.

Category: Rice and Grains

Nutrition Facts

Serving Size 1/6 recipe (208g)
Servings Per Container 6

Amount Per Serving

Calories 150 — Calories from Fat 5

% Daily Value*

Total Fat 0.5g	1%
Saturated Fat 0g	0%
Trans Fat 0g	
Cholesterol 0mg	0%
Sodium 80mg	3%
Total Carbohydrate 33g	11%
Dietary Fiber 3g	12%
Sugars 5g	
Protein 4g	

Vitamin A 60% • Vitamin C 90%
Calcium 6% • Iron 15%

*Percent Daily Values are based on a 2,000 calorie diet. Your daily values may be higher or lower depending on your calorie needs:

		Calories:	2,000	2,500
Total Fat	Less than		65g	80g
Saturated Fat	Less than		20g	25g
Cholesterol	Less than		300mg	300mg
Sodium	Less than		2,400mg	2,400mg
Total Carbohydrate			300g	375g
Dietary Fiber			25g	30g

Calories per gram:
Fat 9 • Carbohydrate 4 • Protein 4

SPICY POLENTA

Once prepared, these strips can be cooked in a large skillet for 1 minute on each side or brushed lightly with olive oil (or spray) and grilled for several minutes on each side.

Makes 24 strips (servings)

Ingredients:

4	cups	fat-free chicken broth
2	Tbsp	butter flavored sprinkles
1	cup	polenta (see page 260)
2	cloves	garlic, minced
1	cup	fat-free or tofu shredded cheese
2/3	cup	roasted red bell pepper, chopped
1/2	cup	Parmesan cheese, non-fat
1/4	cup	green onion, sliced (green tops only)
1/2	tsp	fresh sage, minced
		salt and pepper to taste

Preparation:

- Spray a 13 x 9 inch baking pan with vegetable oil cooking spray; set aside.
- In a medium saucepan, bring broth to a boil.
- Add polenta, cook and stir over low heat for 10 minutes.
- Add remaining ingredients and cook for an additional 5 minutes.
- Pour into prepared pan and let cool to room temperature or chill overnight.
- Cut into 1-by-2 inch strips and transfer to a decorative platter.
- Serve at room temperature.

Nutrition Facts

Serving Size 1x2 inch strip (60g)
Servings Per Container 24

Amount Per Serving

Calories 50 — Calories from Fat 5

% Daily Value*

Total Fat 0.5g	1%
Saturated Fat 0g	0%
Trans Fat 0g	
Cholesterol 0mg	0%
Sodium 220mg	9%
Total Carbohydrate 7g	2%
Dietary Fiber 1g	4%
Sugars 1g	
Protein 4g	

Vitamin A 6% • Vitamin C 10%
Calcium 6% • Iron 4%

*Percent Daily Values are based on a 2,000 calorie diet. Your daily values may be higher or lower depending on your calorie needs:

		Calories:	2,000	2,500
Total Fat	Less than		65g	80g
Saturated Fat	Less than		20g	25g
Cholesterol	Less than		300mg	300mg
Sodium	Less than		2,400mg	2,400mg
Total Carbohydrate			300g	375g
Dietary Fiber			25g	30g

Calories per gram:
  Fat 9 • Carbohydrate 4 • Protein 4

From *Raley's*

Category: Rice and Grains

Vegetable Risotto

Arborio rice is an Italian short-grain rice and the rounded grains are firm, creamy, and chewy, making it the best for risotto.

Makes 2 servings

Ingredients:

½	cup	arborio rice, uncooked
½	cup	mushrooms, chopped
½	cup	celery, diced
⅓	cup	onion, chopped
½	cup	green peas
⅓	cups	vegetable broth (see page 284)
½	cup	tomatoes, chopped

Preparation:

- Combine ingredients in a saucepan.
- Cover and simmer over medium heat 20-25 minutes until rice is done.

Thanks to: Conrad and Phyllis Merrick, Group 26

Category: Rice and Grains

Nutrition Facts

Serving Size 1/2 recipe (371g)
Servings Per Container 2

Amount Per Serving

Calories 250 — Calories from Fat 5

% Daily Value*

Total Fat 0g	0%
Saturated Fat 0g	0%
Trans Fat 0g	
Cholesterol 0mg	0%
Sodium 360mg	15%
Total Carbohydrate 53g	18%
Dietary Fiber 5g	20%
Sugars 8g	
Protein 8g	

Vitamin A 40% • Vitamin C 70%
Calcium 8% • Iron 20%

*Percent Daily Values are based on a 2,000 calorie diet. Your daily values may be higher or lower depending on your calorie needs:

		Calories:	2,000	2,500
Total Fat	Less than		65g	80g
Saturated Fat	Less than		20g	25g
Cholesterol	Less than		300mg	300mg
Sodium	Less than		2,400mg	2,400mg
Total Carbohydrate			300g	375g
Dietary Fiber			25g	30g

Calories per gram:
  Fat 9 • Carbohydrate 4 • Protein 4

VEGETABLES

APPLE SWEET AND SOUR RED CABBAGE

The red cabbage lends beautiful color to this tangy dish.

6 servings

Ingredients:

1	tsp	olive oil
½	cup	green onion, diced
4	cups	red cabbage, shredded
2	medium	red delicious apples, sliced
3	Tbsp	brown sugar
¼	tsp	salt
⅛	tsp	ground black pepper
½	cup	unsweetened apple juice
6	Tbsp	cider vinegar

Preparation:

- Coat a large non-stick skillet with oil and place over medium-high heat until hot.
- Add green onion and sauté until tender, 2-3 minutes. Add all other ingredients and stir well.
- Cook, uncovered, over medium heat 15-18 minutes, or until cabbage is tender, stirring occasionally.

Thanks to: Phyllis Quinn, Group 26

Category: Vegetables

Nutrition Facts

Serving Size about 3/4 cup (185g)
Servings Per Container 6

Amount Per Serving

Calories 110   Calories from Fat 10

% Daily Value*

Total Fat 1g	2%
Saturated Fat 0g	0%
Trans Fat 0g	
Cholesterol 0mg	0%
Sodium 120mg	5%
Total Carbohydrate 25g	8%
Dietary Fiber 3g	12%
Sugars 19g	
Protein 1g	

Vitamin A 15% • Vitamin C 60%

Calcium 4% • Iron 4%

*Percent Daily Values are based on a 2,000 calorie diet. Your daily values may be higher or lower depending on your calorie needs:

		Calories:	2,000	2,500
Total Fat	Less than		65g	80g
Saturated Fat	Less than		20g	25g
Cholesterol	Less than		300mg	300mg
Sodium	Less than		2,400mg	2,400mg
Total Carbohydrate			300g	375g
Dietary Fiber			25g	30g

Calories per gram:
  Fat 9 • Carbohydrate 4 • Protein 4

APPLE SWEET POTATO MEDLEY

You cannot go wrong with sweet potatoes and apples. Perfect for fall.

Makes 6 servings

Ingredients:

1	lb	sweet potatoes, peeled and cubed
⅔	cup	unsweetened apple juice or cider
2	tsp	cornstarch
¼	tsp	ground cinnamon
⅛	tsp	ground nutmeg
2	medium	apples, peeled, cored and cubed

Preparation:

- Place sweet potato cubes in vegetable steamer over boiling water. Cover and steam until tender, about 6-7 minutes
- While potatoes are cooking, peel, core, and chop apples. Transfer potatoes to a serving bowl and cover to keep warm.
- In a medium saucepan, combine apple juice, cornstarch, cinnamon and nutmeg.
- Cook over medium heat, stirring constantly, until thickened and bubbly, about 4 minutes.
- Stir in chopped apple.
- Reduce heat, cover and simmer, stirring frequently, until apples are tender, about 10 minutes.
- Add apple mixture to sweet potatoes; toss gently.

Nutrition Facts

Serving Size 1/6 recipe (177g)
Servings Per Container 6

Amount Per Serving

Calories 110   Calories from Fat 0

% Daily Value*

Total Fat 0g	0%
Saturated Fat 0g	0%
Trans Fat 0g	
Cholesterol 0mg	0%
Sodium 45mg	2%
Total Carbohydrate 28g	9%
Dietary Fiber 4g	16%
Sugars 15g	
Protein 1g	

Vitamin A 70% • Vitamin C 25%
Calcium 2% • Iron 2%

*Percent Daily Values are based on a 2,000 calorie diet. Your daily values may be higher or lower depending on your calorie needs:

		Calories:	2,000	2,500
Total Fat	Less than		65g	80g
Saturated Fat	Less than		20g	25g
Cholesterol	Less than		300mg	300mg
Sodium	Less than		2,400mg	2,400mg
Total Carbohydrate			300g	375g
Dietary Fiber			25g	30g

Calories per gram:
   Fat 0 • Carbohydrate 4 • Protein 4

Category: Vegetables

Baked Eggplant

Makes 3 servings

Ingredients:

1	large	eggplant
4		egg whites
½	cup	skim milk
1½	cups	bread cubes
½	cup	onion, chopped
1	cup	fat-free cheese, shredded
½	tsp	salt

Preparation:

- Preheat oven to 350°F.
- Peel eggplant and cut it into cubes. Boil cubes in salt water until tender. Drain and mash.
- Add eggs, milk, bread cubes, and onion. Mix well.
- Place mixture in an oven safe dish and top with cheese.
- Bake approximately 35 minutes

Category: Vegetables

Note: Caution regarding sodium content

Nutrition Facts

Serving Size (353g)
Servings Per Container

Amount Per Serving

Calories 200 Calories from Fat 10

	% Daily Value*
Total Fat 1g	2%
Saturated Fat 0g	0%
Trans Fat 0g	
Cholesterol 5mg	2%
Sodium 840mg	35%
Total Carbohydrate 27g	9%
Dietary Fiber 7g	28%
Sugars 8g	
Protein 22g	

Vitamin A 8% • Vitamin C 10%
Calcium 45% • Iron 6%

*Percent Daily Values are based on a 2,000 calorie diet. Your daily values may be higher or lower depending on your calorie needs:

		Calories:	2,000	2,500
Total Fat	Less than		65g	80g
Saturated Fat	Less than		20g	25g
Cholesterol	Less than		300mg	300mg
Sodium	Less than		2,400mg	2,400mg
Total Carbohydrate			300g	375g
Dietary Fiber			25g	30g

Calories per gram:
Fat 9 • Carbohydrate 4 • Protein 4

CABBAGE ROLLS

These take a little time, but a good twist on an old favorite.

Makes 16 cabbage rolls, ~ 8 servings.

Ingredients:

2	small	heads cabbage

Sauce:

1		onion, chopped
3	cups	tomato sauce, unsalted
1		bay leaf
½	tsp	ground ginger
¼	cup	honey
¼	cup	vinegar
¼	tsp	thyme leaves
½	tsp	salt or less
		pepper to taste

Filling:

1	large	onion, chopped
1	cup	non-fat cottage cheese
½	cup	fresh parsley, chopped
½	cup	unsalted tomato paste (Page 371, 380, 383)
2	cups	brown rice, cooked
¼	tsp	garlic powder

Nutrition Facts

Serving Size 2 rolls, 1/8 recipe (446g)
Servings Per Container 8

Amount Per Serving

Calories 260   Calories from Fat 10

% Daily Value*

Total Fat 1.5g	2%
Saturated Fat 0g	0%
Trans Fat 0g	
Cholesterol 0mg	0%
Sodium 310mg	13%
Total Carbohydrate 55g	18%
Dietary Fiber 9g	36%
Sugars 19g	
Protein 10g	

Vitamin A 25% • Vitamin C 190%
Calcium 15%   • Iron 20%

*Percent Daily Values are based on a 2,000 calorie diet. Your daily values may be higher or lower depending on your calorie needs:

		Calories:	2,000	2,500
Total Fat	Less than		65g	80g
Saturated Fat	Less than		20g	25g
Cholesterol	Less than		300mg	300mg
Sodium	Less than		2,400mg	2,400mg
Total Carbohydrate			300g	375g
Dietary Fiber			25g	30g

Calories per gram:
   Fat 9 • Carbohydrate 4 • Protein 4

Preparation:

- Steam cabbage 20 minutes, then carefully separate leaves from the head.
- Sauce: Steam onion until transparent; add remaining ingredients and gently simmer for about 30 minutes.
- Preheat oven to 350°F.
- Filling: Steam the chopped onion, add remaining ingredients and heat thoroughly.
- Place about 1 Tbsp on each cabbage leaf, roll up tightly and secure with a wooden tooth pick.
- Assemble dish: Place a small amount of sauce in shallow baking pan and add cabbage rolls. Pour remaining sauce over ingredients.
- Cover pan and bake for 45-60 minutes, until cabbage is soft.

Category: Vegetables

Caponata

Southern Italian, an eggplant 'stew'. Awesome!

4 servings ~ ½ cup each

Ingredients:

1		eggplant, peeled and cut into inch cubes
1	cup	fresh tomatoes, chopped
1	med	green bell pepper, coarsely chopped
1	med	red bell pepper, coarsely chopped
1	med	onion, coarsely chopped
3	cloves	garlic, minced
8		black olives, pitted and chopped
¼	cup	drained capers
¼	cup	fresh Italian parsley, chopped
2	Tbsp	fresh marjoram, chopped
1	Tbsp	red wine vinegar

Nutrition Facts

Serving Size 1/4 recipe (about 1/2 cup) (317g)
Servings Per Container 4

Amount Per Serving

Calories 90   Calories from Fat 15

% Daily Value*

Total Fat 2g	3%
Saturated Fat 0g	0%
Trans Fat 0g	
Cholesterol 0mg	0%
Sodium 330mg	14%
Total Carbohydrate 18g	6%
Dietary Fiber 8g	32%
Sugars 9g	
Protein 3g	

Vitamin A 40%	•	Vitamin C 150%
Calcium 6%	•	Iron 15%

*Percent Daily Values are based on a 2,000 calorie diet. Your daily values may be higher or lower depending on your calorie needs:

	Calories:	2,000	2,500
Total Fat	Less than	65g	80g
Saturated Fat	Less than	20g	25g
Cholesterol	Less than	300mg	300mg
Sodium	Less than	2,400mg	2,400mg
Total Carbohydrate		300g	375g
Dietary Fiber		25g	30g

Calories per gram:
 Fat 9 • Carbohydrate 4 • Protein 4

Preparation:

- In a large non-stick frying pan over medium-high heat, sauté eggplant for 2 minutes:
- Reduce heat, add peppers, onions, and garlic and simmer for 10 minutes, stirring occasionally.
- Add olives, capers, parsley, marjoram and vinegar.
- Turn the Caponata into a large bowl; cover and let sit for 2 hours before serving.
- Refrigerate leftovers.

Thanks to: Jerre Schermerhorn, Group 29

Category: Vegetables

CARROT CASSEROLE

This is a comfort food! If you don't have a food processor, you save time grating carrots by buying them pre-grated.

Makes 6 servings

Ingredients:

6	large	carrots
1½	cups	water
½	tsp	salt
1	med	onion diced
½	cup	water
½	tsp	salt
14	oz	skim milk, evaporated
2	Tbsp	cornstarch
1	Tbsp	butter-flavored sprinkles
¼	tsp	black pepper
5	oz.	non-fat cracker crumbs

Nutrition Facts
Serving Size 1/6 recipe (190g)
Servings Per Container 6

Amount Per Serving

Calories 190   Calories from Fat 5

% Daily Value*

Total Fat 0.5g	1%
Saturated Fat 0g	0%
Trans Fat 0g	
Cholesterol 5mg	2%
Sodium 310mg	13%
Total Carbohydrate 39g	13%
Dietary Fiber 3g	12%
Sugars 13g	
Protein 8g	

Vitamin A 250% • Vitamin C 10%
Calcium 25% • Iron 15%

*Percent Daily Values are based on a 2,000 calorie diet. Your daily values may be higher or lower depending on your calorie needs:

	Calories:	2,000	2,500
Total Fat	Less than	65g	80g
Saturated Fat	Less than	20g	25g
Cholesterol	Less than	300mg	300mg
Sodium	Less than	2,400mg	2,400mg
Total Carbohydrate		300g	375g
Dietary Fiber		25g	30g

Calories per gram:
Fat 9 • Carbohydrate 4 • Protein 4

Preparation:

- Preheat oven to 375 °F.
- Peel and grate carrots. Boil carrots for 5 minutes in 1½ cups of water with ½ tsp of salt.
- Simmer for 10 minutes or until tender. Drain well.
- Simmer onion in ½ cup of water and ½ tsp of salt for 5 minutes. Drain well.
- Add cornstarch to evaporated milk. Mix carrots and onions together, and stir in milk.
- Then fold in 3 oz cracker crumbs. Place mixture in casserole dish and sprinkle with remaining 2 oz cracker crumbs.
- Bake for 30 minutes.

Thanks to: Frank and Minnie Bell, Group 5

Category: Vegetables

Cucumber Raita

The lightened raita increases your veggie servings and is a nice addition to meals with a South Asian flavor.

Makes 4 servings

Ingredients:

1	cucumber	English - sliced very thin
1	cup	non-fat sour cream
2	cloves	fresh garlic, crushed
1	tsp.	fresh ginger, grated
2		green onions, sliced
		salt to taste
		pepper to taste
		paprika for garnish

Preparation:

- Combine all ingredients.
- Chill and allow flavors to blend for at least one hour.

Thanks to: Tissa Kappagoda

Category: Vegetables

Nutrition Facts

Serving Size 1/4 recipe (154g)
Servings Per Container 4

Amount Per Serving

Calories 70 — Calories from Fat 0

% Daily Value*

Total Fat 0g	0%
Saturated Fat 0g	0%
Trans Fat 0g	
Cholesterol 5mg	2%
Sodium 170mg	7%
Total Carbohydrate 14g	5%
Dietary Fiber 1g	4%
Sugars 2g	
Protein 3g	

Vitamin A 10% • Vitamin C 10%
Calcium 10% • Iron 2%

*Percent Daily Values are based on a 2,000 calorie diet. Your daily values may be higher or lower depending on your calorie needs:

		Calories:	2,000	2,500
Total Fat	Less than		65g	80g
Saturated Fat	Less than		20g	25g
Cholesterol	Less than		300mg	300mg
Sodium	Less than		2,400mg	2,400mg
Total Carbohydrate			300g	375g
Dietary Fiber			25g	30g

Calories per gram:
  Fat 9 • Carbohydrate 4 • Protein 4

CUCUMBERS VINAIGRETTE

This provides a tangy, crisp complement to a hearty, hot bowl of soup

Makes 6 servings ~ ½ cup each

Ingredients:

3		cucumbers, thinly sliced (~3-1/2 cups)
½	cup	red onion, vertically sliced
1	Tbsp	chopped fresh basil OR 1 tsp dried basil
1	Tbsp	chopped fresh parsley OR 1 tsp dried parsley
2	Tbsp	red wine vinegar
2½	tsp	Dijon mustard
¼	tsp	salt

Preparation:

- Cucumbers should be peeled, halved lengthwise, seeded, and thinly sliced.
- Mix cucumbers and onion together in a bowl.
- Combine spices, vinegar, mustard and salt in a small container. Pour over cucumber mixture.
- Toss gently.
- Cover and chill.

Category: Vegetables

Nutrition Facts

Serving Size 1/2 cup (172g)
Servings Per Container 6

Amount Per Serving

Calories 30 — Calories from Fat 0

% Daily Value*

Total Fat 0g	0%
Saturated Fat 0g	0%
Trans Fat 0g	
Cholesterol 0mg	0%
Sodium 150mg	6%
Total Carbohydrate 6g	2%
Dietary Fiber 2g	8%
Sugars 4g	
Protein 2g	

Vitamin A 8% • Vitamin C 20%
Calcium 4% • Iron 4%

*Percent Daily Values are based on a 2,000 calorie diet. Your daily values may be higher or lower depending on your calorie needs:

	Calories:	2,000	2,500
Total Fat	Less than	65g	80g
Saturated Fat	Less than	20g	25g
Cholesterol	Less than	300mg	300mg
Sodium	Less than	2,400mg	2,400mg
Total Carbohydrate		300g	375g
Dietary Fiber		25g	30g

Calories per gram:
Fat 9 • Carbohydrate 4 • Protein 4

EGGPLANT PARMESAN

Eggplant Parmesan is usually battered, fried, and loaded with cheese. This is a much healthier version.

Makes 4 servings

Ingredients:

1	med	eggplant, cut in ½ inch slices
12	oz	unsalted tomato sauce (see page 371, 380, 383)
2	tsp	dried parsley
2	tsp	chives, chopped (or 1 tsp. grated onion)
¼	cup	Parmesan cheese, grated non-fat
½	tsp	garlic salt
½	tsp	crushed oregano
3	oz.	non-fat mozzarella cheese, sliced or grated
		dash of pepper

Preparation:

- Preheat oven to 375°F.
- Place slices of eggplant into boiling, slightly salted water in a large saucepan; turn down heat and simmer 3 minutes.
- Drain off water and pat slices with paper towel to dry.
- Mix remaining ingredients except mozzarella cheese.
- Cover the bottom of a shallow, medium-size (about 4 x 8 or 5 x 9 inch) baking pan with a little sauce.
- Cover with slices of eggplant.
- Add ⅓ of mozzarella cheese and repeat alternating layers.
- Top with remaining sauce and a sprinkle of Parmesan cheese.
- Bake for 35 minutes, until very hot.

Thanks to: Walter and Rita Kough, Group 6

Category: Vegetables

Nutrition Facts

Serving Size 1/4 recipe (252g)
Servings Per Container 4

Amount Per Serving

Calories 130	Calories from Fat 5

	% Daily Value*
Total Fat 1g	2%
Saturated Fat 0g	0%
Trans Fat 0g	
Cholesterol 5mg	2%
Sodium 400mg	17%
Total Carbohydrate 19g	6%
Dietary Fiber 6g	24%
Sugars 9g	
Protein 12g	

Vitamin A 15%	•	Vitamin C 25%
Calcium 20%	•	Iron 8%

*Percent Daily Values are based on a 2,000 calorie diet. Your daily values may be higher or lower depending on your calorie needs:

		Calories:	2,000	2,500
Total Fat		Less than	65g	80g
Saturated Fat		Less than	20g	25g
Cholesterol		Less than	300mg	300mg
Sodium		Less than	2,400mg	2,400mg
Total Carbohydrate			300g	375g
Dietary Fiber			25g	30g

Calories per gram:
Fat 9 • Carbohydrate 4 • Protein 4

EGGPLANT STEAK

Sweet, fragrant balsamic vinegar cuts the bitterness of the roasted eggplant and enables the health-conscious cook to cut back on the olive oil of the traditional version.

Makes 4 servings

Ingredients:

2		eggplants (1 ½ lbs. total)
½	tsp	salt (or less)
1	tsp	olive oil, preferably extra-virgin
1	Tbsp	balsamic vinegar
1	Tbsp	fresh mint, chopped
½	tsp	dried oregano
1	clove	garlic, minced
		freshly ground black pepper to taste

Preparation:

- Preheat oven to 450°F.
- Prepare eggplant by trimming ends, cutting crosswise into ¾ inch thick slices. Sprinkle with salt and drain in a colander for 30 minutes.
- Lightly coat 2 baking sheets with non-stick cooking spray.
- Rinse eggplant under cold water and pat dry.
- Arrange the slices in a single layer on the prepared baking sheets. Bake for 20 minutes, turn eggplant over and bake for 5 minutes longer, or until golden brown and tender.
- In a small bowl, stir together oil, vinegar, mint, oregano and garlic.
- Season the eggplant with pepper and brush tops with the oil mixture.
- Serve at room temperature.

Nutrition Facts

Serving Size 1/4 recipe (177g)
Servings Per Container 4

Amount Per Serving

Calories 60   Calories from Fat 15

% Daily Value*

Total Fat 1.5g	2%
Saturated Fat 0g	0%
Trans Fat 0g	
Cholesterol 0mg	0%
Sodium 300mg	13%
Total Carbohydrate 11g	4%
Dietary Fiber 6g	24%
Sugars 5g	
Protein 2g	

Vitamin A 2%	•	Vitamin C 6%
Calcium 2%	•	Iron 2%

*Percent Daily Values are based on a 2,000 calorie diet. Your daily values may be higher or lower depending on your calorie needs:

	Calories:	2,000	2,500
Total Fat	Less than	65g	80g
Saturated Fat	Less than	20g	25g
Cholesterol	Less than	300mg	300mg
Sodium	Less than	2,400mg	2,400mg
Total Carbohydrate		300g	375g
Dietary Fiber		25g	30g

Calories per gram:
    Fat 9 • Carbohydrate 4 • Protein 4

The recipe can be prepared ahead and stored, covered, in the refrigerator for up to 8 hours. Bring to room temperature before serving.

Thanks to: Connie Laventurier, Group 2

Category: Vegetables

Eggplant with Sweet and Sour Sauce

Be mindful the sesame oil and sesame seed are the major source of the fat content of this recipe.

Makes 6 servings

Ingredients:

2	lb	small eggplant (6-12)

Sauce:

1	green	chile pepper
1	clove	garlic, crushed
1	Tbsp	vinegar
2	Tbsp	light soy sauce
1	Tbsp	sugar
½	tsp	sesame oil (optional as added fat)
1	tsp	sesame seeds (optional as added fat)

Preparation:

- Make sauce.
- Seed and slice the chile pepper. Mix pepper, garlic, vinegar, soy sauce, sugar and sesame oil into small bowl.
- Sauté eggplant in non-stick pan, using cooking spray if desired. Turn off heat and add sauce. Sprinkle with sesame seeds if desired.

Thanks to: Marian Ono

Category: Vegetables

Nutrition Facts

Serving Size 1/6 recipe (170g)
Servings Per Container 6

Amount Per Serving

Calories 60	Calories from Fat 5

	% Daily Value*
Total Fat 1g	2%
Saturated Fat 0g	0%
Trans Fat 0g	
Cholesterol 0mg	0%
Sodium 170mg	7%
Total Carbohydrate 12g	4%
Dietary Fiber 5g	20%
Sugars 7g	
Protein 2g	

Vitamin A 2%	•	Vitamin C 35%
Calcium 2%	•	Iron 2%

*Percent Daily Values are based on a 2,000 calorie diet. Your daily values may be higher or lower depending on your calorie needs:

	Calories:	2,000	2,500
Total Fat	Less than	65g	80g
Saturated Fat	Less than	20g	25g
Cholesterol	Less than	300mg	300mg
Sodium	Less than	2,400mg	2,400mg
Total Carbohydrate		300g	375g
Dietary Fiber		25g	30g

Calories per gram:
  Fat 9 • Carbohydrate 4 • Protein 4

GARDEN BAKE

Tasty way to use some of the bounty from your summer garden.

Makes 10 servings

Ingredients:

1½	cups	zucchini, chopped
1	cup	yellow summer squash, chopped
1	cup	tomato, chopped
1	med	onion, chopped
⅓	cup	fat-free Parmesan cheese
1	cup	fat-free mozzarella cheese
1½	cup	skim milk
¾	cup	baking mix (see page 177)
¾	cup	egg substitute
¾	tsp	salt
½	tsp	ground black pepper

Preparation:

- Preheat oven to 400°F. Coat 13 x 9 inch pan with cooking spray.
- Spread zucchini, squash, tomato and onion evenly in pan.
- Blend in blender remaining ingredients until smooth.
- Spread over vegetables in pan.
- Bake 35-40 minutes or until knife inserted in center comes out clean.
- Let stand 5 minutes before cutting.

Thanks to: Ginny Goodrow, Group 25

Category: Vegetables

Nutrition Facts

Serving Size 1/10 recipe (125g)
Servings Per Container 10

Amount Per Serving

Calories 90   Calories from Fat 5

% Daily Value*

Total Fat 0g	0%
Saturated Fat 0g	0%
Trans Fat 0g	
Cholesterol 5mg	2%
Sodium 420mg	18%
Total Carbohydrate 13g	4%
Dietary Fiber 1g	4%
Sugars 4g	
Protein 10g	

Vitamin A 6%   •   Vitamin C 10%

Calcium 20%   •   Iron 6%

*Percent Daily Values are based on a 2,000 calorie diet. Your daily values may be higher or lower depending on your calorie needs:

	Calories:	2,000	2,500
Total Fat	Less than	65g	80g
Saturated Fat	Less than	20g	25g
Cholesterol	Less than	300mg	300mg
Sodium	Less than	2,400mg	2,400mg
Total Carbohydrate		300g	375g
Dietary Fiber		25g	30g

Calories per gram:
  Fat 9   •   Carbohydrate 4   •   Protein 4

Garlicky Kale

Another way to enjoy this tasty, nutrition-packed green.

Makes 6 servings

Ingredients:

2	lb	kale, about 2 bunches
2	tsp	olive oil
4-5	cloves	garlic
	pinch	red pepper flakes
	splash	red wine vinegar
		salt, freshly ground pepper

Preparation:

- Remove stems from the kale and chop the leaves coarsely.
- Wash and drain well but do not dry.
- Heat a large sauté pan, add 1 tsp olive oil and enough kale to cover the bottom of the pan.
- Cook over high heat while stirring to rotate the leaves.
- Add more kale as the leaves wilt.
- When all the kale has been added, season with salt, cover and reduce the heat to medium.
- Cook, stirring occasionally; cooking time will depend on the maturity of the kale. Young kale will be tender after 4-5 minutes.
- It may be necessary to add a splash of water if the leaves begin to scorch.
- When the leaves are tender, remove the lid and allow any excess water to cook away.
- Remove the kale to a warm bowl and set aside.
- Add the remaining 1 tsp of olive oil to the pan along with the garlic and red pepper.
- Sauté just until you smell the aroma of the garlic.
- Sprinkle the garlic and red pepper over the kale and toss with a splash of vinegar.
- Adjust the salt and pepper to taste.
- Serve warm or at room temperature.

Category: Vegetables

Nutrition Facts

Serving Size 1/6 recipe (161g)
Servings Per Container 6

Amount Per Serving

Calories 90 — Calories from Fat 25

	% Daily Value*
Total Fat 2.5g	4%
Saturated Fat 0g	0%
Trans Fat 0g	
Cholesterol 0mg	0%
Sodium 160mg	7%
Total Carbohydrate 16g	5%
Dietary Fiber 3g	12%
Sugars 0g	
Protein 5g	

Vitamin A 470% • Vitamin C 300%
Calcium 20% • Iron 15%

*Percent Daily Values are based on a 2,000 calorie diet. Your daily values may be higher or lower depending on your calorie needs:

		Calories: 2,000	2,500
Total Fat	Less than	65g	80g
Saturated Fat	Less than	20g	25g
Cholesterol	Less than	300mg	300mg
Sodium	Less than	2,400mg	2,400mg
Total Carbohydrate		300g	375g
Dietary Fiber		25g	30g

Calories per gram:
Fat 9 • Carbohydrate 4 • Protein 4

GREEN BEANS WITH MUSTARD

All spices available in East Indian food markets. If you do not wish to invest in special spices, the methods can be mimicked by using curry (a mixture of spices). Young skinny green beans are often cooked for a much shorter time.

Makes 4 servings

Ingredients:

1½	lb	fresh green beans, cut into small pieces.
¼	tsp	garam masala
3	Tbsp	non-fat yogurt, plain
½		fresh hot green chile thinly sliced (optional)
OR		
¼	tsp	cayenne pepper
3	Tbsp	cilantro, Chinese parsley or coriander greens, finely chopped
1	tsp	salt
1	tsp	sugar
¾	tsp	dry mustard
¾	tsp	ground cumin
2	tsp	lemon juice
3	Tbsp	water
1	tsp	olive oil
3	whole	fenugreek seeds
¼	tsp	cumin seeds

Nutrition Facts
Serving Size 1/4 recipe (203g)
Servings Per Container 4

Amount Per Serving
Calories 60   Calories from Fat 15

% Daily Value*
- Total Fat 1.5g — 2%
  - Saturated Fat 0g — 0%
  - Trans Fat 0g
- Cholesterol 0mg — 0%
- Sodium 610mg — 25%
- Total Carbohydrate 10g — 3%
  - Dietary Fiber 4g — 16%
  - Sugars 5g
- Protein 5g

Vitamin A 0% • Vitamin C 6%
Calcium 2% • Iron 4%

*Percent Daily Values are based on a 2,000 calorie diet. Your daily values may be higher or lower depending on your calorie needs:

	Calories:	2,000	2,500
Total Fat	Less than	65g	80g
Saturated Fat	Less than	20g	25g
Cholesterol	Less than	300mg	300mg
Sodium	Less than	2,400mg	2,400mg
Total Carbohydrate		300g	375g
Dietary Fiber		25g	30g

Calories per gram:
Fat 9 • Carbohydrate 4 • Protein 4

Preparation:

- In a cup or small bowl, mix together yogurt, chile, spices, lemon juice, and water. Mix well.
- Heat oil in skillet over medium heat.
- When hot, add fenugreek seeds and cumin seeds. When the fenugreek seeds begin to change color (about 20 seconds) and you smell the aroma of the spices, add the beans and stir for about 5 minutes.
- Beat the yogurt mixture once again and stir into the beans.
- When the skillet begins to make bubbling noises, cover, reduce heat to very low, and allow to cook slowly for 40 minutes.
- Stir every 10 minutes or so.
- Before serving, sprinkle with garam masala.

Thanks to: Annemari Mukherjee, Group 28, from Madhur Jaffrey, An Invitation to Indian Cooking

Category: Vegetables

OKRA CURRY

Okra is commonly used in Indian foods. It contains soluble fiber, vitamin C, calcium, and folate. Good stuff.

Makes 6 servings

Ingredients:

1½	med	onion
1	tsp	olive oil
½	tsp	red chili powder
¼	tsp	turmeric powder
1½	tsp	cumin powder
1	tsp	coriander powder
¼	tsp	garam masala powder (3-spice powder)
1	tsp	salt
2	lb	okra (fresh or frozen, cut off tips and tops)
12	oz	tomato sauce, unsalted
2	cups	water if using frozen okra
OR		
2½	cups	water if using fresh okra
1	handful	fresh cilantro, chopped

Nutrition Facts

Serving Size 1/6 recipe (316g)
Servings Per Container 6

Amount Per Serving

Calories 80 — Calories from Fat 10

% Daily Value*

- Total Fat 1g — 2%
- Saturated Fat 0g — 0%
- Trans Fat 0g
- Cholesterol 0mg — 0%
- Sodium 430mg — 18%
- Total Carbohydrate 18g — 6%
- Dietary Fiber 7g — 28%
- Sugars 6g
- Protein 4g

Vitamin A 15% • Vitamin C 60%
Calcium 15% • Iron 8%

*Percent Daily Values are based on a 2,000 calorie diet. Your daily values may be higher or lower depending on your calorie needs:

	Calories:	2,000	2,500
Total Fat	Less than	65g	80g
Saturated Fat	Less than	20g	25g
Cholesterol	Less than	300mg	300mg
Sodium	Less than	2,400mg	2,400mg
Total Carbohydrate		300g	375g
Dietary Fiber		25g	30g

Calories per gram:
Fat 9 • Carbohydrate 4 • Protein 4

Preparation:

- Sauté onions in oil over medium-low heat until translucent.
- Add in spices, stirring well.
- Add okra, stir, add tomato sauce and water.
- Stir, cover and cook on high heat, stirring occasionally for 5 minutes.
- Reduce heat to medium (curry will be bubbling) for 10 minutes.
- Stir, keep covered.
- Reduce heat to low. Stir and add cilantro.
- Simmer 15 minutes in covered pan.
- Turn off heat and serve.

Category: Vegetables

RATATOUILLE

Mediterranean vegetable stew, an Italian favorite and naturally low in fat.

Makes 4 servings

Ingredients:

1	tsp	olive oil
4	cloves	garlic, crushed
1		bay leaf
1	med	onion, chopped
1	small	eggplant, cubed
3	Tbsp	burgundy (or dry, red wine of your choice)
½	cup	tomato juice
1	tsp	basil
1	tsp	marjoram
½	tsp	oregano
½	tsp	ground rosemary
2	small,	zucchini or summer squash, cubed
2	med	bell peppers, in strips or cubes
2	med	tomatoes, in chunks
2	Tbsp	tomato paste
		fresh parsley, chopped
		non-fat cheddar cheese, grated as garnish (optional)
		black olives, as garnish (optional)
		salt and black pepper to taste
		steamed rice or French bread

Nutrition Facts

Serving Size 1/4 recipe (433g)
Servings Per Container 4

Amount Per Serving

Calories 120   Calories from Fat 20

% Daily Value*

Total Fat 2g	3%
Saturated Fat 0g	0%
Trans Fat 0g	
Cholesterol 0mg	0%
Sodium 125mg	5%
Total Carbohydrate 24g	8%
Dietary Fiber 9g	36%
Sugars 12g	
Protein 4g	

Vitamin A 15% • Vitamin C 160%
Calcium 8% • Iron 10%

*Percent Daily Values are based on a 2,000 calorie diet. Your daily values may be higher or lower depending on your calorie needs:

		2,000	2,500
Total Fat	Less than	65g	80g
Saturated Fat	Less than	20g	25g
Cholesterol	Less than	300mg	300mg
Sodium	Less than	2,400mg	2,400mg
Total Carbohydrate		300g	375g
Dietary Fiber		25g	30g

Calories per gram:
Fat 9 • Carbohydrate 4 • Protein 4

Preparation:

- Heat olive oil in large heavy cooking pot. Crush the garlic into the oil.
- Add bay leaf and onion. Sauté over medium heat until onion begins to turn transparent.
- Add eggplant, wine and tomato juice.
- Add herbs. Stir to mix well, then cover and simmer 10-15 minutes over low heat.
- When eggplant is tender enough to be easily pricked by a fork, add zucchini and peppers.
- Cover and simmer 10 minutes.
- Add salt and pepper, tomatoes and tomato paste. Mix well.
- Continue to stew until all vegetables are tender, to your liking.
- Just before serving, mix in the fresh parsley.
- Serve on a bed of rice, or in a bowl with French bread.

- Top with grated non-fat cheese and chopped black olives (if desired).

Note: Rice, bread, cheese, olives not included in nutritional data. Be sure to consider those if tracking calories/fat content

Thanks to: Lew and Dorothy Watkins, Group 2

Category: Vegetables

ROASTED FALL VEGETABLES

Many fresh vegetables take on a new, rich flavor when roasted or grilled. Other vegetables include: eggplant slices or fingers, mushrooms, all summer squash (zucchini, pattypan etc), carrots, potatoes, sweet potato chunks, onions, peppers, garlic cloves. Other marinades may include fat-free salad dressings, soy sauce, balsamic or rice vinegar, bit of olive oil and Pam spray, but pretty much anything goes. Be sure to check out the marinade recipes in this collection.

makes 4 servings ~ ½ cup each

Ingredients:

2	cups	small broccoli florets
1	large	red bell pepper, cut into squares
1	cup	turnips, peeled, 1-inch cubes
½	cup	onion, diced
2	tsp	olive oil
1	Tbsp	balsamic vinegar or red wine vinegar
½	cup	flavored broth, your choice OR water
4	sprigs	fresh thyme OR ¼ tsp dried thyme leaves
¼	tsp	salt
		black pepper

Preparation:

- Preheat oven to 425°F.
- In a shallow roasting pan, combine vegetables.
- Whisk together oil and vinegar.
- Pour over veggies, tossing to coat.
- Then, pour broth around veggies: and add thyme.
- Roast for about 30 minutes or until tender, stirring occasionally.

Nutrition Facts

Serving Size 1/4 recipe (about 1/2 cup) (155g)
Servings Per Container 4

Amount Per Serving	
Calories 60	Calories from Fat 25

	% Daily Value*
Total Fat 2.5g	4%
Saturated Fat 0g	0%
Trans Fat 0g	
Cholesterol 0mg	0%
Sodium 230mg	10%
Total Carbohydrate 9g	3%
Dietary Fiber 3g	12%
Sugars 4g	
Protein 2g	

Vitamin A 40%	•	Vitamin C 130%	
Calcium 4%	•	Iron 4%	

*Percent Daily Values are based on a 2,000 calorie diet. Your daily values may be higher or lower depending on your calorie needs:

		Calories:	2,000	2,500
Total Fat	Less than		65g	80g
Saturated Fat	Less than		20g	25g
Cholesterol	Less than		300mg	300mg
Sodium	Less than		2,400mg	2,400mg
Total Carbohydrate			300g	375g
Dietary Fiber			25g	30g

Calories per gram:
  Fat 9 • Carbohydrate 4 • Protein 4

- Remove from oven season with salt and pepper to taste.

Thanks to: Terry Lavirgne, Group 29
Category: Vegetables

SEASONED PORTOBELLO MUSHROOMS

These work well on the grill and can be used in place of a 'burger' on a bun.

Makes 4 servings

Ingredients:

2-3		Portobello mushrooms
1	cup	red wine
½	cup	fat-free Italian dressing
½	cup	light soy sauce
1	tsp	minced garlic

Preparation:

- Slice Portobello mushrooms.
- Combine other ingredients as a marinade, add mushrooms and leave 1-2 hours.
- After marinating, place the mushrooms in a pan and broil for 5 minutes, turn them over, and broil for another 5 minutes or until done.

Category: Vegetables

Nutrition Facts

Serving Size 1/4 recipe (188g)
Servings Per Container 4

Amount Per Serving

Calories 80 — Calories from Fat 5

% Daily Value*

Total Fat 0g	0%
Saturated Fat 0g	0%
Trans Fat 0g	
Cholesterol 0mg	0%
Sodium 1400mg	58%
Total Carbohydrate 11g	4%
Dietary Fiber 1g	4%
Sugars 8g	
Protein 4g	

Vitamin A 0% • Vitamin C 0%
Calcium 2% • Iron 4%

*Percent Daily Values are based on a 2,000 calorie diet. Your daily values may be higher or lower depending on your caloric needs:

		Calories:	2,000	2,500
Total Fat	Less than		65g	80g
Saturated Fat	Less than		20g	25g
Cholesterol	Less than		300mg	300mg
Sodium	Less than		2,400mg	2,400mg
Total Carbohydrate			300g	375g
Dietary Fiber			25g	30g

Calories per gram:
Fat 9 • Carbohydrate 4 • Protein 4

Shepherd's Pie

Here's a happy home for leftovers. The vegetables will vary according to the season. A small amount of leftover lentil, pea, or bean soup may be stirred in with the vegetables. If you don't have any tomatoes, you can substitute ¼ cup tomato paste and ½ cup water

Makes 6 servings

Topping:

2	cups	leftover mashed potatoes
OR		
3	med	potatoes
¼	cup	skim milk
½	tsp	salt

Filling:

1		onion, coarsely chopped
1	tsp	olive oil
1	lb.	broccoli
1		green pepper, diced
4	med	carrots, diced
½	tsp	dried basil
1		bay leaf
¾	cup	fresh tomatoes, chopped
1		bunch spinach or Swiss chard
½	tsp	salt

Preparation:

- Preheat oven to 350°F.
- Unless you have leftover mashed potatoes, steam potato chunks or cook them in fast boiling water until soft. Mash well, adding milk and salt.
- Cut broccoli into florets and stems. Peel and slice the stems in ¼ inch rounds.
- Wash spinach thoroughly and cut into bite-size pieces.
- Sauté onion in olive oil.
- Add broccoli, green pepper, and carrots, then the basil and bay leaf.
- Stir well and add tomatoes.
- Bring to a boil, cover, turn heat to low, and simmer for 15 minutes or until vegetables are just tender.
- Stir in spinach. Add salt.
- Put vegetables into a 9 x 13 inch baking dish.

Nutrition Facts

Serving Size 1/6 recipe (336g)
Servings Per Container 6

Amount Per Serving

Calories 130   Calories from Fat 10

% Daily Value*

Total Fat 1.5g	2%
Saturated Fat 0g	0%
Trans Fat 0g	
Cholesterol 0mg	0%
Sodium 490mg	20%
Total Carbohydrate 28g	9%
Dietary Fiber 7g	28%
Sugars 8g	
Protein 7g	

Vitamin A 210%	•	Vitamin C 210%
Calcium 15%	•	Iron 15%

*Percent Daily Values are based on a 2,000 calorie diet. Your daily values may be higher or lower depending on your calorie needs:

	Calories:	2,000	2,500
Total Fat	Less than	65g	80g
Saturated Fat	Less than	20g	25g
Cholesterol	Less than	300mg	300mg
Sodium	Less than	2,400mg	2,400mg
Total Carbohydrate		300g	375g
Dietary Fiber		25g	30g

Calories per gram:
  Fat 9 • Carbohydrate 4 • Protein 4

- Spread potatoes over top and shake paprika over all. Bake for 10 or 15 minutes, until the potatoes are piping hot.
-

Thanks to: Frank and Minnie Bell, Group 5

Category: Vegetables

SHITAKE MUSHROOMS WITH OYSTER SAUCE

Milder tasting than their dried counterparts, fresh shiitake mushrooms give a rich woodsy flavor to this vegetable stir-fry.

Makes 4 servings

Ingredients:

½	cup	carrot, thinly sliced for garnish (optional)
1	lb	fresh shitake mushrooms
1	small head	Napa cabbage
½	cup	non-fat chicken broth
¼	cup	oyster sauce
2	Tbsp	light soy sauce
1	Tbsp	bourbon
2	tsp	sugar
1	tsp	olive oil
1	tsp	cornstarch dissolved in 2 tsp water

Nutrition Facts
Serving Size 1/4 recipe (366g)
Servings Per Container 4

Amount Per Serving
Calories 130 Calories from Fat 15

% Daily Value*
- Total Fat 2g — 3%
- Saturated Fat 0g — 0%
- Trans Fat 0g
- Cholesterol 0mg — 0%
- Sodium 840mg — 35%
- Total Carbohydrate 19g — 6%
- Dietary Fiber 6g — 24%
- Sugars 9g
- Protein 7g

Vitamin A 100% • Vitamin C 80%
Calcium 10% • Iron 4%

*Percent Daily Values are based on a 2,000 calorie diet. Your daily values may be higher or lower depending on your calorie needs:

	Calories:	2,000	2,500
Total Fat	Less than	65g	80g
Saturated Fat	Less than	20g	25g
Cholesterol	Less than	300mg	300mg
Sodium	Less than	2,400mg	2,400mg
Total Carbohydrate		300g	375g
Dietary Fiber		25g	30g

Calories per gram:
Fat 9 • Carbohydrate 4 • Protein 4

Preparation:

- If using carrot garnish, cook in boiling salted water 2 minutes or until crisp-tender.
- Drain, rinse with cold water, and set aside.
- Cut off tough stems from mushrooms. Rinse and drain caps; leave caps whole.
- Trim cabbage, remove outer leaves and save for another use. Cut heart of cabbage lengthwise into quarters.
- Cook in boiling salted water until tender, 3-4 minutes. Drain, rinse with cold water and drain again; arrange cooked cabbage on a serving platter.
- Combine non-fat chicken broth, oyster sauce, soy sauce, bourbon, and sugar in a small bowl; set aside.
- Heat a wok or wide frying pan over medium-high heat until hot.
- Add olive oil, rotating pan to coat sides.

- Add mushrooms and stir-fry for 1 minute.
- Add chicken broth mixture and cook 3-4 minutes or until mushrooms are tender.
- Add cornstarch solution and cook, stirring, until sauce boils and thickens slightly.
- With tongs, lift mushrooms from sauce and arrange attractively around cabbage.
- Pour sauce over all. Garnish with carrot if desired.

Note: Presentation is very important in Chinese cooking and the carrot slices are added for color and show. They can be cut into interesting shapes and special cutters can give you hearts, dragons, even flowing-tailed fish.

Source: *Adapted and Modified from the Lina Fat Cookbook*

SICILIAN STUFFED EGGPLANT

Buying Eggplant: The skin should have a clear, dark, glossy color covering the entire surface. Eggplant should be heavy and firm to the touch. The stem should be green.

Makes 4 servings

Ingredients:

1	med	eggplant (about 1 lb)
1	tsp	olive oil
1	cup	onions, chopped
1	clove	garlic, minced
1	cup	fresh bread crumbs
4	Tbsp	non-fat Parmesan cheese, grated
¼	cup	fresh Italian parsley
1	cup	tomato sauce
¼	cup	fresh basil (optional)
		salt and pepper to taste

Preparation:

- Cut eggplant lengthwise into quarters, and again in half crosswise yielding 8 pieces.
- Put into a large saucepan, cover with water and bring to a boil. Cover, reduce the heat and simmer for 8 minutes, or until the pulp can be removed easily from the peel.
- Spoon the pulp from the peel; save the peel. Mash the pulp and set aside.
- Heat oil in a large non-stick frying pan over medium heat.

Nutrition Facts

Serving Size 1/4 recipe (265g)
Servings Per Container 4

Amount Per Serving

Calories 140	Calories from Fat 20
	% Daily Value*
Total Fat 2.5g	4%
Saturated Fat 0.5g	3%
Trans Fat 0g	
Cholesterol 0mg	0%
Sodium 470mg	20%
Total Carbohydrate 24g	8%
Dietary Fiber 7g	28%
Sugars 8g	
Protein 7g	

Vitamin A 15%	•	Vitamin C 25%
Calcium 10%	•	Iron 10%

*Percent Daily Values are based on a 2,000 calorie diet. Your daily values may be higher or lower depending on your calorie needs:

	Calories:	2,000	2,500
Total Fat	Less than	65g	80g
Saturated Fat	Less than	20g	25g
Cholesterol	Less than	300mg	300mg
Sodium	Less than	2,400mg	2,400mg
Total Carbohydrate		300g	375g
Dietary Fiber		25g	30g

Calories per gram:
Fat 9 • Carbohydrate 4 • Protein 4

- Add eggplant with the onions and garlic and sauté for 7 minutes, or until tender.
- Stir in bread crumbs and 2 tablespoons of the Parmesan cheese.
- Add salt and pepper if desired.
- Place the eggplant peels in a large baking dish or on a baking sheet and spoon the eggplant mixture onto the peels.
- Bake at 350°F for 20 minutes, or until hot and bubbly.
- In a small saucepan, heat tomato sauce and then spoon sauce over the eggplant; top with remaining 2 tablespoons Parmesan cheese and basil.

Thanks to: Jerre Schermerhorn, Group 29

Category: Vegetables

SPAGHETTI SQUASH WITH ARTICHOKES

Make ahead the roasted tomato herb sauce, using the recipe from this collection.

Makes 4 servings

Ingredients:

1		spaghetti squash, halved, seeded, and cooked
1	tsp	olive oil
2	cup	onion, chopped
2		cloves garlic, minced
9	oz	frozen artichoke hearts, thawed, cut into halves
¼	cup	dry white wine or water
3	cups	roasted Tomato Herb Sauce (see page 380)
¼	cup	fat-free (or soy) Parmesan cheese, grated

Preparation:

- Heat oil over medium heat until hot.
- Sauté onion and garlic about 5 minutes.
- Add artichoke hearts and wine; heat to boiling.
- Reduce heat and simmer, covered, until artichoke hearts are tender, about 5 minutes.
- Add tomato sauce and cook over medium heat until hot.

Nutrition Facts

Serving Size 1/4 recipe (581g)
Servings Per Container 4

Amount Per Serving

Calories 220   Calories from Fat 30

% Daily Value*

Total Fat 3g	5%
Saturated Fat 0.5g	3%
Trans Fat 0g	
Cholesterol 0mg	0%
Sodium 260mg	11%
Total Carbohydrate 39g	13%
Dietary Fiber 10g	40%
Sugars 14g	
Protein 9g	

Vitamin A 30%	•	Vitamin C 70%
Calcium 20%	•	Iron 10%

*Percent Daily Values are based on a 2,000 calorie diet. Your daily values may be higher or lower depending on your calorie needs:

		Calories:	2,000	2,500
Total Fat	Less than		65g	80g
Saturated Fat	Less than		20g	25g
Cholesterol	Less than		300mg	300mg
Sodium	Less than		2,400mg	2,400mg
Total Carbohydrate			300g	375g
Dietary Fiber			25g	30g

Calories per gram:
  Fat 9 • Carbohydrate 4 • Protein 4

- Scrape squash with tines of fork to fluff flesh; spoon tomato sauce mixture into squash halves and mix; sprinkle with cheese and serve.

  Squash can be cooked in oven: place squash halves in roasting pan, add 1 inch hot water. Bake, covered at 400° F for about 45 minutes. Or wrap squash loosely in foil; grill over medium hot coals for about 30 to 40 minutes, turn occasionally.

  Using spaghetti squash 'noodles' instead of pasta noodles reduces calories and carbs and increases fiber.

Category: Vegetables

STUFFED ACORN SQUASH WITH BRANDIED FRUIT

Good winter dish. You can use any winter squash: delicata, butternut, buttercup, sweet dumpling, just to name a few. The fruit and alcohol in this first recipe boost the caloric count a lot. When you're not in the position for such a splurge, consider cutting portion size way down or use recipe on page 295.

Makes 2 servings

Ingredients:

1		acorn squash
1	cup	dried fruit, cut into bite size pieces
½	cup	brandy or wine

Preparation:

- Preheat oven to 350°F. Coat shallow baking pan with vegetable oil cooking spray. Cut squash in half, remove seeds and membranes. Place squash halves cut-side down in pan, add ½ cup boiling water. Cover. Bake 30 minutes, remove from oven. Remove cover. Turn squash over and bake another 20 minutes, or until tender.
- While cooking squash, warm dried fruit with brandy or wine in a small saucepan. Do not allow to boil. With slotted spoon place one half of fruit mixture into each acorn half and serve immediately. Add a bit of brown sugar if fruit is not very sweet.

Nutrition Facts

Serving Size 1/2 squash (332g)
Servings Per Container 2

Amount Per Serving

Calories 380	Calories from Fat 0

	% Daily Value*
Total Fat 0g	0%
Saturated Fat 0g	0%
Trans Fat 0g	
Cholesterol 0mg	0%
Sodium 50mg	2%
Total Carbohydrate 66g	22%
Dietary Fiber 8g	32%
Sugars 30g	
Protein 3g	

Vitamin A 30%	•	Vitamin C 40%
Calcium 15%	•	Iron 20%

*Percent Daily Values are based on a 2,000 calorie diet. Your daily values may be higher or lower depending on your calorie needs:

		Calories:	2,000	2,500
Total Fat	Less than		65g	80g
Saturated Fat	Less than		20g	25g
Cholesterol	Less than		300mg	300mg
Sodium	Less than		2,400mg	2,400mg
Total Carbohydrate			300g	375g
Dietary Fiber			25g	30g

Calories per gram:
 Fat 9 • Carbohydrate 4 • Protein 4

Category: Vegetables

STUFFED ACORN SQUASH WITH SLICED APPLES

One apple can go a long way to dress up winter squash, making it special and boosting your fiber intake even more.

Makes 2 servings

Ingredients:

1		acorn squash
1		fresh, tart apple
1	Tbsp	butter substitute
1	Tbsp	brown sugar
		nutmeg to taste

Preparation:

- Prepare squash (see page 294) and bake, covered, for 30 minutes.
- Peel and core apple, then cut in wedges. Turn squash over and fill each half squash cavity with the apple slices. Dot or sprinkle with butter substitute, brown sugar and nutmeg.
- Bake uncovered for 30 minutes longer or until the squash and apples are tender.

Category: Vegetables

Nutrition Facts

Serving Size 1/2 squash (337g)
Servings Per Container 2

Amount Per Serving

Calories 180 — Calories from Fat 5

% Daily Value*

Total Fat 0g	0%
Saturated Fat 0g	0%
Trans Fat 0g	
Cholesterol 0mg	0%
Sodium 280mg	12%
Total Carbohydrate 46g	15%
Dietary Fiber 6g	24%
Sugars 18g	
Protein 2g	

Vitamin A 15% • Vitamin C 50%
Calcium 8% • Iron 10%

*Percent Daily Values are based on a 2,000 calorie diet. Your daily values may be higher or lower depending on your calorie needs:

		Calories:	2,000	2,500
Total Fat	Less than		65g	80g
Saturated Fat	Less than		20g	25g
Cholesterol	Less than		300mg	300mg
Sodium	Less than		2,400mg	2,400mg
Total Carbohydrate			300g	375g
Dietary Fiber			25g	30g

Calories per gram:
  Fat 9 • Carbohydrate 4 • Protein 4

SWEET AND SOUR EGGPLANT

Serve hot as a main dish over pasta or chilled as a dip with crackers or pita bread; top with fat-free cheese if desired

6 servings ~ ¾ cup each

Ingredients:

1	large	eggplant, chopped in cubes (~ 2 lbs)
1	cup	celery, diced
1	cup	red pepper, diced
16	oz	tomato sauce, unsalted (see page 371, 380, 383)
¼	cup	seasoned rice vinegar
3	cloves	garlic, minced
⅛	tsp	cayenne pepper (optional)
1½	Tbsp	ground cumin
2½	Tbsp	brown sugar, packed
¼	tsp	salt
⅔	cup	parsley, chopped

Preparation:

- In a large skillet, sauté the eggplant for a few minutes.
- Add the celery, pepper and all other ingredients except parsley.
- Continue cooking over medium heat for about 15 minutes, stirring often to prevent sticking.
- Mix in the parsley. Cover and simmer for another 10 minutes until the vegetables are tender, stirring to prevent sticking. Add water if mixture becomes too dry.

Potential substitutions:

- Green pepper for the red or for the celery.
- Use a jar of pimentos if fresh red pepper is not available.
- Add additional garlic just before serving the dish.
- Add the parsley just prior to serving as it may help to freshen the breath for those that are not fond of the aftertaste of garlic.

Nutrition Facts

Serving Size about 3/4 cup each (294g)
Servings Per Container 6

Amount Per Serving

Calories 120 Calories from Fat 10

% Daily Value*

Total Fat 1g	2%
Saturated Fat 0g	0%
Trans Fat 0g	
Cholesterol 0mg	0%
Sodium 260mg	11%
Total Carbohydrate 27g	9%
Dietary Fiber 8g	32%
Sugars 17g	
Protein 3g	

Vitamin A 40% • Vitamin C 90%
Calcium 6% • Iron 10%

*Percent Daily Values are based on a 2,000 calorie diet. Your daily values may be higher or lower depending on your calorie needs:

		Calories:	2,000	2,500
Total Fat	Less than		65g	80g
Saturated Fat	Less than		20g	25g
Cholesterol	Less than		300mg	300mg
Sodium	Less than		2,400mg	2,400mg
Total Carbohydrate			300g	375g
Dietary Fiber			25g	30g

Calories per gram:
Fat 9 • Carbohydrate 4 • Protein 4

- Add small white beans to increase the fiber and protein content.
- Apple cider vinegar for the seasoned rice vinegar (you may need to add more salt to enhance the flavor).
- Use diced tomatoes and tomato paste in place of the tomato sauce.

Thanks to: Jill Burns, R.D.

Category: Vegetables

APPETIZERS

Note: some of the dips have no portion sizes in the nutrition labels. They should be used sparingly if they have a high salt content.

Dippables - beyond carrots and celery sticks

apples	peaches	broccoli	green beans	red onions
bananas	pears	cauliflower	jicama	scallions
dried apricots	tangerines	celery hearts	mushrooms	spinach
grapefruit	baby carrots	cherry tomatoes	pea pods	yellow squash
grapes	baby onions	cucumbers	radicchio	yellow tomatoes
oranges	bell peppers	endive	radishes	

CHILES RELLENOS APPETIZERS

A low fat version of the traditional calorie-laden favorite.

Makes 10 servings

Ingredients:

3	cans	whole green chiles (4 oz.)
8	oz.	non-fat cheddar cheese, grated
8	oz	non-fat jack cheese, grated
½	cup	egg substitute
2	Tbsp	flour
¼	cup	evaporated skim milk or regular skim milk
8	oz	unsalted tomato sauce (see page 371, 380, 383)

Preparation:

- Preheat oven to 350°F.
- Wash chiles, remove seeds, pat dry with paper towel.
- Sprinkle small amount of the cheese on an 11 x 8 inch baking pan.
- Layer half of the chiles and half of the cheese. Repeat.
- Save some of the cheese (½ cup or more) for topping after baking.
- Mix egg substitute, flour and milk together in a small bowl until smooth. Pour over the chiles and cheese.
- Bake uncovered for 30 minutes. Remove from oven and spread with tomato sauce. Use just enough to cover nicely.
- Sprinkle with reserved grated cheese.
- Return to oven for 15 minutes. Serve hot as an entree.
- When cold, cut into squares for an appetizer. Eat and enjoy.

Thanks to: Lew and Dorothy Watkins, Group 2

Category: Snacks/Mexican/Appetizers

Nutrition Facts

Serving Size 1/10 recipe (122g)
Servings Per Container 10

Amount Per Serving

Calories 100 — Calories from Fat 0

% Daily Value*

Total Fat 0g	0%
Saturated Fat 0g	0%
Trans Fat 0g	
Cholesterol 5mg	2%
Sodium 490mg	20%
Total Carbohydrate 8g	3%
Dietary Fiber 1g	4%
Sugars 3g	
Protein 16g	

Vitamin A 10% • Vitamin C 25%
Calcium 50% • Iron 2%

*Percent Daily Values are based on a 2,000 calorie diet. Your daily values may be higher or lower depending on your calorie needs:

		Calories:	2,000	2,500
Total Fat	Less than		65g	80g
Saturated Fat	Less than		20g	25g
Cholesterol	Less than		300mg	300mg
Sodium	Less than		2,400mg	2,400mg
Total Carbohydrate			300g	375g
Dietary Fiber			25g	30g

Calories per gram:
Fat 9 • Carbohydrate 4 • Protein 4

DEVILED EGGS

This clever recipe swap loses all the cholesterol found in egg yolks.

Ingredients:

1	dozen	hard boiled eggs, halved (discard yolks)
2	servings	instant mashed potatoes
4	Tbsp	sweet pickles, finely chopped
1	Tbsp	yellow prepared mustard
4	Tbsp	sweet pickle juice
1	Tbsp	celery seeds

Preparation:

- Prepare the instant potatoes enough for 2 servings, omitting margarine.
- Mix in pickles, mustard and pickle juice.
- Place in refrigerator for 30 minutes for flavors to blend.
- Taste and add more pickles, mustard or pickle juice according to your taste preference, mixing well.
- Fill egg white halves with mixture and sprinkle with celery seeds.
- Keep refrigerated.

Thanks to: Josie and Al Davidson

Category: Appetizers

Nutrition Facts

Serving Size 1 egg half (47g)
Servings Per Container 24

Amount Per Serving

Calories 35 Calories from Fat 0

% Daily Value*

Total Fat 0g	0%
Saturated Fat 0g	0%
Trans Fat 0g	
Cholesterol 0mg	0%
Sodium 85mg	4%
Total Carbohydrate 4g	1%
Dietary Fiber 0g	0%
Sugars 1g	
Protein 4g	

Vitamin A 0% • Vitamin C 0%
Calcium 2% • Iron 2%

*Percent Daily Values are based on a 2,000 calorie diet. Your daily values may be higher or lower depending on your calorie needs:

	Calories:	2,000	2,500
Total Fat	Less than	65g	80g
Saturated Fat	Less than	20g	25g
Cholesterol	Less than	300mg	300mg
Sodium	Less than	2,400mg	2,400mg
Total Carbohydrate		300g	375g
Dietary Fiber		25g	30g

Calories per gram:
Fat 9 • Carbohydrate 4 • Protein 4

EGGPLANT GARLIC DIP

Just like Baba Ghanoush, a traditional Middle Eastern dish.

Makes 2 cups

Ingredients:

2	med	eggplants, ends trimmed
1	tsp	olive oil
½	tsp	salt
½	tsp	pepper
½	tsp	cumin
4-8	cloves	garlic, minced
2	Tbsp	lemon juice
		fresh parsley, chopped

Preparation:

- Preheat oven 450°F.
- Cut eggplant in half lengthwise. Score flat side several times with deep gashes. Sprinkle with olive oil.
- Rub in salt, pepper and cumin.
- Bake on trays until soft and partly charred, about 1 hour.
- Let cool. Scrape out pulp, roughly chop, and put in bowl.
- Add garlic, olive oil, and lemon juice and mix well.
- Garnish with parsley.
- Spread on your choice fat-free saltines, thin slices toasted French bread.

Thanks to: Laurie Crider-Vanpal, Group 29

Category: Appetizers

Nutrition Facts

Serving Size (1144g)
Servings Per Container

Amount Per Serving

Calories 330   Calories from Fat 50

	% Daily Value*
Total Fat 6g	9%
Saturated Fat 0.5g	3%
Trans Fat 0g	
Cholesterol 0mg	0%
Sodium 1190mg	50%
Total Carbohydrate 66g	22%
Dietary Fiber 38g	152%
Sugars 26g	
Protein 11g	

Vitamin A 6%	•	Vitamin C 60%	
Calcium 10%	•	Iron 15%	

*Percent Daily Values are based on a 2,000 calorie diet. Your daily values may be higher or lower depending on your calorie needs:

		Calories:	2,000	2,500
Total Fat	Less than		65g	80g
Saturated Fat	Less than		20g	25g
Cholesterol	Less than		300mg	300mg
Sodium	Less than		2,400mg	2,400mg
Total Carbohydrate			300g	375g
Dietary Fiber			25g	30g

Calories per gram:
   Fat 9 • Carbohydrate 4 • Protein 4

Note: Serving Size on Label applies to entire recipe.

Hummus with Garlic

Hummus is a good protein alternative for a sandwich spread and can also be used as a dip.

Ingredients:

2	cloves	garlic
1	Tbsp	fresh parsley
1½	cups	garbanzo beans, cooked
2	Tbsp	lemon juice
		salt, cumin, paprika to taste

Preparation:

- Blend garlic and parsley together in food processor.
- Add in beans and blend together.
- Add lemon juice and spices to taste.
- Add liquid (bean water) until desired consistency.
- Serve as dip for pita bread, cut or torn into chip-sized pieces.

Nutrition Facts

Serving Size (429g)
Servings Per Container

Amount Per Serving

Calories 410	Calories from Fat 30

% Daily Value*

Total Fat 3.5g	5%
Saturated Fat 0g	0%
Trans Fat 0g	
Cholesterol 0mg	0%
Sodium 90mg	4%
Total Carbohydrate 70g	23%
Dietary Fiber 15g	60%
Sugars 3g	
Protein 21g	

Vitamin A 6%	•	Vitamin C 25%
Calcium 15%	•	Iron 25%

*Percent Daily Values are based on a 2,000 calorie diet. Your daily values may be higher or lower depending on your calorie needs:

		Calories:	2,000	2,500
Total Fat	Less than		65g	80g
Saturated Fat	Less than		20g	25g
Cholesterol	Less than		300mg	300mg
Sodium	Less than		2,400mg	2,400mg
Total Carbohydrate			300g	375g
Dietary Fiber			25g	30g

Calories per gram:
  Fat 9 • Carbohydrate 4 • Protein 4

Category: Appetizer

Note: Serving Size on Label applies to entire recipe.

Hummus with Tahini

This hummus recipes calls for the more traditional ingredient, tahini, or sesame paste. Tahini increases the fat content but it is a healthy fat.

Ingredients:

1½	cup	garbanzo beans, cooked (reserve liquid after cooking).
2-3	Tbsp	lemon juice, according to taste
1	large	garlic clove, crushed
¼	tsp	cumin
2	tsp	tahini (sesame paste without oil)
¼	tsp	curry powder (optional)
		salt and pepper to taste
		non-fat milk (optional)
¼	tsp	paprika

Preparation:

- Put garbanzos, lemon juice, garlic, cumin, sesame paste, and ½ cup of drained liquid into blender.
- Whirl until consistency of heavy batter; add more garbanzo liquid if needed.
- Add salt, pepper and curry powder to taste
- For a more creamy taste, substitute a little non-fat milk for liquid as the final addition.
- Put into fridge (covered) to allow flavors blend.
- Sprinkle paprika before serving.

Thanks to: Tissa and Mary Kappagoda

Category: Appetizer

Nutrition Facts

Serving Size (283g)
Servings Per Container

Amount Per Serving

Calories 430   Calories from Fat 100

% Daily Value*

Total Fat 11g	17%
Saturated Fat 1.5g	8%
Trans Fat 0g	
Cholesterol 0mg	0%
Sodium 310mg	13%
Total Carbohydrate 61g	20%
Dietary Fiber 17g	68%
Sugars 11g	
Protein 21g	

Vitamin A 2%	•	Vitamin C 30%
Calcium 25%	•	Iron 45%

*Percent Daily Values are based on a 2,000 calorie diet. Your daily values may be higher or lower depending on your calorie needs:

	Calories:	2,000	2,500
Total Fat	Less than	65g	80g
Saturated Fat	Less than	20g	25g
Cholesterol	Less than	300mg	300mg
Sodium	Less than	2,400mg	2,400mg
Total Carbohydrate		300g	375g
Dietary Fiber		25g	30g

Calories per gram:
   Fat 9 • Carbohydrate 4 • Protein 4

Note: Serving Size on Label applies to entire recipe.

Italian Style Veggie Dip

Makes ~ 3 cups

Ingredients:

2	cups	fat-free sour cream
½	cup	fat-free mayonnaise
⅓	cup	red peppers, roasted and chopped
¼	cup	fresh basil, chopped
¼	cup	green onion, chopped
1	Tbsp	lemon juice
1½	tsp	Mrs. Dash Tomato, Basil and Garlic Blend

Preparation:

- Combine all ingredients in a small bowl.
- Mix well to blend.
- Serve with fresh crudités and dippers.

Source: *Raley's*

Category: Appetizers

Nutrition Facts

Serving Size (769g)
Servings Per Container

Amount Per Serving

Calories 580   Calories from Fat 30

% Daily Value*

Total Fat 3.5g	5%
Saturated Fat 0.5g	3%
Trans Fat 0g	
Cholesterol 60mg	20%
Sodium 2440mg	102%
Total Carbohydrate 111g	37%
Dietary Fiber 4g	16%
Sugars 12g	
Protein 19g	

Vitamin A 70% • Vitamin C 30%
Calcium 70% • Iron 8%

*Percent Daily Values are based on a 2,000 calorie diet. Your daily values may be higher or lower depending on your calorie needs:

		Calories:	2,000	2,500
Total Fat	Less than		65g	80g
Saturated Fat	Less than		20g	25g
Cholesterol	Less than		300mg	300mg
Sodium	Less than		2,400mg	2,400mg
Total Carbohydrate			300g	375g
Dietary Fiber			25g	30g

Calories per gram:
Fat 9 • Carbohydrate 4 • Protein 4

Note: Serving Size on Label applies to entire recipe.

LAYERED MEXICAN DIP

Perfect for Super Bowl Sunday!

Ingredients:

1	large	onion, diced
3	cloves	garlic, or more to taste
3	Tbsp	fat-free chicken broth
3	cups	fat-free refried beans (see page 174)
1	can	green chiles, chopped (4 oz)
2	cups	fat-free mozzarella cheese, grated
1	cup	fat-free cheddar cheese, grated
1	jar	taco sauce (16 oz)
1	cup	fat-free sour cream

Preparation:

- Preheat oven to 400°F.
- Sauté diced onion and garlic in chicken broth.
- Stir in refried beans.
- Spread into a 9 x 13 inch casserole dish.
- Sprinkle green chilies over top of bean mixture.
- Spread ½ of cheese over this.
- Pour taco sauce over cheese.
- Sprinkle remaining cheese on top.
- Bake for 20-25 minutes
- Cool slightly and spoon sour cream to make a cross on top of casserole.
- Serve with fat-free tortilla chips or other dippables.

Thanks to: Doug Cort, Ph.D.

Category: Appetizers

Nutrition Facts

Serving Size (2203g)
Servings Per Container

Amount Per Serving

Calories 1760   Calories from Fat 0

	% Daily Value*
Total Fat 0g	0%
Saturated Fat 0g	0%
Trans Fat 0g	
Cholesterol 85mg	28%
Sodium 8590mg	358%
Total Carbohydrate 228g	76%
Dietary Fiber 41g	164%
Sugars 51g	
Protein 155g	

Vitamin A 60% • Vitamin C 35%
Calcium 360% • Iron 70%

*Percent Daily Values are based on a 2,000 calorie diet. Your daily values may be higher or lower depending on your calorie needs:

	Calories:	2,000	2,500
Total Fat	Less than	65g	80g
Saturated Fat	Less than	20g	25g
Cholesterol	Less than	300mg	300mg
Sodium	Less than	2,400mg	2,400mg
Total Carbohydrate		300g	375g
Dietary Fiber		25g	30g

Calories per gram:
  Fat 9 • Carbohydrate 4 • Protein 4

Note: Serving Size on Label applies to entire recipe.

Mexican Bean Dip

A lighter 7-layer dip. Try Peamole as another layer too.

Ingredients:

1½	cups	fat-free refried beans (see page 174)
8	oz	fat-free cream cheese
8	oz	fat-free sour cream
1	pkg	taco seasoning
½	cup	lettuce, chopped
½	cup	fat-free cheese, grated
½	cup	tomatoes, chopped

Preparation:

- Spread beans neatly on bottom of attractive casserole or other bowl.
- Mix cream cheese, sour cream and taco seasoning together and then spread on top of beans.
- Top with lettuce, cheese, and tomatoes.
- Enjoy with baked fat-free tortilla chips or other dippables.

Category: Appetizers

Nutrition Facts

Serving Size (1156g)
Servings Per Container

Amount Per Serving

Calories 1100   Calories from Fat 50

% Daily Value*

Total Fat 6g	9%
Saturated Fat 1.5g	8%
Trans Fat 0g	
Cholesterol 75mg	25%
Sodium 7150mg	298%
Total Carbohydrate 160g	53%
Dietary Fiber 23g	92%
Sugars 42g	
Protein 93g	

Vitamin A 80%	•	Vitamin C 20%
Calcium 190%	•	Iron 40%

*Percent Daily Values are based on a 2,000 calorie diet. Your daily values may be higher or lower depending on your calorie needs:

		Calories:	2,000	2,500
Total Fat		Less than	65g	80g
Saturated Fat		Less than	20g	25g
Cholesterol		Less than	300mg	300mg
Sodium		Less than	2,400mg	2,400mg
Total Carbohydrate			300g	375g
Dietary Fiber			25g	30g

Calories per gram:
 Fat 9 • Carbohydrate 4 • Protein 4

Note: Serving Size on Label applies to entire recipe.

PEAMOLE

Amazing substitute for guacamole. Eat with baked tortilla chips or crackers or use as a sandwich spread instead of mayonnaise. Could also use this as another layer on a layered Mexican bean dip.

Ingredients:

1½	cups	green peas, cooked
½	jar	green salsa
1	can	green chiles (4 oz)
1	clove	garlic, minced
¼	cup	cilantro, chopped
1	med	tomato, diced

Preparation:

- Put peas, salsa, chiles, garlic and cilantro in blender and blend until desired consistency.
- Pour into a dish and stir in tomato.
- Refrigerate for better flavor.

Nutrition Facts

Serving Size (595g)
Servings Per Container

Amount Per Serving

Calories 280   Calories from Fat 15

	% Daily Value*
Total Fat 1.5g	2%
Saturated Fat 0g	0%
Trans Fat 0g	
Cholesterol 0mg	0%
Sodium 1180mg	49%
Total Carbohydrate 52g	17%
Dietary Fiber 14g	56%
Sugars 24g	
Protein 15g	

Vitamin A 40% • Vitamin C 230%

Calcium 10% • Iron 25%

*Percent Daily Values are based on a 2,000 calorie diet. Your daily values may be higher or lower depending on your calorie needs:

		Calories:	2,000	2,500
Total Fat	Less than		65g	80g
Saturated Fat	Less than		20g	25g
Cholesterol	Less than		300mg	300mg
Sodium	Less than		2,400mg	2,400mg
Total Carbohydrate			300g	375g
Dietary Fiber			25g	30g

Calories per gram:
   Fat 9 • Carbohydrate 4 • Protein 4

Category: Appetizers

Note: Serving Size on Label applies to entire recipe.

Raspberry Lemonade Fruit Dip

Makes 2 cups

Ingredients:

6	Tbsp	thawed raspberry lemonade concentrate (undiluted)
16	oz	fat-free vanilla yogurt

Preparation:

- In a medium bowl, stir yogurt and lemonade concentrate together.
- Serve with fresh fruit.

Source: *Raley's*

Category: Appetizers/Snacks

Nutrition Facts

Serving Size (563g)
Servings Per Container

Amount Per Serving

Calories 650 — Calories from Fat 5

	% Daily Value*
Total Fat 1g	2%
Saturated Fat 0g	0%
Trans Fat 0g	
Cholesterol 10mg	3%
Sodium 370mg	15%
Total Carbohydrate 134g	45%
Dietary Fiber 0g	0%
Sugars 129g	
Protein 24g	

Vitamin A 20% • Vitamin C 40%

Calcium 90% • Iron 0%

*Percent Daily Values are based on a 2,000 calorie diet. Your daily values may be higher or lower depending on your calorie needs:

		Calories:	2,000	2,500
Total Fat	Less than		65g	80g
Saturated Fat	Less than		20g	25g
Cholesterol	Less than		300mg	300mg
Sodium	Less than		2,400mg	2,400mg
Total Carbohydrate			300g	375g
Dietary Fiber			25g	30g

Calories per gram:
  Fat 9 • Carbohydrate 4 • Protein 4

Note: Serving Size on Label applies to entire recipe.

Spicy Bean Dip

Be adventurous. Try the recipe to make your own non-fat refried beans and then use them in this dip.

Ingredients:

1½	cup	fat-free refried beans (see page 174)
¾	cup	mild fresh salsa (or to taste)
3	cloves	garlic, minced

Preparation:

- Mix and let flavors blend for a few hours.
- Serve with baked fat-free tortilla chips and other dippers.

Thanks to: Mary and Jack Lobenberg, Group 3

Category: Appetizer

Nutrition Facts

Serving Size (228g)
Servings Per Container

Amount Per Serving

Calories 180 — Calories from Fat 0

	% Daily Value*
Total Fat 0g	0%
Saturated Fat 0g	0%
Trans Fat 0g	
Cholesterol 0mg	0%
Sodium 290mg	12%
Total Carbohydrate 60g	20%
Dietary Fiber 32g	128%
Sugars 5g	
Protein 17g	

Vitamin A 15% • Vitamin C 25%
Calcium 6% • Iron 6%

*Percent Daily Values are based on a 2,000 calorie diet. Your daily values may be higher or lower depending on your calorie needs:

	Calories:	2,000	2,500
Total Fat	Less than	65g	80g
Saturated Fat	Less than	20g	25g
Cholesterol	Less than	300mg	300mg
Sodium	Less than	2,400mg	2,400mg
Total Carbohydrate		300g	375g
Dietary Fiber		25g	30g

Calories per gram:
  Fat 9 • Carbohydrate 4 • Protein 4

Note: Serving Size on Label applies to entire recipe.

Spinach Dip

This recipe also works well if you substitute ½ to 1 package of dried vegetable soup mix for the spices (omitting garlic, mustard, tarragon, and pepper), but sodium content will be higher. For variety, add in chopped celery.

Ingredients:

2	pkg	frozen spinach, chopped (10 oz. each)
1	cup	green onions, finely minced
1	can	water chestnuts (8 oz)
1	cup	non-fat mayonnaise
1	cup	non-fat sour cream or non-fat yogurt
1-4	cloves	garlic, finely minced (to taste)
1	tsp	dry mustard
¾	tsp	dry tarragon, crushed
½	tsp	black pepper
1	loaf	sourdough bread, hollowed out
		salt to taste (optional)
		fresh vegetables

Preparation:

- Thaw out and squeeze extra water from spinach.
- Mix in green onions.
- Drain and finely chop water chestnuts, mix them in. Set aside.
- Mix together all other ingredients.
- Stir together spinach mixture and dressing.
- Let rest overnight in refrigerator (for best results).
- Serve in hollowed out sourdough loaf with sourdough pieces and fresh vegetables.

Thanks to: Marinda Reed

Category: Appetizers

Nutrition Facts

Serving Size (1551g)
Servings Per Container

Amount Per Serving

Calories 800 — Calories from Fat 80

% Daily Value*

Total Fat 9g	14%
Saturated Fat 1.5g	8%
Trans Fat 0g	
Cholesterol 50mg	17%
Sodium 3290mg	137%
Total Carbohydrate 138g	46%
Dietary Fiber 30g	120%
Sugars 35g	
Protein 27g	

Vitamin A 390% • Vitamin C 60%
Calcium 110% • Iron 45%

*Percent Daily Values are based on a 2,000 calorie diet. Your daily values may be higher or lower depending on your calorie needs:

		Calories:	2,000	2,500
Total Fat		Less than	65g	80g
Saturated Fat		Less than	20g	25g
Cholesterol		Less than	300mg	300mg
Sodium		Less than	2,400mg	2,400mg
Total Carbohydrate			300g	375g
Dietary Fiber			25g	30g

Calories per gram:
  Fat 9 • Carbohydrate 4 • Protein 4

Note: Serving Size on Label applies to entire recipe.

Water-Crisped Corn Tortilla Chips

Yet another suggestion for something to use with the great dip recipes you'll find in this collection.

Ingredients:

12   corn tortillas (6 inch each)
      See page 214 for recipe.

Preparation:

- Preheat oven to 500°F.
- Immerse tortillas one at a time in water. Let drain briefly, then lay flat.
- If desired, sprinkle tops lightly with salt.
- Cut each tortilla into 6 wedges.
- Fill a 10 x 15 inch pan with a single layer of tortilla wedges, salt side up, placed close together (do not overlap).
- Bake for 4 minutes. Turn with a wide spatula, and continue to bake until golden brown and crisp, about 3 more minutes.
- Turn chips out of pan and fill again; repeat until all are baked.
- Serve chips warm or cool.
- Store cool chips airtight at room temperature for up to 2 weeks.

Nutrition Facts

Serving Size 1/6 tortilla (4.5g)
Servings Per Container 72

Amount Per Serving

Calories 10   Calories from Fat 0

	% Daily Value*
Total Fat 0g	0%
Saturated Fat 0g	0%
Trans Fat 0g	
Cholesterol 0mg	0%
Sodium 0mg	0%
Total Carbohydrate 2g	1%
Dietary Fiber 0g	0%
Sugars 0g	
Protein 0g	

Vitamin A --% • Vitamin C --%
Calcium --% • Iron --%

*Percent Daily Values are based on a 2,000 calorie diet. Your daily values may be higher or lower depending on your calorie needs:

		Calories:	2,000	2,500
Total Fat	Less than		65g	80g
Saturated Fat	Less than		20g	25g
Cholesterol	Less than		300mg	300mg
Sodium	Less than		2,400mg	2,400mg
Total Carbohydrate			300g	375g
Dietary Fiber			25g	30g

Calories per gram:
  Fat 9 • Carbohydrate 4 • Protein 4

Category: Appetizers/Snacks/Mexican

Water-Crisped Flour Tortilla Chips

Ingredients:

10   8 inch   whole wheat flour tortillas (fat free)

Preparation:

- Preheat oven to 500°F.
- Immerse tortillas one at a time in water. Let drain briefly, then lay flat.
- If desired, sprinkle tops lightly with salt.
- Cut each tortilla into 8 wedges.
- Fill a 10 x 15 inch pan with a single layer of tortilla wedges, salt side up, placed close together (do not overlap).
- Bake for 4 minutes. Turn with a wide spatula, and continue to bake until golden brown and crisp, about 1 more minute.
- Turn chips out of pan and fill again; repeat until all are baked.
- Serve chips warm or cool.
- Store cool chips airtight at room temperature for up to 2 weeks.

Nutrition Facts

Serving Size 1/8 tortilla (6g)
Servings Per Container 80

Amount Per Serving

Calories 15	Calories from Fat 0

% Daily Value*

Total Fat 0g	0%
Saturated Fat 0g	0%
Trans Fat 0g	
Cholesterol 0mg	0%
Sodium 40mg	2%
Total Carbohydrate 3g	1%
Dietary Fiber 0g	0%
Sugars 0g	
Protein 1g	

Vitamin A --%	Vitamin C --%
Calcium --%	Iron --%

*Percent Daily Values are based on a 2,000 calorie diet. Your daily values may be higher or lower depending on your calorie needs:

		Calories:	2,000	2,500
Total Fat	Less than		65g	80g
Saturated Fat	Less than		20g	25g
Cholesterol	Less than		300mg	300mg
Sodium	Less than		2,400mg	2,400mg
Total Carbohydrate			300g	375g
Dietary Fiber			25g	30g

Calories per gram:
  Fat 9 • Carbohydrate 4 • Protein 4

Category Snacks/Appetizers/Mexican

BAKED PITA TRIANGLES

A healthful suggestion for something to use with the great dip recipes you'll find in this collection.

Ingredients:

6   pitas   (6 inch rounds) split, then quartered to make 48 triangles

Preparation:

- Adjust oven rack to upper-middle position and heat oven to 325°F.
- Place pita triangles directly on the rack.
- Bake until golden brown and completely crisp, about 10 minutes.

Nutrition Facts

Serving Size 1 triangle (8g)
Servings Per Container 48

Amount Per Serving	
Calories 20	Calories from Fat 0

	% Daily Value*
Total Fat 0g	0%
Saturated Fat 0g	0%
Trans Fat --g	
Cholesterol 0mg	0%
Sodium 45mg	2%
Total Carbohydrate 4g	1%
Dietary Fiber 1g	4%
Sugars 0g	
Protein 1g	

Vitamin A 0%	•	Vitamin C 0%
Calcium 0%	•	Iron 2%

*Percent Daily Values are based on a 2,000 calorie diet. Your daily values may be higher or lower depending on your calorie needs:

	Calories:	2,000	2,500
Total Fat	Less than	65g	80g
Saturated Fat	Less than	20g	25g
Cholesterol	Less than	300mg	300mg
Sodium	Less than	2,400mg	2,400mg
Total Carbohydrate		300g	375g
Dietary Fiber		25g	30g

Calories per gram:
  Fat 9 • Carbohydrate 4 • Protein 4

Category Snacks/Appetizers

GOLDEN TOAST ROUNDS

Another dipping suggestion.

Ingredients:

1	long	baguette, sliced a generous ¼ inch thick to make about 48 rounds
1	tsp	olive oil

Preparation:

- Adjust oven rack to upper-middle position and heat oven to 375°F.
- Lay bread rounds on a large wire rack or cookie sheet.
- Brush or drizzle with olive oil-
- Bake until golden and crisp throughout, 10 to 12 minutes.
- If using a cookie sheet, turn over midway.

Category: Snacks

Nutrition Facts

Serving Size 1/4 inch slice (9g)
Servings Per Container 48

Amount Per Serving

Calories 30 — Calories from Fat 0

% Daily Value*

Total Fat 0g	0%
Saturated Fat 0g	0%
Trans Fat 0g	
Cholesterol 0mg	0%
Sodium 70mg	3%
Total Carbohydrate 6g	2%
Dietary Fiber 0g	0%
Sugars 0g	
Protein 1g	

Vitamin A 0% • Vitamin C 0%
Calcium 0% • Iron 2%

*Percent Daily Values are based on a 2,000 calorie diet. Your daily values may be higher or lower depending on your calorie needs:

		Calories:	2,000	2,500
Total Fat	Less than		65g	80g
Saturated Fat	Less than		20g	25g
Cholesterol	Less than		300mg	300mg
Sodium	Less than		2,400mg	2,400mg
Total Carbohydrate			300g	375g
Dietary Fiber			25g	30g

Calories per gram:
Fat 9 • Carbohydrate 4 • Protein 4

Kale Chips

The oil does deliver an added fat, but a clever way to get some nutrition in a chip. Even kids will love this potato chip substitute.

Ingredients:

1	bunch	kale
1	tsp	olive oil
1	tsp	seasoned salt

Preparation:

- Preheat oven to 350°F.
- Line a non-insulated baking sheet with parchment paper.
- Cut stems from kale and tear leaves into bite-sized pieces.
- Wash and thoroughly dry kale, using a salad spinner.
- Drizzle kale with olive oil and sprinkle with seasoned salt.
- Bake for 10-15 minutes until the edges brown but are not burned.

Thanks to: Marie Barone, R.D.

Category: Snacks

Nutrition Facts

Serving Size 1/20 recipe (23g)
Servings Per Container 20

Amount Per Serving

Calories 15   Calories from Fat 5

	% Daily Value*
Total Fat 0g	0%
Saturated Fat 0g	0%
Trans Fat 0g	
Cholesterol 0mg	0%
Sodium 10mg	0%
Total Carbohydrate 2g	1%
Dietary Fiber 0g	0%
Sugars 0g	
Protein 1g	

Vitamin A 70% • Vitamin C 45%
Calcium 4% • Iron 2%

*Percent Daily Values are based on a 2,000 calorie diet. Your daily values may be higher or lower depending on your calorie needs:

		Calories:	2,000	2,500
Total Fat	Less than		65g	80g
Saturated Fat	Less than		20g	25g
Cholesterol	Less than		300mg	300mg
Sodium	Less than		2,400mg	2,400mg
Total Carbohydrate			300g	375g
Dietary Fiber			25g	30g

Calories per gram:
Fat 9 • Carbohydrate 4 • Protein 4

Party Mix

Put into individual snack bags to have on hand for a portion-controlled snack.

Makes 8 servings

Ingredients:

1¼	cups	Cheerios
1¼	cups	Wheat Chex
1¼	cups	Rice Chex
1¼	cups	Corn Chex
2	cups	pretzel sticks
⅓	cup	apple juice
4	tsp	Worcestershire sauce
½	tsp	garlic powder
1	tsp	onion powder

Preparation:

- Combine cereals to make 5 cups, and then add pretzel sticks.
- Combine remaining ingredients and toss with cereals. Mix until all ingredients are damp.
- Place in a shallow non-stick baking pan.
- Bake at 275°F for 1 hour. Stir every 10 minutes.
- Cool before serving.

This can also be made in the microwave by cooking at full power for 6 minutes. Stir every 2 minutes.

Nutrition Facts

Serving Size 1/8 recipe (41g)
Servings Per Container 8

Amount Per Serving

Calories 110 — Calories from Fat 5

	% Daily Value*
Total Fat 0g	0%
Saturated Fat 0g	0%
Trans Fat 0g	
Cholesterol 0mg	0%
Sodium 300mg	13%
Total Carbohydrate 25g	8%
Dietary Fiber 2g	8%
Sugars 3g	
Protein 3g	

Vitamin A 6% • Vitamin C 6%
Calcium 6% • Iron 35%

*Percent Daily Values are based on a 2,000 calorie diet. Your daily values may be higher or lower depending on your calorie needs:

		Calories:	2,000	2,500
Total Fat		Less than	65g	80g
Saturated Fat		Less than	20g	25g
Cholesterol		Less than	300mg	300mg
Sodium		Less than	2,400mg	2,400mg
Total Carbohydrate			300g	375g
Dietary Fiber			25g	30g

Calories per gram:
Fat 9 • Carbohydrate 4 • Protein 4

Thanks to: Roy Kannada, Group 18

Category: Snacks/Appetizers

SPICY GARBANZO NUTS

Wonderful snack. Fill a half-pint mason jar with Spicy Garbanzo Nuts for gifts.

Makes 4 servings ~ ½ cup each

Ingredients:

2	cups	garbanzo beans, cooked and drained
½	tsp	garlic powder
2	tsp	chili powder

Preparation:

- Mix ingredients well on ungreased nonstick baking sheet.
- Bake at 350°F for 45 minutes.
- Remove from baking sheet to let cool.

An unexpected bonus of making this recipe is the wonderful aroma that will fill your kitchen as the garbanzo beans bake. Don't drain the garbanzo beans too well or the spices won't stick to the beans.

Thanks to: Marie Barone, R.D.

Category: Appetizers

Nutrition Facts

Serving Size 1/2 cup (63g)
Servings Per Container 4

Amount Per Serving

Calories 110 — Calories from Fat 15

% Daily Value*

Total Fat 2g	3%
Saturated Fat 0g	0%
Trans Fat 0g	
Cholesterol 0mg	0%
Sodium 25mg	1%
Total Carbohydrate 18g	6%
Dietary Fiber 5g	20%
Sugars 3g	
Protein 6g	

Vitamin A 8% • Vitamin C 2%

Calcium 4% • Iron 10%

*Percent Daily Values are based on a 2,000 calorie diet. Your daily values may be higher or lower depending on your calorie needs:

		Calories:	2,000	2,500
Total Fat	Less than		65g	80g
Saturated Fat	Less than		20g	25g
Cholesterol	Less than		300mg	300mg
Sodium	Less than		2,400mg	2,400mg
Total Carbohydrate			300g	375g
Dietary Fiber			25g	30g

Calories per gram:
  Fat 9 • Carbohydrate 4 • Protein 4

DESSERTS

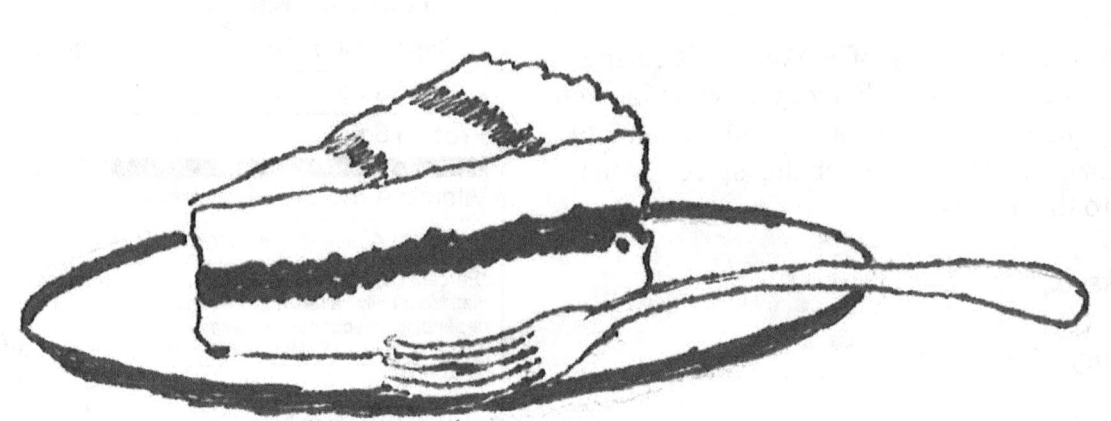

ANGEL FOOD CAKE

So much better than store bought!

Makes 12 servings

Ingredients:

1½	cups	powdered sugar
1	cup	cake flour
1½	cups	egg whites (about 12)
1½	tsp	cream of tartar
1	cup	granulated sugar
1½	tsp	vanilla extract
½	tsp	almond extract
¼	tsp	salt (optional)

Preparation:

- Move oven rack to lowest position. Preheat oven to 375°F.
- Sift powdered sugar and flour together.
- Beat egg whites and cream of tartar until foamy.
- Add granulated sugar, 2 Tbsp at a time, adding vanilla extract, almond extract and salt with last addition of sugar.
- Beat until stiff and glossy—DO NOT UNDERBEAT.
- Sprinkle sugar and flour mixture, ¼ cup at a time, into egg whites, folding in until mixture disappears.
- Pour batter into ungreased 10x4 inch tube pan, and bake for 30-35 minutes.
- When cake is done, turn upside down onto a glass bottle or funnel—let hang for about 2 hours.
- Remove from pan. Use a serrated knife to cut slices.

Thanks to: Clara and Jay Massman

Category: Desserts

Nutrition Facts

Serving Size 1/12 of recipe (77g)
Servings Per Container 12

Amount Per Serving

Calories 180   Calories from Fat 0

% Daily Value*

Total Fat 0g	0%
Saturated Fat 0g	0%
Trans Fat 0g	
Cholesterol 0mg	0%
Sodium 105mg	4%
Total Carbohydrate 40g	13%
Dietary Fiber 2g	8%
Sugars 32g	
Protein 5g	

Vitamin A 0% • Vitamin C 0%
Calcium 0% • Iron 2%

*Percent Daily Values are based on a 2,000 calorie diet. Your daily values may be higher or lower depending on your calorie needs:

	Calories:	2,000	2,500
Total Fat	Less than	65g	80g
Saturated Fat	Less than	20g	25g
Cholesterol	Less than	300mg	300mg
Sodium	Less than	2,400mg	2,400mg
Total Carbohydrate		300g	375g
Dietary Fiber		25g	30g

Calories per gram:
  Fat 9 • Carbohydrate 4 • Protein 4

ANGEL LEMON CAKE.

This makes a good substitute for when the craving for lemon meringue pie strikes.

Makes 12 servings

Ingredients:

1		angel food cake
1	package	lemon pudding mix (fat-free)
½	cup	egg substitute

Glaze (optional):

| ¼ | cup | powdered sugar |
| 1½ | tsp | lemon juice |

Preparation:

- Prepare lemon pudding per package directions, substituting egg substitute for egg yolks.
- Cut angel food cake horizontally into 2-3 layers.
- Reassemble cake, placing slightly cooled pudding in between layers.
- Combine powdered sugar and lemon juice for glaze; drizzle over cake.
- Cut carefully with a serrated knife.

Thanks to: Dianne Hyson, R.D.

Category: Desserts

Nutrition Facts

Serving Size 1/2 recipe (95g)
Servings Per Container 12

Amount Per Serving

Calories 210 — Calories from Fat 5

% Daily Value*

Total Fat 0g	0%
Saturated Fat 0g	0%
Trans Fat 0g	
Cholesterol 0mg	0%
Sodium 160mg	7%
Total Carbohydrate 48g	16%
Dietary Fiber 2g	8%
Sugars 33g	
Protein 6g	

Vitamin A 2% • Vitamin C 0%
Calcium 2% • Iron 2%

*Percent Daily Values are based on a 2,000 calorie diet. Your daily values may be higher or lower depending on your calorie needs:

		Calories:	2,000	2,500
Total Fat	Less than		65g	80g
Saturated Fat	Less than		20g	25g
Cholesterol	Less than		300mg	300mg
Sodium	Less than		2,400mg	2,400mg
Total Carbohydrate			300g	375g
Dietary Fiber			25g	30g

Calories per gram:
 Fat 9 • Carbohydrate 4 • Protein 4

Apple Cake

Prune puree is a good substitute for fat in a baked recipe.

Makes 12 servings

Ingredients:

1	cup	sugar
1½	cups	flour
¼	cup	egg substitute or 2 egg whites
½	cup	prune puree
1	tsp	baking powder
¾	tsp	cinnamon
½	tsp	salt
2	cups	apples, chopped
¼	cup	walnuts, chopped

Topping:

½	tsp	cinnamon
2	Tbsp	sugar

Preparation:

- Preheat oven to 350° F.
- Spray an 8 x 8 inch pan, lightly flour.
- In large mixing bowl, combine sugar, egg and prune puree. Mix on high speed for 2 minutes. Fold in flour, baking soda, cinnamon and salt. Mix until flour is moist.
- Fold in chopped apples and walnuts.
- Pour batter into prepared pan. Sprinkle the top with the sugar and cinnamon mixture. Bake 45-55 minutes until toothpick inserted in center of cake comes out clean.
- Cool cake in pan on rack

NOTE: Prune puree - Combine 1⅓ cups (8 oz pkg.) pitted prunes and 6 tbsp hot water in container of food processor; puree until smooth. Makes about 1 cup. Keep refrigerated for up to 2 months in tightly sealed container. You could also use a 4 oz. jar of baby food prune puree.

Thanks to: Jack and Charlene Phillips

Category: Desserts

Nutrition Facts

Serving Size 1/12 recipe (71g)
Servings Per Container 12

Amount Per Serving

Calories 170 Calories from Fat 15

	% Daily Value*
Total Fat 2g	3%
Saturated Fat 0g	0%
Trans Fat 0g	
Cholesterol 0mg	0%
Sodium 160mg	7%
Total Carbohydrate 38g	13%
Dietary Fiber 2g	8%
Sugars 21g	
Protein 3g	

Vitamin A 6% • Vitamin C 2%
Calcium 2% • Iron 8%

*Percent Daily Values are based on a 2,000 calorie diet. Your daily values may be higher or lower depending on your calorie needs:

	Calories:	2,000	2,500
Total Fat	Less than	65g	80g
Saturated Fat	Less than	20g	25g
Cholesterol	Less than	300mg	300mg
Sodium	Less than	2,400mg	2,400mg
Total Carbohydrate		300g	375g
Dietary Fiber		25g	30g

Calories per gram:
 Fat 9 • Carbohydrate 4 • Protein 4

APPLE CHERRY CRISP

You can alter the fruit filling to reflect which fruits are in season. Pears, peaches, nectarines, raspberries, blueberries, and strawberries are all good choices for crisp. Use a total of 6 cups of prepared fruit.

Makes 8 servings

Ingredients:

4	cups	apples, peeled and sliced
2	cups	pitted fresh or frozen cherries, sweet or tart
½	cup	brown sugar
½	tsp	ground cinnamon
1	tsp	quick-cooking tapioca (not pearl tapioca)

Crisp Topping:

1½	cup	rolled oats or Grape-Nuts cereal
¼	cup	white flour, unbleached
½	cup	brown sugar
½	tsp	ground cinnamon
1		egg white
1	Tbsp	canola oil
1	tsp	vanilla extract
2	Tbsp	apple or orange juice, unsweetened

Preparation:

- Preheat oven to 350°F
- In a bowl, mix together fruit, brown sugar, cinnamon, and tapioca.
- Pour fruit evenly into a 10 inch pie pan or a 9 inch square baking dish and set aside.
- Combine all remaining ingredients for Crisp Topping. Carefully spread the topping over the fruit.
- Cover and bake for 20 minutes, then uncover and continue to bake for another 20 to 30 minutes, until the fruit is soft and bubbly and the topping is crisp and golden.

Thanks to: Ginny Goodrow, Group 25

Category: Desserts

Nutrition Facts

Serving Size 1/8 recipe (162g)
Servings Per Container 8

Amount Per Serving

Calories 280   Calories from Fat 25

% Daily Value*

Total Fat 2.5g	4%
Saturated Fat 0g	0%
Trans Fat 0g	
Cholesterol 0mg	0%
Sodium 125mg	5%
Total Carbohydrate 63g	21%
Dietary Fiber 4g	16%
Sugars 40g	
Protein 4g	

Vitamin A 8% • Vitamin C 6%
Calcium 4% • Iron 50%

*Percent Daily Values are based on a 2,000 calorie diet. Your daily values may be higher or lower depending on your calorie needs:

		Calories:	2,000	2,500
Total Fat	Less than		65g	80g
Saturated Fat	Less than		20g	25g
Cholesterol	Less than		300mg	300mg
Sodium	Less than		2,400mg	2,400mg
Total Carbohydrate			300g	375g
Dietary Fiber			25g	30g

Calories per gram:
  Fat 9 • Carbohydrate 4 • Protein 4

APPLE NUT TORTE

This recipe can be made in advance and frozen. Can be doubled and quadrupled, as seconds are always requested.

Makes 8 servings

Ingredients:

¾	cup	sugar
¼	cup	egg substitute
½	cup	flour
½	tsp	salt
1	tsp	baking powder
½	cup	apples, chopped
2	tsp	nuts such as walnuts or almonds, chopped (optional, but a few finely chopped almonds enhances the flavor)*
1	tsp	almond extract

Preparation:

- Preheat oven to 375°F.
- Mix all ingredients and put in a 9x9 inch non-stick pan. Bake for 35-40 minutes, or until the torte begins to pull away from the sides of the pan.

Note: 2 tsp of nuts counts as approximately 1 added tsp of fat

Thanks to: Connie LaVenturier, Group 2

Category Desserts

Nutrition Facts

Serving Size 1/8 recipe (46g)
Servings Per Container 8

Amount Per Serving

Calories 120   Calories from Fat 10

% Daily Value*

Total Fat 1.5g	2%
Saturated Fat 0g	0%
Trans Fat 0g	
Cholesterol 0mg	0%
Sodium 230mg	10%
Total Carbohydrate 27g	9%
Dietary Fiber 1g	4%
Sugars 20g	
Protein 2g	

Vitamin A 0% • Vitamin C 0%
Calcium 2% • Iron 4%

*Percent Daily Values are based on a 2,000 calorie diet. Your daily values may be higher or lower depending on your calorie needs:

		Calories:	2,000	2,500
Total Fat	Less than		65g	80g
Saturated Fat	Less than		20g	25g
Cholesterol	Less than		300mg	300mg
Sodium	Less than		2,400mg	2,400mg
Total Carbohydrate			300g	375g
Dietary Fiber			25g	30g

Calories per gram:
  Fat 9 • Carbohydrate 4 • Protein 4

Apple-Cot Cobbler

Grape Nuts cereal makes a nice crunchy topping without added fat.

Makes 8 servngs

Ingredients:

6	large	apples
2	Tbsp	lemon juice
2	cups	apricots, dried, halved
3	Tbsp	tapioca
2	cups	apple juice, unsweetened
½	tsp	ground nutmeg
½	tsp	ground cinnamon
1	cup	grape nuts cereal

Preparation:

- Peel, core, thinly slice apples and place in saucepan with lemon juice and dried apricots.
- Soak tapioca with apple juice to soften.
- Add juice to fruit with spices.
- Mix and bring to a boil, lower heat. Stir and cook until all fruit is cooked.
- Pour into serving dish.
- Sprinkle cereal over top before serving.

Thanks to: Phylllis Quinn, Group 25

Category: Desserts

Nutrition Facts

Serving Size 1/8 recipe (279g)
Servings Per Container 8

Amount Per Serving

Calories 250   Calories from Fat 5

	% Daily Value*
Total Fat 1g	2%
Saturated Fat 0g	0%
Trans Fat 0g	
Cholesterol 0mg	0%
Sodium 80mg	3%
Total Carbohydrate 63g	21%
Dietary Fiber 6g	24%
Sugars 42g	
Protein 3g	

Vitamin A 30% • Vitamin C 15%

Calcium 4% • Iron 35%

*Percent Daily Values are based on a 2,000 calorie diet. Your daily values may be higher or lower depending on your calorie needs:

	Calories:	2,000	2,500
Total Fat	Less than	65g	80g
Saturated Fat	Less than	20g	25g
Cholesterol	Less than	300mg	300mg
Sodium	Less than	2,400mg	2,400mg
Total Carbohydrate		300g	375g
Dietary Fiber		25g	30g

Calories per gram:
  Fat 9 • Carbohydrate 4 • Protein 4

BANANA CAKE

Banana is another fruit that can be substituted for fat in baking.

Makes 16 servings

Ingredients:

3	cups	flour
½	cup	brown sugar
1	Tbsp	baking powder
1	tsp	baking soda
1	tsp	cinnamon
¼	tsp	ground nutmeg
8		egg whites
2	cups	banana, mashed (~4 ripe)
1⅓	cup	skim milk
¾	cup	light corn syrup
⅔	cup	dried apricots, snipped into ¼ inch pieces

Preparation:

- Preheat oven to 400° F. Lightly spray 13 x 9 inch baking pan with spray oil. Dust with flour.
- In medium bowl, combine all dry ingredients. Mix together thoroughly.
- In another bowl, beat egg whites until frothy. Stir in bananas, milk, and corn syrup.
- Add dry ingredients to liquid. Mix thoroughly.
- Fold in dried apricots.
- Pour into prepared baking pan.
- Bake for 25 minutes, until toothpick inserted into middle comes out clean.

Category: Desserts

Nutrition Facts

Serving Size 1/16 recipe (117g)
Servings Per Container 16

Amount Per Serving

Calories 220 — Calories from Fat 5

% Daily Value*

Total Fat 0g	0%
Saturated Fat 0g	0%
Trans Fat 0g	
Cholesterol 0mg	0%
Sodium 230mg	10%
Total Carbohydrate 49g	16%
Dietary Fiber 2g	8%
Sugars 18g	
Protein 5g	

Vitamin A 2% • Vitamin C 4%

Calcium 6% • Iron 8%

*Percent Daily Values are based on a 2,000 calorie diet. Your daily values may be higher or lower depending on your calorie needs:

	Calories:	2,000	2,500
Total Fat	Less than	65g	80g
Saturated Fat	Less than	20g	25g
Cholesterol	Less than	300mg	300mg
Sodium	Less than	2,400mg	2,400mg
Total Carbohydrate		300g	375g
Dietary Fiber		25g	30g

Calories per gram:
Fat 9 • Carbohydrate 4 • Protein 4

BLUEBERRY BREAD PUDDING

To prevent spilling hot water when transferring pans to the oven, it is safer to add the hot water after placing the pans in the oven.

Makes 16 servings

Ingredients:

2	cups	skim milk
1	cup	egg substitute
⅔	cup	sugar
1	tsp	vanilla extract
¼	tsp	ground cinnamon
8	slices	bread, cubed (about 4 cups)
1	cup	blueberries, fresh or frozen
		hot water

Preparation:

- Preheat oven to 350°F. Coat an 8 x 8 x 2 inch baking dish with vegetable oil cooking spray.
- In a large bowl, blend together milk, egg substitute, sugar, vanilla extract and cinnamon; set aside.
- Place cubed bread in bottom of pan.
- Sprinkle berries over bread.
- Pour egg mixture evenly over bread mixture.
- Set this pan in a larger pan. Pour hot water around the baking pan to a depth of 1 inch.
- Bake for 1 hour or until set. Serve warm or cold.

Nutrition Facts

Serving Size 2x2 inch square (76g)
Servings Per Container 16

Amount Per Serving

Calories 90   Calories from Fat 5

% Daily Value*

Total Fat 0.5g	1%
Saturated Fat 0g	0%
Trans Fat 0g	
Cholesterol 0mg	0%
Sodium 90mg	4%
Total Carbohydrate 17g	6%
Dietary Fiber 1g	4%
Sugars 12g	
Protein 4g	

Vitamin A 2% • Vitamin C 2%
Calcium 6% • Iron 4%

*Percent Daily Values are based on a 2,000 calorie diet. Your daily values may be higher or lower depending on your calorie needs:

		Calories:	2,000	2,500
Total Fat	Less than		65g	80g
Saturated Fat	Less than		20g	25g
Cholesterol	Less than		300mg	300mg
Sodium	Less than		2,400mg	2,400mg
Total Carbohydrate			300g	375g
Dietary Fiber			25g	30g

Calories per gram:
  Fat 9 • Carbohydrate 4 • Protein 4

Variation: use Raisin Bread with the blueberries or whole grain bread to increase fiber.

Thanks to: Jane Hue, Group 29

Category: Desserts

Blueberry Cobbler

For variety, substitute blackberries or pitted sweet cherries for the blueberries.

Makes 8 servings

Ingredients:

5	cups	blueberries, fresh (or frozen partially thawed)
¼	cup	sugar
2	Tbsp	sugar
3½	tsp	cornstarch
4	tsp	frozen orange juice concentrate, thawed

Biscuit Topping:

¾	cup	unbleached flour
2	Tbsp	unbleached flour
¼	cup	oat bran
⅓	cup	sugar
1¾	tsp	baking powder
½	cup	non-fat buttermilk
1½	tsp	sugar
	pinch	ground cinnamon

Preparation:

- Preheat oven to 375°F. Coat a 2 quart casserole dish with non-stick cooking spray.
- Place berries in a large bowl and set aside.
- Mix sugar and cornstarch well, in a small bowl,.
- Sprinkle the mixture over the fruit, and toss to mix well. (If the fruit is tart you may need to add another couple of Tbsp of sugar.)
- Add juice concentrate and toss to mix well.
- Spread the fruit mixture evenly in the prepared dish. Cover with foil.
- Bake for 30 to 40 minutes, or until hot and bubbly.
- Mix Biscuit Topping ingredients together when filling is hot.
- Drop topping on the hot fruit by spoonfuls. Sprinkle with sugar/cinnamon mixture.
- Bake uncovered for 18 to 20 minutes or until biscuit topping is lightly browned.
- Allow to cool at room temperature for at least 10 minutes before serving warm.

Thanks to: Ginny Goodrow, Group 25

Category: Desserts

Nutrition Facts

Serving Size 1/8 recipe (148g)
Servings Per Container 8

Amount Per Serving

Calories 200 — Calories from Fat 5

% Daily Value*

Total Fat 0.5g	1%
Saturated Fat 0g	0%
Trans Fat 0g	
Cholesterol 0mg	0%
Sodium 130mg	5%
Total Carbohydrate 48g	16%
Dietary Fiber 3g	12%
Sugars 30g	
Protein 3g	

Vitamin A 2%	•	Vitamin C 20%
Calcium 4%	•	Iron 6%

*Percent Daily Values are based on a 2,000 calorie diet. Your daily values may be higher or lower depending on your calorie needs:

		Calories:	2,000	2,500
Total Fat	Less than		65g	80g
Saturated Fat	Less than		20g	25g
Cholesterol	Less than		300mg	300mg
Sodium	Less than		2,400mg	2,400mg
Total Carbohydrate			300g	375g
Dietary Fiber			25g	30g

Calories per gram:
Fat 9 • Carbohydrate 4 • Protein 4

Boston Cream Pie Cake

This is not a pie but really a cake consisting of two layers of cake filled with a vanilla pudding and topped with a chocolate glaze. A bit of work, but worth the trouble.

Makes 15 servings

Ingredients:

1	pkg	light yellow cake mix (18.25 oz)
¼	tsp	baking soda
1⅓	cups	water
4		egg whites
2	tsp	vanilla extract
1	pkg	fat-free instant vanilla pudding mix (3.4 oz)
1⅓	cups	skim milk
½	tsp	vanilla extract
1	cup	powdered sugar
1½	Tbsp	cocoa powder
1½	Tbsp	water
¾	tsp	vanilla extract

Preparation:

- Preheat the oven to 350°F.
- Coat two round 9 inch cake pans with vegetable oil cooking spray. Coat lightly with flour, shaking out any excess. Set aside.
- In a large bowl, combine cake mix and baking soda. Add water, egg whites, and 2 tsp vanilla extract. With an electric mixer, beat on low speed for 30 seconds. Increase speed to medium and beat for 2 minutes. Pour batter into the prepared pans.
- Bake for 30 minutes, or until the cakes pull away from the sides of the pans and spring back when touched lightly in the center.
- Cool in the pan on racks for 10 minutes. Invert the cakes onto the racks and allow to cool completely.
- In a medium bowl, combine pudding mix, milk, and ½ tsp vanilla extract. With an electric mixer, beat on low speed for 2 minutes, or until slightly thickened. Set aside for 5 minutes to thicken.
- Into a medium bowl, sift powdered sugar and cocoa together. Add water and ¾ tsp vanilla extract; mix well. Add a few drops more water, if necessary, for the desired spreading consistency.

Nutrition Facts

Serving Size 1/15 recipe (103g)
Servings Per Container 15

Amount Per Serving

Calories 210   Calories from Fat 20

% Daily Value*

Total Fat 2g	3%
Saturated Fat 0.5g	3%
Trans Fat 0g	
Cholesterol 0mg	0%
Sodium 290mg	12%
Total Carbohydrate 44g	15%
Dietary Fiber 1g	4%
Sugars 14g	
Protein 3g	

Vitamin A 0% • Vitamin C 0%
Calcium 8% • Iron 4%

*Percent Daily Values are based on a 2,000 calorie diet. Your daily values may be higher or lower depending on your calorie needs:

		Calories:	2,000	2,500
Total Fat	Less than		65g	80g
Saturated Fat	Less than		20g	25g
Cholesterol	Less than		300mg	300mg
Sodium	Less than		2,400mg	2,400mg
Total Carbohydrate			300g	375g
Dietary Fiber			25g	30g

Calories per gram:
  Fat 9 • Carbohydrate 4 • Protein 4

- Place 1 cake layer on a serving dish. Spread evenly with the pudding mixture. Top with the remaining cake layer. Spread remaining pudding mixture as glaze evenly over the top.
- Allow to stand for 10 to 14 minutes, or until the glaze sets.

Thanks to: Laurie Crider-Vandal, Group 29

CARROT CAKE WITH CREAM CHEESE FROSTING

What a surprise—an awesome carrot cake with little fat!

Makes 16 servings ~ 2 x 2 inch square each

Ingredients:

3	cups	carrots, shredded
½	cup	raisins
1	cup	light brown sugar, packed
⅓	cup	crushed pineapple, drained
¾	cup	egg substitute
2	cups	flour
1	tsp	baking powder
1	tsp	baking soda
1	tsp	ground cinnamon
¼	tsp	ground allspice
¼	tsp	ground nutmeg
1	tsp	salt

Frosting Ingredients:

8	oz	non-fat cream cheese, softened
2	Tbsp	crushed pineapple, drained
4-5	cups	powdered sugar (enough to make a good consistency for spreading)
1	tsp	vanilla extract

Nutrition Facts

Serving Size 1/16 recipe (2x2 inch square) (119g)
Servings Per Container 16

Amount Per Serving

Calories 280 — Calories from Fat 5

% Daily Value*

- Total Fat 0.5g — 1%
- Saturated Fat 0g — 0%
- Trans Fat 0g
- Cholesterol 0mg — 0%
- Sodium 400mg — 17%
- Total Carbohydrate 65g — 22%
- Dietary Fiber 2g — 8%
- Sugars 49g
- Protein 5g

Vitamin A 70% • Vitamin C 4%
Calcium 10% • Iron 8%

*Percent Daily Values are based on a 2,000 calorie diet. Your daily values may be higher or lower depending on your calorie needs:

	Calories:	2,000	2,500
Total Fat	Less than	65g	80g
Saturated Fat	Less than	20g	25g
Cholesterol	Less than	300mg	300mg
Sodium	Less than	2,400mg	2,400mg
Total Carbohydrate		300g	375g
Dietary Fiber		25g	30g

Calories per gram:
 Fat 9 • Carbohydrate 4 • Protein 4

Preparation:

- Preheat oven to 350° F. Spray two 8 inch cake pans with non-fat cooking spray.
- In a large bowl, mix together carrots, raisins, brown sugar, pineapple, and egg substitute. Combine dry ingredients together then mix into carrot mixture.
- Pour batter equally into prepared pans. Cook 25 to 30 minutes or until toothpick inserted in center comes out clean.
- Cool in pans on rack for 10 minutes; then remove from pans and cool on racks.
- Make frosting by beating cream cheese and pineapple together until smooth.

- Beat in sugar and vanilla extract.
- Place 1 cake layer on serving plate and frost. Top with other layer, frost top and sides.

Thanks to: Phyllis Merrick, Group 26. Adapted from " 1001 Low-Fat Vegetarian Recipes"

Category: Desserts

CHOCOLATE PUDDING CAKE

Makes 16 servings ~ 2 x 2 inch square each

Ingredients:

Cake:

1	cup	flour
¾	cup	sugar
3	Tbsp	cocoa
2	tsp	baking powder
¼	tsp	salt
½	cup	skim milk
3	Tbsp	applesauce, unsweetened
1	tsp	vanilla extract

Topping:

1	cup	brown sugar
5	Tbsp	cocoa
1¾	cups	hottest tap water

Preparation:

- Preheat oven to 350°F.
- Mix flour, sugar, 3 Tbsp cocoa, baking powder and salt in ungreased, square 9 x 9 2 inch pan.
- Mix in milk, applesauce and vanilla extract with fork until batter is smooth.
- Spread evenly around pan.
- Mix brown sugar and 5 Tbsp cocoa together in small bowl. Sprinkle over batter.
- Slowly pour hot water over batter.
- Bake for 40 minutes. Serve warm

Thanks to: Elizabeth Parks and Dianne Hyson, R.D.

Nutrition Facts

Serving Size 2x2 inch square (71g)
Servings Per Container 16

Amount Per Serving

Calories 130   Calories from Fat 5

% Daily Value*

Total Fat 0g	0%
Saturated Fat 0g	0%
Trans Fat 0g	
Cholesterol 0mg	0%
Sodium 115mg	5%
Total Carbohydrate 32g	11%
Dietary Fiber 1g	4%
Sugars 24g	
Protein 2g	

Vitamin A 0%	•	Vitamin C 0%
Calcium 4%	•	Iron 4%

*Percent Daily Values are based on a 2,000 calorie diet. Your daily values may be higher or lower depending on your calorie needs:

	Calories:	2,000	2,500
Total Fat	Less than	65g	80g
Saturated Fat	Less than	20g	25g
Cholesterol	Less than	300mg	300mg
Sodium	Less than	2,400mg	2,400mg
Total Carbohydrate		300g	375g
Dietary Fiber		25g	30g

Calories per gram:
 Fat 9 • Carbohydrate 4 • Protein 4

Category: Desserts

CRANBERRY PEAR CRUMBLE

Pears are ripe when area around stem yields to gentle pressure.

Makes 8 servings

Ingredients:

4½	cups	pears, peeled and diced
½	cup	cranberries, fresh coarsely chopped (or frozen unthawed)
⅓	cup	light brown sugar
2	tsp	cornstarch

Crumble topping:

6	Tbsp	quick cooking oats
6	Tbsp	whole wheat pastry flour
⅓	cup	brown sugar
½	tsp	ground cinnamon
⅓	cup	honey crunch wheat germ

OR

⅓	cup	toasted pecans

Preparation:

- Preheat oven to 375°F.
- Coat a 9 inch deep dish pie pan with non-stick cooking spray.
- Place pears and cranberries in a large bowl and toss to mix well. Set aside.
- Place brown sugar and cornstarch in a small bowl and stir to mix well.
- Sprinkle this mixture over fruit, and toss to mix. (If the fruit is tart, you may need to add another couple of Tbsp of sugar.) Spread the fruit mixture evenly in the prepared pan.
- Mix together Crumble Topping ingredients and sprinkle over filling.
- Bake uncovered for 35 to 40 minutes, or until the filling is bubbly and the topping is golden brown.
- Cover loosely with foil during the last few minutes of baking if the topping starts to brown too quickly.
- Allow to cool at room temperature for at least 15 minutes before serving warm.

Note: Label is shown for using Crumble Topping with wheat germ. If pecans are used, add 17 grams of fat for whole recipe, or 153 calories.

Thanks to: Ginny Goodrow, Group 25

Nutrition Facts

Serving Size 1/8 recipe (135g)
Servings Per Container 8

Amount Per Serving

Calories 190   Calories from Fat 5

	% Daily Value*
Total Fat 1g	2%
Saturated Fat 0g	0%
Trans Fat 0g	
Cholesterol 0mg	0%
Sodium 5mg	0%
Total Carbohydrate 45g	15%
Dietary Fiber 5g	20%
Sugars 30g	
Protein 3g	

Vitamin A 0%	•	Vitamin C 15%
Calcium 4%	•	Iron 6%

*Percent Daily Values are based on a 2,000 calorie diet. Your daily values may be higher or lower depending on your calorie needs:

	Calories:	2,000	2,500
Total Fat	Less than	65g	80g
Saturated Fat	Less than	20g	25g
Cholesterol	Less than	300mg	300mg
Sodium	Less than	2,400mg	2,400mg
Total Carbohydrate		300g	375g
Dietary Fiber		25g	30g

Calories per gram:
 Fat 9 • Carbohydrate 4 • Protein 4

Category: Desserts

CREAMY PEACH CHEESECAKE

The day before drain yogurt to make Yogurt Cheese (see page 386). Use 2 pints of yogurt for this recipe.

Makes 10 servings

Ingredients:

16	oz	yogurt cheese (see page 386)
1½	cups	fat-free cookies, ground into fine crumbs
1	can	peach halves, in juice (16 oz.)
2	Tbsp	quick cooking tapioca
½	cup	honey
1	tsp	vanilla extract
½	tsp	almond extract
1½	Tbsp	arrowroot
2		egg whites

Preparation:

- Preheat oven to 325°F.
- Moisten fingers with water and press cookie crumbs over bottom of 8 inch spring-form pan. Chill.
- Drain peaches and slice thinly. Reserve liquid.
- Combine liquid and tapioca in a saucepan. Set aside for 5 minutes, and then cook over low heat until slightly thickened, about 3 minutes. Cool slightly.
- Beat together yogurt cheese, honey, vanilla, almond extract and arrowroot.
- Gradually add tapioca mixture, stirring until well blended.
- In a separate bowl, beat egg whites to soft peak stage. Fold egg whites into cheese mixture and mix until well blended.
- Pour half of the cheese filling into prepared pan. Cover the cheese filling with half of the peaches. Pour remaining filling on top and smooth with spatula. Arrange the rest of the peach slices on top.
- Bake for 50 minutes, or until center is set and surface is lightly browned.
- Remove from oven, cool to room temperature, then refrigerate until chilled.

Thanks to: George and Ila Kross, Group 8.

Nutrition Facts

Serving Size 1/10 recipe (191g)
Servings Per Container 10

Amount Per Serving	
Calories 260	Calories from Fat 35

	% Daily Value*
Total Fat 4g	6%
Saturated Fat 1g	5%
Trans Fat 0g	
Cholesterol 5mg	2%
Sodium 240mg	10%
Total Carbohydrate 49g	16%
Dietary Fiber 1g	4%
Sugars 25g	
Protein 9g	

Vitamin A 10%	•	Vitamin C 2%
Calcium 20%	•	Iron 6%

*Percent Daily Values are based on a 2,000 calorie diet. Your daily values may be higher or lower depending on your calorie needs:

		Calories: 2,000	2,500
Total Fat	Less than	65g	80g
Saturated Fat	Less than	20g	25g
Cholesterol	Less than	300mg	300mg
Sodium	Less than	2,400mg	2,400mg
Total Carbohydrate		300g	375g
Dietary Fiber		25g	30g

Calories per gram:
Fat 9 • Carbohydrate 4 • Protein 4

Category: Desserts

DATE BARS

Makes 24 bars

Ingredients:

1	cup	sugar
1	cup	flour
3	tsp	baking powder
¾	cup	egg substitute
½	tsp	baking soda
1	tsp	vanilla extract
½	tsp	salt (optional)
20	oz	dates, chopped
½	cup	nuts, chopped (optional)

Preparation:

- Preheat oven to 325°F. Coat 9 x 13 inch pan with cooking spray.
- Mix all ingredients together:
- Pour into prepared pan. Bake about 30-35 minutes.
- Be careful not to over bake! Cut into bars when cooled.

Thanks to: Sharla Bayer, Group 26

Category: Desserts

Nutrition Facts

Serving Size 1/24 recipe (48g)
Servings Per Container 24

Amount Per Serving

Calories 140   Calories from Fat 15

% Daily Value*

Total Fat 1.5g	2%
Saturated Fat 0g	0%
Trans Fat 0g	
Cholesterol 0mg	0%
Sodium 160mg	7%
Total Carbohydrate 32g	11%
Dietary Fiber 2g	8%
Sugars 25g	
Protein 2g	

Vitamin A 0%	•	Vitamin C 0%
Calcium 2%	•	Iron 4%

*Percent Daily Values are based on a 2,000 calorie diet. Your daily values may be higher or lower depending on your calorie needs:

		Calories:	2,000	2,500
Total Fat		Less than	65g	80g
Saturated Fat		Less than	20g	25g
Cholesterol		Less than	300mg	300mg
Sodium		Less than	2,400mg	2,400mg
Total Carbohydrate			300g	375g
Dietary Fiber			25g	30g

Calories per gram:
   Fat 9 • Carbohydrate 4 • Protein 4

DEEP DISH APPLE CRANBERRY CRUMBLE

Makes 16 servings

Ingredients:

2½	cups	cranberries, fresh or frozen
¾	cup	granulated sugar
¼	cup	water
4	large	apples, peeled, cored and thinly sliced
¼	cup	flour
1	tsp	apple pie spice (or cinnamon, cardamom, and nutmeg to equal 1 tsp)

Crumble Topping:

6	Tbsp	quick-cooking oats
6	Tbsp	whole wheat pastry flour
⅓	cup	brown sugar
½	tsp	ground cinnamon
2	Tbsp	frozen orange juice concentrate, thawed
⅓	cup	honey crunch wheat germ
OR		
⅓	cup	pecans, toasted

Nutrition Facts

Serving Size 1/16 recipe (100g)
Servings Per Container 16

Amount Per Serving

Calories 130   Calories from Fat 5

% Daily Value*

- Total Fat 0.5g — 1%
  - Saturated Fat 0g — 0%
  - Trans Fat 0g
- Cholesterol 0mg — 0%
- Sodium 0mg — 0%
- Total Carbohydrate 31g — 10%
  - Dietary Fiber 3g — 12%
  - Sugars 22g
- Protein 2g

Vitamin A 0% • Vitamin C 10%
Calcium 2% • Iron 4%

*Percent Daily Values are based on a 2,000 calorie diet. Your daily values may be higher or lower depending on your calorie needs:

	Calories:	2,000	2,500
Total Fat	Less than	65g	80g
Saturated Fat	Less than	20g	25g
Cholesterol	Less than	300mg	300mg
Sodium	Less than	2,400mg	2,400mg
Total Carbohydrate		300g	375g
Dietary Fiber		25g	30g

Calories per gram:
Fat 9 • Carbohydrate 4 • Protein 4

Preparation:

- Preheat oven to 375°F.
- In a saucepan, stir cranberries, sugar, and water together.
- Cover and heat until sugar is dissolved and cranberries are heated but not soft.
- In medium size mixing bowl, mix cranberries with apples, flour, and spices. Place in 8 x 8 x 2 inch pan.
- Mix together Crumble Topping and spread over top of fruit.
- Bake for about 1 hour. Serve warm. Refrigerate any leftovers.

Thanks to: Jerre Schermerhorn Group 29

Category: Desserts

Forgotten Cookies

So easy and perfect for the holidays. Much tastier than the store-bought variety.

Makes 30 cookies

Ingredients:

4		egg whites
1⅓	cup	sugar
1	tsp	vanilla extract
¼	tsp	cream of tartar
¼	cup	broken peppermint candy canes

Preparation:

- Preheat oven to 350° for 1 hour.
- Best if egg whites are at room temperature. Beat egg whites until foamy, add cream of tartar and vanilla extract.
- Gradually add sugar and beat until stiff. Stir in broken candy canes.
- Drop cookies on foil lined cookie sheet in peaked chunks.
- Place in oven and turn off oven. Leave overnight.
- In morning, place in sealed container.

NOTE: May also use other flavors: 1 tsp. lemon flavor and a few drops of yellow food coloring, or ¼ cup cocoa and a few drops peppermint flavor or vanilla bean.

Thanks to: Laura Schlund, R.N.

Category: Desserts

Nutrition Facts

Serving Size 1 cookie (1/30 recipe) (15g)
Servings Per Container 30

Amount Per Serving

Calories 45	Calories from Fat 0

% Daily Value*

Total Fat 0g	0%
Saturated Fat 0g	0%
Trans Fat 0g	
Cholesterol 0mg	0%
Sodium 5mg	0%
Total Carbohydrate 11g	4%
Dietary Fiber 0g	0%
Sugars 9g	
Protein 0g	

Vitamin A 0%	•	Vitamin C 0%
Calcium 0%	•	Iron 0%

*Percent Daily Values are based on a 2,000 calorie diet. Your daily values may be higher or lower depending on your calorie needs:

		Calories:	2,000	2,500
Total Fat		Less than	65g	80g
Saturated Fat		Less than	20g	25g
Cholesterol		Less than	300mg	300mg
Sodium		Less than	2,400mg	2,400mg
Total Carbohydrate			300g	375g
Dietary Fiber			25g	30g

Calories per gram:
Fat 9 • Carbohydrate 4 • Protein 4

Fresh Strawberry Pie

Follow this same recipe using peaches or raspberries in place of strawberries for other delicious fruit pies.

Makes 12 servings

Ingredients:

1		Grape Nuts pie crust (see page 342)
5	cups	fresh strawberries
½	cup	fruit juice concentrate (apple for example)
2	Tbsp	cornstarch
¼	cup	cold water

Preparation:

- Prepare pie crust. Cool.
- Mash 2 cups of fresh strawberries. Add fruit juice concentrate.
- Whisk cornstarch into cold water and pour into mashed fruit.
- Heat to boiling, stirring constantly. Mixture will become a thick, shiny glaze.
- Fill pie crust with remaining whole berries.
- Pour glaze over top.
- Chill and serve.

Category: Desserts

Nutrition Facts

Serving Size 1/12 recipe (116g)
Servings Per Container 12

Amount Per Serving

Calories 120 — Calories from Fat 5

% Daily Value*

Total Fat 0g	0%
Saturated Fat 0g	0%
Trans Fat 0g	
Cholesterol 0mg	0%
Sodium 75mg	3%
Total Carbohydrate 29g	10%
Dietary Fiber 3g	12%
Sugars 15g	
Protein 2g	

Vitamin A 6% • Vitamin C 70%
Calcium 2% • Iron 30%

*Percent Daily Values are based on a 2,000 calorie diet. Your daily values may be higher or lower depending on your calorie needs:

		Calories:	2,000	2,500
Total Fat	Less than		65g	80g
Saturated Fat	Less than		20g	25g
Cholesterol	Less than		300mg	300mg
Sodium	Less than		2,400mg	2,400mg
Total Carbohydrate			300g	375g
Dietary Fiber			25g	30g

Calories per gram:
Fat 9 • Carbohydrate 4 • Protein 4

Fruit Cocktail Cake

Amazingly simple recipe sure to satisfy your sweet tooth.

Makes 16 servings ~ 2x2 inch square

Ingredients:

1	can	fruit cocktail in juice (~15 oz)
1	tsp	vanilla extract
¼	cup	egg substitute
1	cup	flour
1	tsp	baking soda
½	tsp	salt

Preparation:

- Preheat oven to 350°F. Coat an 8 x 8 inch pan with nonstick spray.
- In a large bowl, mix fruit cocktail, vanilla extract, egg substitute.
- Place flour, baking soda, and salt in flour sifter.
- Sift the dry mixture into the wet mixture and combine gently.
- Pour into prepared pan and bake for 30 minutes.

Thanks to: Frank and Minnie Bell, Group 5

Category: Desserts

Nutrition Facts

Serving Size 1/16 recipe (39g)
Servings Per Container 16

Amount Per Serving

Calories 45   Calories from Fat 0

	% Daily Value*
Total Fat 0g	0%
Saturated Fat 0g	0%
Trans Fat 0g	
Cholesterol 0mg	0%
Sodium 160mg	7%
Total Carbohydrate 9g	3%
Dietary Fiber 0g	0%
Sugars 3g	
Protein 1g	

Vitamin A 2% • Vitamin C 2%
Calcium 0% • Iron 2%

*Percent Daily Values are based on a 2,000 calorie diet. Your daily values may be higher or lower depending on your calorie needs:

		Calories:	2,000	2,500
Total Fat		Less than	65g	80g
Saturated Fat		Less than	20g	25g
Cholesterol		Less than	300mg	300mg
Sodium		Less than	2,400mg	2,400mg
Total Carbohydrate			300g	375g
Dietary Fiber			25g	30g

Calories per gram:
   Fat 9 • Carbohydrate 4 • Protein 4

FRUIT MERINGUE

Vary this delicious dessert by substituting other fruit combinations, selecting from fresh, frozen unsweetened (partially thawed), or canned juice-packed fruits (drained).

Makes 20 servings

Ingredients:

3	cups	strawberries, sliced
2	cups	frozen cherries, partially thawed and halved
¼	cup	apple juice concentrate
1	Tbsp	lemon juice
1	Tbsp	pectin
1	tsp	vanilla extract
1	tsp	lemon extract
6		fresh egg whites (container egg whites will not work)

Nutrition Facts
Serving Size 1/20 recipe (54g)
Servings Per Container 20

Amount Per Serving

Calories 30 — Calories from Fat 0

% Daily Value*

Total Fat 0g — 0%
  Saturated Fat 0g — 0%
  Trans Fat 0g
Cholesterol 0mg — 0%
Sodium 15mg — 1%
Total Carbohydrate 6g — 2%
  Dietary Fiber 1g — 4%
  Sugars 4g
Protein 1g

Vitamin A 0% • Vitamin C 25%
Calcium 0% • Iron 0%

*Percent Daily Values are based on a 2,000 calorie diet. Your daily values may be higher or lower depending on your calorie needs:

		Calories:	2,000	2,500
Total Fat	Less than		65g	80g
Saturated Fat	Less than		20g	25g
Cholesterol	Less than		300mg	300mg
Sodium	Less than		2,400mg	2,400mg
Total Carbohydrate			300g	375g
Dietary Fiber			25g	30g

Calories per gram:
  Fat 9 • Carbohydrate 4 • Protein 4

Preparation:

- Combine all the ingredients except the egg whites in a pot.
- Stir and bring to a boil, then reduce heat and simmer, stirring constantly, for 3-5 minutes, until slightly thickened.
- Pour the fruit mixture into a bowl to cool.
- Beat the egg whites until stiff peaks form and fold into the fruit.
- Transfer mixture to 9 x 13 inch glass or nonstick baking dish.
- Set the dish into a larger ovenproof pan filled with boiling water to reach halfway up the sides of the baking dish.
- Bake uncovered for 20 minutes (325°F).
- Remove the baking dish from the water 2-3 minutes before the end of the baking period, placing it directly on the oven rack to finish baking.
- The meringue should brown only slightly.
- Remove from oven and let set for about 10 minutes or longer before serving, or serve chilled.

Thanks to: Sharon Myers, R.N.

Category: Desserts

FRUITFUL GRAHAM CRACKER PIE CRUST

For use with fruit pies in this collection.

Ingredients:

8	large	graham crackers (1¼ cups crumbs)
3	Tbsp	fruit spread or jam, any flavor

Preparation:

- Preheat oven to 350°F and coat 9 inch pie pan with vegetable oil cooking spray.
- Using blender, processor, or rolling pin, make fine crumbs from graham crackers.
- Mix in jam to make moist and crumbly mixture.
- Press crumbs over bottom and sides of pie pan with back of sugar-coated spoon.
- Bake for 10 minutes or until edges feel firm and dry.
- Cool to room temperature and fill as desired.

Category: Desserts

Nutrition Facts

Serving Size (150g)
Servings Per Container

Amount Per Serving

Calories 520   Calories from Fat 100

	% Daily Value*
Total Fat 11g	17%
Saturated Fat 1.5g	8%
Trans Fat 0g	
Cholesterol 0mg	0%
Sodium 510mg	21%
Total Carbohydrate 100g	33%
Dietary Fiber 6g	24%
Sugars 49g	
Protein 7g	

Vitamin A 0%	•	Vitamin C 0%
Calcium 10%	•	Iron 35%

*Percent Daily Values are based on a 2,000 calorie diet. Your daily values may be higher or lower depending on your calorie needs:

	Calories:	2,000	2,500
Total Fat	Less than	65g	80g
Saturated Fat	Less than	20g	25g
Cholesterol	Less than	300mg	300mg
Sodium	Less than	2,400mg	2,400mg
Total Carbohydrate		300g	375g
Dietary Fiber		25g	30g

Calories per gram:
  Fat 9 • Carbohydrate 4 • Protein 4

GINGERBREAD

Top with light Cool-Whip

Makes 16 cookies

Ingredients:

⅔	cup	non-fat sour cream
⅓	cup	applesauce, unsweetened
⅓	cup	egg substitute
3	Tbsp	brown sugar
2	Tbsp	molasses
¾	cup	whole wheat flour
¾	cup	unbleached all purpose flour
4	tsp	ground ginger
1	tsp	ground cinnamon
½	tsp	ground cloves
1	tsp	baking soda
1	tsp	baking powder
½	tsp	salt

Preparation:

- Preheat oven to 350°F. Prepare a 9 inch round or 8 inch square cake pan, either non-stick or lightly sprayed with vegetable oil.
- In a medium bowl, combine sour cream, applesauce, egg substitute, brown sugar, and molasses.
- Stir until smooth and well-blended.
- In another medium bowl, stir together whole wheat flour, all-purpose flour, ginger, cinnamon, cloves, baking soda, baking powder, and salt.
- Sift them onto a sheet of wax paper.
- Add dry ingredients to the sour cream mixture and stir just until blended; do not over mix. A few lumps are okay.
- Spread the batter evenly in prepared pan. Bake until the gingerbread has risen to the top of the pan and a toothpick inserted in the center comes out clean, about 25 minutes.
- Cool 30 minutes before cutting into wedges or squares.

Category: Desserts

Nutrition Facts

Serving Size 1/16 recipe (78g)
Servings Per Container 16

Amount Per Serving

Calories 220 Calories from Fat 5

% Daily Value*

Total Fat 0g	0%
Saturated Fat 0g	0%
Trans Fat 0g	
Cholesterol 0mg	0%
Sodium 230mg	10%
Total Carbohydrate 54g	18%
Dietary Fiber 1g	4%
Sugars 42g	
Protein 2g	

Vitamin A 2% • Vitamin C 0%
Calcium 6% • Iron 6%

*Percent Daily Values are based on a 2,000 calorie diet. Your daily values may be higher or lower depending on your calorie needs:

		Calories:	2,000	2,500
Total Fat	Less than		65g	80g
Saturated Fat	Less than		20g	25g
Cholesterol	Less than		300mg	300mg
Sodium	Less than		2,400mg	2,400mg
Total Carbohydrate			300g	375g
Dietary Fiber			25g	30g

Calories per gram:
Fat 9 • Carbohydrate 4 • Protein 4

GINNY'S PEACH COBBLER

The peach slices are embedded in a tasty cake with a sherry-laced sauce moistening all.

Makes 16 servings

Ingredients:

1	cup	flour
1	tsp	baking powder
½	tsp	salt
½	cup	egg substitute
1	cup	sugar
1	Tbsp	applesauce, unsweetened
1	Tbsp	non-fat milk
½	cup	sherry
½	cup	sugar
3	cups	sliced fresh peaches (or drained canned)

Preparation:

- Preheat oven to 375°F. Coat 9 inch square pan with vegetable oil cooking spray.
- In large bowl, mix together the dry ingredients.
- In separate bowl, beat egg substitute and sugar together.
- Add in applesauce and milk.
- Add to the dry ingredients and mix well.
- Pour into prepared pan.
- In medium saucepan, simmer sherry and sugar together for 3 or 4 minutes. Add peaches.
- Pour hot peach mixture over batter in pan, arranging the slices evenly.
- Bake for 30 minutes.
- Serve warm or cold.

Nutrition Facts

Serving Size 1/16 recipe (73g)
Servings Per Container 16

Amount Per Serving

Calories 130 Calories from Fat 0

% Daily Value*

Total Fat 0g	0%
Saturated Fat 0g	0%
Trans Fat 0g	
Cholesterol 0mg	0%
Sodium 170mg	7%
Total Carbohydrate 29g	10%
Dietary Fiber 1g	4%
Sugars 22g	
Protein 2g	

Vitamin A 2% • Vitamin C 4%
Calcium 2% • Iron 4%

*Percent Daily Values are based on a 2,000 calorie diet. Your daily values may be higher or lower depending on your calorie needs:

	Calories:	2,000	2,500
Total Fat	Less than	65g	80g
Saturated Fat	Less than	20g	25g
Cholesterol	Less than	300mg	300mg
Sodium	Less than	2,400mg	2,400mg
Total Carbohydrate		300g	375g
Dietary Fiber		25g	30g

Calories per gram:
  Fat 9 • Carbohydrate 4 • Protein 4

Thanks to: Ginny Goodrow, Group 25

Category: Desserts

GRAPE NUTS PIE CRUST

Only a trace of fat and terrific taste for most any pie.

Makes 1 crust

Ingredients:

| 1 | 6 oz | can apple juice concentrate |
| 1½ | cups | Grape Nuts cereal |

Preparation:

- Preheat oven to 350°F.
- Mix juice with cereal and let stand for a few minutes until moisture is absorbed.
- Press into a 9 inch non-stick pie pan. Bake for 12 minutes. Cool.
- Fill with fruit and yogurt or a pudding recipe.

Category: Desserts

Nutrition Facts

Serving Size (344g)
Servings Per Container

Amount Per Serving

Calories 920   Calories from Fat 30

	% Daily Value*
Total Fat 3g	5%
Saturated Fat 0.5g	3%
Trans Fat 0g	
Cholesterol 0mg	0%
Sodium 870mg	36%
Total Carbohydrate 210g	70%
Dietary Fiber 15g	60%
Sugars 88g	
Protein 22g	

Vitamin A 60% • Vitamin C 0%

Calcium 6% • Iron 370%

*Percent Daily Values are based on a 2,000 calorie diet. Your daily values may be higher or lower depending on your calorie needs:

		Calories:	2,000	2,500
Total Fat	Less than		65g	80g
Saturated Fat	Less than		20g	25g
Cholesterol	Less than		300mg	300mg
Sodium	Less than		2,400mg	2,400mg
Total Carbohydrate			300g	375g
Dietary Fiber			25g	30g

Calories per gram:
  Fat 9 • Carbohydrate 4 • Protein 4

Note: Serving Size on Label applies to entire recipe.

HARVEST CAKE

This tasty cake has both vegetables and fruit to increase the nutrient content.

Makes 16 servings

Ingredients:

1½	cups	applesauce, unsweetened
2	cups	brown sugar, packed
1	cup	egg substitute
1	Tbsp	vanilla extract
2	cups	carrots, grated
4	cups	flour
1	Tbsp	baking soda
4	tsp	ground cinnamon
1	tsp	nutmeg
1	tsp	ground ginger
1	tsp	salt
2	cartons	non-fat pineapple yogurt (8 oz each)
½	cup	nuts, finely chopped (optional)
		powdered sugar (optional)

Nutrition Facts
Serving Size 1/16 recipe (150g)
Servings Per Container 16

Amount Per Serving
Calories 300   Calories from Fat 25

% Daily Value*
- Total Fat 3g — 5%
- Saturated Fat 0g — 0%
- Trans Fat 0g
- Cholesterol 0mg — 0%
- Sodium 450mg — 19%
- Total Carbohydrate 64g — 21%
- Dietary Fiber 2g — 8%
- Sugars 37g
- Protein 7g

Vitamin A 50% • Vitamin C 4%
Calcium 10% • Iron 10%

*Percent Daily Values are based on a 2,000 calorie diet. Your daily values may be higher or lower depending on your calorie needs:

	Calories:	2,000	2,500
Total Fat	Less than	65g	80g
Saturated Fat	Less than	20g	25g
Cholesterol	Less than	300mg	300mg
Sodium	Less than	2,400mg	2,400mg
Total Carbohydrate		300g	375g
Dietary Fiber		25g	30g

Calories per gram:
Fat 9 • Carbohydrate 4 • Protein 4

Preparation:

- Preheat oven to 350°F. Coat a 14-cup Bundt pan or crown ring mold with nonstick cooking spray and dust with flour.
- In a large bowl, mix applesauce, brown sugar, egg substitute and vanilla extract.
- In a separate bowl, mix carrots, flour, baking soda, spices and nuts.
- Mix portions of dry mixture (about ⅓ at a time) into egg mixture alternately with yogurt.
- Turn into prepared pan and bake for 1 hour 15 minutes or until pick inserted into cake comes out dry.
- Cool 15 minutes in pan, then loosen top edges and gently invert from pan onto wire rack.
- When cake is completely cool, sift powdered sugar lightly over cake for a final touch.
- Sprinkle with nuts if desired.

Thanks to: Mary Dalzell, Group 22

Category: Desserts

Ice Cream Cake

Add mixed berries to the layers (blueberries, strawberries) to increase nutrients. Use sugar free Angel food cake and ice cream to lower the carbohydrates.

Makes 12 servings

Ingredients:

1		Angel food cake
½	gallon	fat-free, ice cream or frozen yogurt

Preparation:

- Slice cake horizontally into three slices.
- Place one slice on bottom of plate.
- Slice ice cream (1-2 inch thickness as desired), and place over cake to cover.
- Repeat cake layer, ice cream layer and top with final cake layer. Keep in freezer until ready to serve.
- To serve: Top with favorite fruit topping.

Thanks to: Debbie Lucus, R.D.

Category: Desserts

Nutrition Facts

Serving Size 1/12 cake (176g)
Servings Per Container 12

Amount Per Serving

Calories 310 — Calories from Fat 0

% Daily Value*

Total Fat 0g	0%
Saturated Fat 0g	0%
Trans Fat 0g	
Cholesterol 0mg	0%
Sodium 190mg	8%
Total Carbohydrate 68g	23%
Dietary Fiber 2g	8%
Sugars 58g	
Protein 11g	

Vitamin A 0% • Vitamin C 2%
Calcium 15% • Iron 2%

*Percent Daily Values are based on a 2,000 calorie diet. Your daily values may be higher or lower depending on your calorie needs:

		Calories:	2,000	2,500
Total Fat	Less than		65g	80g
Saturated Fat	Less than		20g	25g
Cholesterol	Less than		300mg	300mg
Sodium	Less than		2,400mg	2,400mg
Total Carbohydrate			300g	375g
Dietary Fiber			25g	30g

Calories per gram:
Fat 9 • Carbohydrate 4 • Protein 4

Laura's Reversal Chocolate Cake

Prunes work well to replace fat in chocolate recipes.

Makes 24 servings

Ingredients:

½	cup	cocoa
½	cup	prune paste*
2	cups	sugar
1	cup	fat-free egg substitute
½	cup	skim milk
1	cup	flour
4	tsp	baking powder
2	tsp	vanilla extract

Preparation:

- Preheat oven to 350°F.
- Combine prune paste, sugar, and cocoa.
- Beat until blended.
- Add egg substitute and beat until fluffy. Then add milk and vanilla extract.
- Combine flour and baking powder. Stir.
- Add flour mix to chocolate mixture and beat until thoroughly combined.
- Bake 25-30 minutes in a greased 13x 9 inch baking pan.
- Cool and cut into 24 squares.

Make prune paste by blending 1 cup prunes, 6 Tbsp water, 2 tsp vanilla extract in blender or food processor

Thanks to: Laura Schlund, R.N.

Category: Desserts

Nutrition Facts

Serving Size 1/24 recipe (about 2x2 inch square)2 (46g)
Servings Per Container 24

Amount Per Serving

Calories 110   Calories from Fat 5

	% Daily Value*
Total Fat 0g	0%
Saturated Fat 0g	0%
Trans Fat 0g	
Cholesterol 0mg	0%
Sodium 115mg	5%
Total Carbohydrate 27g	9%
Dietary Fiber 1g	4%
Sugars 20g	
Protein 2g	

Vitamin A 4% • Vitamin C 0%

Calcium 4% • Iron 4%

*Percent Daily Values are based on a 2,000 calorie diet. Your daily values may be higher or lower depending on your calorie needs:

		Calories:	2,000	2,500
Total Fat		Less than	65g	80g
Saturated Fat		Less than	20g	25g
Cholesterol		Less than	300mg	300mg
Sodium		Less than	2,400mg	2,400mg
Total Carbohydrate			300g	375g
Dietary Fiber			25g	30g

Calories per gram:
  Fat 9 • Carbohydrate 4 • Protein 4

Lemon Cheese-like Cake

Start with making "yogurt cheese" (see page 386). Drain yogurt overnight in the refrigerator in coffee filters or cheesecloth to thicken for a cream cheese substitute.

Makes 12 servings

Ingredients:

1½	cups	reduced fat Vanilla Wafers, rolled into crumbs
2	pkg	sugar-free lemon gelatin
1	cup	boiling water
1½	Tbsp	lemon juice
	peel	of one lemon
32	oz	non-fat yogurt, plain
¼	cup	powdered non-fat milk
½	cup	sugar (or sugar substitute)

Preparation:

- **CRUST:** Moisten fingers with water and press cookie crumbs into 9 inch pie plate.
- **FILLING:** Blend gelatin and boiling water until powder is dissolved.
- Cool until slightly set.
- Add lemon juice, lemon peel and then fold in yogurt cheese, milk and sugar or sugar substitute.
- Spoon into pie crust.
- Refrigerate several hours until firm.
- Serve with topping of your choice.

This recipe can also easily be made sugar-free

Nutrition Facts

Serving Size 1/12 recipe (120g)
Servings Per Container 12

Amount Per Serving

Calories 130   Calories from Fat 5

% Daily Value*

Total Fat 0.5g	1%
Saturated Fat 0g	0%
Trans Fat 0g	
Cholesterol 0mg	0%
Sodium 170mg	7%
Total Carbohydrate 24g	8%
Dietary Fiber 0g	0%
Sugars 18g	
Protein 6g	

Vitamin A 8%	•	Vitamin C 8%
Calcium 10%	•	Iron 0%

*Percent Daily Values are based on a 2,000 calorie diet. Your daily values may be higher or lower depending on your calorie needs:

		Calories:	2,000	2,500
Total Fat		Less than	65g	80g
Saturated Fat		Less than	20g	25g
Cholesterol		Less than	300mg	300mg
Sodium		Less than	2,400mg	2,400mg
Total Carbohydrate			300g	375g
Dietary Fiber			25g	30g

Calories per gram:
 Fat 9 • Carbohydrate 4 • Protein 4

Thanks to: Dianne Hyson, R.D, adapted from Connie Laventurier, Group 2

Category: Desserts

Lemon Pie

The graham cracker crumbs are the fat source in this recipe. Using a fat-free substitute crust will make this recipe essentially fat-free. With the graham crackers, it is very low fat.

Makes 12 servings

Ingredients:

½	cup	graham cracker crumbs
½	cup	cornstarch
1½	cups	sugar
½	cup	plus 2 Tbsp. fresh lemon juice
1	tsp	lemon zest (grated lemon rind)
1	Tbsp	cider vinegar
½	cup	egg substitute or 4 egg whites
2½	cups	cold water
2-4	Tbsp	fat-free sour cream

Meringue:

3	egg	whites
½	tsp	cream of tartar
1	tsp	vanilla extract
½	cup	powdered sugar

Nutrition Facts

Serving Size 1/12 recipe (124g)
Servings Per Container 12

Amount Per Serving

Calories 170   Calories from Fat 5

% Daily Value*

Total Fat 0g	0%
Saturated Fat 0g	0%
Trans Fat 0g	
Cholesterol 0mg	0%
Sodium 60mg	3%
Total Carbohydrate 39g	13%
Dietary Fiber 0g	0%
Sugars 31g	
Protein 2g	

Vitamin A 2% • Vitamin C 8%
Calcium 2% • Iron 2%

*Percent Daily Values are based on a 2,000 calorie diet. Your daily values may be higher or lower depending on your calorie needs:

		Calories:	2,000	2,500
Total Fat	Less than		65g	80g
Saturated Fat	Less than		20g	25g
Cholesterol	Less than		300mg	300mg
Sodium	Less than		2,400mg	2,400mg
Total Carbohydrate			300g	375g
Dietary Fiber			25g	30g

Calories per gram:
Fat 9 • Carbohydrate 4 • Protein 4

Preparation:

- Spray the bottom of a Pyrex pie pan with vegetable oil spray. Cover with graham cracker crumbs.
- Preheat oven to 350°F.
- Combine cornstarch, sugar, lemon juice, lemon zest and vinegar (if you don't like your lemon pie tart, leave out the vinegar).
- Use a gradual approach to keep it free from lumps. Beat in egg substitute or whites and water.
- Place mixture in a pan to cook. Stir constantly. Let the filling boil for 3 minutes (or until it comes to a rolling boil).
- Add 2 Tbsp of sour cream.
- Pour hot pie filling over crust. If the filling seems too thick, add an additional spoonful of sour cream.
- Prepare meringue. Beat egg whites just past the frothy stage at high speed and gradually add sugar until very stiff peaks form.

- Spread over hot pie filling, carefully covering the edges.
- Bake for 15-20 minutes until golden brown.

Thanks to: Harriette Miller

Category: Desserts

MEXICAN FLAN

Using egg substitute, you eliminate the cholesterol in this traditional recipe.

Makes 6 servings

Ingredients:

½	cup	egg substitute
2	cups	skim milk
1	tsp	cinnamon
½	tsp	nutmeg
2	cup	sugar, divided
¼	cup	water

Preparation:

- Preheat oven to 325°F.
- Combine eggs substitute, milk, spices, and 1 cup sugar (this makes the custard).
- To make caramelized syrup, put 1 cup sugar into medium sized pan, place on medium heat, and allow sugar to darken.
- Add water.
- Pour syrup into small custard sized cups.
- Pour uncooked custard on top.
- Bake for 30 minutes.
- Allow to cool, loosen around edges with knife and invert onto serving plate.

Nutrition Facts
Serving Size 1/6 recipe (180g)
Servings Per Container 6

Amount Per Serving

Calories 300   Calories from Fat 0

% Daily Value*

Total Fat 0g	0%
Saturated Fat 0g	0%
Trans Fat 0g	
Cholesterol 0mg	0%
Sodium 75mg	3%
Total Carbohydrate 72g	24%
Dietary Fiber 0g	0%
Sugars 72g	
Protein 5g	

Vitamin A 6%   •   Vitamin C 0%
Calcium 10%   •   Iron 2%

*Percent Daily Values are based on a 2,000 calorie diet. Your daily values may be higher or lower depending on your calorie needs:

	Calories:	2,000	2,500
Total Fat	Less than	65g	80g
Saturated Fat	Less than	20g	25g
Cholesterol	Less than	300mg	300mg
Sodium	Less than	2,400mg	2,400mg
Total Carbohydrate		300g	375g
Dietary Fiber		25g	30g

Calories per gram:
Fat 9 • Carbohydrate 4 • Protein 4

Category: Desserts

MICROWAVED KRUNCH CAKE TOPPING

Watch carefully! This mixture burns easily so don't be surprised if you ruin a batch

Ingredients:

1½	cup	sugar
¼	cup	light corn syrup
¼	cup	strong coffee
OR		
1	tsp	lemon extract in ¼ cup water
1	Tbsp	baking soda, sifted (use a small strainer)

Preparation:

- In a one quart glass measuring cup with handle, combine ingredients and stir well.
- Microwave on HIGH for 3 minutes. Stir.
- Microwave again 2 - 3 minutes until candy thermometer reaches 300°F. Watch carefully.
- Stir in baking soda quickly.
- Immediately pour the foamy mass into a 9 inch square pan (ungreased). Do not spread or stir.
- When cool, break into pieces and sprinkle liberally over marshmallow cream-frosted angel food cake.

Thanks to: Jane Hue, Group 29

Category: Desserts

Nutrition Facts

Serving Size (463g)
Servings Per Container

Amount Per Serving

Calories 1420   Calories from Fat 0

% Daily Value*

Total Fat 0g	0%
Saturated Fat 0g	0%
Trans Fat 0g	
Cholesterol 0mg	0%
Sodium 3830mg	160%
Total Carbohydrate 370g	123%
Dietary Fiber 0g	0%
Sugars 325g	
Protein 0g	

Vitamin A 0% • Vitamin C 0%

Calcium 2% • Iron 0%

*Percent Daily Values are based on a 2,000 calorie diet. Your daily values may be higher or lower depending on your calorie needs:

		Calories:	2,000	2,500
Total Fat		Less than	65g	80g
Saturated Fat		Less than	20g	25g
Cholesterol		Less than	300mg	300mg
Sodium		Less than	2,400mg	2,400mg
Total Carbohydrate			300g	375g
Dietary Fiber			25g	30g

Calories per gram:
 Fat 9 • Carbohydrate 4 • Protein 4

MICROWAVED TAPIOCA

Makes 4 servings

Ingredients:

⅓	cup	sugar (OR Splenda OR - Equal)
3	Tbsp	quick cooking tapioca
2	cups	skim milk
¼	cup	egg substitute, beaten
1	tsp	vanilla extract

Preparation:

- Mix ingredients in a large microwaveable bowl.
- Microwave on High for 10 to 12 minutes until mixture comes to a full boil stirring every 3 minutes.
- Beware of the 3rd 3 minutes as mixture may overflow.
- Stir in vanilla extract.
- For creamier pudding, place plastic wrap on surface of pudding while cooling for 20 minutes.
- Stir before serving.

Category: Desserts

Nutrition Facts

Serving Size 1/4 recipe (165g)
Servings Per Container 4

Amount Per Serving

Calories 150 — Calories from Fat 0

% Daily Value*

Total Fat 0g	0%
Saturated Fat 0g	0%
Trans Fat 0g	
Cholesterol 0mg	0%
Sodium 85mg	4%
Total Carbohydrate 31g	10%
Dietary Fiber 0g	0%
Sugars 23g	
Protein 6g	

Vitamin A 6% • Vitamin C 0%
Calcium 15% • Iron 2%

*Percent Daily Values are based on a 2,000 calorie diet. Your daily values may be higher or lower depending on your calorie needs:

	Calories:	2,000	2,500
Total Fat	Less than	65g	80g
Saturated Fat	Less than	20g	25g
Cholesterol	Less than	300mg	300mg
Sodium	Less than	2,400mg	2,400mg
Total Carbohydrate		300g	375g
Dietary Fiber		25g	30g

Calories per gram:
Fat 9 • Carbohydrate 4 • Protein 4

MOCHA PUDDING CAKE

This chocolaty dessert forms two layers as it bakes; a creamy pudding on the bottom and a soft cake on the top.

Makes 16 servings

Ingredients:

1	cup	flour
⅔	cup	sugar
¼	cup	unsweetened cocoa
1½	Tbsp	instant coffee granules
2	tsp	baking powder
¼	tsp	salt
½	cup	skim milk
3	Tbsp	prune purées (e.g. baby food)
1	tsp	vanilla extract

Topping:

⅓	cup	sugar
2	Tbsp	unsweetened cocoa
1	cup	boiling water
32	Tbsp	non-fat vanilla yogurt, frozen

Preparation:

- Preheat oven to 350°F.
- Coat an 8 inch square baking pan with vegetable oil cooking spray.
- Combine flour, sugar, cocoa, instant coffee, baking powder and salt in a bowl.
- Combine milk, prunes, and vanilla extract separately.
- Add liquids to dry ingredients and stir well.
- Spoon batter into prepared pan.
- Combine sugar and cocoa for topping and sprinkle over batter.
- Then pour the boiling water over the batter, do not stir.
- Bake for 30 minutes or until cake springs back when lightly touched in center.
- Serve warm with 2 Tbsp non-fat vanilla frozen yogurt for each serving.

Category: Desserts

Nutrition Facts

Serving Size 2x2 inch square (62g)
Servings Per Container 16

Amount Per Serving

Calories 110 — Calories from Fat 5

% Daily Value*

Total Fat 0g	0%
Saturated Fat 0g	0%
Trans Fat 0g	
Cholesterol 0mg	0%
Sodium 120mg	5%
Total Carbohydrate 26g	9%
Dietary Fiber 1g	4%
Sugars 18g	
Protein 2g	

Vitamin A 2%	•	Vitamin C 0%
Calcium 4%	•	Iron 4%

*Percent Daily Values are based on a 2,000 calorie diet. Your daily values may be higher or lower depending on your calorie needs:

		Calories:	2,000	2,500
Total Fat	Less than		65g	80g
Saturated Fat	Less than		20g	25g
Cholesterol	Less than		300mg	300mg
Sodium	Less than		2,400mg	2,400mg
Total Carbohydrate			300g	375g
Dietary Fiber			25g	30g

Calories per gram:
  Fat 9 • Carbohydrate 4 • Protein 4

OATMEAL BARS WITH CHEWY FRUIT

Low-fat and cholesterol free, these bars make great snacks.

Makes 24 bars

Ingredients:

¾	cup	brown sugar, firmly packed
½	cup	granulated sugar
8	oz	non-fat vanilla yogurt
2		egg whites, lightly beaten
2	Tbsp	canola oil
2	Tbsp	skim milk
1½	cups	flour
1	tsp	baking soda
1	tsp	cinnamon
½	tsp	salt (optional)
3	cups	oats, quick or old-fashioned
1	cup	mixed fruit, dried and diced, raisins, or cranberries

Preparation:

- Preheat oven to 350°F.
- In a large bowl, combine brown sugar, white sugar, yogurt, egg whites, oil and milk and mix well.
- Into a medium bowl, combine flour, baking soda, cinnamon, and salt, mixing well.
- Add dry ingredients to yogurt ingredients and mix well.
- Stir in oats and mixed fruit.
- Spread dough onto bottom of ungreased 9 x 13 inch baking pan.
- Bake 28-32 minutes, until light golden brown.
- Cool completely on wire rack. Cut into 24 bars.
- Stored tightly covered.

Thanks to: Sharla Bayer, Group 26

Category: Desserts

Nutrition Facts

Serving Size 1 bar (50g)
Servings Per Container 24

Amount Per Serving

Calories 140   Calories from Fat 20

	% Daily Value*
Total Fat 2g	3%
Saturated Fat 0g	0%
Trans Fat 0g	
Cholesterol 0mg	0%
Sodium 120mg	5%
Total Carbohydrate 29g	10%
Dietary Fiber 1g	4%
Sugars 16g	
Protein 3g	

Vitamin A 0% • Vitamin C 0%
Calcium 2% • Iron 6%

*Percent Daily Values are based on a 2,000 calorie diet. Your daily values may be higher or lower depending on your calorie needs:

		Calories:	2,000	2,500
Total Fat	Less than		65g	80g
Saturated Fat	Less than		20g	25g
Cholesterol	Less than		300mg	300mg
Sodium	Less than		2,400mg	2,400mg
Total Carbohydrate			300g	375g
Dietary Fiber			25g	30g

Calories per gram:
Fat 9 • Carbohydrate 4 • Protein 4

OATMEAL CORN SYRUP RAISIN COOKIES

Makes 30-36

Ingredients:

1	cup	flour
1	cup	quick oats
½	cup	sugar (or less)
½	tsp	salt
½	tsp	cinnamon
½	tsp	baking soda
⅛	tsp	ginger
⅛	tsp	nutmeg
2		egg whites
⅓	cup	corn syrup (dark or light)
1	tsp	vanilla extract
½	cup	raisins

Preparation:

- Preheat oven to 375°F. Use a non-stick cookie sheet for best results.
- In a large bowl combine dry ingredients.
- Stir in egg whites, corn syrup, and vanilla.
- Mix well.
- Add raisins. Batter will be stiff.
- Drop by teaspoonfuls onto cookie sheet.
- Bake 10 minutes, or until firm. DO NOT OVERBAKE.
- Cool on wire rack.

Nutrition Facts

Serving Size 1 cookie (about 2 1/2 dozen yield) (16g)
Servings Per Container 36

Amount Per Serving

Calories 50	Calories from Fat 0

% Daily Value*

Total Fat 0g	0%
Saturated Fat 0g	0%
Trans Fat 0g	
Cholesterol 0mg	0%
Sodium 55mg	2%
Total Carbohydrate 11g	4%
Dietary Fiber 0g	0%
Sugars 5g	
Protein 1g	

Vitamin A 0%	•	Vitamin C 0%
Calcium 0%	•	Iron 2%

*Percent Daily Values are based on a 2,000 calorie diet. Your daily values may be higher or lower depending on your calorie needs:

		Calories:	2,000	2,500
Total Fat	Less than		65g	80g
Saturated Fat	Less than		20g	25g
Cholesterol	Less than		300mg	300mg
Sodium	Less than		2,400mg	2,400mg
Total Carbohydrate			300g	375g
Dietary Fiber			25g	30g

Calories per gram:
  Fat 9 • Carbohydrate 4 • Protein 4

Thanks to: Dianne Hyson, (modified from Karo recipe)

Category: Desserts

Oatmeal Walnut Cookies

Since these have walnuts, they will have slightly more fat than other cookies. Accommodate appropriately and drop them in smaller sizes.

Makes ~ 24

Ingredients:

⅓	cup	dark brown sugar, packed
½	cup	sugar
1	Tbsp	olive oil
¼	cup	applesauce, unsweetened
1	tsp	vanilla extract
¼	cup	egg substitute
¾	cup	flour
1	cup	oats
¼	tsp	salt
⅔	cup	golden raisins
¼	cup	walnuts, toasted, chopped

Preparation:

- Preheat oven to 350°F.
- Coat cookie sheet with vegetable oil cooking spray.
- In a large bowl, beat brown sugar, white sugar, oil, applesauce, vanilla extract and egg substitute with a mixer until well blended.
- Add flour, oats, and salt; beat well.
- Stir in raisins and walnuts.
- Drop by level tablespoons, 1½ inches apart on sprayed cookie sheet.
- Bake for 12 minutes or until lightly browned.
- Remove from pan and cool on wire racks.

NOTE: Food that is low or lacking in fat will not brown as easily as fatter foods, so things may be cooked and "done" although not browned. Be careful to not overcook and dry out low-fat baked goods.

Thanks to: Mary Dalzell, Group 22

Category: Desserts

Nutrition Facts

Serving Size 1 cookie (26g)
Servings Per Container 24

Amount Per Serving

Calories 80	Calories from Fat 15

	% Daily Value*
Total Fat 1.5g	2%
Saturated Fat 0g	0%
Trans Fat 0g	
Cholesterol 0mg	0%
Sodium 30mg	1%
Total Carbohydrate 16g	5%
Dietary Fiber 1g	4%
Sugars 10g	
Protein 1g	

Vitamin A 0%	•	Vitamin C 0%
Calcium 0%	•	Iron 2%

*Percent Daily Values are based on a 2,000 calorie diet. Your daily values may be higher or lower depending on your calorie needs:

	Calories:	2,000	2,500
Total Fat	Less than	65g	80g
Saturated Fat	Less than	20g	25g
Cholesterol	Less than	300mg	300mg
Sodium	Less than	2,400mg	2,400mg
Total Carbohydrate		300g	375g
Dietary Fiber		25g	30g

Calories per gram:
Fat 9 • Carbohydrate 4 • Protein 4

Peach and Raspberry Cloud Cake

Amazing low calorie and moderate carbohydrate dessert!

Makes 12 servings

Meringue Ingredients:

5	large	egg whites
½	tsp	cream of tartar
1	cup	sugar
1	tsp	vanilla extract
1	tsp	anise seed, crushed

Filling and Sauce:

1	lb	peaches, ripe, peeled
1½	cup	raspberries
3	Tbsp	sugar
3	Tbsp	lemon juice
½	tsp	lemon peel, grated

Preparation:

- Preheat oven to 275°F.
- Coat an 8 inch cheesecake pan with removable rim with vegetable oil spray and then dust with flour.
- **Prepare Meringue:** In a deep bowl, beat egg whites with cream of tartar, using a mixer on high speed until frothy.
- Continue beating, and add sugar at rate of about 1 Tbsp every 30 seconds until whites hold stiff peaks and all sugar is blended.
- Then beat in vanilla extract and anise seed.
- Spread meringue in prepared pan, smoothing to make it level.
- Bake until pale golden, 1¼ to 1½ hours.
- Run a thin-bladed knife between meringue cake and pan rim to release.
- Cool meringue in pan on a rack, about 20 minutes.
- **Prepare filling**: Thinly slice peaches.
- Mix together 2 cups of the peach slices with ½ cup raspberries, 1 Tbsp sugar, lemon peel and 1 Tbsp lemon juice.
- **Prepare Sauce**: In a blender or food processor, whirl until smooth the remaining peaches and 1 cup raspberries with 2 Tbsp sugar and 2 Tbsp lemon juice. Rub purée through a fine strainer into a bowl; discard residue.

Nutrition Facts

Serving Size 1/12 recipe (91g)
Servings Per Container 12

Amount Per Serving

Calories 110 — Calories from Fat 0

	% Daily Value*
Total Fat 0g	0%
Saturated Fat 0g	0%
Trans Fat 0g	
Cholesterol 0mg	0%
Sodium 20mg	1%
Total Carbohydrate 26g	9%
Dietary Fiber 1g	4%
Sugars 23g	
Protein 2g	

Vitamin A 2%	•	Vitamin C 10%
Calcium 0%	•	Iron 2%

*Percent Daily Values are based on a 2,000 calorie diet. Your daily values may be higher or lower depending on your calorie needs:

	Calories:	2,000	2,500
Total Fat	Less than	65g	80g
Saturated Fat	Less than	20g	25g
Cholesterol	Less than	300mg	300mg
Sodium	Less than	2,400mg	2,400mg
Total Carbohydrate		300g	375g
Dietary Fiber		25g	30g

Calories per gram:
  Fat 9 • Carbohydrate 4 • Protein 4

- Remove pan rim and set meringue cake on a plate. Spoon sliced peaches and whole berries onto cake and drizzle with about 2 Tbsp fruit sauce.
- Cut cake into wedges and add remaining sauce to taste.

Note: Use a flat-bottomed glass to crush anise seed.

Thanks to: Ginny Goodrow, Group 25

Category: Desserts

PINEAPPLE CAKE WITH CREAM CHEESE FROSTING

A fruity cake guaranteed to suit your sweet tooth.

Makes 24 servings ~ 2 x 2 inch square

Ingredients:

½	cup	egg substitute
2	cups	granulated sugar
2	cups	all-purpose flour
2	tsp	baking soda
2½	cups	crushed pineapple (20 oz)
1	tsp	vanilla extract
¼	cup	nuts, chopped (optional)

Frosting:

8	oz	fat-free cream cheese, softened
1½	cups	powdered sugar
¼	tsp	vanilla extract

Preparation:

- Preheat the oven to 350°F.
- Coat a 13 x 9 x 2 inch pan with vegetable oil cooking spray.
- In a medium large mixing bowl, beat together egg substitute and sugar with an electric mixer.
- Mix together flour and baking soda and beat into egg mixture.
- Add pineapple and continue to beat
- When well blended, stir in vanilla extract and nuts.
- Pour into the prepared pan, scraping the

Nutrition Facts

Serving Size 2x2 inch square (77g)
Servings Per Container 24

Amount Per Serving

Calories 170   Calories from Fat 10

% Daily Value*

Total Fat 1g	2%
Saturated Fat 0g	0%
Trans Fat 0g	
Cholesterol 0mg	0%
Sodium 180mg	8%
Total Carbohydrate 37g	12%
Dietary Fiber 1g	4%
Sugars 29g	
Protein 3g	

Vitamin A 0% • Vitamin C 4%
Calcium 4% • Iron 4%

*Percent Daily Values are based on a 2,000 calorie diet. Your daily values may be higher or lower depending on your calorie needs:

		Calories:	2,000	2,500
Total Fat	Less than		65g	80g
Saturated Fat	Less than		20g	25g
Cholesterol	Less than		300mg	300mg
Sodium	Less than		2,400mg	2,400mg
Total Carbohydrate			300g	375g
Dietary Fiber			25g	30g

Calories per gram:
  Fat 9 • Carbohydrate 4 • Protein 4

sides of the bowl.
- Bake for 35 to 45 minutes, until a wooden pick inserted in the center of the cake comes out clean.
- Meanwhile, mix the frosting by stirring cream cheese with a wire whisk, not the mixer.
- Gradually add in sugar. Then stir in vanilla extract.
- Let the cake cool about 10 minutes and frost. Sprinkle with additional nuts if desired.

Thanks to: Carolanne Stoller, Group 21

Note: Fat-free cream cheese has a water base and gets runny easily. If the frosting is runny, don't be alarmed. Use it anyway if you have left your cake in a pan. If making a layer cake, add just a tiny bit of instant vanilla pudding, about 1 tsp at a time, until you have the consistency desired.

POACHED PEARS

This is a fun addition to your fruit tally for the day.

Makes 6 servings, 1 pear each

Ingredients:

6		fresh pears peeled and cored but left whole
1	cup	port
½	cup	sugar

Preparation:

- Combine port and sugar.
- Pour over pears and bake for 10-15 minutes at 375°F basting occasionally.
- Remove pears, allow to cool
- Bring remaining poaching liquid to boil.
- Thicken with cornstarch if necessary and sweeten to taste.

Category: Desserts

Nutrition Facts

Serving Size 1 pear each (286g)
Servings Per Container 6

Amount Per Serving

Calories 260 Calories from Fat 0

% Daily Value*

Total Fat 0g — 0%
 Saturated Fat 0g — 0%
 Trans Fat 0g
Cholesterol 0mg — 0%
Sodium 5mg — 0%
Total Carbohydrate 58g — 19%
 Dietary Fiber 7g — 28%
 Sugars 42g
Protein 1g

Vitamin A 2% • Vitamin C 15%
Calcium 2% • Iron 2%

*Percent Daily Values are based on a 2,000 calorie diet. Your daily values may be higher or lower depending on your calorie needs:

		Calories:	2,000	2,500
Total Fat	Less than		65g	80g
Saturated Fat	Less than		20g	25g
Cholesterol	Less than		300mg	300mg
Sodium	Less than		2,400mg	2,400mg
Total Carbohydrate			300g	375g
Dietary Fiber			25g	30g

Calories per gram:
 Fat 9 • Carbohydrate 4 • Protein 4

Pumpkin Cream Cheese Swirl Cake

Finished product looks terrific and is simpler to accomplish than it appears. The day before, prepare yogurt cream cheese (see page 386).

Makes 24 Servings

Ingredients:

2	cups	flour
2	tsp	baking powder
1	tsp	baking soda
¾	tsp	salt
2	tsp	ground cinnamon
1½	cups	sugar
1	can	pumpkin (packed 16 oz)
½	cup	skim milk
½	cup	plain non-fat yogurt
1	tsp	vanilla extract
¼	tsp	maple flavor

Cream cheese swirl:

8	oz	non-fat yogurt cheese (see page 386)
1	cup	sugar
⅛	tsp	salt
¼	cup	egg substitute OR 2 egg whites
½	tsp	vanilla extract
¼	tsp	maple flavor

Nutrition Facts

Serving Size 2x2 inch square (83g)
Servings Per Container 24

Amount Per Serving

Calories 140 — Calories from Fat 0

% Daily Value*

- Total Fat 0g — 0%
- Saturated Fat 0g — 0%
- Trans Fat 0g
- Cholesterol 0mg — 0%
- Sodium 220mg — 9%
- Total Carbohydrate 33g — 11%
- Dietary Fiber 1g — 4%
- Sugars 24g
- Protein 3g

Vitamin A 50% • Vitamin C 0%
Calcium 6% • Iron 4%

*Percent Daily Values are based on a 2,000 calorie diet. Your daily values may be higher or lower depending on your calorie needs:

	Calories:	2,000	2,500
Total Fat	Less than	65g	80g
Saturated Fat	Less than	20g	25g
Cholesterol	Less than	300mg	300mg
Sodium	Less than	2,400mg	2,400mg
Total Carbohydrate		300g	375g
Dietary Fiber		25g	30g

Calories per gram:
 Fat 9 • Carbohydrate 4 • Protein 4

Preparation:

- Preheat oven to 325°F. Spray a 9 x 13 inch pan with vegetable oil cooking spray and wipe with a paper towel to spread cooking spray evenly and absorb the excess.
- In a medium-sized bowl, combine flour, baking powder, baking soda, salt, and cinnamon and mix well.
- In a large bowl, combine sugar, pumpkin, milk, yogurt, vanilla extract, and maple flavor; mix well.
- Add dry mixture to wet mixture and mix well. Spread batter evenly in pan.
- **Cream cheese swirl:** In a medium-sized bowl, combine and mix together well yogurt, sugar, salt, egg substitute, vanilla extract and maple flavoring. Spread evenly over batter.
- Scoop up spoonfuls of batter through cream cheese on top and turn each spoonful over so that there are dots of batter showing. Use a fork to swirl the batter and cream cheese.

- Bake for 40 minutes. Cool cake completely.

Thanks to: Carolanne Stoller, Group 21

Category: Desserts

PUMPKIN LOG ROLL

Perfect for the holidays. Pumpkin is high in vitamin A.

10 servings, 1 inch slice

Roll Ingredients:

¾	cup	egg substitute
10	oz	pumpkin, canned
1	cup	granulated sugar
1	tsp	baking soda
¾	tsp	ground cinnamon
¾	cup	flour
		vegetable oil cooking spray

Filling:

½	tsp	butter flavored sprinkles
8	oz	fat-free cream cheese
¾	tsp	vanilla extract
½	cup	powdered sugar (optional)

Preparation:

Roll: Preheat oven to 375°F.
- Mix all roll ingredients together.
- Pour onto a 10 x 15 inch cookie sheet sprayed with vegetable oil cooking spray.
- Bake for 15 to 20 minutes or until done in the middle.
- When done, loosen cake with a spatula, turn it onto a towel. Cover with a small amount of granulated sugar. Cool completely.

Filling: Mix all ingredients until smooth.
- Spread onto cooked cake. Roll (like a jelly roll).
- Cut in half. Place in plastic wrap and refrigerate or freeze.
- Before serving, garnish with powdered sugar if desired.
- Cut into 1 inch slices.

Nutrition Facts

Serving Size 1 inch slice (106g)
Servings Per Container 10

Amount Per Serving

Calories 180 — Calories from Fat 5

% Daily Value*

Total Fat 0g	0%
Saturated Fat 0g	0%
Trans Fat 0g	
Cholesterol 5mg	2%
Sodium 330mg	14%
Total Carbohydrate 38g	13%
Dietary Fiber 2g	8%
Sugars 29g	
Protein 7g	

Vitamin A 70% • Vitamin C 0%
Calcium 10% • Iron 6%

*Percent Daily Values are based on a 2,000 calorie diet. Your daily values may be higher or lower depending on your calorie needs:

	Calories:	2,000	2,500
Total Fat	Less than	65g	80g
Saturated Fat	Less than	20g	25g
Cholesterol	Less than	300mg	300mg
Sodium	Less than	2,400mg	2,400mg
Total Carbohydrate		300g	375g
Dietary Fiber		25g	30g

Calories per gram:
Fat 9 • Carbohydrate 4 • Protein 4

Thanks to: Mary Sheikh

Category: Desserts

Punch Bowl Trifle

Using coconut extract instead of coconut eliminates artery-clogging saturated fat.

Makes 24 servings

Ingredients:

1	box	yellow cake mix (18.25 oz)
⅓	cup	applesauce, unsweetened
¾	cup	egg substitute
2	tsp	coconut extract
2	boxes	instant fat-free vanilla pudding mix
2	20 oz	cans crushed pineapple with juice with
3	jars	marshmallow cream
½	cup	pecans, finely chopped maraschino cherries

Preparation:

- In large bowl, mix together cake mix, applesauce, egg substitute, and coconut extract.
- Bake according to package directions. Let cool.
- Crumble into large pieces.
- Prepare pudding according to package directions.
- Have ready crushed pineapple, marshmallow cream, nuts and cherries.
- In a large punch bowl, layer ⅓ of crumbled cake, followed by other ingredients ⅓ at a time, in the following order: pudding, pineapple with juice, marshmallow cream, pecans.
- Repeat for a total of 3 layers. Garnish with maraschino cherries. Chill.

Thanks to: Laurie Crider-Vanpal Group 29

Category: Desserts

Nutrition Facts

Serving Size 1/24 recipe (116g)
Servings Per Container 24

Amount Per Serving

Calories 250 Calories from Fat 25

% Daily Value*

Total Fat 3g	5%
Saturated Fat 0g	0%
Trans Fat 0g	
Cholesterol 0mg	0%
Sodium 210mg	9%
Total Carbohydrate 53g	18%
Dietary Fiber 1g	4%
Sugars 25g	
Protein 2g	

Vitamin A 2% • Vitamin C 8%
Calcium 4% • Iron 4%

*Percent Daily Values are based on a 2,000 calorie diet. Your daily values may be higher or lower depending on your calorie needs:

		2,000	2,500
Total Fat	Less than	65g	80g
Saturated Fat	Less than	20g	25g
Cholesterol	Less than	300mg	300mg
Sodium	Less than	2,400mg	2,400mg
Total Carbohydrate		300g	375g
Dietary Fiber		25g	30g

Calories per gram:
Fat 9 • Carbohydrate 4 • Protein 4

Rhubarb Strawberry Cobbler

Rhubarb can be used in sweet or savory dishes. It blends well with strawberries here.

Makes 16 servings ~ 2x2 inch square

Ingredients:

¾	cup	sugar
1	cup	water
1	cup	strawberries, sliced
2	cups	rhubarb, ends and green removed, finely diced

Biscuit Topping:

¾	cup	flour
2	Tbsp	flour
¼	cup	oat bran
⅓	cup	sugar
1¾	tsp	baking powder
½	cup	non-fat buttermilk

OR

Make sour milk by placing ½ Tbsp vinegar in measuring cup and add non-fat milk to make ½ cup.

1½	tsp	sugar
		pinch ground cinnamon

Preparation:

- Preheat oven to 400°F and coat 9 x 9 x 2 inch pan with nonstick cooking spray.
- In a medium saucepan, simmer sugar and water for 5 minutes.
- Add fruit and reheat well.
- Pour into prepared pan. Put in oven to keep hot if biscuit topping is not ready.
- Mix together Biscuit Topping ingredients and drop by tablespoons over the hot fruit, sprinkle with sugar/ cinnamon mixture.
- Cook for 20 minutes until top is golden and juice bubbles up around the edge.
- Serve warm.

Note: Putting dough over HOT fruit/syrup will make it less likely that the underside of the biscuit will be uncooked and yucky when the top is done.

Thanks to: Ginny Goodrow, Group 25

Category: Desserts

Nutrition Facts

Serving Size 1/16 recipe (71g)
Servings Per Container 16

Amount Per Serving

Calories 90 — Calories from Fat 0

% Daily Value*

Total Fat 0g	0%
Saturated Fat 0g	0%
Trans Fat 0g	
Cholesterol 0mg	0%
Sodium 65mg	3%
Total Carbohydrate 22g	7%
Dietary Fiber 1g	4%
Sugars 15g	
Protein 1g	

Vitamin A 0%	•	Vitamin C 10%
Calcium 4%	•	Iron 2%

*Percent Daily Values are based on a 2,000 calorie diet. Your daily values may be higher or lower depending on your calorie needs:

		Calories:	2,000	2,500
Total Fat		Less than	65g	80g
Saturated Fat		Less than	20g	25g
Cholesterol		Less than	300mg	300mg
Sodium		Less than	2,400mg	2,400mg
Total Carbohydrate			300g	375g
Dietary Fiber			25g	30g

Calories per gram:
Fat 9 • Carbohydrate 4 • Protein 4

So So So Low Fat Brownies

Who doesn't love brownies?

Makes 16 servings

Ingredients:

½	cup	flour
5	Tbsp	cocoa powder
½	tsp	baking powder
4		egg whites
¾	cup	sugar
3	Tbsp	skim milk
1	tsp	vanilla extract
1	Tbsp	instant coffee
1	Tbsp	hot water

Preparation:

- Preheat oven to 300°F.
- Mix cocoa, flour, and baking powder in a bowl.
- In separate bowl, beat the egg whites until frothy.
- Add cream of tartar and continue to beat.
- Slowly add sugar, one tablespoon at a time.
- Add milk and vanilla extract, several drops at a time.
- Dissolve instant coffee in the hot water and slowly add to whites while beating.
- Continue beating until mixture is glossy and forms peaks.
- Fold into flour mixture.
- Pour into an 8 x 8 inch nonstick baking pan.
- Bake for 35 minutes.

Thanks to: Lance and Valerie McIntyre, Group 1

Category: Desserts

Nutrition Facts

Serving Size 2x2 inch square (28g)
Servings Per Container 16

Amount Per Serving

Calories 60   Calories from Fat 5

	% Daily Value*
Total Fat 0g	0%
Saturated Fat 0g	0%
Trans Fat 0g	
Cholesterol 0mg	0%
Sodium 35mg	1%
Total Carbohydrate 14g	5%
Dietary Fiber 1g	4%
Sugars 10g	
Protein 2g	

Vitamin A 0%	•	Vitamin C 0%
Calcium 2%	•	Iron 2%

*Percent Daily Values are based on a 2,000 calorie diet. Your daily values may be higher or lower depending on your calorie needs:

		Calories:	2,000	2,500
Total Fat	Less than		65g	80g
Saturated Fat	Less than		20g	25g
Cholesterol	Less than		300mg	300mg
Sodium	Less than		2,400mg	2,400mg
Total Carbohydrate			300g	375g
Dietary Fiber			25g	30g

Calories per gram:
  Fat 9 • Carbohydrate 4 • Protein 4

Strawberry Divinity Candy

Makes 80 pieces

Ingredients:

¾	cup	water
¾	cup	light corn syrup
1	pkg	strawberry gelatin (3 oz)
3	cups	sugar
2		egg whites, beaten stiff

Preparation:

- Combine water, sugar, gelatin, and corn syrup in a 3 quart sauce pan over medium heat. Stir constantly until sugar and gelatin dissolved. Continue cooking to the "hard ball" stage (252 °F).
- Meanwhile beat the 2 egg whites until they are stiff but not dry. Blend gelatin mixture in beaten egg whites, beating constantly with electric mixer on medium speed. Beat as long as possible. Pour into a 9 x 9 inch pan sprayed generously with vegetable oil cooking spray (or drop by teaspoonful onto waxed paper).
- Cut into one-inch squares when hardened.

Thanks to: Harriette Miller

Category: Desserts, Candy

Nutrition Facts

Serving Size 1x1 inch square (15g)
Servings Per Container 80

Amount Per Serving

Calories 45   Calories from Fat 0

% Daily Value*

Total Fat 0g	0%
Saturated Fat 0g	0%
Trans Fat 0g	
Cholesterol 0mg	0%
Sodium 5mg	0%
Total Carbohydrate 11g	4%
Dietary Fiber 0g	0%
Sugars 9g	
Protein 0g	

Vitamin A 0% • Vitamin C 0%

Calcium 0% • Iron 0%

*Percent Daily Values are based on a 2,000 calorie diet. Your daily values may be higher or lower depending on your calorie needs:

		Calories:	2,000	2,500
Total Fat	Less than		65g	80g
Saturated Fat	Less than		20g	25g
Cholesterol	Less than		300mg	300mg
Sodium	Less than		2,400mg	2,400mg
Total Carbohydrate			300g	375g
Dietary Fiber			25g	30g

Calories per gram:
  Fat 9 • Carbohydrate 4 • Protein 4

Truffles de Light

A fun portion-controlled dessert, (low calorie and low carbohydrate).

Makes ~ 48

Ingredients:

6	oz	fat-free cream cheese
½	cup	sugar
1¾	cup	graham cracker crumbs
⅓	cup	cocoa
½	cup	Rice Krispies cereal

Preparation:

- Combine cream cheese, sugar and vanilla extract in a bowl and beat until mixed smooth.
- Add graham cracker crumbs, cocoa and cereal, mixing well.
- Shape dough into 3/4 inch small balls.
- Roll balls in additional crushed cereal if desired.
- Best kept refrigerated and eaten cool.

Thanks to: Debbie Lucus, R.D.

Category: Snacks and Desserts

Nutrition Facts

Serving Size 3/4 inch ball (10g)
Servings Per Container 48

Amount Per Serving

Calories 25 — Calories from Fat 5

% Daily Value*

Total Fat 0g	0%
Saturated Fat 0g	0%
Trans Fat 0g	
Cholesterol 0mg	0%
Sodium 40mg	2%
Total Carbohydrate 5g	2%
Dietary Fiber 0g	0%
Sugars 3g	
Protein 1g	

Vitamin A 0% • Vitamin C 0%
Calcium 2% • Iron 2%

*Percent Daily Values are based on a 2,000 calorie diet. Your daily values may be higher or lower depending on your calorie needs:

		Calories:	2,000	2,500
Total Fat	Less than		65g	80g
Saturated Fat	Less than		20g	25g
Cholesterol	Less than		300mg	300mg
Sodium	Less than		2,400mg	2,400mg
Total Carbohydrate			300g	375g
Dietary Fiber			25g	30g

Calories per gram:
 Fat 9 • Carbohydrate 4 • Protein 4

YAM PIE

A lighter version of sweet potato pie. Look at all the vitamin A!

Makes 12 servings

Crust:

2	cups	graham cracker crumbs
3	Tbsp	jam

Filling:

4	large	or 8 small yams, cooked
¾	cup	egg substitute
¼	tsp	ground nutmeg
¼	tsp	ground allspice
¼	tsp	ground ginger
1	Tbsp	vanilla extract
½	cup	brown sugar
½	cup	skim milk

Preparation:

- Preheat oven to 350°F.
- Spray 10 inch pie pan with vegetable oil cooking spray.
- Mix crust ingredients together and press to to line pan.
- Mash yams and blend with remaining ingredients.
- Pour mixture into crust.
- Bake for 45-50 minutes, until center of pie is firm.
- Cool and refrigerate.

Category: Desserts

Nutrition Facts

Serving Size 1/12 pie (95g)
Servings Per Container 12

Amount Per Serving

Calories 160   Calories from Fat 15

	% Daily Value*
Total Fat 1.5g	2%
Saturated Fat 0g	0%
Trans Fat 0g	
Cholesterol 0mg	0%
Sodium 120mg	5%
Total Carbohydrate 32g	11%
Dietary Fiber 2g	8%
Sugars 20g	
Protein 4g	

Vitamin A 160% • Vitamin C 15%
Calcium 4% • Iron 6%

*Percent Daily Values are based on a 2,000 calorie diet. Your daily values may be higher or lower depending on your calorie needs:

		Calories:	2,000	2,500
Total Fat	Less than		65g	80g
Saturated Fat	Less than		20g	25g
Cholesterol	Less than		300mg	300mg
Sodium	Less than		2,400mg	2,400mg
Total Carbohydrate			300g	375g
Dietary Fiber			25g	30g

Calories per gram:
  Fat 9 • Carbohydrate 4 • Protein 4

SAUCES / MISCELLANEOUS

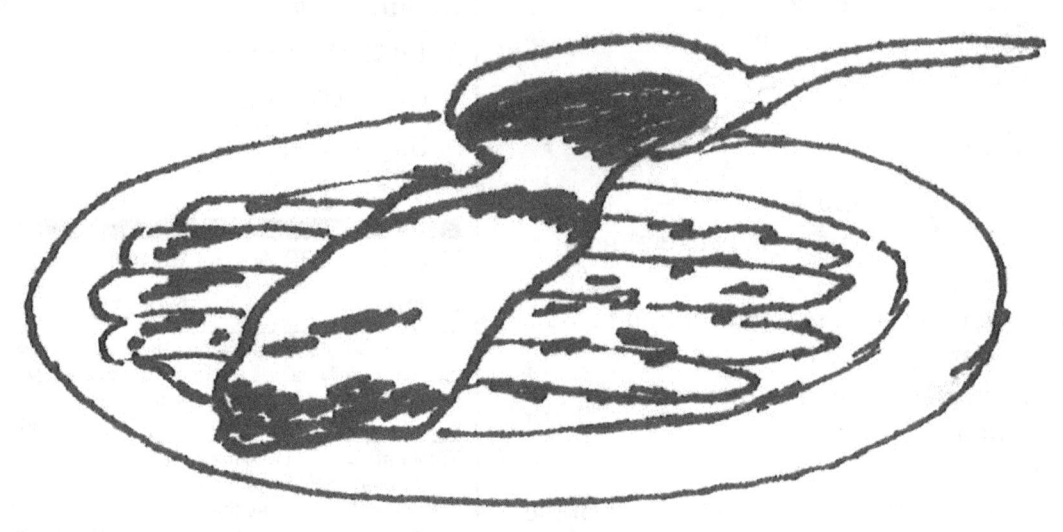

Note: some of the items in this section have no portion sizes in the nutrition labels. They should be used sparingly, especially if they have a high salt content.

BLACK BEAN SAUCE

Use as dipping sauce for salad rolls, or grilled vegetables.

Makes about 2 cups

Ingredients:

1	cup	hoisin sauce
¼	cup	water
5	Tbsp	vinegar
¼	cup	yellow onion, minced
1	tsp	chili paste (or less to taste)
		chiles (for garnish)

Preparation:

- Put hoisin sauce, water, vinegar and onion into a saucepan and bring to a boil.
- Add a little water to thin if needed.
- Set aside to cool.
- Add chili paste to taste.
- Transfer mixture to a sauce dish and
- garnish with chiles.

Thanks to: Mai Pham, Lemon Grass Restaurant

Note: High sodium content.

Use sparingly

Nutrition Facts

Serving Size (436g)
Servings Per Container

Amount Per Serving

Calories 600   Calories from Fat 80

	% Daily Value*
Total Fat 9g	14%
Saturated Fat 1.5g	8%
Trans Fat 0g	
Cholesterol 10mg	3%
Sodium 4420mg*	184%
Total Carbohydrate 117g	39%
Dietary Fiber 8g	32%
Sugars 72g	
Protein 9g	

Vitamin A 0% • Vitamin C 25%
Calcium 10% • Iron 15%

*Percent Daily Values are based on a 2,000 calorie diet. Your daily values may be higher or lower depending on your calorie needs:

	Calories:	2,000	2,500
Total Fat	Less than	65g	80g
Saturated Fat	Less than	20g	25g
Cholesterol	Less than	300mg	300mg
Sodium	Less than	2,400mg	2,400mg
Total Carbohydrate		300g	375g
Dietary Fiber		25g	30g

Calories per gram:
  Fat 9 • Carbohydrate 4 • Protein 4

Chunky Enchilada Sauce

Much more tasty than the canned variety.

Makes 5 cups

Ingredients:

1		onion, chopped
2		cloves garlic, crushed
½	cup	water
3	cups	tomatoes, chopped
1	can	green chiles, chopped (4 oz.)
3	Tbsp	chili powder
½	tsp	ground cumin
1½	cups	water
1	Tbsp	light soy sauce
3	Tbsp	cornstarch

Preparation:

- Place the onion, garlic, and water in a large saucepan.
- Cook, stirring, for 5 minutes, until the onion softens slightly.
- Add the tomatoes, chiles, and spices. .
- Stir, cover and cook over low heat for 15 minutes.
- Add 1 cup of the water and the soy sauce.
- Mix the cornstarch in the remaining ½ cup water. Add to the sauce while stirring.
- Cool, stirring, until thickened.

Thanks to: Kitty Oulicky, Group 5

Category: Mexican

Nutrition Facts

Amount in Recipe 1709 g (5 cups)

Calories/cup : 88
Calories from fat 9.

	% Daily Value*
Total Fat 6g	9%
Saturated Fat 1g	5%
Trans Fat 0g	
Cholesterol 0mg	0%
Sodium 1430mg	60%
Total Carbohydrate 90g	30%
Dietary Fiber 23g	92%
Sugars 37g	
Protein 14g	

Vitamin A 290% • Vitamin C 230%
Calcium 25% • Iron 45%

*Percent Daily Values are based on a 2,000 calorie diet. Your daily values may be higher or lower depending on your calorie needs:

	Calories:	2,000	2,500
Total Fat	Less than	65g	80g
Saturated Fat	Less than	20g	25g
Cholesterol	Less than	300mg	300mg
Sodium	Less than	2,400mg	2,400mg
Total Carbohydrate		300g	375g
Dietary Fiber		25g	30g

Calories per gram:
Fat 9 • Carbohydrate 4 • Protein 4

CRANBERRY SAUCE

Use light (low sugar) orange juice to further reduce the carbohydrate content.

Makes 6 servings

Ingredients:

12	oz	cranberries (discard stems, soft berries)
1	rind	orange, grated (the zest)
3	Tbsp	sugar-free maple syrup
3	Tbsp	Splenda
1	cup	orange juice (8 oz)

Preparation:

- Place all ingredients in a saucepan.
- Bring to a boil - be careful the berries will pop (which is what you want them to do).
- Cook on medium heat until all berries have popped.
- Lower heat and cook for a total of 30 minutes.
- Refrigerate overnight before serving.
- May add arrowroot or cornstarch to thicken.

Thanks to: Mary Davis, Group 29

Category: Miscellaneous

Nutrition Facts

Serving Size 1/6 recipe (107g)
Servings Per Container 6

Amount Per Serving

Calories 50 Calories from Fat 0

% Daily Value*

Total Fat 0g	0%
Saturated Fat 0g	0%
Trans Fat 0g	
Cholesterol 0mg	0%
Sodium 0mg	0%
Total Carbohydrate 14g	5%
Dietary Fiber 3g	12%
Sugars 6g	
Protein 1g	

Vitamin A 2% • Vitamin C 40%
Calcium 2% • Iron 2%

*Percent Daily Values are based on a 2,000 calorie diet. Your daily values may be higher or lower depending on your calorie needs:

	Calories:	2,000	2,500
Total Fat	Less than	65g	80g
Saturated Fat	Less than	20g	25g
Cholesterol	Less than	300mg	300mg
Sodium	Less than	2,400mg	2,400mg
Total Carbohydrate		300g	375g
Dietary Fiber		25g	30g

Calories per gram:
 Fat 9 • Carbohydrate 4 • Protein 4

CREAM SAUCE

Great for pasta, pizza sauce, over veggies

Makes ~ 3 cups

Ingredients:

1½	cans	evaporated skim milk (15 oz)
1¼	cups	fat-free low sodium chicken broth
1	oz	white wine
1	tsp	garlic powder
¾	tsp	white pepper
2	Tbsp	non-fat butter substitute
3	Tbsp	cornstarch

Preparation:

- Combine 1 cup of the evaporated skim milk, chicken broth, wine, garlic powder, white pepper and powdered butter substitute in a saucepan.
- Simmer for 10 minutes.
- Mix cornstarch and remaining milk in a separate bowl and slowly add to simmering mixture.
- Stir constantly for 20 minutes on a very low heat.

Thanks to: Michele Lites, RD

Category: Miscellaneous

Nutrition Facts

Serving Size (822g)
Servings Per Container

Amount Per Serving

Calories 550   Calories from Fat 10

% Daily Value*

Total Fat 1g	2%
Saturated Fat 0.5g	3%
Trans Fat 0g	
Cholesterol 20mg	7%
Sodium 2090mg	87%
Total Carbohydrate 84g	28%
Dietary Fiber 1g	4%
Sugars 51g	
Protein 42g	

Vitamin A 35% • Vitamin C 10%
Calcium 130% • Iron 10%

*Percent Daily Values are based on a 2,000 calorie diet. Your daily values may be higher or lower depending on your calorie needs:

	Calories:	2,000	2,500
Total Fat	Less than	65g	80g
Saturated Fat	Less than	20g	25g
Cholesterol	Less than	300mg	300mg
Sodium	Less than	2,400mg	2,400mg
Total Carbohydrate		300g	375g
Dietary Fiber		25g	30g

Calories per gram:
  Fat 9 • Carbohydrate 4 • Protein 4

Hearty Tomato Sauce

Use this in recipes calling for "tomato sauce". Much fresher and much lower sodium content.

Makes ~ 2 quarts.

Ingredients:

2	tsp	olive oil
1	large	onion, finely chopped (1
3-6	cloves	garlic, pressed or minced
1	med	carrot, finely chopped
1	med	parsnip, finely chopped (1
1	med	turnip, finely chopped
1	large	bell pepper, finely chopped
2½	cups	mushrooms, sliced
2	tsp	dried basil, crushed
¾	tsp	dried oregano, crushed
¼	tsp	dried thyme, crushed
8	cups	fresh tomatoes, peeled and chopped
		freshly ground black pepper to taste

OR

4	cans	tomatoes, chopped (16 oz)
¼	cup	dry red wine
2	Tbsp	parsley, finely chopped fresh
2	Tbsp	dark miso (or 1 tsp. salt)

Preparation:

- In a large, heavy-bottomed pot, heat oil.
- Add onion, garlic, carrot, parsnip and turnip, and sauté until onion is translucent.
- Add bell pepper, mushrooms, herbs and a generous amount of black pepper, and continue to sauté for several minutes.
- Stir in tomatoes and wine.
- Cover pot and bring to just a simmer.
- Partially uncover and cook at a low simmer, stirring occasionally, until sauce reaches a thick consistency, about 2 to 3 hrs.
- Stir in parsley and remove from heat. Add salt.

Source: Vegetarian Times

Category: Miscellaneous

Intimidation Pasta Sauce

A traditional pasta sauce for noodles, lasagna, pizza.

Ingredients:

1	med	onion, chopped
4	cloves	garlic, crushed
1	lb	mushrooms, sliced
1	tsp	olive oil
6	oz	tomato paste, unsalted
1	tsp	anise seed
1	tsp	Italian seasoning
1	Tbsp	molasses
½	tsp	chili powder
2¼	cups	water
½	cup	carrots, grated
½	cup	celery, chopped
½		bell pepper, chopped
3	cups	tomatoes, diced/chopped
1½	cups	tomato sauce (canned or homemade)
½	cup	red wine
		salt and pepper to taste

Nutrition Facts

Serving Size (2787g)
Servings Per Container

Amount Per Serving

Calories 860 — Calories from Fat 70

	% Daily Value*
Total Fat 8g	12%
Saturated Fat 1g	5%
Trans Fat 0g	
Cholesterol 0mg	0%
Sodium 1880mg	78%
Total Carbohydrate 163g	54%
Dietary Fiber 33g	132%
Sugars 102g	
Protein 35g	

Vitamin A 300% • Vitamin C 430%

Calcium 60% • Iron 130%

*Percent Daily Values are based on a 2,000 calorie diet. Your daily values may be higher or lower depending on your calorie needs:

		Calories:	2,000	2,500
Total Fat		Less than	65g	80g
Saturated Fat		Less than	20g	25g
Cholesterol		Less than	300mg	300mg
Sodium		Less than	2,400mg	2,400mg
Total Carbohydrate			300g	375g
Dietary Fiber			25g	30g

Calories per gram:
Fat 9 • Carbohydrate 4 • Protein 4

Preparation:

- Sauté onions, mushroom and garlic in oil until transparent, then add tomato paste, and cook for additional 5 minutes over low heat, stirring often.
- Add anise seed, Italian seasoning, molasses, chili powder, and water (¾ cup). Simmer for 10 minutes.
- Add carrots, celery, pepper, tomatoes, tomato sauce and water (1½ cups).
- Cook partially covered for 1 hour. Add red wine.
- Cook for an additional 40 minutes uncovered or longer until sauce thickens.
- Season with salt and pepper to taste.

Note: Serving Size on Label applies to entire recipe.

Thanks to: George Jacobs, Group 5

Category: Sauces

Low Sodium Pickles

Pickles are generally a sodium nightmare. Try this to satisfy your pickle cravings without loading up on sodium.

Makes 1 quart

Ingredients:

3-4	small		garlic cloves
1	Tbsp		turmeric
1	bunch		fresh dill
OR			
1	Tbsp		dried dill
½	Tbsp		peppercorns
1	Tbsp		pickling spice
1	Tbsp		prepared mustard
1½	cup		cider vinegar
1½	cup		water
2	lbs		cucumbers, peeled and sliced

Preparation:

- Place garlic and spices in a quart jar.
- If fresh dill is used, place half on the bottom of the jar and half on top.
- Fill jar with cucumbers.
- Heat vinegar and water to boiling point.
- Cover cucumbers with heated vinegar dilution.
- Allow to stand overnight and then pickles are ready to eat.

Category: Miscellaneous

Nutrition Facts

Serving Size (1223g)
Servings Per Container

Amount Per Serving

Calories 180   Calories from Fat 20

                                                                % Daily Value*

Total Fat 2g	3%
Saturated Fat 0g	0%
Trans Fat 0g	
Cholesterol 0mg	0%
Sodium 220mg	9%
Total Carbohydrate 22g	7%
Dietary Fiber 6g	24%
Sugars 8g	
Protein 5g	

Vitamin A 10%	•	Vitamin C 35%
Calcium 20%	•	Iron 35%

*Percent Daily Values are based on a 2,000 calorie diet. Your daily values may be higher or lower depending on your calorie needs:

	Calories:	2,000	2,500
Total Fat	Less than	65g	80g
Saturated Fat	Less than	20g	25g
Cholesterol	Less than	300mg	300mg
Sodium	Less than	2,400mg	2,400mg
Total Carbohydrate		300g	375g
Dietary Fiber		25g	30g

Calories per gram:
  Fat 9 • Carbohydrate 4 • Protein 4

Note: Serving Size on Label applies to entire recipe.

Note: some of the dips have no portion sizes in the nutrition labels. They should be used sparingly, especially, if they have a high salt content.

FAVORITE MARINADES

Fun marinades for tofu. Just marinade tofu slice for 30 minutes, then grill, bake, or pan sauté. Or use with grilled veggies.

BALSAMIC VINEGAR & SOY

Ingredients:

1	small	red onion, finely chopped (½ cup)
3	Tbsp	balsamic vinegar
2	Tbsp	light soy sauce
1	Tbsp	olive oil
¼	tsp	salt
2	tsp	dried thyme (or 2 Tbsp fresh)

Preparation:

- Combine ingredients in a non-aluminum bowl.
- Cover and refrigerate.

Nutrition Facts

Serving Size (182g)
Servings Per Container

Amount Per Serving

Calories 230   Calories from Fat 130

% Daily Value*

Total Fat 14g	22%
Saturated Fat 2g	10%
Trans Fat 0g	
Cholesterol 0mg	0%
Sodium 1610mg	67%
Total Carbohydrate 21g	7%
Dietary Fiber 2g	8%
Sugars 15g	
Protein 4g	

Vitamin A 2%   •   Vitamin C 10%
Calcium 8%   •   Iron 15%

*Percent Daily Values are based on a 2,000 calorie diet. Your daily values may be higher or lower depending on your calorie needs:

		Calories:	2,000	2,500
Total Fat	Less than		65g	80g
Saturated Fat	Less than		20g	25g
Cholesterol	Less than		300mg	300mg
Sodium	Less than		2,400mg	2,400mg
Total Carbohydrate			300g	375g
Dietary Fiber			25g	30g

Calories per gram:
Fat 9   •   Carbohydrate 4   •   Protein 4

Note: Serving Size on Label applies to entire recipe.

Ginger and Soy

Ingredients:

¼	cup	ginger root, grated
4	cloves	garlic, minced
3	Tbsp	light soy sauce
4	Tbsp	water
2	tsp	olive oil
4		green onions, sliced

Preparation:

- Combine ingredients in a non-aluminum bowl.
- Cover and refrigerate.

Nutrition Facts

Serving Size (259g)
Servings Per Container

Amount Per Serving

Calories 200 — Calories from Fat 90

	% Daily Value*
Total Fat 10g	15%
Saturated Fat 1.5g	8%
Trans Fat 0g	
Cholesterol 0mg	0%
Sodium 1540mg	64%
Total Carbohydrate 22g	7%
Dietary Fiber 3g	12%
Sugars 9g	
Protein 7g	

Vitamin A 20% • Vitamin C 40%

Calcium 10% • Iron 10%

*Percent Daily Values are based on a 2,000 calorie diet. Your daily values may be higher or lower depending on your calorie needs:

		Calories:	2,000	2,500
Total Fat	Less than		65g	80g
Saturated Fat	Less than		20g	25g
Cholesterol	Less than		300mg	300mg
Sodium	Less than		2,400mg	2,400mg
Total Carbohydrate			300g	375g
Dietary Fiber			25g	30g

Calories per gram:
  Fat 9 • Carbohydrate 4 • Protein 4

Note: Serving Size on Label applies to entire recipe.

LEMON AND ROSEMARY

Ingredients:

¼	cup	dry Marsala wine
2	Tbsp	fresh lemon juice
1	tsp	olive oil
2	cloves	garlic, minced
1	Tbsp	lemon peel, grated
1	Tbsp	fresh rosemary, chopped (1 tsp. dried)
¼	tsp	salt and pepper

Preparation:

- Combine ingredients in a non-aluminum bowl.
- Cover and refrigerate.

Category: Miscellaneous

Nutrition Facts

Serving Size (111g)
Servings Per Container

Amount Per Serving

Calories 150 — Calories from Fat 45

% Daily Value*

Total Fat 5g	8%
Saturated Fat 0.5g	3%
Trans Fat 0g	
Cholesterol 0mg	0%
Sodium 960mg	40%
Total Carbohydrate 12g	4%
Dietary Fiber 1g	4%
Sugars 8g	
Protein 1g	

Vitamin A 2% • Vitamin C 35%
Calcium 2% • Iron 2%

*Percent Daily Values are based on a 2,000 calorie diet. Your daily values may be higher or lower depending on your calorie needs:

		2,000	2,500
Total Fat	Less than	65g	80g
Saturated Fat	Less than	20g	25g
Cholesterol	Less than	300mg	300mg
Sodium	Less than	2,400mg	2,400mg
Total Carbohydrate		300g	375g
Dietary Fiber		25g	30g

Calories per gram:
Fat 9 • Carbohydrate 4 • Protein 4

Note: Serving Size on Label applies to entire recipe.

PICKLING JUICE

Every once in a while a recipe calls for "pickling juice". Rather than use some from a jar of commercial pickles (major sodium!), make your own. Use more chile peppers if you like it hot.

Ingredients:

½	cup	water
½	cup	vinegar
2	Tbsp	sugar or honey
2	Tbsp	crushed bay leaves
1	Tbsp	cardamom seeds
1	Tbsp	dried ginger root
1	stick	of cinnamon
1		whole dried chili pepper
1	Tbsp	mustard seeds
1	Tbsp	whole allspice
1	Tbsp	coriander
1	Tbsp	peppercorns

Preparation:

- Bring water and vinegar to a boil in a saucepan.
- Add sugar or honey and spices.
- Bring back to boil and take off heat.
- After allowing it to cool, strain the liquid, store in refrigerator for use in recipes calling for pickling juice.

- Note: The items contributing to the fat content of this recipe are the mustard seed and the dried pepper. Keep that in mind if you want to reduce the fat content.

Nutrition Facts
Serving Size (307g)
Servings Per Container

Amount Per Serving

Calories 230 Calories from Fat 45

	% Daily Value*
Total Fat 5g	8%
Saturated Fat 1g	5%
Trans Fat 0g	
Cholesterol 0mg	0%
Sodium 30mg	1%
Total Carbohydrate 45g	15%
Dietary Fiber 10g	40%
Sugars 20g	
Protein 5g	

Vitamin A 80%	•	Vitamin C 10%
Calcium 15%	•	Iron 30%

*Percent Daily Values are based on a 2,000 calorie diet. Your daily values may be higher or lower depending on your calorie needs:

		Calories:	2,000	2,500
Total Fat	Less than		65g	80g
Saturated Fat	Less than		20g	25g
Cholesterol	Less than		300mg	300mg
Sodium	Less than		2,400mg	2,400mg
Total Carbohydrate			300g	375g
Dietary Fiber			25g	30g

Calories per gram:
 Fat 9 • Carbohydrate 4 • Protein 4

Category: Miscellaneous

Note: Serving Size on Label applies to entire recipe.

PINEAPPLE-HONEY MUSTARD DRESSING

This is good on vegetable salads as well as fruit.

Makes 1 cup. Serving size: 1 Tbsp

Ingredients:

⅓	cup	pineapple juice, unsweetened
¼	cup	lime juice
¼	cup	honey
2	Tbsp	Dijon mustard
1 ½	Tbsp	light soy sauce
¼	tsp	garlic powder
⅛	tsp	red pepper, dried and crushed

Preparation:

- Combine ingredients in a small bowl, stirring well with a wire whisk.

Thanks to: Laurie Crider-Vanpal, Group 27

Category: Miscellaneous

Nutrition Facts
Serving Size (298g)
Servings Per Container

Amount Per Serving

Calories 500   Calories from Fat 0

% Daily Value*

Total Fat 0g	0%
Saturated Fat 0g	0%
Trans Fat 0g	
Cholesterol 0mg	0%
Sodium 1490mg	62%
Total Carbohydrate 127g	42%
Dietary Fiber 1g	4%
Sugars 115g	
Protein 4g	

Vitamin A 4%   •   Vitamin C 100%

Calcium 6%   •   Iron 8%

*Percent Daily Values are based on a 2,000 calorie diet. Your daily values may be higher or lower depending on your calorie needs:

	Calories:	2,000	2,500
Total Fat	Less than	65g	80g
Saturated Fat	Less than	20g	25g
Cholesterol	Less than	300mg	300mg
Sodium	Less than	2,400mg	2,400mg
Total Carbohydrate		300g	375g
Dietary Fiber		25g	30g

Calories per gram:
Fat 9   •   Carbohydrate 4   •   Protein 4

Note: Serving Size on Label applies to entire recipe.

Roasted Tomato Herb Sauce

Traditional pasta sauce created with clever cooking methods.

Makes ~ 3 cups

Ingredients:

2 ½	lbs	Italian plum tomatoes, halved
1		leek (white part only), cut into ¾ inch pieces
1	med	onion, cut into wedges
2	med	carrots, cut into ¾ inch pieces
3	cloves	garlic, peeled
1	tsp	dried oregano leaves
1	tsp	dried marjoram leaves
⅛	tsp	pepper
½	cup	loosely packed basil leaves
		salt and pepper, to taste

Preparation:

- Preheat oven to 425°F.
- Spray aluminum-foil-lined jelly roll pan with vegetable oil cooking spray.
- Arrange vegetables in single layer on pan.
- Spray vegetables with cooking spray and sprinkle with oregano, marjoram, and ⅛ tsp pepper.
- Roast in oven until vegetables are browned and tender, about 60 minutes.
- Process vegetables and fresh basil in food processor or blender until almost smooth.
- Season to taste with salt and pepper.

Nutrition Facts

Serving Size (1560g)
Servings Per Container

Amount Per Serving

Calories 390   Calories from Fat 25

	% Daily Value*
Total Fat 3g	5%
Saturated Fat 0g	0%
Trans Fat 0g	
Cholesterol 0mg	0%
Sodium 200mg	8%
Total Carbohydrate 88g	29%
Dietary Fiber 24g	96%
Sugars 53g	
Protein 16g	

Vitamin A 460% • Vitamin C 330%
Calcium 35% • Iron 45%

*Percent Daily Values are based on a 2,000 calorie diet. Your daily values may be higher or lower depending on your calorie needs:

		Calories:	2,000	2,500
Total Fat	Less than		65g	80g
Saturated Fat	Less than		20g	25g
Cholesterol	Less than		300mg	300mg
Sodium	Less than		2,400mg	2,400mg
Total Carbohydrate			300g	375g
Dietary Fiber			25g	30g

Calories per gram:
  Fat 9 • Carbohydrate 4 • Protein 4

Category: Miscellaneous

Note: Serving Size on Label applies to entire recipe.

Saucy Dip

Dipping sauce for use in Baked Golden Tofu Dumpling recipe.

Ingredients:

¾	cup	apple juice
2	tsp	maple syrup or brown sugar
1-2	tsp	tamari sauce
1-2	tsp	apple cider vinegar
½	tsp	ginger, grated (optional)
2	cloves	garlic, pressed
1-2	tsp	arrowroot powder (or cornstarch)
1-2	tsp	water

Preparation:

- Combine apple juice, syrup or sugar, tamari sauce and vinegar in a small saucepan.
- Stir in ginger and garlic.
- Bring to a simmer and cook for 1 to 2 minutes.
- Dissolve arrowroot or cornstarch in water and add to saucepan. Cook for one minute while stirring. Remove from heat.

Category: Miscellaneous

Nutrition Facts

Serving Size (254g)
Servings Per Container

Amount Per Serving

Calories 160   Calories from Fat 5

	% Daily Value*
Total Fat 0.5g	1%
Saturated Fat 0g	0%
Trans Fat 0g	
Cholesterol 0mg	0%
Sodium 680mg	28%
Total Carbohydrate 37g	12%
Dietary Fiber 0g	0%
Sugars 30g	
Protein 1g	

Vitamin A 0% • Vitamin C 0%
Calcium 2% • Iron 2%

*Percent Daily Values are based on a 2,000 calorie diet. Your daily values may be higher or lower depending on your calorie needs:

		Calories:	2,000	2,500
Total Fat	Less than		65g	80g
Saturated Fat	Less than		20g	25g
Cholesterol	Less than		300mg	300mg
Sodium	Less than		2,400mg	2,400mg
Total Carbohydrate			300g	375g
Dietary Fiber			26g	30g

Calories per gram:
   Fat 9 • Carbohydrate 4 • Protein 4

Note: Serving Size on Label applies to entire recipe.

SPICY SAUCE FOR COUSCOUS

Here's something for a very quick and easy, yet flavorful, meal.

Ingredients:

1	can	Mexican stewed tomatoes (15oz)
8	oz	favorite salsa (try garlic salsa)
12	oz	firm tofu, diced

Preparation:

- Mix ingredients together and heat.
- Add broccoli or other veggies as desired.
- Serve over couscous.

Thanks to: Jill Burns, R.D.

Nutrition Facts

Serving Size (992g)
Servings Per Container

Amount Per Serving

Calories 420   Calories from Fat 80

	% Daily Value*
Total Fat 9g	14%
Saturated Fat 0g	0%
Trans Fat 0g	
Cholesterol 0mg	0%
Sodium 1900mg	79%
Total Carbohydrate 53g	18%
Dietary Fiber 11g	44%
Sugars 29g	
Protein 34g	

Vitamin A 190% • Vitamin C 80%

Calcium 140% • Iron 50%

*Percent Daily Values are based on a 2,000 calorie diet. Your daily values may be higher or lower depending on your calorie needs:

	Calories:	2,000	2,500
Total Fat	Less than	65g	80g
Saturated Fat	Less than	20g	25g
Cholesterol	Less than	300mg	300mg
Sodium	Less than	2,400mg	2,400mg
Total Carbohydrate		300g	375g
Dietary Fiber		25g	30g

Calories per gram:
  Fat 9 • Carbohydrate 4 • Protein 4

Note: Serving Size on Label applies to entire recipe.

Tomatillo Sauce

Fresh tomatillos and a couple of choice recipes from this collection give you yet another ingredient to use in many dishes. Try this sauce in Dave's Hearty Burrito recipe from the same collection. Don't be intimidated by the tomatillos. They are quick and easy to use.

Makes ~ 3 ½ cups.

Ingredients:

1	lb.	tomatillos
1	cup	roasted tomato herb sauce (see page 380)
½	cup	vegetable broth (see page 384)
1	tsp	ground cumin
2	tsp	chili powder
½	tsp	garlic powder

Preparation:

- Drop tomatillos in warm water to remove outer husks.
- Chop coarsely, place in pan.
- Add remaining ingredients.
- Bring to boil, lower heat and cook for 15-30 minutes, until tomatillos are very soft.
- Let sit several minutes. Puree if desired.

Thanks to: Linda Paumer

Category: Miscellaneous

Nutrition Facts

Serving Size (1130g)
Servings Per Container

Amount Per Serving

Calories 340   Calories from Fat 60

	% Daily Value*
Total Fat 7g	11%
Saturated Fat 1g	5%
Trans Fat 0g	
Cholesterol 0mg	0%
Sodium 210mg	9%
Total Carbohydrate 67g	22%
Dietary Fiber 21g	84%
Sugars 38g	
Protein 13g	

Vitamin A 290% • Vitamin C 270%
Calcium 25% • Iron 50%

*Percent Daily Values are based on a 2,000 calorie diet. Your daily values may be higher or lower depending on your calorie needs:

		Calories:	2,000	2,500
Total Fat	Less than		65g	80g
Saturated Fat	Less than		20g	25g
Cholesterol	Less than		300mg	300mg
Sodium	Less than		2,400mg	2,400mg
Total Carbohydrate			300g	375g
Dietary Fiber			25g	30g

Calories per gram:
Fat 9 • Carbohydrate 4 • Protein 4

Note: Serving Size on Label applies to entire recipe.

Vegetable Broth

Wonderful broth to have on hand for soups, sauces, and a variety of recipes from this collection. Wonderful use of healthy vegetables and wonderful way to control sodium content of recipes.

Makes ~ 2 quarts

Ingredients:

3		celery stalks
3	med	carrots
1	large	onion
2	large	leeks
8	oz	mushrooms
1	bunch	parsley

Preparation:

- Peel and quarter carrots.
- Quarter onion and celery stalks.
- Roughly chop white and light green part of leeks.
- Put all ingredients in a large pot and add water to cover.
- Bring to a boil and spoon off any foam that forms on top.
- Reduce heat and simmer until broth is reduced by half, 2½ -3 hours.
- Pour mixture through a strainer into a bowl and let broth cool; discard vegetables in the strainer.

Ladle broth into quart-size freezer bags or containers (great for soups) or ice cube trays (handy for sauces). Freeze for up to 6 months; transfer the cubes to bags once they are solid.

Category: Miscellaneous

Nutrition Facts

Serving Size (2364g)
Servings Per Container

Amount Per Serving

Calories 510	Calories from Fat 50

	% Daily Value*
Total Fat 5g	8%
Saturated Fat 1g	5%
Trans Fat 0g	
Cholesterol 0mg	0%
Sodium 650mg	27%
Total Carbohydrate 103g	34%
Dietary Fiber 31g	124%
Sugars 34g	
Protein 27g	

Vitamin A 1560% • Vitamin C 1090%

Calcium 100% • Iron 190%

*Percent Daily Values are based on a 2,000 calorie diet. Your daily values may be higher or lower depending on your calorie needs:

	Calories:	2,000	2,500
Total Fat	Less than	65g	80g
Saturated Fat	Less than	20g	25g
Cholesterol	Less than	300mg	300mg
Sodium	Less than	2,400mg	2,400mg
Total Carbohydrate		300g	375g
Dietary Fiber		25g	30g

Calories per gram:
   Fat 9 • Carbohydrate 4 • Protein 4

Note: Serving Size on Label applies to entire recipe.

Vegetable Marinara Sauce for Pasta

If you are stuck on using jarred sauce for pasta, consider dressing it up a bit with this recipe.

Ingredients:

¼	cup	water or just enough to steam
2		carrots, cut into coin shapes
1		red onion, diced
1		zucchini, grated
1	jar	fat free pasta sauce (28 oz)
¼	cup	red wine, or more to taste
1	tsp	Italian seasoning or to taste
1	tsp	garlic powder, or to taste
2	cups	cauliflower, cut into bite sized pieces

Preparation:

- In a kettle put only enough water to steam vegetables, add carrot, and onion.
- Steam until you can pierce carrots with a fork.
- Add the pasta sauce to the vegetables, followed by red wine.
- Mix and heat.
- Add grated zucchini. Stir and adjust the thickness of the sauce with added wine or water if desired.
- Season with Mrs. Dash Italian Seasoning and garlic powder.
- Add cauliflower, stir, bring to a low simmer and cover until soft.

Thanks to: Lyn and Jim Livingston, Group 8

Category: Sauces, Miscellaneous

Nutrition Facts

Serving Size (1708g)
Servings Per Container

Amount Per Serving

Calories 650   Calories from Fat 80

	% Daily Value*
Total Fat 8g	12%
Saturated Fat 0.5g	3%
Trans Fat 0g	
Cholesterol 0mg	0%
Sodium 2170mg	90%
Total Carbohydrate 118g	39%
Dietary Fiber 26g	104%
Sugars 61g	
Protein 24g	

Vitamin A 560% • Vitamin C 360%
Calcium 60% • Iron 70%

*Percent Daily Values are based on a 2,000 calorie diet. Your daily values may be higher or lower depending on your calorie needs:

	Calories:	2,000	2,500
Total Fat	Less than	65g	80g
Saturated Fat	Less than	20g	25g
Cholesterol	Less than	300mg	300mg
Sodium	Less than	2,400mg	2,400mg
Total Carbohydrate		300g	375g
Dietary Fiber		25g	30g

Calories per gram:
  Fat 9 • Carbohydrate 4 • Protein 4

Note: Serving Size on Label applies to entire recipe.

YOGURT CHEESE

Yogurt cheese is one of the most versatile foods you can have in your kitchen! You can use it as a replacement for cream cheese and sour cream and you can use it to make spreads, dips, whipped cream and cake frosting! Originally from *The Eat-Clean Diet® Cookbook*.

YIELD: 1 cup

Ingredients:

2 cups non-fat plain yogurt

Preparation:

- Place yogurt in a fine mesh sieve or colander lined with two layers of cheesecloth.
- Place the sieve over a large bowl to catch the liquid that drips out of the yogurt.
- Place in the refrigerator and let stand overnight.
- Discard the liquid in the bowl below and you are left with rich, creamy yogurt cheese in the cheesecloth.

Category: Miscellaneous

Nutrition Facts

Serving Size (907g)
Servings Per Container

Amount Per Serving

Calories 400	Calories from Fat 0

% Daily Value*

Total Fat 0g	0%
Saturated Fat 0g	0%
Trans Fat 0g	
Cholesterol 20mg	7%
Sodium 540mg	23%
Total Carbohydrate 76g	25%
Dietary Fiber 0g	0%
Sugars 52g	
Protein 40g	

Vitamin A 80%	•	Vitamin C 80%	
Calcium 120%	•	Iron 0%	

*Percent Daily Values are based on a 2,000 calorie diet. Your daily values may be higher or lower depending on your calorie needs:

	Calories:	2,000	2,500
Total Fat	Less than	65g	80g
Saturated Fat	Less than	20g	25g
Cholesterol	Less than	300mg	300mg
Sodium	Less than	2,400mg	2,400mg
Total Carbohydrate		300g	375g
Dietary Fiber		25g	30g

Calories per gram:
Fat 9 • Carbohydrate 4 • Protein 4

INDEX

Acetyl-CoA	27
Alcohol	38-41
Benefits of Drinking	40
Cardiovascular Risks	40
Chemistry	40
Alcohol Proof	38
Alcoholic Beverages (Calories in Common Beverages)	39
All Vegetable Chili	135
Alpha-linolenic Acid	27
Alternative Seasonings to Salt	36
American Heart Association's Nutrition Committee Recommendations	29
Angel Food Cake	319
Angel Lemon Cake	320
<u>Appetizers</u>	298
Baked Pita Triangles *(dippers)*	313
Chile Rellenos Appetizers	299
Deviled Eggs	300
Eggplant Garlic Dip	301
Golden Toast Rounds (dippers)	314
Hummus with Garlic	302
Hummus with Tahini	303
Italian Style Veggie Dip	304
Kale Chips	315
Layered Mexican Dip	305
Mexican Bean Dip	306
Party Mix	316
Peamole	307
Raspberry Lemonade Fruit Dip	308
Spicy Bean Dip	309
Spicy Garbanzo Nuts	317
Spinach Dip	310
Water-crisped Corn Tortilla Chips	311
Water-crisped Flour Tortilla Chips	312
<u>Apples</u>	
Apple cake	321

Apple Carrot Muffins with Flaxseed	61
Apple Cherry Crisp	322
Apple Nut Torte	323
Apple Sweet and Sour Red Cabbage	272
Apple Sweet Potato Medley	273
Apple-Cot Cobbler	324
Deep Dish Apple Cranberry Crumble	334
Fresh Apple Coffee Cake	74

Apricots

Apple-Cot Cobbler	324
Apricot Bread	62

Asian Noodle Salad	94

Asparagus

Asparagus Potato Bisque	136
Spring Asparagus Soup	158

Atherosclerosis	29
Baked Beans, Plymouth-style	165
Baked eggplant	274
Baked Golden Tofu Dumplings	188
Baked Pita Triangles *(dippers)*	313
Baking Mix	177

Bananas

Banana Cake	325
Chocolate Banana Muffins	66

Barbecue Bean Casserole	166

Barley

Barley & Mushroom Pilaf	253
Barley Bean Salad	95
Hearty Barley Salad	115

Basal Calorie Requirement	6,7
Basic Pasta Salad	96
Basic Pasta Salad Italiano	97
Basic Pasta Salad Party	97
Basic Pasta Salad South of the Border	98

Beans

Bean and Corn Enchiladas	206
Baked Beans, Plymouth-style	165
Barbecue Bean Casserole	166
Cajun Pinto Beans	167
Classic Baked Beans	168

Curried Garbanzo Beans & Potatoes	169
Dave's Hearty Burrito	170
Lazy Baked Beans	171
Lazy Baked Beans with Pineapple	172
Lentils with Spinach	173
Refried Beans	174
Soft Lentils	175
Benefits of Improving Diet	47
Biscuits	178

<u>Black Beans</u>

Black Bean and Mango Salad	98
Black Bean and Rice Soup	137
Black Bean Salad	99
Black Bean Sauce	367
Black Bean Soup	138
Couscous and Black Bean Salad	106
Cowboy Caviar	107

<u>Blueberries</u>

Blueberry Bread Pudding	326
Blueberry Cobbler	327
Body Mass Index	9
Determining BMI	10
Ethnicity	11,12
Formula	9
Interpretation of BMI	11
Boston Cream Pie Cake	328

<u>Breads</u>

Apple Carrot Muffins with Flaxseed	61
Apricot Bread	62
Baking Mix	177
Biscuits	178
Breakfast Rolls	65
Chocolate Banana Muffins	66
Corn Bread	179
Date Bread	70
English Muffin Loaf	71
Flaxseed Pancakes	72
French Toast	73
Fresh Apple Coffee Cake	74
Honey Corn Bread	180

	Honey Wheat Bread	181
	Honey Wheat Rolls	182
	Indian Corn Bread	183
	Low Fat Pizza	184
	Oatmeal Navy Beans Muffins	78
	Oatmeal Pumpkin Muffins	79
	Oil-Free Muffins	80
	Orange Cranberry Bread	81
	Overnight Coffee Cake	82
	Sourdough Oatmeal Bread	86
	Stout Bread	186
	Stuffed French Toast	87
	Yogurt Muffins	91
	Yogurt Muffins with Streusel Topping	91
Breakfast Frittata		63
Breakfast Parfait		64
Breakfast Parfait with Yogurt		64
Breakfast Rolls		65
Broccoli Lasagna Rolls		223
Broccoli Salad		100
Broccoli Soup		139
Butternut Squash Enchiladas		207
C and W Green Pea Soup		140
<u>Cabbage</u>		
	Apple Sweet and Sour Red Cabbage	272
	Cabbage Rolls	275
	Oriental Cabbage Slaw	119
	Winter Red Cabbage Salad	126
Caloric Needs (Estimated)		7
Calorie		6
Calories Burned in One Hour of Activity		16
Calories in Different Types of Food		18
Calories in Alcoholic Drinks		39
Cholesterol		25-30
	Content in Milk and Meat Products	30
	High	28
Chylomicrons		28
"CIS" Bonds		26
Cajun Pinto Beans		167
Campfire Vegetable-Bean-Pasta Soup		141

Can Opener Chili	142
Caponata	276
<u>Carrots</u>	
Apple Carrot Muffins with Flaxseed	61
Carrot Cake with Cream Cheese Frosting	329
Carrot Casserole	277
Copper Carrot Pennies	105
Glorified Carrot Raisin Salad	114
<u>Cereal</u>	
Breakfast Parfait	64
Breakfast Parfait with Yogurt	64
Cranberry Orange Breakfast Barley	68
Hot Quinoa Breakfast Cereal	75
Muselix	77
Overnight Oatmeal	83
Party Mix	316
<u>Chiles</u>	
Chile Relleno Appetizers	299
Chile Relleno Casserole	208
Chile Relleno Tofu Casserole	209
Chili Mole	143
Chili Rico	144
Chunky Enchilada Sauce	368
Sweet Potato Jalapeno Soup with Tomatillo Cream	160
Chile Rellenos con no Manteca	210
Chipotle Mashed Sweet Potatoes	240
<u>Chocolate</u>	
Chocolate Banana Muffins	66
Chocolate Pudding Cake	330
Laura's Reversal Chocolate Cake	345
Mocha Pudding Cake	351
So So So Low Fat Brownies	362
Chunky Enchilada Sauce	368
Citrus Pasta Salad	101
Classic Baked Beans	168
Cold Tomato-Yogurt Soup	145
Confetti Bean Salad	102
Cool Green Fruit Salad	103
Cool Meal Potato Salad	104
Copper Carrot Pennies	105

Corn
- Corn Chowder — 146
- Lu's Tortilla Soup — 154
- Pilgrim Corn Salad — 120

Corn Bread — 179
Corn Frittata — 67

Cottage Cheese
- Broccoli Lasagna Rolls — 223
- Cottage Cheese Stuffed Manicotti — 224
- Fettuccine with Cottage Cheese Alfredo Sauce — 226
- Herbed Cottage Cheese Spread — 130
- Lentil and Kale Loaf — 189
- Millet Applesauce Enchiladas — 217
- Special K Cottage Cheese Loaf — 195
- Stuffed Shells — 235
- TVP and Tofu Loaf — 201
- Zucchini Lasagna — 237

Cottage Style Twice Baked Potatoes — 241

Couscous
- Campfire Vegetable-Bean-Pasta Soup — 141
- Couscous and Black Bean Salad — 106
- Couscous with Veggies — 254
- Curry Spiced Couscous — 256
- Spicy Sauce for Couscous — 382

Cowboy Caviar — 107

Cranberries
- Cranberry Orange Breakfast Barley — 68
- Cranberry Raspberry Jello with Pineapple — 108
- Cranberry Sauce — 369
- Cranberry Velvet Salad — 109
- Cranberry-Pear Crumble — 331
- Deep Dish Apple Cranberry Crumble — 334
- Orange Cranberry Bread — 81
- Cranberry Glazed Sweet Potatoes — 242

Cream Sauce — 370
Creamy Peach Cheesecake — 332
Crepes — 69
Cucumber Raita — 278
Cucumbers Vinaigrette — 279
Curried Garbanzo Beans and Potatoes — 169

Curried Rice and Sweet Potatoes	255
Curry Spiced Couscous	256
Date Bars	333
Date Bread	70
Dave's Hearty Burrito	170
Debbie's Taco Soup	147

<u>Desserts</u>

Angel Food Cake	319
Angel Lemon Cake	320
Apple cake	321
Apple Cherry Crisp	322
Apple Nut Torte	323
Apple-Cot Cobbler	324
Banana Cake	325
Blueberry Bread Pudding	326
Blueberry Cobbler	327
Boston Cream Pie	328
Carrot Cake with Cream Cheese Frosting	329
Chocolate Pudding Cake	330
Cranberry-Pear Crumble	331
Creamy Peach Cheesecake	332
Date Bars	333
Deep Dish Apple Cranberry Pie	334
Forgotten Cookies	335
Fresh Strawberry Pie	336
Fruit Cocktail Cake	337
Fruit Meringue	338
Fruitful Graham Cracker Pie Crust	339
Gingerbread	340
Ginny's Peach Cobbler	341
Grape Nuts Pie Crust	342
Harvest Cake	343
Ice Cream Cake	344
Laura's Reversal Chocolate Cake	345
Lemon Cheese-Like Cake	346
Lemon Pie	347
Mexican Flan	348
Microwaved Krunch Cake Topping	349
Microwaved Tapioca	350
Mocha Pudding Cake	351

Oatmeal Bars with Chewy Fruit	352
Oatmeal Corn Syrup Raisin Cookies	353
Oatmeal Walnut Cookies	354
Peach and Raspberry Cloud Cake	355
Pineapple Cake with Cream Cheese Frosting	356
Poached Pears	357
Pumpkin Cream Cheese Swirl Cake	358
Pumpkin Log Roll	359
Punch Bowl Trifle	360
Rhubarb Strawberry Cobbler	361
So So So Low Fat Brownies	362
Strawberry Divinity	363
Truffles de Light	364
Yam Pie	365
Deviled Eggs	300
<u>Dips/Dippers</u>	
Baked Pita Triangles *(dippers)*	313
Eggplant Garlic Dip	301
Golden Toast Rounds (dippers)	314
Hummus with Garlic	302
Hummus with Tahini	303
Italian Style Veggie Dip	304
Layered Mexican Dip	305
Mexican Bean Dip	306
Peamole	307
Raspberry Lemonade Fruit Dip	308
Saucy Dip	381
Spicy Bean Dip	309
Spinach Dip	310
Water-crisped Corn Tortilla Chips	311
Water-crisped Flour Tortilla Chips	312
Easy Enchiladas	211
Easy Pineapple Yam Bake	243
<u>Egg/Meat Substitutes</u>	
Baked Golden Tofu Dumplings	188
Breakfast Frittata	63
Corn Frittata	67
Crepes	69
Joe's Special Frittata	76
Lentil and Kale Loaf	189

Maple Brandy Meat Substitute	190
Nan's Stroganoff	191
Quick and Easy Stroganoff	192
Sloppy Joes	193
Southwest Surprise	194
Special K Cottage Cheese Loaf	195
Spicy Bean and Lentil Loaf	196
Stuffed Green Peppers	197
Stuffed Portobello Mushrooms	198
Tempeh Taco Salad	199
Tofu Scramble	88
Tofu Stir Fry	200
TVP and Tofu Loaf	201
TVP Loaf	202
Vegetable Omelet	89
Vegetarian Loaf	203
<u>Eggplant</u>	
Baked eggplant	274
Caponata	276
Eggplant Garlic Dip	301
Eggplant Parmesan	280
Eggplant Steak	281
Eggplant with Sweet and Sour Sauce	282
Ratatouille	287
Sicilian Stuffed Eggplant	292
Enchilada Casserole	212
Energy	5
Energy Requirements (Estimated)	7
English Muffin Loaf	71
Essential Fatty Acids	27
Estimated Energy Requirements Formula for Men & Women	7
Falafel Sandwich	128
Fancy Coleslaw	110
Fat in Food	20-31
Fatty Acids	27, 28
<u>Favorite Marinades</u>	374
Balsamic vinegar & Soy	375
Ginger and Soy	376
Lemon and Rosemary	377

Fettuccine with Cottage Cheese Alfredo Sauce	226
Fiber	33
Foods Rich In	33
Health Benefits	32
<u>Flaxseed</u>	
Apple Carrot Muffins with Flaxseed	61
Flaxseed Pancakes	72
Food and Nutrition Board and Institute of Medicine Recommendations	42
Food Diary	14-16
Advantages	14
Examples of "Small Sacrifices"	17
Instructions	15
Sample	15
Food Labels	23
Making Sense of	23
Reading	30
Forgotten Cookies	335
French Toast	73
Fresh Apple Coffee Cake	74
Fresh Strawberry Pie	336
Fruit Cocktail Cake	337
Fruit Meringue	338
Fruitful Graham Cracker Pie Crust	339
<u>Garbanzo Beans</u>	
Curried Garbanzo Beans & Potatoes	169
Falafel Sandwich	128
Garbanzo and Pomegranate Salad	111
Garbanzo Bulgur Tomato Pilaf	257
Garbanzo Salad	112
Garbanzo Stew	148
Hummus with Garlic	302
Hummus with Tahini	303
Spicy Garbanzo Nuts	317
Garden Bake	283
Garlicky Kale	284
Getting Started	50
Ginger Noodle Salad	113
Gingerbread	340
Ginny's Peach Cobbler	341

Glorified Carrot Raisin Salad	114
Glycerol	26
Golden Toast Rounds (dippers)	314
Grape Nuts Pie Crust	342
Green Beans with Mustard	285
<u>Green Peppers</u>	
Quinoa Stuffed Peppers	261
Stuffed Green Peppers	197
Grilled Cheese with Tomato and Basil	129
Harvest Cake	343
Healthy Ingredient Substitutions	58-60
Heart Disease Reversal Program Recommendations	42
Hearty Barley Salad	115
Hearty Tomato Sauce	371
Herbed Cottage Cheese Spread	130
High Density Lipoprotein (HDL)	25,28
Homemade Tortillas	213
Honey Corn Bread	180
Honey Wheat Bread	181
Honey Wheat Rolls	182
Hot Quinoa Breakfast Cereal	75
Hot Vegetable Hero	131
Huaraches	215
Hummus with Garlic	302
Hummus with Tahini	303
Hydrogenated Vegetable Oil	26
Ice Cream Cake	344
Indian Corn Bread	183
Insoluble Fiber	32
Intimidation Pasta Sauce	372
Italian Style Veggie Dip	304
Jane's No-Boil Lasagna	227
Joe's Special Frittata	76
<u>Kale</u>	
Garlicky Kale	284
Kale and Potato Soup	149
Kale Chips	315
Lentil and Kale Loaf	189
Kasha Southwest Salad	116
Kidney Bean Gumbo	150

Kilocalorie	6
Laura's Reversal Chocolate Cake	345
Layered Mexican Dip	305
Lazy Baked Beans	171
Lazy Baked Beans with Pineapple	172
Lemon Cheese-Like Cake	346
Lemon Pie	347
Lemon Rice with Spinach	258
<u>Lentils</u>	
Lentil and Kale Loaf	189
Lentil Stew	151
Lentil Salad	117
Lentil Soup	152
Lentil Sweet Potato Stew	153
Lentils with Spinach	173
Linguine with Lentils	228
Soft Lentils	175
Spicy Bean and Lentil Loaf	196
Linoleic Acid	27
Lipase	28
Lipoproteins	28
Low Density Lipoproteins (LDL)	28
Low Fat Pizza	184
Low Sodium Pickles	373
Lu's Tortilla Soup	154
Macaroni & Cheese	229
Macaroni Salad	118
Maple Brandy Meat Substitute	190
Meal Planning	50
Meat Substitutes	52
Meatless Jambalaya	259
<u>Mexican</u>	
Bean and Corn Enchiladas	206
Butternut Squash Enchiladas	207
Chile Relleno Casserole	208
Chile Relleno Tofu Casserole	209
Chile Rellenos con no Manteca	210
Corn Tortilla	214
Easy Enchiladas	211
Enchilada Casserole	212

Homemade Tortillas	213
Huaraches	215
Mexican Lasagna	216
Millet Applesauce Enchiladas	217
Mushroom Quesadillas	218
Quickie Quesadillas	84
Tamale TVP Pie	219
Tamale Vegetable Pie	220
Vegetable Quesadillas	90
Mexican Bean Dip	306
Mexican Flan	348
Microwaved Krunch Cake Topping	349
Microwaved Tapioca	350
Millet Applesauce Enchiladas	217

Miscellaneous

Favorite Marinades	374
Low Sodium Pickles	373
Pickling Juice	378
Saucy Dip	381
Smoothies	85
Yogurt Cheese	386
Mocha Pudding Cake	351
Modifying Your Recipes with Healthy Substitutions	59-60
Monoglycerides	25-27
Mono-unsaturated Fat	25-27
Muselix	77
Mushroom Quesadillas	218

Mushrooms

Mushroom Quesadillas	218
Seasoned Portobello Mushrooms	289
Shiitake Mushrooms with Oyster Sauce	291
Stuffed Portobello Mushrooms	198
Nan's Stroganoff	191
National Cholesterol Education Program Adult Treatment Panel (NCEP II and III)	47
New Potatoes and Peas	244
Nutritional Content Sample Meal	20

Oatmeal

Oatmeal Bars with Chewy Fruit	352
Oatmeal Corn Syrup Raisin Cookies	353

Oatmeal Navy Beans Muffins	78
Oatmeal Pumpkin Muffins	79
Oatmeal Walnut Cookies	354
Overnight Oatmeal	83
Sourdough Oatmeal Bread	86
Oil-Free Muffins	80
Okra Curry	286
Omega-3 and Omega – 6 fatty acids	27
Orange Cranberry Bread	81
Oriental Cabbage Slaw	119
Oven Baked French Fries	245
Overnight Coffee Cake	82
Overnight Oatmeal	83
Party Mix	316

Pasta

Broccoli Lasagna Rolls	223
Cottage Cheese Stuffed Manicotti	224
Fettuccine with Cottage Cheese Alfredo Sauce	226
Jane's No-Boil Lasagna	227
Linguine with Lentils	228
Macaroni & Cheese	229
Pasta Al Pesto	230
Pasta Primavera	231
Pasta with Mock Cream Sauce	232
Pasta with Spinach and Beans	233
Pauline's Macaroni & Cheese	234
Stuffed Shells	235
Vegetable Lasagna	236
Zucchini Lasagna	237

Peaches

Creamy Peach Cheesecake	332
Ginny's Peach Cobbler	341
Peach and Raspberry Cloud Cake	355

Pears

Cranberry-Pear Crumble	331
Poached Pears	357
Spinach Salad with Pears	124

Peas

C and W Green Pea Soup	140
Peamole	307

Snow Pea Salad with Sesame Dressing	123
Personal Activity Level (PAL)	7
Pickling Juice	378
Pilgrim Corn Salad	120
Pineapple Cake with Cream Cheese Frosting	356
Pineapple-Honey Mustard Dressing	379

Pizza

Low Fat Pizza	184
Pita Pizza	132
Zucchini Pizza	133
Poached Pears	357
Polenta	260
Pomegranate, Mandarin & Kiwi Salad	121
Potassium	35

Potatoes

Chipotle Mashed Sweet Potatoes	240
Cottage Style Twice Baked Potatoes	241
Cranberry Glazed Sweet Potatoes	242
Easy Pineapple Yam Bake	243
New Potatoes and Peas	244
Oven Baked French Fries	245
Roasted New Potatoes with Garlic	246
Roasted New Potatoes with Rosemary	247
Roasted Sweet Potatoes	248
Southern Sweet Potatoes	249
Two Potato Casserole	250
Pumpkin Cream Cheese Swirl Cake	358
Pumpkin Log Roll	359
Punch Bowl Trifle	360
Quick and Easy Stroganoff	193
Quick Meal Combos	52
Quickie Quesadillas	84

Quinoa

Hot Quinoa Breakfast Cereal	75
Quinoa Garden Salad	122
Quinoa Stuffed Peppers	261
Quorn	52

Raspberries

Peach and Raspberry Cloud Cake	355
Raspberry Lemonade Fruit Dip	308

Ratatouille	287
Red Wine and Heart Disease	40
Refried Beans	174
Relationship Between Food Eaten, Energy Spent and Fat Stores in the Body	13,14
Reversal Diet Recommendations	42

Rhubarb
- Rhubarb Strawberry Cobbler — 361

Rice & Grains
- Barley & Mushroom Pilaf — 253
- Couscous with Veggies — 254
- Curried Rice and Sweet Potatoes — 255
- Curry Spiced Couscous — 256
- Garbanzo Bulgur Tomato Pilaf — 257
- Lemon Rice with Spinach — 258
- Meatless Jambalaya — 259
- Polenta — 260
- Quinoa Stuffed Peppers — 261
- Rice Casserole — 262
- Rice Paper Wrapped Salad Rolls — 263
- Rice Pilaf — 265
- Southwestern Rice — 267
- Spanish Rice — 268
- Spicy Polenta — 269
- Vegetable Risotto — 270

Risotto Mollynese	266
Roasted Fall Vegetables	288
Roasted New Potatoes with Garlic	246
Roasted New Potatoes with Rosemary	247
Roasted Red Pepper and Sweet Potato Soup	155
Roasted Sweet Potatoes	248
Roasted Tomato Herb Sauce	380

Salads
- Asian Noodle Salad — 94
- Barley Bean Salad — 95
- Basic Pasta Salad — 96
- Basic Pasta Salad Italiano — 97
- Basic Pasta Salad Party — 97
- Basic Pasta Salad South of the Border — 98

Black Bean and Mango Salad	98
Black Bean Salad	99
Broccoli Salad	100
Citrus Pasta Salad	101
Confetti Bean Salad	102
Cool Green Fruit Salad	103
Cool Meal Potato Salad	104
Copper Carrot Pennies	105
Couscous and Black Bean Salad	106
Cowboy Caviar	107
Cranberry Raspberry Jello with Pineapple	108
Cranberry Velvet Salad	109
Fancy Coleslaw	110
Garbanzo and Pomegranate Salad	111
Garbanzo Salad	112
Ginger Noodle Salad	113
Glorified Carrot Raisin Salad	114
Hearty Barley Salad	115
Kasha Southwest Salad	116
Lentil Salad	117
Macaroni Salad	118
Oriental Cabbage Slaw	119
Pilgrim Corn Salad	120
Pomegranate, Mandarin & Kiwi Salad	121
Quinoa Garden Salad	122
Snow Pea Salad with Sesame Dressing	123
Spinach Salad with Pears	124
Surprise Cole-Slaw	125
Winter Red Cabbage Salad	126
Salt (Sodium Chloride)	35
Alternative Seasonings to Salt	36
Sample Menus	56,57
<u>Sandwiches</u>	
Falafel Sandwich	128
Grilled Cheese with Tomato and Basil	129
Herbed Cottage Cheese Spread	130
Hot Vegetable Hero	131
Pita Pizza	132
Zucchini Pizza	133
Saturated Fat	25-30

Saturated Fatty Acid Diagram — 26

Sauces
- Black Bean Sauce — 367
- Chunky Enchilada Sauce — 368
- Cranberry Sauce — 369
- Cream Sauce — 370
- Hearty Tomato Sauce — 371
- Intimidation Pasta Sauce — 372
- Roasted Tomato Herb Sauce — 380
- Spicy Sauce for Couscous — 382
- Tomatillo Sauce — 383
- Vegetable Broth — 384
- Vegetable Marinara Sauce — 385

Saucy Dip — 381
Seasoned Portobello Mushrooms — 289
Seven Areas of Interest for Patients with Coronary Artery Disease — 3
Shepherd's Pie — 290
Shiitake Mushrooms with Oyster Sauce — 292
Sicilian Stuffed Eggplant — 292
Sloppy Joes — 193
Smoothies — 85
Snow Pea Salad with Sesame Dressing — 123
Sodium Chloride — 35
Soluble Fiber — 32

Soups
- All Vegetable Chili — 135
- Asparagus Potato Bisque — 136
- Black Bean and Rice Soup — 137
- Black Bean Soup — 138
- Broccoli Soup — 139
- C and W Green Pea Soup — 140
- Campfire Vegetable-Bean-Pasta Soup — 141
- Can Opener Chili — 142
- Chili Mole — 143
- Chili Rico — 144
- Cold Tomato-Yogurt Soup — 145
- Corn Chowder — 146
- Debbie's Taco Soup — 147
- Garbanzo Stew — 148

Kale and Potato Soup	149
Kidney Bean Gumbo	150
Lentil Stew	151
Lentil Soup	152
Lentil Sweet Potato Stew	153
Lu's Tortilla Soup	154
Roasted Red Pepper and Sweet Potato Soup	155
Spring Asparagus Soup	158
Sweet and Sour Soup	159
Sweet Potato Jalapeno Soup with Tomatillo Cream	160
Sweet Potato Stew	161
Winter Vegetable Soup	162
Special K Cottage Cheese Loaf	195
Speedy TVP Stew	156
Spicy Bean and Lentil Loaf	196
Spicy Bean Dip	309
Spicy Garbanzo Nuts	317
Spicy Polenta	269
Spicy Sauce for Couscous	382

Spinach

Lemon Rice with Spinach	258
Pasta with Spinach and Beans	233
Shepherd's Pie	290
Spinach Dip	310
Spinach Salad with Pears	124
Vegetable Lasagna	236
Spring Asparagus Soup	158

Squash

Stuffed Acorn Squash with Apple Slices	295
Stuffed Acorn Squash with Brandied Fruit	294
Butternut Squash Enchiladas	207
Spaghetti Squash with Artichokes	293

Strawberries

Fresh Strawberry Pie	336
Fruit Meringue	338
Rhubarb Strawberry Cobbler	361
Strawberry Divinity	363
Stuffed French Toast	87
Stuffed Green Peppers	197
Stuffed Portobello Mushrooms	198

Stuffed Shells	235
Substitutions, Modifying Recipes	50-59
Suggested Daily Proportion of Calories in Each Meal for a 2000 Calorie/Day Diet	44
Surprise Cole-Slaw	125
Sweet and Sour Eggplant	296
Sweet and Sour Soup	159
Sweet Potato Jalapeno Soup with Tomatillo Cream	160
Sweet Potato Stew	161
Tamale TVP Pie	219
Tamale Vegetable Pie	220
Tempeh Taco Salad	199
Textured Vegetable Protein (TVP)	52
<u>Tofu</u>	52
Baked Golden Tofu Dumplings	188
Tofu Scramble	88
Tofu Stir Fry	200
TVP and Tofu Loaf	201
Tomatillo Sauce	383
"Trans" Bonds	26
Trans-fatty Acids	26
Triglyceride Diagram	26
Truffles de Light	364
TVP Loaf	202
Two Potato Casserole	250
Unsaturated Fat	28
Unsaturated Fatty Acid Diagram	28
Vegetable Broth	384
Vegetable Lasagna	236
Vegetable Marinara Sauce	385
Vegetable Omelet	89
Vegetable Quesadillas	90
Vegetable Risotto	270
<u>Vegetables</u>	
Apple Sweet and Sour Red Cabbage	272
Apple Sweet Potato Medley	273
Baked eggplant	274
Cabbage Rolls	275
Caponata	276
Carrot Casserole	277

Cucumber Raita	278
Cucumbers Vinaigrette	279
Eggplant Parmesan	280
Eggplant Steak	281
Eggplant with Sweet & Sour Sauce	282
Garden Bake	283
Garlicky Kale	284
Green Beans with Mustard	285
Okra Curry	286
Ratatouille	287
Roasted Fall Vegetables	288
Seasoned Portabello Mushrooms	289
Shepherd's Pie	290
Shiitake Mushrooms with Oyster Sauce	291
Sicilian Stuffed Eggplant	292
Spaghetti Squash with Artichokes	293
Stuffed Acorn Squash with Apple Slices	295
Stuffed Acorn Squash with Brandied Fruit	294
Sweet and Sour Eggplant	296
Winter Red Cabbage Salad	126
Winter Vegetable Soup	162
Yam Pie	365
Vegetarian Loaf	203
Vegetarian Pantry	51
Very Low Density Lipoproteins(VLDL)	24,28
Water-crisped Corn Tortilla Chips	311
Water-crisped Flour Tortilla Chips	312
What's for Breakfast?	53
What's for Lunch?	53
What's for Dinner?	54

Yams

Easy Pineapple Yam Bake	243
Yam Pie	365

Yogurt

Breakfast Parfait with Yogurt	64
Cold Tomato-Yogurt Soup	145
Raspberry Lemonade Fruit Dip	308
Yogurt Cheese	386
Yogurt Muffins	91
Yogurt Muffins with Streusel Topping	91

Zucchini

Garden Bake	283
Ratatouille	287
Zucchini Lasagna	237
Zucchini Pizza	133